Springer
Tokyo
Berlin
Heidelberg
New York
Hong Kong
London
Milan
Paris

F. Saito

Decentralization and Development Partnerships

Lessons from Uganda

With 31 Figures

 Springer

Fumihiko Saito
Associate Professor
Faculty of Intercultural Communication
Ryukoku University
Seta, Otsu 520-2194, Japan
URL: http://www.world.ryukoku.ac.jp/~fumisait/

Photographs
Front cover: Training session for LC 3 councillors in Tororo
Back cover: LC 1 meeting in a village in Mukono

ISBN 4-431-40835-5 Springer-Verlag Tokyo Berlin Heidelberg New York

Library of Congress Cataloging-in-Publication Data

Saito, Fumihiko, 1961-
    Decentralization and development partnerships : lessons from Uganda / F. Saito.
       p. cm.
    Includes bibliographical references and index.
    ISBN 4-431-40835-5 (soft : alk. paper)
     1. Decentralization in government--Uganda. I. Title.

  JS7649.3.A3 S25.2003
  320.8'096761--dc22

                                                                   2003061290

Printed on acid-free paper

Typesetting: Author
Printing and binding: Nihon Hicom, Japan
SPIN: 10955819

Preface

Public institutions in developing countries are often blamed for being too remote from the daily realities of poor people's lives. Decentralization measures are often recommended as a solution. These measures are intended to improve economic efficiency in the middle of resource scarcity in low-income countries. Locally provided services are, as argued, more likely to match different realities in different localities. This way of providing services is considered to be less bureaucratic in processing and more efficient in resource utilization. It is also intended to achieve participatory development in ways that respond to the needs of local communities. When people are assured of their rights to access key information, incentives would work to make decisions best suited to local needs. This will give the participants the responsibility for political, economic and social consequences of their decisions. This process contributes to democratization, which is also much needed in developing countries. Decentralization is, therefore, often advocated as a policy solution for many developing countries for both economic and political reasons.

The emphasis on local governments by those who have been following development issues in general, and those in Africa since independence in particular, is not entirely new. Retrospectively, W. Arthur Lewis, a Nobel Laureate in economics made an impressive remark in the mid 1960s, based on his observations in West Africa. He stated:

> All that is asked is a reasonable degree of provincial decentralization. Countries with this kind of problem need both a strong centre and strong provincial governments; and this is not a contradiction, since government functions are now so numerous that there is plenty of room for both. It is quite true that a country needs a strong central government to hold it together, meaning by this a government which acts boldly in all spheres which are of common interest. But it is equally true that a country with sharp regional differences needs to give its provinces the opportunity to look after their own affairs, if they are to feel content with the political union. Whether one calls this federalism or provincial devolution makes no difference (Lewis, 1965, p. 55)

Curiously enough, his shrewd observation did not receive much acceptance in academic or parishioners' circles. It was an era when development planning in tropical countries, conducted by central government experts, had a very big influence in modernizing the newly born countries. For various reasons, his recommendation was forgotten for many years.

On the other hand, even among those who support decentralization endeavors, it is frequently observed that various issues, which are not easily resolved, emerge during its implementation process. These issues are often related to very fundamental political, economic, and social problems in developing countries in general and in Africa in particular. Political patronage penetrates into local politics, and new autonomy given to local governments is abused by locally powerful leaders. Limited resources of various kinds in rural areas often prevent community efforts from improving livelihoods. Relaxed restrictions rejuvenate associational activities, but sometimes the result is increased inter-ethnic rivalries.

Thus, debate over decentralization has been revolving around many issues and has certainly contributed to improving our understanding of the process. The various arguments are presented both by supporters and critics of decentralization measures. But, the way in which the arguments are contrasted between pro- and anti-decentralists is not entirely productive. Instead, since most of the contested points are empirical matters, it is more useful to conduct a careful and comprehensive examination of complex decentralization processes based on real situations. This research is, therefore, intended to contribute to this empirical approach by analyzing one pioneering example in Africa.

This empirical study aims to generate useful lessons in order to overcome difficulties associated with decentralization. This book is, therefore, addressed not only to academics concerned with policy design but also to political and administrative leaders who are in a position to lead institutional reform processes. This study looks at Africa, since research on African experiences in decentralization measures is most lacking despite the fact that the continent receives considerable assistance for decentralization reforms. Uganda, being one of the most advanced countries on the African continent, provides a very useful case study for understanding more clearly what should and should not be done in design and implementation stages of this reform agenda. By looking into education and health, this book will examine whether decentralizing these essential public services contributes to ameliorating poverty.

The study looks into how decentralizing the state structure changes the way in which individuals and organizations engage with central and local governments. The study describes in what way people's perceptions of their relationship to local authorities are changing. Then, it addresses questions such as the conditions under which public, private, and non-governmental organizations become more willing to collaborate for mutually beneficial outcomes. What are the crucial factors distinguishing success from failure in such collaborations? Does decentralization offer hope to overcome persistent problems in developing countries? My short answer to this last question is cautiously affirmative. The study explains why I have come to this conclusion.

Acknowledgments

This research originates from my experience at the United Nations Development Programme (UNDP) in Kampala, Uganda, from 1991 to 1993. During that time, a new initiative in human development was being introduced in Uganda, and consultation with the government and others was very interesting in many ways. Against this background, it was in 1998 that I began this research project, taking more than five years to complete it.

During this process, enormous numbers of people provided me with assistance, suggestions, ideas, warm support, and critical comments, without which this research could not have been completed.

The list of people and organizations to whom I would like to express my appreciation is too long to complete. In Kampala, Dr. Zie Gariyo at Uganda Debt Network has been providing me with all sorts of practical suggestions on how to carry out research. Mr. Haruna Kyamanywa at UNDP has been supportive, both officially and personally. Several government officials in Kampala have equally been helpful to me, and special appreciation should be passed on to the staff of Uganda Participatory Poverty Assessment Project (UPPAP).

In the various districts I visited, different people collaborated with me by sacrificing their personal time and energy. In Mukono, Food for the Hungry International and Mrs. Margaret Nsubuga were helpful in introducing me to the communities. In Rakai, various different NGOs offered me assistance: Rakai AIDS Information Network, Concern Worldwide, and the Irish Foundation for Cooperative Development Ltd. In Tororo, since NGO activities were not so widespread as in the other two areas, Mr. Fred Etiang at the Development Office of the Bukedi Diocese of the Church of Uganda was immensely helpful. Obviously, political leaders and administrative staff at various levels in these areas were also very kind to me in responding to the questions I had during my visit. Some names appear as footnotes in the main text, but these people reflect only a fraction of those who helped me during my fieldwork in Uganda. During my stay in Uganda, I was affiliated with the Makerere Institute of Social Research at Makerere University, and am thankful to the staff there as well. I also had opportunities to interact with researchers at the Centre for Basic Research in Kampala. Seminars at Makere and the DBR were helpful in shaping my ideas.

From September 2000 to March 2001 I was in London, associated with the Department of Development Studies at the School of Oriental and African Studies (SOAS), University of London, and this affiliation provided me with a rare opportunity to concentrate on the early drafts of this manuscript. During this stay, I had chances to meet with numerous people inside and outside of the meetings of the

Development Studies Association in the UK. I was given opportunities to present my preliminary arguments in seminars organized by DSA and several institutions of the university. These opportunities were certainly very effective in clarifying my arguments. My special thanks go to Dr. Machiko Nissanke at SOAS and Dr. Robert Cassen at the London School of Economics (LSE), who were very helpful in many respects.

I would also like to thank those with whom I started to exchange ideas and manuscripts by e-mail. These include Dr. Nelson Kasfir, Dr. Per Tidemand, and Dr. Dan Ottemoeller.

Some seeds of the ideas developed in this book appeared in working papers published by Ryukoku University and posted on my personal website. A substantial part of this book was taken from my doctoral thesis submitted to Ryukoku University in 2001. I have benefited from suggestions from members of the thesis committee at Ryukoku University. Prof. Hisashi Nakamura and Prof. Minoru Obayashi provided various kinds of support. I also received critical comments and suggestions from Prof. Norman Uphoff at Cornell University, who served as an external examiner for my thesis. His insights, based on his long experience in development studies, have been truly valuable to me on a number of occasions.

During the process of trying to seek publication possibilities, a couple of anonymous reviewers gave me very critical, yet helpful, comments. These critical remarks, in fact, have helped me to refocus my arguments. I have reorganized the earlier thesis manuscript in order to respond to their suggestions.

Last but surely not least, Dr. Steve Wolfe, a colleague of mine at Ryukoku has meticulously checked my manuscript. Without his careful review, this writing would not appear as clear as it is now. Mr. Ken-ichiro Arai has been kindly assisting me in preparing the manuscript. In addition, Dr. Tsuyoshi Kawasaki at Simon Fraser University, an old friend from college days, has been offering me a variety of tips on how to "craft a research project" during the entire process of research and publication. I would also express my appreciation to publisher Springer-Verlag Tokyo, which has extended all manner of assistance.

I would also like to thank Aili Mari Tripp and James Currey Ltd. for kindly granting me their permission to use the two excellent maps of Uganda drawn by Aili's sister. I am also grateful to Dr. Sam Okuonzi for allowing me to use some materials in Chapter 8, which earlier appeared in Uganda Health Bulletin, Vol. 7, No.1, 2001. The UPPAP office also kindly allowed me to use one table in the text.

This research received financial assistance from various sources. In 1998, the Socio-Cultural Research Institute, Ryukoku University provided me with a modest amount to enable the preliminary study in Uganda. In 1999, the generous Grant-in-Aid for Scientific Research under the Ministry of Education, Culture, Sports, and Technology was helpful in carrying out the fieldwork in Uganda. In 2000, during my year-long sabbatical, Ryukoku University funded a relatively long four-and-a-half-month period of fieldwork in Uganda. In addition, from 1998 to 2000, a joint research project of Comparative Analysis of Participatory Development in Low Income Countries was funded by the Research Institute of Social Sciences at Ryukoku University, under which a series of stimulating discussion sessions were held in Kyoto, Japan. Finally, Ryukoku was again very generous in providing me with a publication subsidy, without which this book would not reach its intended readers. This publication coincides with a start of a new five-year project of an Open Research Center for Local System Development at Ryukoku which has provided logistic support. (This new project will conduct further research on some issues that are examined in this book.) All of them assisted in the execution of this project, and I do hope that the book merits the grants provided.

Fumihiko SAITO
Otsu, Shiga, Japan

Table of Contents

List of Tables and Figures

TABLES

FIGURES

Acronyms

AIDS	acquired immunodeficiency syndrome
BFP(s)	Budget Framework Paper(s)
CAO(s)	Chief Administrative Officer(s)
CBO(s)	Community-Based Organization(s)
CDRN	Community Development Resource Network
CFO(s)	Chief Finance Officer(s)
DANIDA	Danish International Development Assistance
DDHS	District Director of Health Services
DDP(s)	District Development Plan(s)
DEO(s)	District Education Officer(s)
DfID	Department for International Development, the UK
DREPS	District Resource Endowment Profile Survey
DS	Decentralization Secretariat
DSC(s)	District Service Commission(s)
EMIS	Education Management Information System
ESIP	Education Sector Investment Plan
FY	financial year/ fiscal year
GDP	gross domestic product
GER	gross enrollment ratio
GNI	gross national income
HDI	Human Development Index
HIPC	Highly Indebted Poor Countries
HIV	human immunodeficiency virus
HMIS	Health Management Information System
HPI	Human Poverty Index
HSD(s)	Health Sub-District(s)
HUMC(s)	Health Unit Management Committee(s)
IMF	International Monetary Fund
LC(s)	Local Council(s)
LGDP	Local Government Development Program
LGFC	Local Government Finance Commission
MISR	Makerere Institute for Social Research
MoES	Ministry of Education and Sports
MoFPED	Ministry of Finance, Planning and Economic Development
MoGCD	Ministry of Gender and Community Development
MoH	Ministry of Health
MoLG	Ministry of Local Government

MP	Member of Parliament
NAOWU	National Association of Women's Organizations of Uganda
NGO(s)	non-governmental organization(s)
NPM	New Public Management
NRA	National Resistance Army
NRM	National Resistance Movement
OPD(s)	Out-Patients Department(s)
PAF	Poverty Action Fund
PEAP	Poverty Eradication Action Plan
PHC	primary health care
PMA	Plan for Modernisation of Agriculture
PPA	participatory poverty assessment
PTA(s)	Parent Teachers Association(s)
RAIN	Rakai AIDS Information Network
RC(s)	Resistance Council(s)
RDC(s)	Resident District Commissioner(s)
RUWASA	Rural Water and Sewage Authority
SAP(s)	Structural Adjustment Programme(s)
SFG	School Facilities Grant
SMC(s)	School Management Committee(s)
SNG(s)	Sub-National Government(s)
STD(s)	sexually transmitted disease(s)
SWAP	sector-wide approach
TASO	The AIDS Support Organization
TDMP	Teacher Development Management Plan
Ush	Uganda Shilling
ULAA	Uganda Local Authorities Association
UNCDF	United Nations Capital Development Fund
UNDP	United Nations Development Programme
UNICEF	United Nations Children's Fund
UPDN	Uganda Participatory Development Network
UPE	Universal Primary Education
UPPAP	Uganda Participatory Poverty Assessment Project
USAID	United States Agency for International Development

UGANDA DISTRICTS

Source: Aili Mari Tripp [2000] *Women & Politics in Uganda* (Oxford: James Currey). Reprinted with permission.
Note: This map matches the district boundaries in the study, although the number of districts has subsequently increased. For the latest map, see http://www.un.org/Depts/Cartographic/map/profile/uganda.pdf.

UGANDA ETHNIC GROUPS

Source: Aili Mari Tripp [2000] *Women & Politics in Uganda* (Oxford: James Currey).
Reprinted with permission.

Mukono District Council
Building

LC 5 Chairperson's visit
to his constituencies

A newly elected LC 5
chairperson visits an LC
3 meeting in Rakai

People make voluntary contributions to build schools

Women express their views in a village gathering in Rakai

A drama is performed to inform the public about the LC system

1 Introduction: Why Decentralization Matters?

Debates about decentralisation are characterised by a number of fallacies. Major among them is the tendency to view decentralisation as a singular process rather than a multi-dimensional set of relationships; the treatment of decentralisation and centralisation as opposites in a zero-sum relationship; and attempts to formulate optimum arrangements for all programmes at all times, without regard for variation in values, technologies and geography. Many debates ... ignore [that] the advantage to be gained from any shift in central-local relations depends upon its conformance to feasible division of power and practical division of work - practical in terms of both the nature of public programmes and the resources of existing institutions.

Walsh, 1969, p. 179 quoted in Golooba-Mutebi, 1999, chapter 2[1]

Decentralization is a process through which a central government transfers authority and functions to sub-national units of the government. Normally there is a cluster of measures involved in this process, and thus decentralization is a shorthand expression. It is one of the most frequently pursued institutional reforms in developing countries, particularly since the late 1980s. The rationale for decentralizing measures derives from diverse origins and is intended to contribute to democratization, to more efficient public administration, to more effective development, and to "good governance."

Recently there is a growing literature on the subject. Yet, a serious void exists. Many of the contributions tend to assume that once organizations are decentralized formally and legally, the intended results will be attained. But there have been few tests to compare critically the assumptions and the decentralization results by establishing coherent frameworks. The comparison can be made by solid empirical investigation. Such investigation has significant implications for both theoretical clarifications and practical applications of decentralization in policy formulation and project management.

This study intends to help fill this gap with a case study from Uganda. Uganda, under the current National Resistance Movement (NRM) government, is one of the most interesting examples of an attempt at decentralization. In sharp contrast

---

[1] Golooba-Mutebi kindly made his dissertation available to this author by electronic files, whose format does not correspond with the printed version. Thus, specifying the pages of quotations is very difficult.

to Uganda in the 1970s and the 1980s, in which the country experienced disorder, civil strife and collapse of the state, Uganda today is one of the most promising economic reformers within Sub-Saharan Africa (Reinikka and Collier, 2001; Bigsten and Kayizzi-Mugerwa, 2001; and Holmgren et al., 1999).[2] While various factors have undoubtedly supported this significant recent transformation, one of the crucial issues is how the government attempted to divide responsibilities and functions in its central-local relations and how this process has been carried out. This realigning of duties between central and local governments, which has contributed to the impressive transition from a symbol of "hopelessness" in the past to one of the "hopefuls" in the African continent today, deserves careful scrutiny.

On the basis of field research, this study argues that properly implemented decentralization can facilitate strategic partnership formations. The partnership arrangements present one promising option for realizing integrated multi-dimensional solutions to a set of compounded political, economic, and social problems in developing countries in general, and in Africa in particular. The partnerships enable improved resource allocation and mutually beneficial results. Decentralization measures do not proceed within one dimension only. Instead they result in a kind of pluralization of relationships, through which partnerships emerge. This aspect of decentralization has seldom been investigated. Although the processes of decentralization are double-edged, the partnerships present at least a potential for making decentralization attempts more successful.

In Uganda's case, several important partnerships among stakeholders have been appearing. A first example is *the relationship between central and local governments*. While the central government mostly controlled local authorities previously, now a mutual central-local partnership has been evolving. Although the current partnership is far from fully matured, the central and local governments have started to engage each other as partners through the harmonization of respective budgeting.

A second example can be traced in *the relationship between the government and the private sector including non-governmental organizations* (NGOs), especially at local levels. Representatives of the business community, various associations, and NGOs now interact more frequently with local governments in pursuing mutually beneficial outcomes. These partnerships have yielded improved provision of services, which has benefited the poor and the disadvantaged.

A third instance is *the collaborative relation between service providers and recipients*, as exemplified in the sphere of primary education. Without the collaboration of recipients, the massive increase of primary education coverage would not have been possible.

A fourth example of partnership is *the relation among local authorities*, which now have their own association. This association has been effective in advancing the interests of local governments vis-à-vis the central government. The association's role will become even more crucial as local authorities exchange ideas and information in order to focus on solutions to mutual problems and difficulties.

---

[2] In this study, Africa and the African continent refer to Sub-Saharan Africa unless otherwise specified.

In order to solidify the strategic partnerships emerging from the decentralization processes, three elements need urgent attention and strengthening. A first crucial issue is incentives. In order to improve public services in the process of decentralization, both providers and recipients need to be motivated for mutual collaboration. Unless their motivation is enhanced through coherent mechanisms of rewarding performers and sanctioning non-performers, "bringing services closer to people" could result in a superficial shifting of ineffective and inefficient services from central to local levels.

Second, more accurate information should be provided to all stakeholders about their new roles, rights and responsibilities in the decentralized context. At the moment, each stakeholder understands "decentralization" in its own way. Improved information dissemination should help various stakeholders to form consensus which can guide them toward mutually beneficial solutions in order to improve respective livelihoods. The information, especially related to local policies and budgets, should be more thoroughly provided in order to enhance transparency.

Third, the current legal framework does not clarify procedures for conflict resolution in the case of political stalemates caused by uncompromising opponents at local levels. Serious efforts are, thus, urgently needed to provide accessible conflict-resolution mechanisms. Improved circulation of information can reduce unnecessary conflicts of views among stakeholders.

These findings have important policy implications. Unless adequate measures in the areas of incentives, information, and conflict-resolution mechanisms accompany decentralization, providing local services to people does not necessarily lead to effective development processes and outcomes. Inadequate services provided by the center may simply be replaced by equally unsatisfactory local services. This danger is the central finding of this study, something which has not been sufficiently addressed in earlier works on decentralization.

In this introductory chapter, the following issues are discussed. First, the different factors behind the decentralizing rationale are presented followed by corresponding criticism. In the second section, unanswered questions are identified, followed by explanations of how this study focusing on Ugandan experiences fills this remaining gap. Third, the framework for this investigation is presented by clarifying essential concepts and themes. Finally, the main points of each subsequent chapter are laid out for the convenience of readers.

1 Decentralization in Development Thinking

Decentralization entails transfer of political, economic, and administrative authority and functions from central to sub-national units of the government.[3] Although decentralization and centralization are often presented in a mutually exclu-

---

[3] Authority is essentially concerned with the idea of legitimate power or the right to exercise influence over others along superior-inferior lines often associated with hierarchies.

sive way, it is evident that the notions of centralization and decentralization form a continuum in which various possibilities in dividing tasks and responsibilities between central and local governments can be established. While centralization emphasizes the role of a national government, decentralization pays more attention to the role of local governments. Obviously, this relative emphasis does not signify that the other levels of government have no role to play.

Decentralizing public service provisions supported by fiscal as well as political autonomy granted to sub-national units of government are often advocated by donor agencies, especially by the World Bank and the International Monetary Fund (IMF).[4] Developing countries often accept this recommendation and undertake decentralization measures as one of the most frequently implemented institutional reforms. Decentralization policies are usually packaged together with Structural Adjustment Programmes (SAPs), which attempt to minimize state interventions in economic activities and to liberalize markets by privatization and deregulation.[5] It is estimated that more than 80% of developing and transitional countries including those in Eastern and Central Europe are experimenting with decentralization in one form or another (Manor, 1999, p. viii). Decentralization measures are certainly common in Africa.

But this is not the first time that decentralizing attempts have been proposed for developing countries. Some colonial administrators considered that decentralized state apparatus would be suitable for Africa, which consisted of many religious and linguistic groups. The newly independent countries, however, strove for economic modernization, which was considered possible by centralized planning and consolidated bureaucracy. When "strong" states were needed in the newly independent areas, the political leaders opted for centralized state structures (Thomas-Slayter, 1994, p. 1483). Unfortunately, this centralization neither produced political liberalism, economic growth, or human development. Instead, the office holders and their close associates in the central governments monopolized both political power and economic resources for their own benefit, which created long-lasting negative consequences such as political turmoil and economic devastation in Africa (Wunsch and Olowu, 1990; and Wunsch, 2000). (The next chapter will provide more explanations of centralization.)

1.1 Pro-decentralization Arguments

Proponents argue that decentralizing measures can bring numerous improvements, politically as well as developmentally. The prime rationale of decentralists is economic efficiency. By bringing public services "closer to people," locally

---

[4] See, for instance, World Bank, 1999a and 2000a.

[5] For the impacts of the SAP on Uganda, see Bigsten and Kayizzi-Mugerwa, 1995 and 1999; Brett, 1996; Jamal, 1991; Kayizzi-Mugerwa, 1993; Mamdani, 1991; and Sverrisson, 2000. For the SAP in general, the literature is large. See, for instance, Engberg-Pedersen et al., 1996; van der Geest and van der Hoeven, 1999; van der Hoeven and van der Kraaij, 1994; and Sandbrook, 1996.

specific issues are more easily identified and tailor-made solutions can be implemented. Public services provided by local governments are also delivered more speedily than by central governments, since decision making at local levels shortens time-consuming bureaucratic procedures.

Second, with decentralized governments, people have increased opportunities on a grassroots level to participate more actively in the decision-making processes of government. Effective participation allows the exercise of people's rights to shape decisions which affect their own lives (e.g. Friedmann, 1992, pp. 34-35).[6] As a result, people can better understand and demonstrate deeper commitment to development policies and projects. Both the consultative processes and results of collaborative activities are empowering to the poor in developing countries.

Third, participatory development increases satisfaction of service users, which in turn increases locally generated revenues. People who value the services they receive become more willing to pay for those services. The increased willingness for cost sharing contributes to sustainable local service provisions.

Fourth, local participation also contributes to improving accountability of public services. With more transparency, decentralized states can accommodate competing interests more favorably than centralized states and are more suitable for multi-ethnic and multi-religious societies in developing countries, particularly in Africa. In other words, social harmony across the nation can be better facilitated by decentralization measures.

Decentralists also offer other reasons which include democratization, nurturing civil society,[7] and harnessing social capital for development.[8] Decentralizing measures increase social opportunities, in which civic organizations can become active. Popular participation in local affairs enhances civic consciousness, and the enhanced civil society checks the state from abusing its power.[9] This process also contributes to improving service provisions by complementing the weak public sector. Empowered local institutions facilitate development of diverse social net-

---

[6] There is a growing literature on participatory development. See, for example, Abram and Waldren, 1998; Blair, 2000; Charlick, 2001; Cleaver, 1999; Craig and Mayo, 1995; Harris, 1996; Johnson and Wilson, 2000; Kaufman and Alfonso, 1997; Lovell, 1998; McGee, 2000b; Narayan and Chambers et al., 2000; Narayan and Patel et al., 2000; Valderrama and Hamilton, 1999; and Warburton, 1998. See also Sen, 1999.

[7] "Civil society" can be understood as an arena within a society at large where interactions between the state and society take place. State-society relations can be analyzed by seeing the state within society rather than looking at the state as antithesis to society (Migdal et al., 1994).

[8] Social capital, similar to physical capital, human capital and natural resources, can be defined as assets which people consider worth investing in, and can produce various forms of material and non-material benefits. See some of the following recent work: Fine, 2001; Fukuyama, 1995 and 2001; Lyon, 2000; Uphoff, 1992, chapter 13; and Uphoff and Wijayaratna, 2000.

[9] For the controversial concept of civil society, see, for instance, Chabal and Daloz, 1999, especially chapter 2; Fatton, 1995; Harbeson et al., 1994; Hyden and Bratton, 1992; Kasfir, 1998; Migdal et al., 1994; Ndegwa, 1996; Robinson and White, 1998; Rudebeck et al., 1998; Sandbrook, 1996; Smith, 1996; Van Rooy, 1998; and Woods, 1992.

works, through which social capital develops. As a result, decentralization is often correlated with "good governance."

1.2 Critiques Against Decentralization

Criticism against decentralization, especially in the developing country context, is not uncommon. Opponents of decentralization offer counterpoints to almost all the arguments provided by decentralists. The following points are presented in opposition to the corresponding views presented by the decentralists.

The critics point out, first of all, that increased efficiency and effectiveness of public resources will not be realized, since capital, human and even social resources available at local levels in low-income countries are very limited. Tailor-made solutions in poor localities remain as a mere slogan. These scarce resources are instead more effectively utilized when they are concentrated at the center. The improvement of public services can be more adequately obtained by consolidating capacities of the central government.

Second, local power structures are likely to influence the way in which participation of the poor is organized. Newly created local autonomy can be abused by local elites seeking personal benefit at the cost of the general population. Thus, consultative processes are not necessarily empowering to the poor.

Third, without significant improvement of public services, the public does not wish to pay more taxes for what it receives. The increased revenue generation locally remains a hope more than a fact.

Fourth, decentralization measures do not mitigate separatist tendencies and may threaten national integration by reemphasizing social divisions along, *inter alia*, ethnic and religious lines. Even a very small locality may not be completely homogeneous in ethnic and religious backgrounds. Because bringing power closer to the people underlines identity issues in local politics, decentralization, on the contrary, may reinforce social divisions.

While decentralists consider decentralization will foster civil society, its opponents reject such an argument since civil society cannot be distinctively independent from the state (Karlström, 1999b, p. 114). Decentralization would not automatically enhance independent civil society from the state, particularly because the boundary between the state and society becomes more blurred at local levels. It would be naïve to anticipate that decentralizing states would necessarily harness associational activities for collective gains at local levels. The hope placed in civil society to check the abuses of state power is unlikely to be realized. Consequently decentralizing attempts are likely to end up with "bad governance." (The next chapter explains the pros and cons of decentralization issues in more detail.)

1.3 Unanswered Issues in Decentralization

Given that decentralization options have been contemplated and even tested for some time, this unresolved debate between supporters and critics is certainly puzzling. This situation is well captured by the analogy of proverbs. Some have already asserted, "arguments for and against decentralisation are often 'like proverbs' with most principles answerable by an equally plausible and acceptable contradictory principle.... Decentralisation promotes efficiency and reduces it. Decentralisation enhances national unity and inhibits it" (Larmour and Qalo 1985, quoted in Regan, 1995, p. 279).

What becomes evident in the literature is that both supporters and critics use the same rationale very differently. The current controversies over decentralization policies and activities suggest that both the supporters and the opponents of decentralization have a certain validity in their arguments at the same time that their criticisms do not suggest any inherent fraud in the opponents' justification. Moreover, close scrutiny of the debate denote that even the critics tend to consider that the ideas behind decentralization policies are correct, however they insist most of the local governments in the developing world do not possess the necessary capacity to implement such policies. The critics of decentralists are not "centralists." Ironically, even the critics appear to assume that once adequate capacity is engendered, decentralization would succeed. In short, realities kill ideals.

The decentralization issue, then, essentially becomes an empirical question. It is argued that decentralization is promising for reducing poverty. But because developing countries are poor, they cannot successfully implement well-intended decentralization measures. The key question, then, is whether decentralization measures present a hope for poor countries? Under what conditions do decentralization measures enjoy a greater chance of success rather than failure?

The most acute problem in the debates is a wide gap, both among supporters and critics of decentralization, between assumed outcomes and empirical evidence. There are several reasons for this gap. First, the available literature on decentralization experiences in developing countries tends to focus on formal and legal aspects (Cohen and Peterson, 1999). Much attention has been paid to realignment of offices, including the shift of duties and responsibilities from one branch of the government to another. However, it has not yet been fully investigated as to how this kind of reorganization is perceived by relevant stakeholders, especially the grassroots poor, and whether the administrative reforms actually have improved relationships between service providers and recipients.

Second, most of the literature tends to examine "decentralization" as a monolithic policy, although its goals are normally numerous: public administration restructuring, economic efficiency, political legitimacy and democratization, and ultimately, poverty reduction. It is not very useful to argue whether "decentralization" as a totality in a given country is "successful" or not, as it was succinctly pointed out by the quotation at the beginning of this chapter. There usually is a mixture of some elements of success and failure. In addition, the attempt to reach these multiple goals at the same time can be contradictory. It has to be recognized, therefore, that decentralization processes often carry ambitious and unrealistic expectations to transform societies in a number of agendas in developing countries, particularly in Africa, which have been suffering from compounded political problems and economic stagnation (Crook and Manor, 1998, p. 302).

Third, decentralizing attempts are often justified by normative values, and this inclination has led to decentralization not being examined critically (e.g. Olowu, 2001; and Smoke, 2001). The decentralists have often argued that decentralization should be good in itself, especially for local democratization. The normative dimension has tended to blind analysts to the complex processes of bargaining and accommodations of competing interests of stakeholders initiated by decentralization measures. Decentralization measures are in fact neither good nor bad in themselves for economic and/or political reforms, and their effects depend on institutional designs and how such designs can be implemented in a given context of complex political, social, economic and cultural backgrounds (Brohman, 1996; and Litvack, et al., 1998, p. vii).

There have been a few attempts (Crook and Manor, 1998; and Crook and Sverrisson, 1999) to verify whether the intended objectives of decentralization policies have actually been achieved by adopting participation and institutional performance as the main variables for analysis. These attempts are in the right direction in overcoming the narrow focus on the formal and legalistic analyses. Unfortunately, even these pioneering studies have exhibited some limitations. "Participation in rural development efforts" was excluded from the main consideration (Crook and Manor, 1998, p. 7). Considering attitudinal aspects of participation was also excluded. These exclusions are serious omissions because decentralization options are often adopted for the sake of promoting rural development by changing the norms of people's participation.[10]

2 Framework for the Research

This study starts from the following broad questions: Is it likely that decentralization measures can actually achieve intended goals in the harsh realities encountered by developing countries? Under what circumstances can decentralization policies actually yield the intended results? What factors are behind the creation of such conducive circumstances?

Although there are various factors for making decentralization successful, a possible missing link between decentralization assumptions and intended results is partnerships (Brinkerhoff, 2002: and Plummer, 2002). This partnership issue has not been sufficiently studied in the decentralization literature (Cohen and Peterson, 1999), even if sporadic evidence of effective partnerships have been reported (UNDP, 2000b). Partnership is a type of collective action that requires coordinated efforts by more than two actors in order to improve the well-being of participants.[11] Apparently no single actor alone, even the state, can provide all the

---

[10] Thus, although Crook and Manor (1998) attempted to measure the degree of responsiveness of local governments to the needs of the poor, they used the budget allocations for essential social services as a proxy barometer. No views of the poor are incorporated to verify if this barometer is reasonable or not.

[11] On collective action see Olson, 1965; Ostrom, 1990 and 1998; and Sandler, 1992.

social services efficiently and effectively. Partnerships, particularly those between public and private organizations, replace the ineffective "traditions of techno-bureaucracy" (Carley and Christie, 2000, p. 181). If collective actions are facilitated by partnerships, anticipated results can be pro-poor. Whether decentralization attempts are successful, particularly in low-income countries, depends on how participatory decision-making processes induce attitudinal changes of stakeholders for mutual collaboration.

Partnership can be conceptualized in its ideal form as an agile relationship among diverse actors aiming to achieve common goals which are based on agreed objectives and principles. This pursuit is usually arranged through rational division of labor reflecting comparative strengths. The partnership represents a careful mix of respective autonomy (mutual respect for organizational independence) and synergy effects (enabled by mutual learning and influences in such forms as innovative experiments and adaptations) (Brinkerhoff, 2002; and Fowler, 2000).[12]

Although this kind of ideal partnership rarely exists in difficult situations in developing countries, especially in Africa, the merits of forging partnerships are significant and deserve careful attention. First, partnerships create results which are more than the sum of what each actor can accomplish independently. Thus, partnerships for development are probably the most acutely needed strategic alliances for realizing sustainable socio-economic development. Partnerships enable engaged actors to access crucial resources which would otherwise be inaccessible. The resources can be, *inter alia*, valuable information, financial resources, useful technologies, and experienced visions on development practices. These resources do not have to be owned by partners initially. Instead, partners can expand opportunities for resource availability by contacts and networks. Second, partnerships lower transaction costs by bringing these resources together for more efficient and effective management. Sometimes, this can be achieved by the economies of scale. Other times, it can be facilitated by mutual trust building and information sharing. Third, partnerships facilitate mutual learning by merging different experiences, skills and perceptions of common problems. Innovative experiments are conducted, which would often be very difficult if one organization attempted them alone. In this process, there would be a further refinement utilizing comparative advantages of respective partners. This readjustment rationalizes the application of available resources. Fourth, as partnerships grow, the capacity of participating organizations would be improved through the experiences of working together. Examples of such capacity improvement may include acquiring new technologies of certain products and/or services, improved customer relations, and reduced organizational vulnerabilities in times of crises (Brinkerhoff, 2002, chapter 1).

The most essential task, therefore, is to identify under what circumstances different stakeholders can form partnerships in order to achieve mutually beneficial results. Do decentralization measures create opportunities among stakeholders to

---

[12] Fowler (1997 and 2000) discusses related notions of ally, collaborator, funder, and supporter. See also Carley and Christie (2000) on networking; Rondinelli (2002) for public-private partnerships in a privatization context; and Goss (2001) in local governance.

form partnerships, including the central and local governments? To what extent would it be feasible for stakeholders attempt to produce mutually beneficial outcomes?

It would be more appropriate to analyze these questions according to the following subcategories. As illustrated in Figure 1.1, there are various steps of causality which eventually lead to mutually beneficial situations. The hypothesized chain of causality is a "decomposed" framework to investigate dynamic stakeholder relations in decentralization processes. The central government establishes a policy framework of decentralization, supported by fiscal transfers to subnational units of the government. At local levels, the relevant governments initiate consultative processes to discuss common issues for mutually agreeable solutions. Increased interaction among different participants, including the poor and the dis-

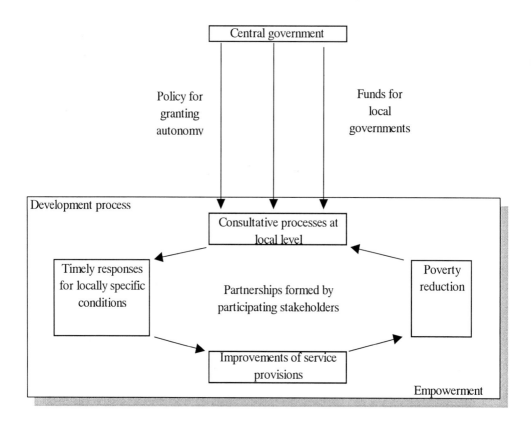

Figure 1.1 Hypothetical framework of successful decentralization measures[13]

[13] Unless otherwise indicated, all tables and figures throughout this study are compiled by the author.

advantaged, fosters mutual understanding and help to create partnerships for common benefits. Constant consultations have better chances to institutionalize democratic decision-making structures. A more frequent and wider scope of participation is considered to contribute to improved transparency and accountability in stakeholder relations. Solutions adopted in these processes tend to be more timely responses to locally specific concerns. Improved essential services provided by local governments contribute to the empowerment of the poor who sincerely appreciate these services. As a result, these processes should enhance responsiveness, which is defined as the degree of congruence between service output and the needs of ordinary people. Both the processes and the outcomes contribute to mitigate poverty, an ultimate goal of decentralization attempts. Empowerment can be defined as a process as well as an outcome of gaining various abilities, confidence and visions for positive transformations in the lives of the poor and the socially disadvantaged. This transformation takes place individually as well as collectively.[14]

In order to test whether the hypothesis is accurate, this study pays particular attention, first of all, to the dynamic interplay between social structures and agencies. This is especially important, as will be examined in the next chapter more closely, because the fluid, unstable, disengaged relations between the state and society in Africa negates the perception of the state as an organic, fixed and unchallenged entity. Restructuring the state is far from an automatic process. Reorganization of government offices affect the way in which stakeholders are aligned and also influence the complex web of relations among stakeholders who exercise influence over the processes of reforms. Assessing the interplay between the structures and agencies might reveal a broad picture of dynamic social change.

Second, this study pays attention to different and often contradictory views of different stakeholders, including the poor and the disadvantaged, concerning decentralization measures. It is important to note that these perceptions are never static and change over time. Perceptions guide the way in which stakeholders interact. Some ally and others conflict over different issues. These assessments help us to overcome the danger of self-righteousness associated with normative values. This approach allows us to see real situations as opposed to the idealized conceptual models such as those of the modern state, democratization, participation, empowerment, and others. The actor-oriented perspective is suitable for analyzing formations and break-ups of alliances in terms of mutual benefits (Lister, 2000, p. 237; and Long, 2001).

3 Case Study in Uganda

This study, therefore, aims to contribute to the illumination of theoretical assumptions and realities of decentralization measures through a case study from

---

[14] For more discussions of empowerment, see Brohman, 1996; Cheater, 1999; Craig and Mayo, 1995; Friedmann, 1992; and Moser, 1993.

Uganda, Africa. There are two important reasons why this study focuses on Africa. First, Africa is a region where relatively little empirical research has been conducted in comparison to Asia and Latin America.[15] This is surprising because Africa receives the highest proportion of World Bank funded decentralization programmes (Olowu, 2001). Another reason is that Africa is the place where the degree of incongruence between the modern nation state system and indigenous societies is the gravest (as elaborated in the next chapter). State-society relations in Africa are the least ideal for anticipating synergy effects of mutual collaboration. Yet, this is the continent where integrated and multi-dimensional solutions are most critically needed. Therefore, focusing on African experiences is to meet timely demands for attempting to fill the research gap.

Among the countries in Africa, Uganda is considered particularly valuable for research on decentralization, since Uganda has been pursuing one of the most systematic decentralization policies in Africa. (Table 1.1 presents basic information of Uganda.) Uganda's living conditions are generally more problematic than other African countries. But, some of the leading district governments in Uganda attract frequent visits of policy makers of African countries and donors (Dawa, 2001).[16] In addition, although Uganda is still heavily dependent on foreign assistance for government activities,[17] the series of decentralization measures are not imposed by external aid agencies as in the case of most other African countries (Smoke, 2001, p. 20). Therefore, it is especially useful to present the complex processes of decentralization attempts as accurately as possible and to generate lessons from Ugandan experiences. These lessons should be valuable for academics, policy makers, and practitioners who are involved in similar decentralizing attempts in other countries.

When the NRM formed a government in 1986, it undertook various structural reforms seriously. Uganda in the 1970s was a typical example of Sub-Saharan Africa, suffering from virtual state collapse and economic bankruptcy (Semboja and Therkildsen, 1995). This experience created a situation whereby ordinary people needed to avoid (over)dependence on the state for essential services in order to secure their day-to-day survival. On the other hand, it also created a certain degree of political apathy and cynicism.

Faced with this situation, the NRM attempted to restore local democracy and to improve the livelihood of ordinary people by the "movement system." The Resistance Council (RC) system - a hierarchy of councils and committees - was a core institution for movement polity. The polity has not allowed political parties but individual people to stand in elections including RC leaders. The NRM has

---

[15] For a review of decentralization in Asia, see Aziz and Arnold, 1996. On Latin America, see Burki et al., 1999.

[16] The number of districts as of April 2003 is 56, but for consistent historical comparisons, this study is based on district information when the number was 45 in 2000.

[17] In the early 1990s, roughly half of the government's total expenditures were financed by aid resources (records provided by UNDP Kampala office, August 1998). This trend applies to today; according to government figures, in FY 2002/03 aid covered 52% of total government expenditures and 12% of GDP (Lister and Nyamugasira, 2003, p. 97).

Table 1.1 Uganda at a glance

Indicators	Uganda	Developing countries	Sub-Saharan Africa
Surface Area (1,000 sq. km, 1999)*	241	101,487	24,267
Population (million, 2001)	22.8	5,178	673.9
Population density (people per sq. km, 2001)	116	52	29
GDP (billion US$, 2001)	5.7	6,179.3	315.3
GNI per capita (PPP US$, 2001)	1,250	3,930	1,620
Human Development Index (2000)**	0.444	0.654	0.471
Life expectancy at birth (years, 2000)	42	64	47
Adult illiteracy rate (% of 15 and above, 2000)	33	25	39
Under 5 mortality rate (per 1,000 births, 2000)	161	85	162
Average annual population growth rate (%, 1990-2001)	3	1.5	2.6

Sources: * World Bank [2000a] *World Development Report 2000/2001* (Oxford: Oxford University Press for the World Bank); ** UNDP [2002] *Human Development Report 2002* (Oxford: Oxford University Press); and the rest from World Bank [2003] *World Development Report 2003* (Oxford: Oxford University Press for the World Bank).
Note: Uganda's surface area is comparable to that of the United Kingdom (245), and its population is about 35% of Britons.

argued that this system has allowed free and fair participation of all Ugandans in a bottom-up decision-making process. It has been one of the aspirations of the NRM that the RC system would promote collective action for both democracy and development. This attempt has been no small endeavor. Indeed, the RC system has often been praised as one of the few institutional attempts to promote democratization that has not been imposed by the West (Brett, 1992, 1994, and 1995; Ottemoeller, 1996; and Tidemand, 1994b, p. 3).

On the other hand, under this movement system, opportunities for people's participation outside of the RC system have been severely limited. The unitary polity in Uganda is very different from liberal democracy often adopted in multi-party democracy in the West. Therefore, numerous analysts consider Uganda as "hostile to democracy" (Human Rights Watch, 1999).[18] Uganda's political system can be most suitably characterized as "semi-authoritarianism." This type of polity usually displays some procedural democracy including constitutional separation of powers, contested presidential and parliamentary elections as well providing some degree of political freedom to their citizens. Nevertheless, the regimes in power shrewdly maneuver to protect themselves from open competition that might threaten the tenure of incumbents. As a result, the same "strongman" remains in power for a considerable period of time (Ottaway, 1999a).[19]

Because the RC system was indivisible from decentralization, NRM's endeavor for decentralization has mainly been implemented as institution building of the RC system. In October, 1992 President Yoweri Museveni officially launched the decentralization policy (Museveni, 1993). Especially since 1993 the pace of decentralization measures has been accelerated. The new constitution adopted in 1995 stipulates that decentralization is a national policy, and the RC system was renamed as the Local Council (LC) system. The Local Governments Act, 1997, provides a legal framework within which decentralization is pursued. (A more detailed background of Uganda's political system is provided in Chapter 3).

There are earlier studies of decentralization measures in Uganda.[20] Most of them evaluate the LC system favorably as it provided a first formal mechanism for the poor to participate in decision-making processes, and as also contributed to empower the poor and the socially disadvantaged. It is only recently that negative aspects have started to receive due attention in attempts to reach a more balanced judgment of the LC system. Less sanguine points include the elite domination of local offices and the continued political apathy among the public (Golooba-Mutebi, 1999).

Unfortunately, almost all of the empirical research with a particular focus on Uganda was carried out before the Local Governments Act, 1997, was passed. Then, a new accountability relationship between political leaders and constituencies was established in subsequent local elections. In addition, significant policy-relevant changes have recently taken place. For instance, the successful pioneering attempts in the early 1990s by some districts have convinced several international aid agencies as well as NGOs to enhance direct collaboration with local governments. Because these events have significantly altered the policy environment, it would be essential to reinvestigate whether the current situation is making any contribution to its policy objectives, including both the attainment of

---

[18] See Bratton and Van de Walle (1997) in classifying Uganda in the current Africa's democratization wave.

[19] Using the typology of Dahl (1971), "semi-authoritarianism" comes close to what he calls inclusive hegemony in which, while the degree of participation is high, the extent of political competition is limited.

[20] The earlier studies include Brett, 1992; Dauda, 1999; Ddungu, 1994 and 1998; Golooba-Mutebi, 1999; Kisubi, 1999; Magyezi, 1998; MISR, 1997; Ottemoeller, 1996; Porter and Onyach-Olaa, 1999; Regan, 1995 and 1998; Tidemand, 1994a and 1994b; and Villadsen and Lubanga, 1996.

democratic participation and reduction of the pervasive poverty in the country. This situation presents a very unique opportunity for this research.

4 Research Methodology

Complex processes of decentralization require systematic assessment based on a variety of indicators, which were collected by a range of complementary methods in field research. The evaluation involves objective (structural) as well as subjective (attitudinal) aspects, since perceptions and attitudes revealed by the qualitative assessment complement formal and quantitative information of organizational changes. Together, a more holistic understanding of decentralization should emerge.

Even though Uganda is one of the pioneering countries in Africa in terms of decentralization, the degree of decentralization measures differs from one place to another. In order to obtain a balanced picture, three districts were chosen for this study: Mukono, Rakai, and Tororo.[21] In Rakai, which borders on Tanzania, a large amount of assistance by Danish International Development Assistance (DANIDA) has been provided, and various stakeholders have figured out the working relationships with each other reasonably clearly.[22] Mukono, located adjacent to Kampala (the capital of Uganda), is another good example. Mukono has pride as the "best" district in Uganda. Mukono has been implementing decentralization measures reasonably successfully until recently without much donor support and held the chairpersonship of the association of local governments for some period.

Other districts are attempting to follow these pioneering districts. One such example is Tororo, which is in the east bordering Kenya. Although it is one of the first districts which was decentralized in 1993, this district suffers from several problems including a large domestic debt. The problems encountered by Tororo District represent dangers and risks of the decentralization endeavors in Uganda, which can happen in other districts as well. Tororo was, therefore, selected as a contrasting example with the other two districts. While NGOs are relatively active in income generation in Mukono and in HIV/AIDS prevention and care in Rakai, NGO activities are not so widespread in Tororo. (More explanation of the three districts is provided at the beginning of Chapter 4.)

In the three districts, empirical investigation was carried out by listening to approximately 160 stakeholders, including political leaders, administrative officials, NGO activists, in addition to 80 stakeholders of various kinds in Kampala. In some cases, observations of the council meetings were conducted. Documents

---

[21] While urbanization cannot be dismissed in Uganda, this study focuses on the rural areas. This does not mean that urban areas are insignificant for development studies. But since poverty is largely a rural issue in Uganda, where the majority reside and engage in farming in one way or another, this choice is deemed justified.

[22] Concern Worldwide et al. (1999) provide a useful poverty analysis in the case of Rakai.

concerning the LC activities were analyzed where they were available. Additional investigations were also made where small-scale development activities were carried out in order to highlight both the potential and limitations of the LC system.

To understand the views of people at the grassroots level, two survey methods were employed, both of which are participatory.[23] The first one was focus group discussions, in which some topics were presented for discussions but participants were not constrained in expressing their opinions on any relevant subjects. The second one was a short survey questionnaire to obtain some quantitative assessment. Visits to rural areas were made in collaboration with NGOs and community development persons active in each district, who also served as interpreters for the languages spoken in each location. On average, one visit to a community took about two-and-a-half-hours; an-hour-and-a-half for focus group discussions and an additional hour for filling out the questionnaire. After the preliminary investigations in 1998, 35 group discussions were held in 1999 and 2000 in 30 different locations (with a total number of 428 respondents), and the average attendance in a visit was 13 people.[24]

In the fieldwork, particular attention was paid to two service delivery sectors for examining the relevance and effectiveness of decentralization: education and health. The selection of these two services is considered appropriate, firstly because the poor at the grassroots level consider education and health as the most essential community priorities if any sincere efforts for poverty reduction are to be attempted. It is also because education, in particular, is normally the sector in which the largest proportion of public expenditures is allocated. Thus, it is essential to examine whether these decentralizing service delivery modalities prove to be efficient and effective.

In examining these sectors, the following areas of concern which form the basis of the hypothesis of Figure 1.1, were investigated. It is crucial to examine what kind of participation is taking place at various levels of local governments, particularly by the poor, women and ethnic minorities by looking into: 1) the degree of voter turnout in local elections; 2) grassroots attendance at LC meetings; 3) constituencies' contact with local councillors on some issues; and 4) the degree of people's collaboration on communal activities. In addition, relations among other stakeholders, including central-local government relations, were examined.

---

[23] This study employs participatory methodologies, although this study itself is not a "participatory evaluation" in that my stake differs from that of Ugandans who collaborated during this study. Participatory evaluation differs from the conventional evaluation in several important aspects. Essentially it is a reflective process in which a series of social changes are interpreted by the stakeholders in order to pursue the process of transformation further into the future. This is a process of mutual learning, while conventional evaluation presents a neutral judgment made by a third party who usually is not involved in the transformative process. On the subject of participatory evaluation, see, for instance, Estella, 2000; and Jackson and Kassam, 1998.

[24] In 1999, 12 discussion sessions were conducted at 11 locations. These served as a test for subsequent implementation of an expanded number of discussions as well as for the improved design of the survey questionnaire.

Investigations are also needed to identify what kinds of roles are played by political leaders, administrators, NGOs, the private sector, and grassroots people in the complex processes of decentralization. It is also essential to find out whether the LC system serves as a useful forum for interaction between the authorities and ordinary people. In addition, it is necessary to analyze whether development planning processes become more transparent and if the LC system's financial allocations match the people's aspirations and desires. The examinations also include whether the speed of response by local governments is increased, and whether collaboration between public and private (NGO) service providers contributes to improved responsiveness.

It is important to consider whether the poor themselves feel more empowered than before due to decentralization measures in general and to the performance of the LC system in particular. More specifically, the proportion of positive change that the poor perceive in their lives in terms of decreasing material and non-material deprivation is to be identified. The degree of maturing local social networks, which can reduce isolation and insecurity of the poor and the marginalized, was also examined. Attention was also paid to examine whether the LC system contributes to the cohesiveness of local communities so that issues can be resolved locally, or whether it simply perpetuates local power inequalities.

It needs to be verified what kind of pro-poor outcomes, if any, are realized as a result of the changes in the processes. Whether the national priority goals for poverty reduction in Uganda (in such areas as agriculture, roads, education, health, and water and sanitation) are met by increased output, possibly by augmented resources made available on both the national and local levels, is an important area for investigation. It is also necessary to examine whether financial support from central to local governments is sufficient in both quality and quantity. Examination into whether locally generated revenues are increasing, possibly supported by greater willingness of local tax payers, is also carried out. Other issues include whether the regional disparities are widening or shrinking due to more autonomy granted to local governments, as well as whether there are any attempts to redistribute income and/or wealth from richer to poorer areas. (The beginning section of Chapter 3 and the Appendix provide more information on the methodology.)

5 Some Clarification of Concepts

Before proceeding further, it would be appropriate to clarify relevant notions. First, while the notions of a stakeholder and an agency are not identical, in this study these terms are employed more or less interchangeably. Stakeholders have an interest either individually or collectively in a particular decision (Hemmati, 2002). They may influence such decisions or be influenced by them. Generally, the notion of an agency assumes that individual actors possess a certain capacity to apply social experiences and to devise mechanisms to cope with changing situations, even under coercion. Within the limits of socio-economic resources, availability of information, and uncertainties, these actors make adaptations (Long,

2001, p. 16). The notion of agency emphasizes the role of actors vis-à-vis social structures. While it may be preferable to use agency rather than stakeholders since the latter tends to connote homogeneity of stakeholders even though the degree of influences encountered by actors are diverse in quality and quantity, the difference is not significant enough to influence the diagnosis of this study.

Second, the following distinction is made between organizations and institutions. While organizations can be defined as structures of recognized and accepted roles for particular purposes, institutions are complexes of norms and behaviors that persist over time because they serve common purposes (Uphoff, 1986, pp. 8-9). Some, but not all, organizations are institutions at the same time. Constant interactions among stakeholders may create certain norms which are useful for mutually beneficial outcomes. Thus, decentralization may facilitate institution building at local levels. A particular form of local government is an organization which may become an institution if people recognize it as serving to create useful norms and behaviors for common benefits. The local government also needs to be durable in order to be recognized as an institution.

The third is concerned with the definition of "decentralization." One of the commonly adopted classifications of various measures associated with decentralization is to distinguish deconcentration, delegation, and devolution (e.g. Carley and Christie, 2000; Litvack et al., 1998; and Turner and Hulme, 1997). *Deconcentration* refers to a situation whereby certain responsibilities are assigned and services transferred from central government to its regional offices and branches. *Devolution* normally indicates a situation in which authority for decision making and financing is transferred from central to sub-national units of government which enjoy a reasonably high degree of autonomy. Deconcentration takes place normally within administrative structures, while devolution mainly centers around political bodies. In short, while deconcentration simply relocates authority at different levels of government, devolution removes authority from central to sub-national units of the government. Another crucial difference between deconcentration and devolution is the way in which accountability works. In deconcentration, even though decision makers are located in local offices, they are still held accountable to authorities at the central level. In contrast, in devolution, locally based decision makers are accountable to the public on a local level (Uphoff, 1986, pp. 221-222).

While distinction between deconcentration and devolution is warranted, defining *delegation* in relation to these two concepts is problematic. Delegation usually involves transfer of responsibilities in decision making as well as management of public administration from central to local governments. Delegation is somewhere in between deconcentration and devolution, but it is normally related to both political and administrative spheres. The problem is that because delegation is vaguely defined, the common typology of classifying decentralization into three categories does not prove really useful (Mawhood, 1993; and Uphoff, 1986). In reality, there are several forms which bear more than one of the three forms of decentralization.[25]

Instead, decentralization in this study is defined as the process through which central government transfers various forms of authority and functions to subnational units of the government for timely adaptation to locally specific conditions. This is a broad definition but is suitable to gauge the degree of autonomy and authority granted to local governments in decision making, including planning, financing, and implementing their activities. This general definition relates to both political and administrative spheres. What is essential is not whether one particular form of decentralization takes place, but what sort of decisions can be made autonomously at what level of the hierarchy within the public realm. Because decentralization entails complex processes, it is useless to try and fit a country's decentralization measures into one category such as either devolution or deconcentration. Instead, it is more useful to see how various resources, political, economic as well as social, are shared among stakeholders in order to evaluate both assumptions and realities of decentralization.

Inevitably, decentralization changes the way in which power is shared between central and local governments. But as we shall see later, this power-sharing does not have to be zero sum (Ostrom et al. 1993, p.164). The "zero sum" and "positive sum" notions are the fourth important concepts in this study. In a zero-sum situation, increased benefits for some can take place only at the expense of others. Gains by some and losses by others would be equal, and therefore the sum becomes zero. Zero-sum transaction is essentially a redistribution of welfare and hardships across the society, and is a very crude method in which compromises cannot be easily made. This type of transactions is politically unpopular and does not generate a high-degree of legitimacy. On the other hand, in a positive-sum situation, improvements of benefits to some do not take place at the cost of others. Participating stakeholders mutually gain from such improvements. This kind of transaction can enjoy a higher level of political legitimacy, and chances for reaching compromises through negotiations would increase (Alfonso, 1997, p. 176). If those resources, including political power, can be shared in a mutually empowering way for both the central and local governments, as well as for both the state and society, this transaction can present "win-win" solutions.[26]

Fifth, the notion of "governance" needs to be explained.[27] Broadly, it relates to both processes and outcomes of (formal and informal) rules that guide and regulate common social concerns among constituent members. Stakeholders, includ-

---

[25] Smith (1997) introduces a dimension in which local councils address single or multi purpose activities.

[26] These terms of "zero sum" and "positive sum" used in this study are more general than those defined by game theorists. For the notions of "zero sum" and "positive sum," see Uphoff, 1992, pp. 284-289.

[27] Pierre (2000) provides an inter-disciplinary review of "governance," and points out that the concept has two meanings. First, it refers to the ways in which the state adapts itself to changing environments especially in the late twentieth century; second, it also relates to co-ordination of social mechanisms (p. 3).

ing governors and the governed, interact in order to find mutually beneficial solutions.[28] The negotiations become acute if and when they are concerned with allocations of benefits and losses across the society, especially by changing allocation of limited public resources. This signifies that governance is in essence a set of social institutions to determine who obtains what kind of benefits and/or losses. The "benefits" and "losses" are not only material but also non-material satisfactions and sacrifices as well. Good governance can, therefore, be established when stakeholders (both the powerful and the powerless) are reasonably satisfied with the way in which benefits and losses are generated as well as distributed. Attaining this goal can be facilitated by reaching a clear, common vision, which guides the stakeholders to identify their positions in relation to others.[29] It is at the level of local governments where the state (governors) and society (the governed) interact most frequently and readily. Therefore, the concept of "local governance" is useful to consider whether the interactions at local levels enhance chances to reach such a common vision.[30]

Sixth, one of the crucial links between participation and good governance lies in accountability. Broadly, governments are considered to be accountable if citizens can distinguish representative from non-representative governments and can thus sanction them appropriately, by retaining in office those who perform well while ousting the non-performers. Governments are obligated to provide explanations related to their performance. Essentially, accountability can be understood as a relational concept and involves reciprocal relationships between the rulers and the ruled as well as between service providers and their recipients.[31] In order for this accountability to be effective, appropriate mechanisms of rewards and sanctions are necessary in which good performances are appreciated and bad ones are penalized. Thus, adequate incentive schemes are indispensable. One of the critical problems, however, is that reciprocity is difficult to maintain between the rulers and the ruled. Some practical measures to overcome this imbalance are necessary.

---

[28] While analysts of international relations and comparative politics tend to emphasize the notions of rules and order provided by governance without government, public administration scholars and development agencies are inclined to emphasize those of control, "steering," and guidance of governance (Hyden and Court, 2001; and Pierre, 2000).

[29] Sharing normative values for collective actions among the stakeholders usually facilitates such consensus building processes.

[30] Reviews of the governance concept are found in, *inter alia*, Commission on Global Governance, 1995; Goss, 2001; Harbeson et al., 1994; Healey and Robinson, 1994; Hollingsworth and Boyer, 1997; Hyden and Court, 2001; Hyden and Bratton, 1992; Hyden, 1998a and 2000; Rosenau, 1995; Schacter, 2000; Schneider, 1999a and 1999b; Thomas, C., 2000; Thomas, V. et al., 2000; UNDP, 2000a, p. 54; UNDP and BMZ, 2000; and Young 1994.

[31] Analyses of different dimensions of the concept and tools for promoting accountability are found in Healey and Robinson, 1994; Olowu, 1999a; Przeworski et al., 1999; Rasheed and Olowu, 1993; Ribot, 2001, Annex C; Robinson and White, 1998; Schneider, 1999a and 1999b; Shah, 1998; and Turner and Hulme, 1997, pp. 122-126.

Finally, the notion of "community" needs to be clarified, since decentralization measures are to serve community development. Efforts have often been made to define this elusive concept geographically, but communities do not necessarily share common geographical spaces. Thus, it would be more suitable to define it functionally. Community can be defined as a social manifestation of often dense personal interactions with the actual or potential cohesion, demarcation, legitimacy, and resilience to organize themselves for effective collective action at levels often beyond the reach of the management of state bureaucracies. Community is related to cohesion since it refers to common identities and interests which serve not only to differentiate the members from others but also to support them in uniting for collective action. Commonalities of identities and interests set social boundaries and determine membership. Thus community has a demarcation function by clarifying the boundaries of jurisdiction in which collective endeavors are organized. This demarcation is commonly based on spatial criteria but can also be based on socially sanctioned access to given resources. Community is also closely related to legitimacy, because effective collective action requires that power exercised by leadership needs to be accepted by the members without a high-degree of hesitation. Community is also somewhat organic. Resilience is the organizational capacity to adapt the community structures and functions in dynamic socio-political and economic changes. Resilience is a key for risk management for members (Barrow and Murphree, 2001, pp. 26-27).[32]

6 Main Arguments and Structure of This Study

It is evident that decentralization by itself should not be viewed normatively as a good policy. Norms and attitudes are influenced by the way in which stakeholders interact with each other to negotiate their benefits and disadvantages. Social dynamics affect norms, just as normative values influence social dynamism. Empirical investigation unfolds a systematic picture of the decentralization measures in Uganda. At the national level, a well-defined policy framework is now in place. The central government is committed to provide funds for decentralized services through inter-government fiscal transfers. At local levels, the local council, formed by elected representatives, is the main interface between authorities and grassroots people. Administrators are held accountable to the councillors who serve as political representatives. At the grassroots level, people participate in local decision-making processes, and small-scale development activities are increasingly carried out. The outcomes usually fulfill the needs of the poor and the disadvantaged. NGOs often support this process by helping community leaders to mobilize villagers, as well as providing some financial assistance.[33] Throughout

---

[32] On the notion of community, see Craig and Mayo, 1995; Kaufman and Alfonso, 1997; and Warburton, 1998.

[33] Concerning the roles of NGOs in Uganda, there are numerous controversies. See Dicklitch, 1998; Howes, 1997; Riddel et al., 1998; and Semboja and Therkildsen, 1995.

the processes, strategic partnerships have started to emerge for mutually beneficial results. This progress appears very impressive.

On the other hand, Uganda certainly faces remaining challenges. Even if participation at the local levels is increasing and can facilitate more collaboration for collective action, it can also frustrate such activities if people's expanding demands are not met. Increased participation can lead to more harmony as well as more conflict within the Ugandan multi-ethnic society. Clearly, partnerships are still fragile and can be solidified by concomitant improvements in incentives, information, and conflict-resolution mechanisms.

Decentralization measures are much bolder attempts to transform a wide range of social interactions among different stakeholders than what is often assumed in the literature, especially those adopted among donor agencies. Decentralization processes are clearly very complex and are not a simple social engineering based on a blueprint which can be used anywhere. Political support is indispensable for successful decentralization. However, the way in which such support is provided is crucial to shape power relations between various levels of the government. In the Ugandan experience, the political commitment by the NRM government has both advantages and disadvantages at the same time. The very fact that the LC system is fused with the NRM polity is advantageous because the NRM is committed politically to pursuing decentralization. The other side of the coin is, however, that since the support for the LC system is at least partly motivated by political reasons for securing the NRM's grip on power, social autonomy granted to the LC system is indeed confined by the political ideas and objectives of the NRM. This contradiction is one of the characteristics of the process of decentralization in Uganda.

The following chapters are to examine both the potential and limitation of the decentralization experience in Uganda. Chapter 2 reviews the evolution of modern statehood and its extension into Africa through colonialism. Attributes usually associated with modern states are not easily found among African states, and reforming them is both necessary and difficult. The pros and cons of decentralization are presented and center around economic efficiency and political democratization. The diverse origins of decentralization rationale and the criticisms against them imply tensions between different perspectives.

In Chapter 3, the historical evolution of Uganda's decentralization endeavors is traced. When the NRM took power in 1986, it created a new RC system. The original establishment of the RC system influenced the way in which the socially disadvantaged would relate to the RC/LC system. But the actual development of the RC system is based more on the experiences at the grassroots level rather than the penetration of the NRM slogans. Although the lower-level LC is central to people's daily concerns today, the LC system is not free from difficulties. In fact, numerous councillors themselves do not wish to seek reelection since they think this job is too time-consuming without much reward.

In Chapter 4, views of people at the grassroots are presented. Their views demonstrate that the LC system is useful for participation and does contribute to some elements of empowerment of the poor, including women, the elderly and the youth. But the LC is more effective as a forum for discussions than as a problem-solving institution. The poor at the grassroots are not familiar with the higher levels of the LC, and their satisfaction with the system deteriorates as the LC moves upwards along the hierarchy.

Chapter 5 looks at the relationships between the LC system and the disadvantaged, including women, the youth, and ethnic minorities. These social groups reveal interesting patterns of collaboration and struggles at the same time. The similarities and differences of these marginalized people in their engagement with the LC within the overall framework of the current polity illustrate the potential as well as limitations of participation and empowerment of the poor.

Chapter 6 is focused on fiscal decentralization. The government has shown commitment in increasing the grants transferred from the central to local governments, especially in the form of conditional grants. This predominance of conditional grants makes local governments implementers of centrally determined activities, which is a contradiction in decentralization. However, there has been much progress in creating a more coherent budgeting process between the central and local governments.

In Chapter 7, one of the essential public services, primary education, is presented within the framework of decentralizing service provisions. The Universal Primary Education (UPE) policy launched in 1996 has succeeded in a massive increase of pupil enrollment at primary schools thanks to collaboration with people at the grassroots level through the LC structure. But this improvement has also led to other serious challenges, including a decline in the quality of education, teachers' lack of motivation, and poor supervision. The current situation urgently calls for a set of consistent and coordinated remedial actions. The role of communities still remains essential for sustaining the gains in this area.

Chapter 8 addresses another important area of service delivery: health. In contrast to education, decentralized local governments actually have reduced resources allocated for health. To improve health conditions, measures to improve funding arrangements, to provide more information, and to engage people closely in monitoring policy outcomes are urgently needed. The area of health is a test case to convince the public that decentralization efforts indeed lead to improved public services.

The comparison of education and health is useful. Whereas both sectors now adopt a sector-wide approach (SWAP) in which donor coordination is improved, the contrast is also striking. In education, decentralization has brought improved grassroots services mainly through constructing classrooms. Noticeable improvement of health service delivery derives not so much from grassroots participation as from increased collaboration between public and private (NGO) service providers. Both are "pro-poor" results of decentralizing service provisions, but the ways in which outcomes are generated are very different. If education can be an example of "demand driven" outcome, then health is "supply driven."

Chapter 9 concludes this study. The LC system is more likely to be "pro-poor" than previous government structures of the country. The LC system is conducive to facilitate strategic partnership formations of stakeholders for mutually beneficial outcomes. The partnerships are still fragile and need to be strengthened by improved incentive mechanisms, wider information dissemination, and adequate conflict-resolution mechanisms. Prospects of successful decentralization measures depend on whether these measures to support partnerships are coherently provided both at the central and at local levels. Granting new autonomy to local governments alone does not necessarily lead to effective development processes and outcomes, unless similar efforts are coordinated nationally. In addition, because many developing countries, particularly those in Africa, depend heavily on donors for development activities, the need for central-local coordination calls for the donors' urgent attention to ameliorate their contradictory aid policies toward developing countries. Supporting both SWAP and decentralization measures is not necessarily coherent.

2 Decentralization Debate: Democracy, Development and Collective Action

The key to resolving the problems of African administration lay[s] in the development of an efficient and democratic system of local government…. I wish to emphasize the words: efficient, democratic and local…. I used these words because they seem to me to contain the kernel of the whole matter; local *because the system of government must be close to the common people and their problems,* efficient *because it must be capable of managing local services in a way which will help to raise the standard of living, and* democratic *because it must not only find a place for the growing class of educated men, but at the same time command the respect and support of the mass of the people.*

Lord Creech Jones, 1947, Secretary of State for Colonies, emphasis in original[1]

The background in which decentralization measures are implemented in developing countries, especially in Africa, is complicated. The modern state was born in a particular historical context of sixteenth to eighteenth century Europe. This form of political order was extended to different parts of the world, including Africa, by the expansion of Europe which was then the dominant world power. The transition from colonial to native authorities did not necessarily improve democratic practices or economic well-being for the majority of Africans. Legacies of colonialism, although they are not the only factor contributing to contemporary difficulties faced by the tropical countries, still exert profound influences on today's political and economic affairs.

On the other hand, development issues that African leaders face have also been becoming increasingly complex and difficult to resolve. In attempting to modernize economies in Africa, leaders opted for state intervention. The failure of these government initiatives was gradually replaced by more market-friendly approaches on the continent. The alternative economic management attempted in Africa has not been effective either. Thus, today's complex development cannot be resolved by states or markets alone. In addition, new challenges of global environmental degradation and increased competition of goods and services in global markets, to name a few, inevitably involve African countries.

---

[1] This famous dispatch is quoted in Apter, 1997, p. 236; Kasfir, 1993, p. 26; and Olowu, 1999b, p. 286, and referred in Turner and Hulme, 1997, p. 163.

Faced with this extremely demanding task to achieve development in an ever globalizing world, a new thinking is necessary for effective solutions. Since no single actor alone can provide sustainable solutions to these complex issues, different segments of the government, private sector, NGOs, as well as ordinary people themselves have respective roles to play. Decentralization has been advocated as a promising mechanism for facilitating collaboration among different actors for mutual benefit. While hierarchy in the past was effective for politico-administrative coordination, today's circumstances demand different forms of effective coordination: partnerships and networks at local levels. In central-local relations, both the central government and local agents need to agree on their division of labor to address common concerns. Decentralizing measures require, accordingly, a new coordination style reflecting a redefined division of tasks between different layers of the government.

This chapter starts with a review of the state-society relations in Africa, against which decentralization measures have been implemented in various countries. What becomes clear from this review is that Africa is the place where probably the most acute imbalances between modern statehood and local realties are manifested in the world. Since the magnitude of such imbalances is daunting, a remedy is needed for both economic and political reasons, both of which favor decentralization over centralization. To those who emphasize economic efficiency, neo-liberalists, decentralized states are compatible with their emphasis on markets and are for bringing locally responsive and speedier solutions to diverse problems. To those who appreciate political reform toward democratization, neo-populists, decentralization is a promising avenue by enlarging the scope for citizen participation. Pro-decentralization advocacy, thus, originates from diverse reasons, which do not necessarily constitute a single consolidated justification. There are certain tensions between different arguments of the neo-liberalists and the neo-populists. This alliance between the neo-liberalists and the neo-populists itself is unique since these two groups often display different orientations on economic and political affairs. This uniqueness constitutes one of the reasons why in the current literature decentralization is often uncritically accepted while centralization is given negative connotations.

The debate over decentralization is, at the same time, polarized between these different orientations (Carley and Christie, 2000, p.123). For decentralization to be successful, there must be a link between these two camps. Although there may be many possibilities to bridge these two arguments, the theory of collective action presents a promising potential to forge such linkage. Especially, partnerships are one form in which collective action can be manifested. However, this bridge is often assumed rather than proved. In their arguments, the logic becomes tautology. On the one hand, in order to reduce tensions between individual behaviors and socially (un)desirable results, collective action is needed that can be facilitated less problematically at local levels. On the other hand, collective action needs to be facilitated by the decentralized state since externalities cannot be resolved by markets alone. Accordingly, the tautological debate implies that decentralization presents in essence an empirical question (Mackintosh and Roy, 1999; and Smoke, 2001). This chapter, therefore, looks critically into both the merits and demerits of decentralization arguments. The review, thus, presents an interesting set of on-the-ground issues which are explored in Uganda's case study in the subsequent chapters.

1 Formation of the Modern State and its Spread into Africa

Europe underwent the establishment of a new political system in the sixteenth and the seventeenth centuries. The evolution of the new nation-state was gradual but unquestionable. By the beginning of the eighteenth century, each state consolidated its power. The development of state sovereignty was essential to this process in which the state was granted the exclusive rights for rule within its jurisdiction that went much beyond the localized territories ruled by the earlier feudal kings. The essential characteristics of the modern state include the centralization of power, monopoly of forces by standing armies and police, the expansion of state administration (bureaucracy), territorial rule, and the diplomatic system for inter-state relations. The state sovereignty then needed to be respected in relations to other states which could also govern in their bounded territories without interference by other states (Held, et al., 1999, chapter 1).[2]

Defining the modern state has been controversial, but it can be defined as a rule-based impersonal political machinery, with exclusive autonomy granted over jurisdiction in a demarcated territorial area, reinforced by a claim to monopolize coercive power, and which enjoys legitimacy by winning loyalty from the citizens (Held, 1995, p. 48). The ideal type of the modern state hardly exists in any one form. Nonetheless, it would be useful to consider the following four characteristics of modern statehood (ibid, pp. 48-50; and Held et al., 1999, p. 45). These dimensions not only distinguish modern states from other forms of political order but also serve as a yardstick to gauge their maturity in relation to time and place, even if these yardsticks are rough.

1.1 Attributes of Modern Statehood

First, although sovereignty itself is a complex notion, it is only the modern state system that defined borders as exactly as they are known. No territory can belong to two sovereign states at the same time, at least formally. The second element is the concentration of force. The modern state lays claim to monopolize the means of coercion by standing armies and police. This monopoly became possible by breaking down rival powers within the jurisdiction.[3] Thirdly, the modern state re-

---

[2] This equality between the states formed the basis of the Westphalian inter-state system, named after the treaty of 1648.

[3] Bates (2001) provides interesting arguments over the relations between economic development and control of force.

flects the notion of legally structured power with supreme jurisdiction over a bounded territory. This impersonalization of power (rule of law) is in part the result of secularization of power from divine and religious authorities.

Fourth, the modern state can ascertain its legitimacy by winning the support of its citizens through responding to the views and interests expressed by them and/or their representatives. An important way to win citizen support is to improve the welfare of the population. But economic improvement is not the only part of securing legitimacy. If the population shares a common socio-cultural and/or religious identity, the state may win legitimacy relatively easily.[4] But nationalism and nation-states are two distinct issues.[5] Ideally, well-performing states would satisfy all of these criteria which are mutually related. But in reality most of the states do not fit into this pure model, and the degree of qualification differs from one case to another.

1.2 Colonialism and Extension of the Modern State to Africa

The modern state was disseminated to different parts of the world through European expansion. The colonial administrations in different places adopted different forms depending on local situations and the historical experiences of the colonial powers at home. Generally, the colonial states were an expanded hierarchical administration through the concentration of political and administrative functions in the hands of a colonial civil service backed by a well-managed coercive apparatus. The fundamental nature of the colonial states was militaristic and authoritarian.

As anti-colonial movements gained support, colonial powers were faced with the forthcoming handover of power to indigenous hands. Retrospectively, it is interesting to note that some colonial officials were paying significant attention to local self-determination. In the 1950s and the early 1960s, when the transition to African administrations was sought, these officials appreciated that fostering local democracy would become essential for the state to provide necessary services to the populations. Because African countries were composed of multi-ethnic and multi-religious societies, the decentralized state structures were deemed a promising approach among colonial administrations (Crook and Manor, 1998, p. 1; and Mawhood, 1993, p. 7). Although the famous dispatch of Lord Jones quoted at the opening of this chapter did not realize his intention, his view was echoed by other colonial officials in the same period (Apter, 1997, p. 237).

---

[4] Legitimacy is also a complex notion. Put simply, power is legitimate when it corresponds to (formal and informal) rules backed not only by the dominant but also by the subordinate (Ribot, 2001). Thus, there are multiple notions of legitimacy in a society which is under transformation.

[5] Those who conceptualize the state as an organization of power emphasize the first three elements, while other analysts consider the state as a political community by emphasizing democratic and representation functions within it. The latter view puts much emphasis on the fourth dimension of legitimacy.

But this appreciation of local governments was perhaps ahead of its time. After the independence of new African states from the middle of the 1960s, centralization became the norm. It was the system in place in the colonial states that independent African leaders inherited in the 1960s. The handover of power from colonial to African leaders did not fundamentally alter the attributes of the states.

Immediately after independence, the new leaders were faced with a paradoxical situation. Although their political experiences had been based on the colonial context which emphasized centralized, bureaucratic and authoritarian control over the populations, they were asked to govern pluralist institutions of foreign origins such as parliaments and political parties. Their dilemma was acute. Anti-colonial movements did not necessarily promote the formation of national consciousness in societies among their diverse social groups. Many segments of the population demanded various public services from the meager state resources. Economic conditions were hardly supportive of rapid growth. Yet in many countries new political rules were written immediately before independence, which demanded democratic rule in the decolonized era.

The new leaders, on the other hand, had to consolidate their political base when their legitimacy was fragile. The actual options available for them were limited. The result was to consolidate the state as an organ of coercive force, elaborated as follows by some analysts:

> The formal agencies transferred to African hands were thus alien in derivation, functionally conceived, bureaucratically designed, authoritarian in nature, and primarily concerned with issues of domination rather than legitimacy. During decolonization these patterns were, in most cases, elaborated rather than transformed (Chazan et al., 1999, p. 43).

The legacies of this inheritance affect the nature of African states fundamentally, which still exist at the current time (Sahn and Sarris, 1994).[6]

1.3 Centralization After Independence

Soon after independence, generally, political competition was curtailed, and rival political parties were outlawed in Africa. Various measures were applied to circumvent constitutional provisions, and one-party systems were consolidated. Administrative and coercive structures were expanded, and decision-making processes were largely centralized in the hands of top leaders and their close associates. The leaders in Sudan, Mauritania, Kenya, Uganda, Zambia, Zimbabwe, to name a few, considered this centralization justifiable since they were faced with the political and administrative paradox and considered it a realistic option for achieving economic growth and welfare.

The new African leaders gave priority to national integration, which was considered to be better served by centralization. They thought that decentralization

---

[6] For historical implications, see Olowu, 2001; Tordoff, 1994; de Valk and Wekwete, 1990; World Bank, 1999a, chapter 5; Wunsch, 2000; and Wunsch and Olowu, 1990.

would create opportunities for the opposition to become threats to their power (Mawhood, 1993).[7] Thus the idea of the government being democratic became secondary. Local governments were put directly under the control of central institutions. Furthermore, the political leaders often used "ethnic cards" to win popular support. As a consequence, local governments became battlefields of ethnic rivalries rather than being a branch of the government that was either authoritarian or democratic.

The tendency toward centralization and personalization of power was consolidated in the 1960s and the 1970s. During the 1960s, the African civil service expanded on average at 7% annually. This trend continued, and by 1980 on average approximately half of the total government expenditures on the continent went for salaries of civil servants (Chazan et al., 1999, p. 55).

This expansion was supported by the then common economic prescription: modernization could be best achieved by state intervention supported by modern bureaucracy (Carley and Christie, 2000; Mawhood, 1993; and Wunsch and Olowu, 1990). National planning was deemed rational for building a sound economic base in new countries (Brohman, 1996).[8] The state intervention and control by, for instance, utility companies and export commodity marketing boards, became common in Africa. Although this kind of intervention did not deny social and cultural traditions on the continent, it was reinforced by the then widespread belief in the supremacy of experts in modern development planning that originated from the West (Wunsch and Olowu, 1990, p. 294). Interestingly enough, this tendency for central planning and government intervention was accepted both by capitalist as well as by socialist regimes in Africa (Brohman, 1996). Within capitalist states, economic growth would be achieved by rational planning and "trickle-down" effects. In socialist governments, plans were decided through a one-party system to bring remarkable progress. Thus, regardless of political ideologies, the central governments became the main engine for economic growth, and the status granted to local governments in Africa was marginal without sufficient political and economic autonomy.

Yet, while bureaucracy became more extensive, it at the same time did not increase its effectiveness. Rather, bureaucratic expansion without meritocracy created a new social division between some who were close to state resources (civil servants and government employees) and majority African populations, which became a fundamental problem (Bates, 1981). Mismanagement of personnel, political appointees, financial misappropriation, corruption, lack of accountability, *inter alia*, prevented what was supposed to be institutions for making new countries

---

[7] De Valk puts a politically oriented explanation differently. After the independence of newly born countries in Africa, decentralization was attempted. Because providing essential social services was costly, fiscal decentralization was thought of as a low-cost solution. Earlier decentralization was clearly motivated by political reasons of the central ruling elite (de Valk, 1990, chapter 1).

[8] Numerous ideas which are mutually related within the neoclassical economics supported this planning stance: functional integration of urban-industrial growth, hierarchical diffusion of innovations, trickle-down, etc (Brohman, 1996, chapter 7).

striving forward for a promising future from being efficient and responsive to the aspirations of Africans.

Similarly, coercive apparatus were enlarged.   Armies and police, taken over from colonial regimes as a symbol of state sovereignty, were augmented to contain anti-government activities and to provide badly needed support to fragile regimes in power. African military expenditures as a proportion of GNP rose from 1.8 % in 1963 to 3.4% in 1971 (Chazan et al., 1999, p. 58). This significant expansion of the coercive apparatus was not only incohesive internally but also created tensions with the civil service and other social groups. In several places of Africa, for instance in Ghana, Nigeria, Uganda, Somalia, and Liberia,[9] faulty lines of command, inadequate salaries, politicization of the military, and undisciplined soldiers contributed to lawlessness of the state on which the very coercive apparatus relied.

Judicially, the most fundamental problem in post-independent Africa was the notion of the rule of law. It is not hard to find examples of gross human rights violations on the continent. Authoritarian regimes exercised state repression. Rapid expansion of bureaucracy and coercive apparatus generally affected the separation of powers and judicial autonomy, although judicial structures remained relatively resilient in some countries.

Moreover, the two decades after independence witnessed the systematic subordination of political organizations under the executive branch. Even in some single-party systems, parties quickly changed their role from an organization of representation to a mere extension of state administration and political control. Legislatures were undermined, although the degree of autonomy and stability differed from country to country. As succinctly summarized already in examining the situations in the 1960s, "The single-party thus fails in all its claims. It cannot represent all the people; or maintain free discussion; or give stable government; or above all, reconcile the differences between various regional groups" (Lewis, 1965, p. 63).[10] The end result of this type of African politics is a high degree of socio-political instability. The political apparatus were not grounded in clearly delineated popular foundations. Even with "strong" authoritarian military rule, the sources of power remained un-clarified, and no articulated rules existed between political institutions and the African populations. The leaders did not establish effective links with societies in Africa and needed to depend on physical force more than at the time of independence (Chazan et al., 1999, chapter 2).[11]

---

[9] The period in which this lawlessness resulted differs from place to place.

[10] In retrospect, Lewis's emphasis on decentralization, or rather more balanced central-local relations in political systems in Africa in his classic work (1965), should have attracted more serious attention.

[11] Useful review of the often paradoxical nature of the state in developing countries and in Africa can be found in Bayart, 1993; Chabal and Daloz, 1999; Comaroff and Comaroff, 1999; Evans, 1995; Joseph, 1999; and Migdal et al., 1994. In Uganda's context, Bunker (1987) demonstrates that the state depended on peasants for export crop production, which put the state in a vulnerable position.

1.4 Failures of Centralization

As a consequence of a series of centralization movements, most, if not all, African countries faced fundamental crises in the late 1970s and the 1980s (Chazan, et al., 1999). Although the precise degree was different in each country, there was a strong preference for a unitary state model based on the powerful executive within a de facto single party system. Not only did the central government become more dominant vis-à-vis local governments, but the executive branch of the government came to be too powerful vis-à-vis legislative and judicial authorities. This centralization, however, could not achieve significant modernization through economic growth or through political democratization, (Mawhood, 1993).[12] There are several important points in assessing these failing states in post-independent Africa, although there are controversies over the reasons. These reasons still bear importance today.

First, as for territoriality of modern statehood, the physical boundaries of the African states were imposed on indigenous populations by the colonial governments. The new independent African states inherited the same boundaries, which created a separation between political and socio-cultural units. This disjuncture has been an important consequence of legitimacy.

The second dimension of the statehood is monopolization of resources and force. The expanded state bureaucracy was overstaffed and costly. The administrations were inefficient in using public resources and ineffective in delivering public services. Even if there were some improvements in health and education in the first couple of decades after independence, lack of improvement in welfare for the majority of Africans since the 1960s was unmistakably evident.

Development planning by experts has not succeeded in economic growth. These plans were often imposed in a top-down fashion without reflecting popular aspirations and were soon shelved without much effect. Bureaucracy did not prove to be rational and efficient, partly because of political interference. While the bureaucracy would prove suitable for administering routine tasks, situations in Africa were far from certain and thus the classic Weberian model was unsuitable (Wunsch and Olowu, 1990).[13] As a consequence, the more centralized the African state became, the further economic situations became exacerbated, which profoundly undermined state legitimacy. Even if African economies deteriorated since the 1960s, partly because of unfairness within the international system, a se-

---

[12] Some countries, faced with these failures, attempted to increase the degree of autonomy for local governments. But this modification did not entirely change central-local relations; local governments remained implementers of centrally decided activities (Mawhood, 1993, chapter 1).

[13] In Asia and Latin America, problems associated with central planning and state intervention became apparent in the 1970s. One way to resolve this problem was integrated regional development planning (IRDP) in which more spatially balanced growth by emphasizing the role of small and intermediate towns was sought. But the IRDI did not alter spatial planning fundamentally (Brohman, 1996, chapter 7).

ries of initiatives taken by most of the African states became an inherent part of the compounded problem rather than an effective solution (Bates, 1981).

The third yardstick for the modern state is a rule-based political system with impersonality of power. African leaders, on the contrary, personalized power. Although their control was far from complete, they became the hub between political parties and the military, as well as between political leaders and administrators. Public office holders became synonymous with private wealth. The distinction between public and private was almost completely blurred. Under this system, economic resources were allocated as rents, which were manipulated by officers and others (ibid.). (Rents are material benefits politically traded between those who seek and those who distribute political influences.) These transactions are in essence zero sum; somebody's gains are losses for others. Thus, those who held the hub positions became influential for allocation of political power and economic resources. This precipitated neo-patrimonialism whereby "relationships to a person (rather than an officeholder) thrived within a purportedly legal-rational administrative system" incurring detrimental social costs (Chazan et al., 1999, p 54; and Chabal and Daloz, 1999).

In addition, even if physical force was extremely concentrated and often abused, power was not articulated. The way it was exercised by the post-independent leaders demonstrated that power was divorced from social foundations, economic conditions and culturally acceptable notions of authority. Ironically, exercises of brutal power by the strongmen were the signs of their fragility in holding power (Kohli and Shue, 1994). Personalized power invited politics of terror for opponents of incumbents, which further promoted social fragmentation and conflict. Monopolized forces also reduced social space that was necessary not only for political oppsition but also for small-scale autonomous organizations striving for development. Small-scale organizations and actors, who can otherwise engage in development activities, including labor unions, cooperative organizations, private enterprises, universities, churches, and voluntary associations, were undermined in this process (Wunsch and Olowu, 1990; and Migdal et al., 1994).

This kind of exercise of power was, again, not considered legitimate, thus not satisfying a prerequisite for modern statehood. Many state leaders were unable to win the trust of large segments of their populations. As the polity became illegitimate, politics became a competition by rent-seeking elites for diminishing state resources behind the scenes. The societies were then more divided than before. This kind of state-society relations is inherently unstable and possibly self-defeating. The state is "strong" in the sense that it is predatory, but extremely "weak" because it is ineffective (Evans, 1995; and Thomas-Slayter, 1994). Thus, centralized structures left extremely compounded inadequacies. The majority of Africans have been forced to pay unbearable costs even today (Mawhood, 1993; Olowu, 2001; and Wunsch and Olowu, 1990).

2 Arguments over Merits and Demerits of Decentralization

Little progress in economic advancement and democratization in Africa in the 1980s was considered a result of the failed centralized state. In particular, central governments from the 1980s onward have been facing severe budget deficits in attempting to keep up with increasing demands for more services (Smoke, 2001). The donors to Africa were then in need of reviewing their past understanding of African states and socio-economic situations. Structural adjustment lending dominated the economic reform agenda in the 1980s. There was also a trend for political reform as well. After the fall of the Berlin Wall in 1989, the international community started to pay more attention to the necessity for global democratization. Africa became a target of such attention, since the lack of progress both in economic and political fronts was so evident.

Against this background, it was considered urgent to redefine the role of the public sector in developing countries for the purpose of improving its performance. A major component of such reform was to decentralize the functions and responsibilities of governments. The World Bank, one of the most influential donors, presented its case for decentralization:

> State institutions are often accused of being too remote from the daily realities of poor pepole's lives, and decentralization is often recommended as a solution. Decentralization can be powerful for achieving development goals in ways that respond to the needs of local communities, by assigning control rights to people who have the information and incentives to make decisions best suited to those needs, and who have the responsibility for the political and economic consequences of their decisions (2000a, p. 106).

This quotation places a high hope on decentralization that it may be more successful in satisfying the four attributes of modern statehood. At local levels, the mismatch between territorial boundaries and socio-cultural communities may be reduced. At the community level, the legacies of imposed colonial boundaries are less important than daily interactions among diverse social groups for various transactions, which facilitates dense social networks. Participatory decision-making systems pre-suppose consultations with others, and have a chance of transforming personal rule in African states to more impersonal and rule-based governance. Socially inclusive processes also have a potential to reverse the monopolization of power and resources. Local elections may bring coercive apparatus under the control of political representatives. Finally, these practices apparently respond to popular needs and have a greater chance to enhance the legitimacy of the state. Indeed, because the process of defining legitimacy itself needs to be consultative, rejuvenated local consultations have more of a chance to establish satisfactory legitimacy for stakeholders.

However, given the compounded instability of African states and their skewed relations with social groups resulting from recent history, this anticipation of decentralization may be too optimistic to be sustained. The experiences of recent African history demonstrate that there have already been trials and errors in decentralization, albeit the degree of decentralization attempts was relatively small. In fact, rationales behind institutional arrangements were associated both with centralization and decentralization depending on the prevailing understanding of political and economic systems both in international as well as domestic arenas.[14] The historical swings between relatively centralized vs. decentralized states provide useful materials for reviewing merits and demerits of decentralization in developing countries, especially in Africa.[15]

2.1 Economic Efficiency

Economic efficiency is probably the most prominent point in debate between supporters and opponents of decentralization policies. Decentralists argue that decentralization measures are especially efficient for the utilization of resources. Because local governments are located closer to people, they argue, the local governments are more suitable than the central government to identify what kinds of services are needed by the people. This advantage in identifying public needs suggests that local authorities can produce services that are more *responsive* to public aspirations (Blair, 2000; Oates, 1999; and Olowu and Smoke, 1992). In addition, public needs differ from one locality to another. Local governments can provide "tailor-made" solutions in each area, whereas the central government tends to impose standardized services across the country (Turner and Hulme, 1997, chapter 7).

Furthermore, it is insisted that since local governments' proximity to people enable decisions to be made much more speedily than the central government. Decentralization cuts through complex chains of bureaucratic red-tape within administrative hierarchies. In addition, reduced red-tape makes coordination among different administrative offices less troublesome. Effective coordination reduces duplication between agencies and facilitates integrated planning of local initiatives. From an economic standpoint, this is considered a substantial gain in efficiency in allocating scarce public resources and improving welfare of the population at large (Shin and Ho, 1998; Smith, 2002; and Smoke, 2001).

---

[14] The historical swings between decentralization and centralization in Africa are discussed in Mawhood, 1993; Olowu, 2001; and Ribot, 2001.

[15] Academic origins of decentralization are diverse. Some of the essential (normative) notions derive from classical liberal democratic theory. In economics it is often associated with public choice theory, among others. In public administration, so-called New Public Management is influential (Iversen et al., 2000; and Werlin, 1992). Participatory development also relates to decentralization. Reviews of decentralization are found in Adamolekun, 1999, chapter 4; Agrawal and Ribot, 1999; Brohman, 1996, chapter 7; Carley and Christie, 2000, chapter 6; Cohen and Peterson, 1999; Gershberg, 1998; Harbeson, 2001; Johnson, 2001; Klugman, 1994; Litvack et al., 1998; Mackintosh and Roy, 1999; Manor, 1999; Mawhood, 1993; Moore and Putzel, 1999; Olowu and Smoke, 1992; Ostrom et al., 1993, chapter 8; Ribot, 2001; Smith, 1996 and 1998; Therkildsen, 1993; Turner and Hulme, 1997, chapter 7; UNDP, 2000b; de Valk, and Wekwete, 1990; World Bank, 1999a; Wunsch and Olowu, 1990; and Wunsch, 2000 and 2001.

This argument is further reinforced by issues related to *transaction costs*. Centralized services normally require very complex institutional arrangements for service delivery. Similarly, complex structures are also needed for monitoring and evaluation. These mechanisms are very costly in developing countries, especially because communication between different levels of government is not fully in place. Decentralized service provisions, in contrast, are much less costly, since local agents are located close enough to monitor services on the ground and necessary adjustment can be made relatively quickly (Smoke, 2001).[16]

Although there are problems in interpreting conflicting situations, Ethiopia may be closest to a positive example in attaining economic efficiency on the continent (Olowu, 2001). Botswana is also an exceptional case in which relative improvements in resource utilization are noted (Wunsch, 2001).[17]

On the other hand, critics respond that these arguments are plausible, but realities of decentralization implementation have not supported them. The anti-decentralists maintain that these arguments are simply assumptions without sufficient proof. In order for efficiency to be gained, the local governments are urged to translate their advantage of proximity into practice. In reality, this translation is often difficult, if not impossible. First, it is not always the case that local people are knowledgeable in local issues. The anti-decentralists maintain that "it is not necessarily true that local citizens have superior ability - or even any ability at all - for identifying both local needs and the optimal amount of resources and services needed to meet them" (Golooba-Mutebi, 1999, chapter 2). Proximity is not equal to knowledge being collected and used effectively (Ostrom et al., 1993, p. 169).

Several factors are considered necessary, if proximity is to yield the intended results of knowledgeability. Attitudes on the part of officials have to be changed in order to facilitate interactions with the people at the grassroots level, especially the poor and the marginalized. In many parts of the developing world, officials working for local authorities do not necessarily consider their affiliation with locality as a matter of professional prestige or a factor in their career development (Ostrom et al., 1993). Instead, most of them prefer to work at the central government, which they consider fulfills their professional aspirations more satisfactorily.

In addition, whether this kind of attitudinal change takes place depends on particular organizational culture, which must foster interaction with populations under its jurisdiction. If such culture prevails within any government, either central or local, it is in a better position to interact with the users of services. Proximity alone does not guarantee such supportive organizational culture (Smith, 2002).

---

[16] The efficiency argument is also supported by the "subsidiarity principle" which states that tasks should be undertaken at the lowest political-administrative levels in societies for efficiency. Upper levels should support lower ones to ensure that they have adequate means to discharge responsibilities (e.g. Carley and Christie, 2000, p. 135).

[17] The countries referred to in this section are tentative indications due to complexities in evaluating decentralization performances.

Second, it is indispensable to avoid *elite capture* for the efficiency argument to hold true. There is no logic to prove that local political leaders are more benevolent than their central counterparts (Manor, 1999), and several countries, including Kenya and Mali, exemplify this fallacy (Charlick, 2001). It is often pointed out that many decentralization programs, particularly those initiated by foreign donors, were implemented without coherent planning as in Guinea (ibid.), and the newly available opportunities of local autonomy are abused by local leaders. Elite capture has a devastating consequence in poverty stricken rural Africa (Crook and Manor, 1998; Smith, 2002; and Smoke, 2001).

Decentralization detractors also insist that allocative efficiency may be at odds with other considerations. Certain measures should be taken by national governments. This includes redistributional and stabilizing functions. It is normally the responsibility of the central government to ensure that people in poorly endowed parts of the country can enjoy a reasonable standard of living through redistribution of revenues. Stabilization functions of macro-economy through monetary and fiscal policies should also be undertaken by the national government (Mackintosh and Roy, 1999; and Shin and Ho, 1998). Furthermore, opponents suggest, decentralization undermines the merit of scale economies. Certain activities should be undertaken by the central government to take advantage of scale merit. For instance, electric utilities, nation-wide transportation systems, and procurement of standard health equipment may be more adequately provided in bulk amount.[18]

2.2 Enhanced Local Revenues

Local revenue raising is another economic issue on which pro- and anti-decentralists disagree. Decentralists maintain that if service improvements take place in areas where people place a high priority on overcoming poverty, this improvement would be highly appreciated at the grassroots level. This appreciation leads to an increased willingness to share the costs of services. It is often pointed out based on experiences in many developing countries that even the poor become more willing to pay for the services if they are considered to be of adequate in quality and quantity. As long as the local population is convinced that their taxes are used for more satisfactory services, they are willing to pay such taxes. This conviction is much more easily established with local rather than centralized taxes (Klugman, 1994). As a result, the revenue available to local governments through user contributions is enhanced. At the local level, expenditure decisions can be more closely linked to actual revenues, which makes public services more sustainable in the long run. Creating this kind of sustainability is an important factor in structural adjustment programmes (Litvack et al., 1998; and World Bank, 1999a).

Criticism is voiced against the decentralist view here as well. The critics argue that limitation of various resources does not allow improvement of services. Im-

---

[18] But this does not mean that scale economies increase without any limits. Therefore, it is advisable to balance competing considerations of certain public services in a given context.

plementing decentralization is too complicated to be coped with by limited resources, skills, and knowledge available to local governments, as shown, for example, by the early decentralization experiences in Malawi (Tordoff, 1994).[19] The economic base for local governments is too narrow to realize the benefits of local autonomy. Rural democracy in developing countries is far from mature enough to handle complex representation and accountability issues at the community level. Furthermore, central government is often unwilling to relinquish necessary political, administrative, financial and technical resources to local governments, which become more dependent on inter-governmental fiscal transfers as well as administrative and technical guidelines issued by the central government. Consequently, the intended result in which people become more willing to pay for the services does not come to fruition (Manor, 1999).[20]

Often, local governments are asked to deliver certain public services even when corresponding resources are not delegated to them. This particularly applies to *fiscal decentralization* (Bird and Vaillancourt, 1998; Bird and Smart, 2002; Smoke, 2001; and Oates, 1999). In Africa particularly, the tax base is very narrow, and national budgets normally face severe shortages. The central government is reluctant to handover authority to collect taxes to local governments. Local governments in effect either must depend on grants transferred from the center or attempt to implement additional taxation measures. Furthermore, the inter-governmental fiscal transfer is usually dominated by central influences, and local authorities are passive recipients of these grants, Kenya being a prime example (Crook and Sverrisson, 1999; and Smoke, 2001). Because the central government controls most of the valuable tax basis, what is left for local governments is not promising as a source for independent revenue. For instance, property tax and user charges are often collected by local governments. But, taxable properties in rural areas are very limited, and the poor are often unable to pay taxes. In addition, these taxes are extremely costly to administer. Many of the local authorities are, therefore, very frustrated by the gap between their mandate and actual resources for fulfilling it.

2.3 Participation for Sustainable Development

Arguments over decentralization relate to the political dimension as well. Notions of participation and democracy are used both by supporters and opponents of decentralization measures. Participation is often considered valuable both as processes and as ends. Participation signifies that people have the legitimate right to voice their concerns in affairs which affect their lives. The consultative process in

---

[19] Critics argue that these limited resources can be better utilized at the central level. Instead of spreading resources too thinly, concentration of the resources at the center can yield more promising results.

[20] Davis et al., report (1994) that the decentralization situation in the Gambia in the late 1980s and the early 1990s showed institutional confusion and ineffective services. They argue that decentralization "by default" was pursued by NGOs. See also Tordoff, 1994.

which the socially marginalized – the poor, the youth, women, ethnic minorities, etc. – are entitled to participate in designing and implementing public policies are valuable as a process itself. Throughout these processes, the socially weak are given precious opportunities to reflect critically on their current situations, which may lead to possible solutions. Often these reflections are *empowering* to the poor. Social gatherings can also provide occasions for overcoming social isolation. If the officials are elected by popular mandate, the relations between leaders and the population become more trustful and accountable.[21]

The participatory processes, in addition, are more likely to yield effective results. Through consultations, development initiatives come to reflect grassroots aspirations and can win the support of the local population. The ready acceptance of activities among the population is significant in comparison to the earlier projects being imposed by the center in a very top-down fashion (Manor, 1999; Olowu 2001; and Wunsch and Olowu, 1990). When developing countries often suffer from under-developed markets and institutions, a consultative decision-making mechanism at the grassroots is deemed a realistic option for articulating essential public services (Litvack et al., 1998; and World Bank, 1999a).[22]

But, there are criticisms expressed against the merits of participation as well (Craig and Mayo, 1995; Cleaver, 1999; Cooke and Kothari, 2001; and Crook and Manor, 1998). Local officials are often not geared toward facilitating popular participation. Political and administrative leaders often unmistakably look down upon the socially disadvantaged. This attitudinal problem, part of which may derive from elitist education, clearly hampers consultative processes to evolve (cf. Green, 1999; and Smith, 2002). Newly given local autonomy may reinforce this tendency. Elected leaders may consider themselves as all-mighty governors in "their small kingdoms." They may not be willing to meet the popular demand for more transparent and accountable decision making.

The local population is not necessarily accustomed to participation practices either. The grassroots poor are not used to being consulted by government officials. Nor do they usually demand the government to be responsive to their needs either. The disadvantaged in Africa, after long years of civil strife and economic mismanagement, have come to devise their own survival strategies without depending on government services. Although this strategy itself is commendable, it has in-

---

[21] Up to the 1980s, some analysts pointed out that decentralization and increased local participation were promising avenues for mitigating profound resistance to social change in rural areas of developing countries. Granting the grassroots people the right to elect their representatives is to win support for change (Smith, 2002). Although this claim may still apply today to some extent, there has been evidence that the local population is not necessarily resistant to social change. When they are convinced of the merits of such changes, they do support changes.

[22] A corollary of this argument is that when people are dissatisfied with services provided by local governments, they can move to another area where they can receive more satisfactory services. This option provides a similar opportunity to what mature markets can accomplish. Although this argument is too simplistic, it is important to acknowledge that people can make choices (Smoke, 2001, p. 6).

grained certain attitudes in interacting with other stakeholders. Therefore, putting participatory forms of development into practice requires a change in the attitude of both leaders as well as followers.

Furthermore, participatory development is costly (Moore and Putzel, 1999). Inclusive processes need a lot of time and energy in order to be properly managed. Since most of rural Africa has not been accustomed to participatory processes, certain types of facilitations are critical, particularly at the initial stage. Often, required skills are not available locally. In this situation, some may be frustrated by the gap between rhetoric and realities of participation. Promoting participation of the socially weak is less promising than rhetoric (Cooke and Kothari, 2001; and Manor, 1999), as Kenya and Côte d'Ivoire (Crook and Sverrisson, 1999) and Mali (Charlick, 2001) may, for instance, illustrate.

In addition, its advantages also need to be balanced with its drawbacks. Local initiatives are certainly desirable in certain types of activities. But community-based activities alone do not mitigate poverty. They need to complement other initiatives such as national infrastructure development, for instance. Certain activities can make sense in one locality, but may become negative externalities in a different locality.[23] Thus, officials are required to pay close attention to a wide range of delicate issues. They also need to collaborate with other stakeholders to realize the complementality.

2.4 National Unity in Multi-ethnic and Multi-religious Societies

The delicate issues of ethnic harmony and regional diversity are also themes contested by pro- and anti-decentralists. Among the decentralists, there is a widespread belief that democratization, especially at local levels, is a prerequisite for building national unity in multi-ethnic and multi-religious societies in developing countries, especially in Africa. It is argued that increased local autonomy can better accommodate competing interests of diverse social groups including ethnic and religious groups. Unless the local population is reasonably satisfied with their legitimate political claims, national unity and harmony cannot be established. Local governments are in a better position than central governments in facilitating diverse claims by the population.

These considerations particularly apply to Africa where the states are formed on the basis of colonial legacies (Smith, 2002). Côte d'Ivoire and Ghana may be presented as examples of improved spatial equity (Crook and Sverrisson, 1999). In Zambia and South Africa, strengthened local governments have helped to recreate national unity (Ribot, 2001).

But, the critics refute such optimistic views. They argue that decentralization measures tend to jeopardize equity among different localities. The critics continue

---

[23] This kind of inter-locality tension applies to, for instance, natural resource management. This tension often requires an external arbitrator, whose role is often played by the central government. The central government often protects common interests beyond local considerations.

that decentralization endeavors may also undermine the traditional Weberian ideal that administration should be conducted rationally; local officials being exposed to competing claims may face significant difficulties in maintaining their objectivity and rationality (Olowu, 1999b, p. 288). In addition, resource-rich areas may take advantage of opportunities of autonomy created by decentralizing attempts, leaving relatively poor areas behind. Therefore, it is argued that development in a country can become severely unbalanced unless central governments take necessary steps to rectify this imbalance.[24] Unless the local revenue base is consolidated, the poor areas are likely to remain behind relatively wealthy areas. This issue of equity in turn has political consequences. Decentralizing attempts may foster great attachment to regional identities rather than national unity in multi-ethnic and multi-religious societies of Africa. As a result, national integrity becomes threatened (Bates, 1999; Ottaway, 1999b; Rothchild, 1997; and Smith, 2002). The military rebellion in Sierra Leone in 1997 was partly caused by decentralization (Rosenbaum and Rojas, 1997).

2.5 Further Controversies

There are additional controversies between supporters and critics of decentralization. First, whether decentralized states improve accountability, particularly between leaders and citizens and thereby reduce corruption, is a hotly debated theme (Agrawal and Ribot, 1999; Johnson, 2001; and Mackintosh and Roy, 1999). In various countries, including Senegal for example, accountability works primarily upward to the center instead of downward to the grassroots (Agrawal and Ribot, 1999). The decentralists argue that local people's participation contributes to improving accountability of public services, because residents can scrutinize local governments more closely than central governments. Thus, the decentralized states reduce the magnitude of corruption and misappropriation of public funds by political representatives and administrators, which is quite serious in developing countries (Manor, 1999). But the opponents argue that local corruption may increase because public resources would then be allocated at local levels. This danger is acute in Africa where patronage plays a significant role in politics and public affairs management (Leonard, 1987). The peril becomes even more real when competition for resources becomes tougher, especially in times of economic hardship partly due to austerity measures of the SAPs (Chabal and Daloz, 1999). Thus, decentralization processes would not necessarily improve accountability.[25]

Second, the question is also raised whether decentralization measures lead to smaller state apparatus. Pro-decentralists argue that decentralization measures make the public sector smaller, as more functions are delegated to local authorities

---

[24] The way in which the central government intervenes is controversial. As attested to by the Nigerian experience, such intervention tends to invite acute struggles over who would benefit from resources.

[25] For the issue of corruption, see Doig, 1995; Stapenhurst and Kpundeh, 1999; and Transparency International, 2000.

with improved inter-office coordination. Improved efficiency and effectiveness of public resource management at local levels no longer requires large bureaucracies at the center. But opponents refute that decentralized states are not necessarily smaller than centralized ones. Since decentralization transfers authority and resources from central to local governments, this shift in fact inevitably demands more sophisticated skills at the central level in order to secure national integrity (Tendler, 1997, p. 143). This is called a paradox of decentralization, that decentralizing measures may require bigger central governments.[26]

3 Discussion of Decentralization Debate

What immediately becomes evident form the review of decentralization arguments is that the same rationales are used toward their own ends both by the supporters and opponents. Economic efficiency, according to the decentralists, can be attained by decentralization measures, whereas the critics argue proximity of local governments is not identical with efficiency. While decentralists advocate the merit of enhanced local revenues, the anti-decentralization camp disputes that limited local capacities prevent this enhancement. Likewise, participatory development through decentralized measures is empowering, as presented by the decentralists, but no previous experiences exist in facilitating participation according to the critics. Even if social harmony across various divisions in Africa can be attained by rejuvenated local interaction, as the decentralists advocate, the critics argue that decentralization results in more regional inequality and instability. These contrasts surely suggest that the debate about decentralization is like proverbs as pointed out in the first chapter of this study.

More importantly, the review suggests there is no singularly proven logic for decentralization. Among the major issues around which the debate revolves, the issues of economic efficiency and local resource enhancement are more emphasized by neo-liberalists than neo-populists. In contrast, the points of participation and national harmony among social divisions are backed more significantly by the neo-populists than the neo-liberalists. The neo-liberal views, closely associated with economic justifications, mainly focus on economic gains such as allocative efficiency and reduced transaction costs to be derived from strengthened local governments. The main advocates include international finance institutions of the World Bank and the IMF.[27] The neo-populists, including leaders of social movements and NGO activists, also support decentralization, although their main stress

---

[26] This paradox parallels Friedmann's view (1992) as he argues that alternative development that responds to the concerns of the disempowered requires the strong state (pp. 7 and 36).

[27] This does not mean that the international finance institutions impose the neo-liberal ideology to recipient countries unilaterally. A notion of "post-conditionality regime," pointed out by Harrison (2001), is useful for more nuanced understanding of donor-recipient relations.

is more on democratic values than on economic efficiency. They appreciate participation and empowerment both as processes and ends. Curiously enough, the neo-liberalists and the neo-populists are in alliance in supporting decentralization, while these two camps are often in confrontation on other issues, for instance the role of markets in the global politico-economic system. The neo-liberalists tend to be politically more conservative than neo-populists who are inclined to present politically alternative views to the mainstream socio-political systems.

This unique alliance symbolizes that rationales for decentralization derive from different origins and backgrounds. Decentralization is proposed for political democratization as well as economic restructuring. Furthermore, the alliance reveals a tension in the political and economic aspects of decentralization. For example, although participatory development is considered a promising alternative to conventional economic modernization, there is no logical proof that political empowerment leads to economic growth. Likewise, whether economic prosperity can satisfy democratic values is an open question, which has been debated hotly. The relationship between political democracy and economic growth is a complicated one, and solutions are highly context specific.[28]

More fundamentally, the views of the neo-liberalists and the neo-populists present a stark contrast in their conceptualization of the relations between individuals and societies. In the neo-liberal views, individuals are to pursue their respective benefits based on their rational judgment. Markets are anticipated to provide an "invisible hand" for coordination. Also with the aid of non-market institutions, social harmony is maintained. In contrast, the neo-populists conceive that people are receptive to collaboration for mutually beneficial activities. It is believed that since the poor have experienced bitterly the limits of individual activities due to their isolation from society, they are interested in possibilities of collective gains. This contrast demonstrates that people are anticipated to behave differently in the neo-liberal and the neo-populist arguments. This difference suggests a contradiction in decentralization rationales.

Problems can be found not only in the justifications but also in criticism of decentralization. Clearly, criticism against decentralization consists largely of empirical arguments rather than theoretical ones (Johnson, 2001; and Smoke, 2001). Elitism and attitudinal difficulties are prime examples. Even if these are real difficulties, they do not mean that these issues are completely beyond the scope of change. Attitudes can be changed, albeit slowly. Elites can become responsive to the aspirations of the socially disadvantaged if appropriate socio-economic incentives are provided. Even if resources are bargained for through patronage networks, patronage can become less problematic if it is publicly disposed through appropriate structures. Certainly skills are deficient at local levels in developing countries, but should this be a reason for not attempting any social change? There have been some interesting attempts to build skills even in poor African countries. True, central governments are not ready to relinquish promising tax resources to local authorities. This reluctance, however, highlights the necessary role of external agencies in changing the relationship between central and local governments.

---

[28] For these complicated relations, see for instance Leftwich, 1996; and UNDP, 2002.

Although decentralization may widen the disparities between rich and poor areas, the classic method of imposing a rigid national standard in many respects would not win the support of the majority of the population in this ever changing world. In short, the anti-decentralists are not entirely "centralists" in their arguments.

The decentralization debate suggests that both sides cannot totally eliminate opposing views, partly because of different interpretations of human nature. The relations between individuals and societies are diverse and may be contradictory, which negates simple theorization. In the decentralization debate, the extent of contradictions is clearly underemphasized. While in the neo-liberal view, individuals are selfish entities driven by their own rationality, in the neo-populist view people are interdependent and collaborative. What is critically absent is a link between the neo-liberal and the neo-populist arguments.

While there are various possibilities of such linkage between these two (contradictory) views,[29] one promising link lies in the theory of collective action. Collective action is an extension of individual rationality combined with the hope to attain collective gains, and presents solutions to various social dilemmas. There are some situations in which individual "rational" choice may end up in socially undesirable outcomes, as symbolized by well-known situations of "tragedy of the commons" and the "prisoners' dilemma." For maximizing economic returns, people may prefer to let others provide public goods which can be enjoyed by non-collaborators as well. This "free riding" matches "rational" calculation by individuals, since benefits can be enjoyed without cost. But if everyone did this free riding, the entire social outcome would be undesirable such as the depletion of public goods on which everyone depends. The tragedy of the commons is the situation in which common pool resources are depleted "rationally." The prisoners dilemma is, similarly, a situation whereby rational decisions by individuals result in sub-optimal consequences. In fact, there are numerous examples by which these kinds of social dilemma can be presented.

Although there have been controversies on the notion of collective action, the main direction of research has been to emphasize some elements under which collective action can be provided to overcome free-riding problems. It is usually considered that collective action can be organized relatively easily if the number of participants is limited as well as if the degree of homogeneity in preferences and capabilities is high among participants. It is also envisaged that such actions tend to take place when the density of interactions by stakeholders is high. Through these interactions, stakeholders would anticipate that other participants would reciprocate contributions toward the common good (values) and goods (materials). Reputation is at stake by reciprocity, and certain norms would emerge that facilitate trust (Ostrom, 1998).[30] On the other hand, collective action often requires institutional support, and markets alone are not sufficient for coordination. The role of the state is often emphasized, and local governments are more suitable,

---

[29] This broad area of interaction between individualistic economic activities and social-level collaboration has been studied in the academic fields of political economy, sociology of economics, and public choice theory (economic study of politics).

[30] The controversial notion of social capital has relevance here as well.

it is argued, to provide much needed support. It is at the local level where a relatively homogenous and limited number of stakeholders engage in day-to-day interactions, from which collective action can develop.[31] Collective action may take many forms, such as partnership which has been receiving increasing attention in development studies.

The relations between decentralization schemes and types of services are complex. The same services can be provided either by the agents of central governments (by deconcentration) or by autonomous local governments (devolution).[32] Generally, policies to redistribute wealth among different local authorities tend to depend more on deconcentration (dispersing functions to local offices), while provisions to provide public goods tend to devolve to local governments (by delegating political authority to local officials). Hospital management, for instance, is often very technical and certain standards need to be met and is considered to be more effective through deconcentration (Shin and Ho, 1998, pp. 107). Thus, standard setting and monitoring of compliance by hospitals may be better managed by a capable central government. Providing certain support for primary education may be more suitably managed by local governments by encouraging involvement of local communities. It may be loosely hypothesized that the more likely certain services tend to generate socially desirable effects beyond individual merits, the more suitable they would be undertaken by local authorities which have sufficient decision-making autonomy (cf. Turner and Hulme, 1997).

However, this anticipated role of bridging economically individualistic and socio-political results by collective action is often assumed rather than proven (cf. Wunsch, 2000). Perhaps, the most acute problem is that its logic almost becomes tautology. Collective action takes place when externalities are taken care,[33] which often needs the supportive role of non-market institutions for coordination, particularly the state. It is at local levels where such coordination can be more readily facilitated than at the central level (Oates, 1999). Simply put, collective action needs decentralization, which itself needs collective action for alleviating economic and political tensions. This circularity does not present a convincing explanation, and is a serious concern. The purpose of this study is, therefore, to resolve the logical contradiction. Especially, how local partnerships emerge is open for more critical investigation.

In addition, the collective action theory assumes that the spheres of public and private can be distinguished. This assumption does not hold in developing countries, particularly in Africa (Semboja and Therkildsen, 1995, p. 3). The blurred boundaries between the public and private realms are partly caused by the rent-seeking behavior of office holders, as seen in the earlier part of this chapter. This case is a negative disjuncture in which resources flow from the public to private consumption. But there have been more positive examples in which lack of public sector activities have been supplemented by private initiatives. These supple-

---

[31] On collective action, see; Olson, 1965; Ostrom, 1990 and 1998; and Sandler, 1992.

[32] See Chapter 1 for the explanation of deconcentration and devolution.

[33] Externalities are negative consequences endured by persons that originate from economic transactions of others. They cannot be resolved by the price and market system.

ments include community-based voluntary activities and small-scale self-help initiatives organized around religious and ethnic groups. Both positive and negative examples complicate the collective action theory. Collective action may be hindered in African socio-cultural contexts, but at the same time, it may be facilitated. The theory shows no clear explanation to reflect African realities. This is why this particular study focuses on the issue of partnership to examine whether the conflicting economic and political rationales can be synthesized reflecting the experiences of an innovative example of decentralization in Uganda.

4 Summary and Conclusion

The incongruence between modern statehood and the African socio-political landscape is daunting. Contemporary history of this continent is full of paradoxes. The "strong" state in monopolizing wealth and repressing opponents is "weak" in facilitating social change much needed for the majority of the population. The African states have been unstable, dismissing a view of the state as an unchallenged power (Joseph, 1999). As the initial hope for independence waned, the politics of Africa has instead become the politics of permanent economic crisis (Van de Walle, 2001). Thus, it is no wonder attempts to redefine the role of the state have become so urgent. In such attempts, relations between central and local governments are crucial. But precisely because pursuing decentralization in this context has been difficult, realizing these goals by supporting local governments is far from an easy task.

As reviewed in this chapter, the debate over decentralization suggests that both pro- and anti-decentralists present only partially convincing arguments. Intuitively, decentralization measures may enjoy a better chance to ameliorate the imbalances of precarious African states, and encourages decentralists. The supporting views of decentralization, on the other hand, derive from different origins, which create unique (yet potentially conflicting) alliances between those who value economic efficiency primarily by markets and others who appreciate social justice largely by collective empowerment of the socially marginalized. The decentralization debate has been revolving around many issues and has certainly contributed to our understanding of decentralization processes. However, there has not yet been a fully completed theorization of the issues. This incompletion strongly implies that the issues related to decentralization are essentially empirical questions. The same incompletion also suggests that there is room for improving our understanding of the widespread policy reforms of decentralization.

Furthermore, it should be noted that decentralization measures have recently been implemented in changing policy contexts. The most imminent change is globalization: A current wave of ever-speedier, much more intense and more influential interactions among actors in different parts of the world have put local governments in developing countries in the forefront in managing complex issues

(Smith, 2002, p. 395).[34] These shifts once again reinforce the positions of both supporters and opponents of decentralization. Certainly the debate over decentralization issues are confusing, because both pro- and anti-decentralists present certain validities in their arguments. The pro-decentralists would argue that precisely because today's situations are more complex, the right remedy for effective statehood is decentralization. On the other hand, the anti-decentralists would insist that decentralization is not a solution precisely because the difficult situations are becoming less conducive to decentralization.

It would, therefore, be inappropriate to approach the controversies by either-or-analyses that gauge only one side of the argument rightly without appreciating opposing views. It is no surprise that among the analysts of decentralization debate there are few "purists" either in supporting or opposing an ideal form of centralization or decentralization, and most exhibit sensitivity to various pro and con arguments (e.g. Manor, 1999; Shin and Ho, 1998; Smoke, 2001; and Smith 2002). The decentralization issues, therefore, need to be examined in real-world contexts. While decentralization may improve congruence between African states and societies, realization depends on how the measures are implemented. The decentralization debate are largely empirical; it is crucial to maintain a reasonable balance in considering various issues related to decentralization. The most desirable solution is to find out how the proposed outcomes can be attained while at the same time minimizing the undesirable side-effects. What would be the characteristics of new local governments? How have perceptions among essential actors been changing over decentralized activities? Do evolving dynamics of stakeholders lead to confrontations or collaborative relations? Are there any possibilities whereby partnerships emerge in the dynamics? Can the partnerships provide a form of collective action, particularly for pro-poor outcomes? Because most of these points are empirical, it is more useful to conduct a careful and comprehensive examination of complex decentralization processes based on real situations. This research is, therefore, intended to contribute to this empirical approach by analyzing one pioneering example in Africa. The case study in Uganda is of value in answering these questions of decentralization, to which this study now turns in subsequent chapters.

---

[34] Globalization is transformative processes of social relations and transactions yielding trans- and inter-regional flows and networks of activities (Held, et al., 1999, p. 16).

3 Evolution of Decentralization in Uganda: Opportunities, Perceptions and Constraints

> *Unless people are equipped in the way they want, any talk of decentralised governance would be mere sloganising. Reservation of seats for the weaker sections is one way of giving them access to decentralised governments. But having done that, if these persons were not trained in the art of governance through the creation of social awareness among them and not provided with the requisite information, then they would be no better off then they were earlier.*

Rajni Kothari, 1996, p. 39

This chapter examines the historical background of Uganda in order to clarify the context in which decentralization measures are currently implemented. The post-independent history of Uganda since 1962 reveals long-lasting civil strife, decaying state institutions and economic bankruptcy. When the National Resistance Movement (NRM) seized power in 1986, it did not want to repeat this painful past (The name of "resistance" reflected their guerrilla struggle and political desire of rejecting instability in their regime). The NRM wished to pursue decentralization to widen popular support by increasing people's participation in decision making through local governments. This policy was intended to contribute to more effective socio-economic development with the ultimate goal of reducing persistent poverty in the country.[1] The NRM's decentralization efforts, with donor support, have been accelerated since 1993. The Constitution, 1995, and the Local Governments Act, 1997, provide rights and responsibilities for local governments. While these legislations have created opportunities for stakeholders to negotiate mutually agreeable outcomes, turning the opportunities into sustained improvement of local livelihood remains a serious challenge.

This chapter first traces the recent history of decentralization measures and outlines the present structure of the Local Council (LC) system. Second, a brief review of the political aspect of decentralization, autonomy in personnel management, and financial resources for local authorities are sketched out. Third, an attempt is made to diagnose how different stakeholders perceive the process of decentralization. Finally, some unique features of decentralization in Uganda are

---

[1] For a recent poverty assessment, see Appleton, 1996 and 1998; CDRN, 1996; Concern Worldwide et al., 1999; Evans, 1994; Jamal, 1998; Kyeyune and Goldey, 1999; Mamdani, 1992; and Uganda, MoFPED, 1999b, 2000e, and 2000g.

considered. It is argued that Uganda's decentralizing attempts have been at least partially motivated by the interests of maintaining the NRM in power. This consideration puts decentralization measures in conflict with other objectives of development and poverty reduction in the country.

1 Evolution of Local Government System

1.1 Historical Background of Uganda

Uganda shares common attributes of imbalances between modern statehood and society as reviewed in the previous chapter. In the late nineteenth century, European powers carved out spheres of influence in East Africa. In 1894, a British protectorate was established in the territories of East Africa including Uganda. In the first half of the twentieth century, the British promoted the agricultural cash crops of coffee and cotton as a basis of colonial economy. But in Uganda no large-scale European settlement took place. The acute social division was not entirely between the whites and Africans but between different ethno-religious African groups. This division was used by the colonial government. The British recruited the northern ethnic group of Nilotics for military and police forces, while the southern Bantus were often employed for administrative posts.

Uganda's transition to an independent state was relatively smooth compared with other countries. The British plan to maintain the integrity of Uganda in its handover of power involved a complex federal constitution. In this arrangement, *kabaka*, the traditional king of Buganda, the largest and wealthiest ethnic group in the country, would serve as the president and Milton Obote, an ethnic Niotlic, as prime minister. In 1962 Uganda became independent, but this north-south alliance did not last long. In 1966, Obote suspended the constitution that allowed traditional kingdoms significant autonomy. Previously, the four traditional kingdoms taxed their own "subjects" and made budgets. Community efforts were mobilized through chiefs. Outside of the kingdoms, in the 1960s, district offices received very limited funds from the center and provided limited services. With the suspension of the constitution, Obote aimed to establish a one-party system to personalize and monopolize political power and economic wealth.

This suspension opened the unfortunate post-independence history, which is tainted with extreme suffering of the Ugandans. The government changed eight times since independence, and four of these changes were forced by military coups. The extent of oppression against civilians did not find comparable examples even in coup-devastated Africa. Ethnic association with formal jobs started during the colonial period is one cause for the severe instability. But political manipulation of ethnicity by post-independent leaders should receive more blame.

Obote became a dictator, becoming dependent on coercive apparatus. Ironically, in 1971 he was deposed by his chief army officer, Idi Amin, who became

Figure 3.1 Central-local relations before NRM's decentralization

the head of state. Amin also played the ethnic card to maintain his grip on power. His army was filled with soldiers from his home area in the north, and he eliminated the ethnic group of Obote from state institutions. It is estimated that approximately 300,000 people were killed. In 1979, Amin was ousted by Tanzanian troops when Uganda and Tanzania were in conflict.

The new government installed by the Tanzanians did not last long either. The country was then in considerable confusion in establishing political order. Obote sought opportunities to return to power and was declared the winner in the December 1980 election. But the election results were contentious, and irregularities were pointed out by many, including Yoweri Museveni, who went into the bush to organize his guerrilla struggle against the declared-winner of the election.

When Museveni came to power in 1986, the consequences of 15 years of civil turmoil were conspicuous. State institutions were destroyed. The living standard for the majority of Ugandans deteriorated. The GDP per capita in 1960 was 100; it reached its peak of 112 in 1969 and deteriorated to the lowest of 60 in 1986 (Bigsten and Kayizzi-Mugerwa, 2001, pp. 16-18). Even when limited services were provided in the 1960s, they did not meet the increasing demands of a growing population. From the 1970s, essential public services were no longer provided. During these difficult times, church-based services and other small-scale self-help groups were the only available support for the majority of the rural population. The "pearl of Africa" was ruined.[2]

The way in which local governments "worked," if at all, since independence is graphically presented in Figure 3.1. Although the figure is simplified, the general pattern is worth emphasizing. The central government fully controlled local governments. The center nominated most local political leaders. At the village level, councils in the late 1960s included two or three village chiefs (appointed officials), clan leaders, a few elected villagers, and representatives of religious leaders (Vincent, 1971, p. 54). The civil servants working at local levels belonged to ministries and answered to remote superiors within ministerial hierarchies not to local

---

[2] For historical background, see Brett, 1992; Hansen and Twaddle, 1991 and 1998; and Semboja and Therkildsen, 1995.

political leadership. The chiefs were appointed salaried-officers who were neither local men nor holders of traditional authority in the particular area. They were outsiders and disliked by villagers.[3] There were few checks on their abuse of power. They did not enjoy prestige (ibid., pp. 52-54).[4] Grassroots people were given little, if any, chance to participate in decision-making processes which affected their lives. The direction of accountability for both political leaders and administrators existed only upwards to the center. Thus, local governments were largely ineffective and inactive, and even the poor were not counting on their services. There was little effort on the side of the private sector or civil society to engage local authorities.

1.2 NRM Seizure of Power in Uganda

When the NRM was still "in the bush" in the middle of the 1980s, it established the Resistance Council (RC) system in areas which it brought under its control.[5] The NRM used the RC system primarily for mobilizing grassroots support to help fight the guerrilla war. The RC was found very effective for maintaining communications between the commanders and grassroots people and proved useful for political mobilization.

The RC was a five-tier hierarchical structure of councils, as illustrated in Table 3.1. The grassroots RC 1 was at the village level; RC 2 for parish; RC 3 for sub-county; RC 4 for county: and RC 5 for district. The people at the grassroots level elected their representatives as councillors at RC 1. There were nine RC 1 councillors in charge of various local matters including information, mobilization, education, finance, security, and concerns of youth and women. These RC 1 councillors in turn elected the same number of councillors for RC 2. This process was repeated up to the level of RC 5. When the NRM took power in 1986, the new government introduced this RC system nationwide.[6]

The RC system is indivisible from the NRM's "movement" polity. The current polity forbids the activities of political parties. Any candidates for elections need to compete on individual merits. The NRM's justification is that political parties in the past divided Uganda along ethnic and religious lines and thereby contrib-

---

[3] Vincent (1971), based on her fieldwork in the late 1960s, compared political leaders with chiefs: The village leaders are typically described as "active men, men who have strong voices politically, men who are fond of asking questions, reasonable men, and above all, popular men. Parish chiefs, by contrast, are thought of as cunning, out to trick people, choleric and unpopular" (p. 247).

[4] On the role of traditional chiefs in decentralization in Africa, see Ribot, 2001, p. 22.

[5] In the Buganda area, almost all the NRM's initial contacts with rural communities were made through "village establishments," which were composed of middle- to large-scale landlords resident in villages (Tidemand, 1994b, p. 70).

[6] For historical background of the RC system, see Brett, 1992, chapter 3; Ottemoeller, 1996, especially chapter 2; Regan, 1995 and 1998; Tidemand, 1994a and 1994b; UPDN, 2000; and Villadsen and Lubanga, 1996.

Table 3.1 Five-tier RC/LC system

Name	Political representatives	Election	Administrative head	Technical team	Numbers *
District RC/LC 5	Chairman and councillors	Direct	CAO	Full team	45
County RC/LC 4	Chairman and councillors	Indirect election	Assistant CAO		214
Sub-county RC/LC 3	Chairman and councillors	Direct election	Subcounty Chief	Sub-accuntant, extension and others	893
Parish RC/LC 2	Chairman and councillors	Indirect	Parish Chief		4,517
Village RC/LC 1	Chairman and councillors	Direct election			39,692

Source: * Uganda, MoH [1999] *National Health Policy* (Kampala: MoH), p. 17.

uted to the prolonged civil war. Instead, the RC system arguably would enable all Ugandans to participate in decision making equally without being discriminated against by their gender, age, religious or political affiliations. Without the RC system, the movement system presents few opportunities for popular participation. The NRM maintains that people can fully participate in politics through the RC system and not through competition by political parties. The RC system and the movement polity are two sides of the same coin. This polity is severely criticized by those who favor multi-party democracy including the old political parties.[7]

The NRM regime also started to investigate what sort of local government system would be desirable in Uganda. The NRM established the Commission of the Inquiry into the Local Government System with 11 members. About a year later, the Commission, in 1987, recommended that the RC should not be a state nor an NRM organ but "democratic organs of the people" in order to establish "effective, viable and representative Local Authorities." In the view of the Commission, both extremes of narrow administrative deconcentration and full political devolution would pose risks, since they would be unable to balance between cohesive national planning, and flexibility required to facilitate local participation. Instead, the RC, the Commission argued, would be able to form a basis for such a balance and hoped to constitute viable democratic local governments (Uganda, 1987).

---

[7] There are numerous works on the assessment of the nature of NRM polity. See, for instance, Bratton and van de Walle, 1997; and Hansen and Twaddle, 1991, 1995, and 1998.

The RC system, in the meantime, spread throughout the country and was generally welcomed by the people as a new political space opened up after prolonged repression. This acceptance was primarily because the people regarded the RC system "not only as protectors against insecurity and custodians of local interests, but also as valuable intermediaries in their relations with higher authorities" (Golooba-Mutebi, 1999, chapter 4). Simply, villagers were not arrested without consultation with the RC leaders; chiefs would no longer treat people harshly;[8] and soldiers would report to the village RCs (Tidemand, 1994b, p. 85). The RC system was really a new political order in the post-independent Ugandan villages.[9]

One of the main reasons for this uniqueness was that the country in 1986 was virtually devoid of any state institutions. This institutional vacuum left much room to maneuver for the NRM which then created new institutions from those past (Brett, 1994, p. 64; and Kasfir, 1999 and 2000). Politically, the RC was installed to solidify people's support for the NRM, which was facing tough challenges from more experienced political parties. In fact, in early elections, the RCs were filled more by candidates of opposition than NRM sympathizers.

The development of the RC system up to the early 1990s was, on the other hand, basically driven by actual experiences gained on the ground. The RC committees functioned continuously with regular elections in 1986, 1989, and 1991. In these years, the NRM Secretariat did not politicize the RC significantly, mainly because the NRM could not penetrate local levels. It was also because the NRM could not articulate local political agendas. Thus, RC 1 was not regarded as an extension of the state apparatus or the political regime (Tidemand, 1994b, p. 95).

On the other hand, the national political situation in fact accelerated the pace of decentralization. In the Buganda Kingdom, the most politically influential kingdom, "decentralization" was interpreted as a federal arrangement in which the King of Buganda would be granted more political and economic autonomy in addition to the cultural symbolism then allowed by the NRM. This Buganda interpretation was obviously against the unitary polity of the NRM. The successive governments in Uganda, including the current NRM, have attempted to control the traditional kingdoms. In order to preempt Buganda's assertion of federalism, rapid decentralization was considered necessary in the early 1990s.[10]

Decentralization attempts were, then, accelerated. In 1993, a first group of 13 districts were decentralized. In the same year, the Local Government (Resistance Councils) Statute, 1993, was passed. This statute provided the legal basis for the

---

[8] Historically, chieftainship in Uganda, particularly in Buganda, went through significant transformations during the British colonial rule and the post-independence periods (Tidemand, 1994b).

[9] Some attempts were made to trace the origin of this RC system, and it is considered that the FRELIMO experience in Mozambique, among other experiences in Africa and developing countries, must have inspired Museveni to devise the RC system. (FRELIMO in English is the Front for the Liberation of Mozambique.) See Brett, 1992, chapter 3; Ottemoeller, 1996, especially chapter 2; and Tidemand, 1994a and 1994b.

[10] This tension between Buganda's federalism and the NRM's policy on decentralization still persists today (Englebert, 2002; and Kayunga, 2000).

earlier practices of the RC system and rationalized the confused lines of authority caused by the five-tiered hierarchy. It also clarified that public servants were answerable to the respective councils.

In the meantime, another significant effort to develop a new constitution was embarked on.[11] The new constitution, adopted in 1995, advocates, *inter alia*, principles of democracy, national unity, human rights, the role of people in development, gender equality, and environmental protection. Chapter 11 describes the principles and structures of the local government. The new constitution renamed Resistance Councils as Local Councils. Following Article 206 of the constitution, the Local Governments Act, 1997 was enacted. This fairly comprehensive act provides the legal framework for the current local government system by laying out responsibilities and functions in relation to the central government.

The recent government plans take decentralization processes into full account. For instance, the Poverty Eradication Action Plan (PEAP) considers decentralizing service provisions as a critical institutional framework to achieve a 50% reduction in Uganda's poverty by 2017 through cost-effective services, particularly in the areas of health, education, agricultural production, feeder roads, and safe drinking water (Uganda, MoFPED, 2000e).

The Decentralization Secretariat, created in 1992, has been vigorously supporting decentralization processes by providing resources and technical support for local authorities. This secretariat is a semi-autonomous organization of the Ministry of Local Government (MoLG). Its training programs target a variety of stakeholders: councillors (elected representatives), civil servants, and concerned citizens. The secretariat also prepares and issues various manuals and guidebooks to enable the councillors and administrators to manage their diverse duties: most notably *The Local Governments Financial and Accounting Regulations, 1998* (Uganda, 1998). The secretariat, with the support of donors, has been generally performing satisfactorily despite shortages of financial resources and manpower.[12]

1.3 Changes from the RC to the LC System

The renaming of RC to LC accompanied fairly significant changes. First, with the Local Governments Act, 1997, a much more articulated structure of accountability was put in place which dispelled the earlier confused line of authority. The council now became the supreme political organ in its jurisdiction. At the LC 5 (district) level, for instance, the chairperson, who is the political head of the council,[13] forms the executive wing together with six other councillors to perform im-

---

[11] For the process of devising this constitution and its significance, see Hansen and Twaddle, 1994; and Hyden, 1998b.

[12] For the role of the Decentralization Secretariat, see, for instance, Villadsen, 1996.

[13] The chairperson nominates his/her core councillors, who form the executive wing, from the list of all councillors. The nomination normally reflects the experience and competence of the candidates and considerations to balance political representation. This nomination has to be approved by the council.

portant functions. These councillors are called secretaries of sector committees: finance and administration, production and extension services, education and sports, health and environment, and works and technical services. The council also forms a legislative forum where all elected councillors serve as representatives of the people. The technical staff under the Chief Administrative Officer (CAO), who is the head of the civil service, implements policy decisions of the council. A typical LC organizational structure is shown in Figure 3.2.

Second, while the RC was a five-tier system, the LC has basically three levels. Although there are still LC 2 and LC 4 units (equivalent to RC 2 and 4 respectively), they are not essential in delivering public services. LC 5 and 3, the focal points for such services, now enjoy corporate status. Especially LC 5 is now the target of various institutional building efforts in collaboration with donors. Gradually some donors started to provide direct assistance to LC 3.[14]

A third significant change is democratization in local elections. In the RC system, RC 1 leaders were elected by universal suffrage of adults by lining up behind the candidates. This form of direct election did not apply to the elections of RC 2 upwards. Therefore, as the councils moved from grassroots to upper levels of the hierarchy, opportunities for reflecting public views were immensely reduced. In the current LC system, the range for direct election has significantly increased. Basically, at the levels of LC 5, 3, and 1, all leaders are elected by universal adult suffrage. Most important is that the election of the LC 5 chairperson, equivalent to a governor in other countries, is now elected by a secret ballot of universal adult suffrage. Additionally, the secret ballot is now a common method of voting. The elected councillors serve for a term of four years.

Fourth, women's representation has significantly improved. While the minimum requirement of female representation in the RC system was only one out of nine councillors, now women must be at least one-third of the entire number of representatives. This change has increased proportional representation of women at the councils significantly. Especially at the lower LC 1 and 2 levels, women tend to occupy more than the mandatory requirement of one-third. When the RC included at least one woman secretary (only), it was often reported that women's voiceswere not seriously heard by male colleagues (Tripp, 2000 and 1998b; and Mulyampiti, 1994). Now men can no longer ignore women's voices as a woman in Mukono stated the representative views:

> In meetings, it is now more comfortable to speak up. But this was not the case before. Husbands mistreated wives before. Husbands either did not allow their wives to attend meetings, or did not allow them to speak in meetings.[15]

---

[14] LC 5 and LC 3 can receive grant aid but are not allowed to borrow funds from donors.

[15] Focus group discussion, Lunbugu, Rakai, 25 August 1999. It was agreed that this statement and the other remarks made throughout this study by rural people during focus group discussions would remain anonymous to assure that participants expressed their views freely without fear of government reprisals.

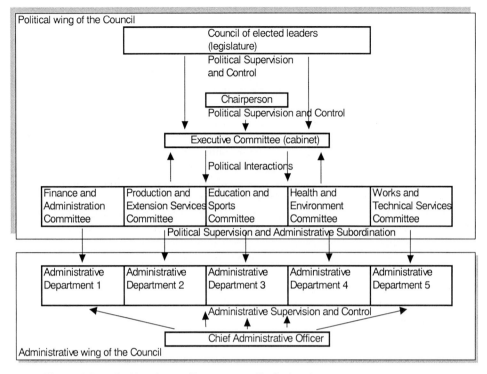

Figure 3.2 Typical local council structure at district level

Fifth, under the RC system, fulfilling responsibilities by councillors was voluntary without any official remuneration. Now essential members of the LC are paid full-time at LC 3 and 5 levels. This includes, the chairperson, the vice chairperson, five secretaries, and the speaker and the vice speaker of the legislative wing of the council. The remuneration has undoubtedly contributed to boost incentives of the councillors, although it is not totally free from problems.[16] In the future, a similar remuneration may be needed for LC 2 and 1 levels.

Accordingly, there have been efforts to enhance the institutional capacity of the LC system. As a result, the LC 1 at the grassroots level is an indispensable institution for ordinary people, since the LC is now a part of complex norms that have existed for more than a decade, and serves socially valuable objectives. The LC 1 has become a genuine institution sensitive to the people's heartfelt concerns, in

---

[16] One problem arises, for instance, from the fact that while the Local Governments Act, 1997 puts a limit on a proportion of funds being used for remuneration for the councillors, this ceiling is often not followed in practice. In addition, because the amounts paid for executive and non-executive members are different, this can disrupt the LC system when it is entangled with social cleavages such as ethnicity and religion.

contrast to other layers of LCs.[17] This is particularly noteworthy because there are numerous local groups and networks in rural Uganda ranging from clan and kinship associations to church groups.[18]

LC 1 is a familiar local forum for the common people to participate and discuss local issues. Today LC 1 can, therefore, be characterized as "a half public, half civic" institution. It is public in a sense that it is a part of the local governments. It is civic because it is a grassroots forum for residents to discuss mutual concerns. At this level, LC meetings are usually similar to those of community-based organizations. There are some elements of volunteerism in organizing activities (Ottemoeller, 1996). Linguistically, the executive committees of the LC 1 and 2 are not referred to by people as a part of government, as rulers, or as chiefs. Instead, the "lower-level LCs are quite explicitly conceived as a form of local self-rule, by contrast with the rule of chiefs, who since the abolition of the kingdom [of Buganda] in 1967, have been imposed from above" (Karlström, 1999b, p. 112).[19]

This characteristic of the LC is largely welcomed by the people. With the LC system, people generally support the current political system, although opposing views are also evident. A national referendum was conducted on 29 June 2000, in which people were asked whether they prefer the movement "non-party" polity to multi-party democracy. The result was overwhelming support for the current movement polity. Although the results cannot be taken at face value due to the problems associated with the referendum, people, especially in rural areas, demonstrated their clear preference for the movement polity to multi-party politics, which in the past brought miserable results to the population in Uganda.[20]

---

[17] Ottemoeller (1996) reports that many considered that the RC would be the first choice for settling local disputes. Many people also thought of the RC as a place where they would be able to exert influence over local affairs, although they did not necessarily use all opportunities in such a way to influence the RC/LC system (chapter 7).

[18] Some of the common grassroots associations include women's groups which conduct joint activities like income generation, skill learning and/or social activities; student groups; youth groups; music and drama groups; farmers groups; mothers' unions of churches; fathers' unions of churches; cash savings groups in selected areas; and associations to organize funerals. See Concern Worldwide et al., 1999 on social networks. The networks are related to social capital (Widner and Mundt, 1998).

[19] On the notion of civil society, and its applicability in Uganda, see Hearn, 1999; and Karlström, 1999b.

[20] According to the local newspaper, Sunday Vision, 2 July 2000, the voter turnout was about 45%, and 92% of the ballots cast showed support for the NRM. But the regional variation was quite wide. The turnout was 98.1% in one county in Rukungiri (where Museveni is from), while it was only 10.5% in Lira Municipality (New Vision, 4 July 2000). Likewise, whereas 57% of voters in Gulu voted for the multiparty system discrediting the NRM, 98% of voters of Nakasongola supported the NRM (ibid., 5 July 2000). Thus, although the referendum was "won" by the NRM, the views of Ugandans were never unanimously behind the NRM. Bratton and Lambright (2001), based on a public attitude survey conducted shortly before the referendum, argue that the voters tended to confuse the referendum with an election of office-holders.

2 Characteristics of Current Local Government System

The decentralization processes in Uganda have evolved gradually since the inception of the NRM. This kind of institutional adaptation is not often found in Africa and is of some significance (Ottemoeller, 1996). The gradual progression and phased approach, reflecting progress and obstacles encountered on the ground, is considered realistic and suitable in resource- and skill-scarce Africa (Tordoff, 1994). This gradual evolution is also based, at least partly, on popular aspirations of, and support for, democratic decision-making processes at local levels. Obviously, this process is not free from contradictions and problems, and the five major characteristics of the LC system merit our discussion.

2.1 Political Decentralization

Decentralization measures enable ordinary people to have opportunities to participate in decision-making processes for the first time since colonial rule was imposed. This is a very significant change because before decentralizing measures, people felt little connection with the administrative offices except being asked to pay taxes and perform other duties. Now the people can exercise their rights in elections as well as voice their concerns at LC meetings.

With the Local Governments Act, 1997, a series of local elections were held throughout the country in 1997 and 1998. Although the level of turnout varied from one type of election to another, it tends to be high for elections of chairpersons of LC 3 and LC 5, while the tendency is low for elections of women candidates, especially in lower administrative units. Nonetheless, these local elections are important enough for the people to realize quickly the significance of decentralization measures.

The election results also indicate a high turnover rate, and many representatives elected during the last elections are new. For instance, 161 candidates stood for the posts of 44 chairpersons of rural LC 5, and only one was elected without any opposing candidates.[21] Voters did not prefer the incumbent to stay on in leadership positions when they felt their representatives were incompetent, and/or corrupt. Among the 45 posts of chairpersons of LC 5, only three incumbent candidates were reelected.[22] This is one area where accountability is put to work. The fact that most incumbent leaders were rejected in the election is of no small significance for the LC system in which grassroots constituencies actually demanding accountability from their leaders.

---

[21] In the case of LC 5 councillors, elections in rural areas, 2,652 people stood for 886 posts. The competition ratio was just about one out of three. At the level of LC 3 chairpersons (both rural and urban), 992 people were elected among 2,561 candidates; one out of 2.5 candidates won election (Uganda, the Electoral Commission, 1999).

[22] There were 38 new chairpersons; 3 incumbents; and 4 unidentifiable (information by the Electoral Commission in Kampala, August 1998).

The real challenge to the political aspect of accountability lies at the heart of the polity. Since the LC system is fused with the movement polity, the LC cannot be separated from NRM politics. On the one hand, in the current system, local political leaders are relatively autonomous. Therefore, political decentralization in Uganda is really devolution. The representatives and executive members are elected by their constituency, and they are held accountable in managing their jurisdiction. On the other hand, the NRM also attempts to ensure that their control over the autonomous local authorities will not be lost. The NRM passed the Movement Act in 1997, which followed the passage of the Local Governments Act by five months. Then in 1998, a new post of NRM Representative was introduced in order to reinforce the "no-party democracy." The act ensures that all essential leaders of the LC system are also members of the movement committees of administrative hierarchical levels. Because the local councillors are representatives of the people and at the same time required to answer to the NRM government, the councillors are required to meet competing demands. One LC 2 chairman explained: "You are caught in between, so who do you serve first? How can I be on the side of the government on an issue that I feel oppressive. This is my constituency" (Tripp, 2000, p. 226).[23]   In short, almost all local political leaders are co-opted into the NRM structure. For the critics of the NRM, this situation creates further alienation. Although it is too early to judge the new NRM attempts, there are signs that the NRM is still uneasy with full democratization. This new cooptation in reality increases the scope for conflicts between supporters and opponents of the NRM and disempowers the latter (UNDP, 1998, p. 57).

2.2 Development Planning

The LC system introduced another important change in relation to the process in which policies are made. All districts are now expected to compile respective District Development Plans (DDPs) reflecting the needs of grassroots people. Rakai and Mukono Districts, for instance, are relatively advanced. Under the Rakai District Development Project assisted by the Danish International Development Assistance (DANIDA), Rakai was the first district to produce its DDP in 1994, a year following the real beginning of decentralization in 1993. Mukono produced a similar DDP in 1997 without much donor support. Throughout the planning process, it was the councillors who had to initiate actions, including organizing meetings to listen to the views of lower administrative units and of local opinion leaders. The councillors also needed to prioritize activities for coherent planning. The planning process in Rakai, in fact, became the de facto standard for making similar DDPs in Uganda (Kasumba, 1997; and Nielsen, 1996a and 1996b), and it has been emulated not only by other districts but by other African countries as well.

Of significance is the change of leadership in the planning process. While previously local administrators made the "sector" plans which were reported to the

---

[23] This may be similar to a predicament faced by district assembly members in Ghana (Crook and Manor, 1998, chapter 5).

central ministries, now the local administrators report to their local council which in turn is held accountable to the people in each jurisdiction. This is the relationship of accountability, which enhances the people's feeling of having more influence on the LC system. Even if the technical staff still advise elected representatives, on the planning processes, the role of political leaders are more significant than before, and the technical staff are subordinate to them. At least structurally, local people now have more chances to participate in the planning process, although this does not automatically mean that the process itself is "pro-poor."

The pioneering district of Rakai, in fact, attempts to make the planning process really function from the bottom up. Rakai District in 2000 was preparing the second 5-year DDP. Based on the self-critical review that the first DDP did not allow sufficient participation of the poor at the grassroots level, the planning process was amended for more inclusive and time-consuming consultations with the grassroots people.[24] All LC 1s were asked to have grassroots consultations and to submit their priority projects to the upper levels, which in turn prioritized their selected activities. This process continued all the way up to the district. Even if some LC 1 councillors showed enthusiasm for the participatory process, this bottom-up planning was a challenge for both political and administrative leaders to adjust their attitudes vis-à-vis the weak. To facilitate this process, the Planning Department of Rakai District conduced training sessions for lower-level administrators on how to solicit and compile ideas in designated formats. One cannot assume that the intentions of participatory planning are fully realized only by a one-time planning exercise. But, this Rakai example demonstrates that at least some districts take participatory planning seriously, instead of treating it as a mere slogan often used by African governments in trying to appease donors.

2.3 Personnel Management

Decentralization measures also drastically changed personnel management. Previously, civil servants belonged to the ministries of the central government, including those people who were posted at local governments. Now, they belong to the respective LCs. Currently, responsibilities for managing personnel fully reside with districts. For this purpose, the District Service Commission (DSC) was formed with the mandate to hire and fire personnel. In theory, the respective DSCs can adjust staff requirements reflecting local needs more speedily and effectively than could the central government. The DSCs process recruitment, promotion, and sanctions of staff members. The reality is, however, different. Many of the newly recruited staff by the local governments in 1998 and 1999 were those who had to fill administrative positions created by the new Local Governments Act, 1997. In 1999 and 2000, additional personnel in service provision positions

---

[24] As Ribot (2001) observes, decentralization and participatory policies can be contradictory if these policies are used by the center to serve pre-determined goals (pp. 37-38). Clearly the process is as important as the outcome, and there may be tensions between the ends and means of participatory planning.

were recruited with increased funding from the central government. The additions contributed to expanding service coverage, including education and health.

With decentralization efforts, however, local autonomy in personnel management in reality has been limited. This limitation is mainly because local governments are still heavily dependent on the resources transferred from the central government. Because most of the districts are suffering from a severe shortage of funds, they cannot easily hire additional manpower to match the increased scope of local services. What is more problematic is that even if the central government transfers funds, DSCs cannot proceed speedily since many districts cannot provide sitting allowances for DSC members to conduct interviews! As a result, roughly only 60% of the posts at district offices are filled, according to a recent study (MISR, 2000, pp. 14-15).

2.4 Financial Resources and Autonomy

These are probably most crucial to make any decentralization attempts effective. Without sufficient autonomy to generate and spend significant funds, locally initiated activities rarely take place. The amount of funds transferred from the central to local governments has increased significantly from Ush 31 billion (approximately US$ 28.5 million) in FY 1993/94 to Ush 331 billion (US$ 236 million) in FY 1999/2000 in nominal terms. (The fiscal year in Uganda is from July to June.) The real value, adjusted by inflation, has increased more than seven times during this period. Financial support by the central government to local authorities includes conditional, unconditional and equalization grants.

This increase, however, does not mean that the local governments enjoy fiscal autonomy as well. On the contrary, approximately 80% of the resources available to local governments are transferred by the central government. On average nationally, less than 20% of the revenue is locally generated (Uganda, MoFPED, 2000f, p. 150). A large proportion of the total transfers to local governments needs to be spent on recurrent costs including personnel salaries. Very little is left for new development activities, which local leaders may wish to initiate otherwise.

A main reason why local governments suffer from a narrow tax base is that more promising tax sources are still controlled by the central government. In addition, conditional grants (funds need to be disbursed for certain purposes usually determined by the central government) now account for about 80% of total intergovernment transfers. While, on the one hand, the increased funds, particularly in the areas of education, health, agriculture, roads, and water/sanitation, have undoubtedly contributed to improved service provisions, this, on the other hand, means that local authorities are de facto implementers of centrally decided activities (Chapter 6 will examine this important theme in much more detail.)

2.5 Donors' Assistance

Since Uganda is a heavily donor dependent country, an important financial source for local government is donors. Donors' collaboration with the LC system has been changing. The particular way in which donor funds are channeled has been modified to suit decentralization requirements. Previously, all donor assistance needed to be based on an agreement between foreign donors and the central government of the Republic of Uganda. The Rakai Project assisted by DANIDA has been innovative. In this project, DANIDA, while maintaining its agreement with the central government, also negotiated a parallel agreement with Rakai District. This allows DANIDA to channel funds directly to Rakai while notifying the Kampala government. Approximately US$ 9 million was provided between 1992 and 1995.[25] This assistance increased the financial autonomy of Rakai District. Although the project encountered some problems, it undoubtedly contributed to enhancing the capacity of local government offices. In the past the central government did not believe that local governments could handle large development budgets. Now, the Rakai project experience has demonstrated that local governments can manage this magnitude of resources if appropriate support is provided.

The Rakai model in fact has been followed by other donors. Encouraged by the DANIDA experience in Rakai, the United Nations Capital Development Fund (UNCDF) implemented the District Development Project in five districts from 1998 to 2000. Under this project, the amount disbursed for each community at the grassroots is very small, but had a tangible impact. In the project areas, for instance, local schools received many desks and chairs. There were other examples of small-scale grassroots development activities organized through the LC system and assisted by the project fund.

The UNCDF project was followed by the Local Government Development Program funded by the World Bank. Since the World Bank is one of the most significant donors in Uganda, its involvement in developing the local government system further in Uganda is of no small importance. It is anticipated that donors are generally more in favor of assisting local governments in building their capacities for improved governance and service delivery.

3 The Relationship between Leaders and Followers in the LC System

Now that the LC structure is in place, the question arises whether the LCs are fulfilling the expectations of creating democratic decision-making processes at local levels. The representatives and their constituencies are supposed to play their respective roles mainly through the LC system. Is this really taking place?

---

[25] A Rakai District Council document in 1994.

3.1 Background of Councillors

The first query is what kind of people are the councillors? Although there has been no systematic analysis of councillors' profiles in Uganda, some generalizations can be made. Depending on the level of the LC system, the profiles of local leaders are quite different. At the grassroots level of LC 1 and LC 2, the councillors are not necessarily the rich and the powerful although they do not suffer from severe poverty either. They are selected primarily because other villagers consider them as trustworthy leaders. For those with farming backgrounds, most of them are middle-scale peasants.[26] But what is essential is not the candidate's farm size, but long residency in the locality (fully settled with a proper home), maturity, marriage, and good behavior.[27] Councillors often have teachers or community activists backgrounds. In the case of women, they tend to have some experience in organizing women's group activities, often in association with NGOs. Material wealth plays a certain role in the elections. For instance, people prefer to choose somebody as their leader, if he/she can provide stationery items for the LC meetings and committees.[28]

A rural woman described the characteristics of capable leaders as follows:

> It is someone who does not discriminate, someone who assists others, and those who correct mistakes. The good leaders should treat everyone equally regardless of religion, ethnicity, gender, and the level of income. And the leaders should try to resolve problems and conflicts, to visit other areas to obtain good ideas for development, to visit homes of the people, and to give guidance on home hygiene, farming, etc. The leaders should also improve our lives through introducing modern farming and mobilizing us for immunization, and so on. The leader should more than just call for meetings.[29]

But the profile of leaders differs at the LC 3 and LC 5 levels. There the councillors tend to be more elite and to come from an establishment background. Among the district-level councillors, quite a few have a university degree and have impressive careers in the formal sector, either in public service, the military,

---

[26] Tidemand (1994a) implies that the mean figure of the candidates' land size is around four acres (p. 107) in the 1992 local elections. Tidemand, based on his fieldwork in Buganda, adopts the following social stratification in rural Buganda: 1) landless and near landless; 2) small peasants who own 1-5 acres; 3) middle peasants who own 5-20 acres; 4) big farmers or landlords of more than 20 acres ownership (ibid., p. 106).

[27] Vincent (1971) found that marital status (polygamy), occupation (farming and land rights and cattle ownership), and permanency in local residence are the status symbols of village leaders (p. 114).

[28] This may be different from the conventional notion of patron-client relationship, which is often viewed as harmful for African political as well as socio-economic development.

[29] Focus group discussion, Nsube, Mukono, 26 May 2000. As hinted in this quotation, villagers like their leaders to be innovative too. Similar views were also heard in Allupe, Tororo, 30 May 2000, and Katana, Rakai, 2 August 2000. Innovativeness was also observed as one of the important characteristics of village leaders earlier (Vincent, 1971, p. 247).

or the private sector (Tidemand, 1994a, p. 34). Most of them are fluent in English. Their profiles are by no means associated with poverty in Uganda. Women councillors at higher levels are no exception, and they also tend to be elite.

The councillors' motivations to become political leaders vary. Some do not necessarily seek economic benefits, while others become councillors for the sake of salaries and allowances. Where the local economy is reasonably strong, such as in Mukono, most of the councillors have private business activities either in Mukono or in Kampala. If one is serious in trying to make money, it is better to do something other than politics in these districts. But in a place like Tororo, where employment opportunities are limited, attempts to become councillors may derive primarily from economic reasons in order to augment their income. Thus, these variations certainly affect the way in which local politics are conducted.

Asked in one village in Rakai why they wanted to become councillors, a newly elected councillor said: "We wanted to participate in politics in order to bring development to this village." A returning incumbent also said: "I wanted to be re-elected. I had a work plan in my last term, but could not fulfill it. And I wanted to finish what I initiated." One of their colleagues added, "We served in the council before, and with that experience, we can lead the village."[30] These statements echo what other councillors in different places said: they basically would like to bring development to their areas. In some cases they replied that they wanted to bring more specific improvements to homes in their village, to send children to schools, to modernize agriculture, and to increase income-generating opportunities in handicraft-making, bread-making, etc.[31]

A LC 1 councillor assessed the job of being a councillor in the following way:

> It is rewarding if we can resolve various simple problems in the village: feeder roads, digging and cleaning of wells, improvement of school buildings, sanitation and home hygiene, cultivation of food, combating deforestation and utilization of wetland. For example, we managed to provide a police post without any outside assistance. This gives us a feeling of accomplishment. But this is purely voluntary work, and since there is no financial facilitation, sometimes it is difficult to get things done.[32]

This sense of accomplishment is greater if the councillors are in collaboration with NGOs and other organizations. In one area, the councillors said that with assistance by a NGO, women formed some groups which received training, for instance, on the subjects of home care, sanitation and health. Many of the councillors consider such visits of dignitaries encouraging. They also say that opportunities for attending seminars and workshops and meeting with visitors (including researchers!) are also good incentives, despite the fact that the councillors at LC 1 and 2 are not paid at all for their work.

---

[30] Focus group discussion with councillors, Kasambya, Rakai, 12 July 2000.

[31] For instance this was revealed by councillors in Ksege, Rakai, 1 August 2000.

[32] Focus group discussion, Kasambya, Rakai, 12 July 2000.

3.2 Degree of Participation in LC System

The LC system led by these councillors is expected to harness popular participation at the grassroots to discuss and resolve daily issues. The meetings are to be convened every other month, but the actual frequency of gatherings varies in different localities. What would be the average attendance of people in LC meetings? There has been no systematic survey on the subject. Based on discussions in numerous villages during this study, the average attendance appears to be approximately one-third to one-half of local residents attend LC meetings.[33] The degree of participation differs in different areas. Although no comparable data is available, the proportion is relatively high in the west and the center,[34] while lower in the northern and eastern areas. Whether this degree can be considered high or low depends on the standard of judgment. Considering the pervasive poverty in rural Uganda, the attendance probably appears to be moderately high. Even if exact comparison of the data is difficult, comparable figures in Ghana and C te d'Ivoire are 32% and 18% respectively (Crook and Manor, 1998, pp. 153 and 217).

Not all meetings attract a similar level of attendance (Ottemoeller, 1996). A councillor informed us of the typical situation:

> There are certain topics which tend to attract more people to come to meetings. They are security, donor assistance projects, and visits of officials like MPs and councillors from higher levels. The topics related to development do not necessarily attract high attendance. People do not appreciate the importance of cleaning roads and wells. Some are ignorant and irresponsible. Some are selfish and let others take care of these things.[35]

It is often a common tendency that education, for instance, attracts more people than other subjects including health and road maintenance. The high attendance facilitates collaboration of grassroots people on school classroom construction. The problem is that other issues do not attract much participation by people at the grassroots. For instance, even if people consider it desirable for water sources to be protected and roads to be maintained, it is not easy to organize community work. It is partly because some consider that it is the job of the councillors and not for themselves to do such work. Some people even consider that since the

---

[33] Based on Table 3.1, the average population per LC 1 is about 500. Because one person per household is usually expected to attend the meetings, the full number of participants may be in the range of 80-100. This crude estimate is largely in line with the field study findings. Tukahebwa also reports that 63% of the people he asked said that they participate in the decision-making process of the LC 1 (Tukahebwa, 1997, p. 52).

[34] The average LC 1 attendance is about 90 among 150 in Kasambya, Rakai and about 40 out of 100 in Ksege, Rakai (interviews on 12 July and 1 August 2000 respectively). The regional difference partly derives from historical reasons of RC/LC system. The NRM fought the war from western to central areas where residents have been exposed to the system more than those in other areas.

[35] Focus group discussion, Kasambya, Rakai, 12 July 2000.

councillors receive allowances (although this is not true for LC 1 and 2 councillors), why cannot they do the work instead of asking the poor to carry out such dirty work. For them, these services are precisely what political leaders promised during the election campaign, and they should be responsible for undertaking these tasks. But for leaders, they cannot easily sacrifice their personal wealth for such activities since they already spent substantial funds for the elections. As a result, *bulungi bwansi*, community development activities, remain unorganized.[36]

In addition, not all social groups attend to a comparable degree. The least participative are the youth. Their main concern is immediate income, since the unemployment rate is very high among the youth, particularly those who are not well educated. Therefore, their attendance at council meetings is normally lower than the older population. One councilor explained that "if we wish to attract the youth to come, we have to organize beer drinking in conjunction with the meetings."[37] (This issue of youth participation will be reviewed in detail in Chapter 4.)

Attendance by itself does not mean that ordinary people can effectively participate in the discussion of issues and contribute to possible solutions. Although there has been no systematic survey on how effective the actual participation of the local population in LC meetings is, such effectiveness tends to be modest to low in most areas. Even if the participants express their views and the councillors promise to take action, mostly nothing happens. When matters are communicated to the upper levels of the LC hierarchy, usually no feedback is given to the lower levels. Thus, they feel that whatever views they express, there is no change. A farmer in Mukono typically complained that "the concerns raised by people at the bottom do not seem to attract enough attention for problem resolving. This makes us to feel that we are ignored."[38]

Another measure of participation is the frequency of contact between councillors and ordinary people outside of meetings. At LC 1 level, councillors and villagers reside in the same neighborhood. Thus, the contacts are very frequent, and many of them are not formal. But the degree of frequency in contacts is drastically reduced when it comes to interacting with councillors and officials at higher levels. Most of the grassroots people do not know their councillors at LC 3 through 5 levels. The contacts diminish tremendously, particularly at the LC 5 level.[39] Testimonies over the frequency of contact between LC 5 councillors and grassroots people are in conflict. On the one hand, LC 5 councillors maintain that when they are invited to the LC 3 and 1 meetings, they attend. But the ordinary people insist they only see LC 5 councilors "maybe once a year." A young man in Rakai expressed his views as follows.

---

[36] This is also because the government in the past provided public services mostly free of charge to the rural population (when they were provided). This sense of dependency of people on the government is still significant. It is also because people have devised their coping mechanism without too much reliance on public services.

[37] Interview, Keefa Ssengendo Kaweesa, Mukono, District Council, 13 August 1999.

[38] Focus group discussion, Kilowooza, Mukono, 18 August 1999.

[39] One study points out that more than 70% of the grassroots people do not interact with their LC 5 councillors over the issues of local communities (Tukahebwa, 1997, p. 53).

For LC 3 councillors, we do not see them often. Maybe once a year or even none. For LC 5 councillors, we never see them. They just pass by in cars, and never stop and see us. They are worse than LC 3 councillors.[40]

The rural people consider the LC 5 leaders not to be seriously interested in hearing the views of "marginal people" at the grassroots level. Therefore, as a woman in Mukono put it, "democracy sleeps once the elections are over."[41]

Furthermore, the hierarchy of the LC system is supposed to work in two ways. It is, on the one hand, supposed to disseminate government policies from the top downwards. On the other hand, the councils are supposed to reflect people's views and needs and to pass them upwards. In reality, they tend to function more as a top-down and less as a bottom-up mechanism. Grassroots people frequently point out that the meetings are often called on short notice, and when the gatherings take place the agenda is often already decided, and what the ordinary people wish to propose cannot be easily accommodated in the council meetings. Farmers in Mukono District stated, "LC policy making is a top-down process. We, the farmers, are not given chances to express our views. We do not believe that farmers are well represented in the council."[42]

Some of the councillors frankly expressed their frustrations about organizing this kind of community work. One of them said, "Before we became councillors, we thought that people would be mobilized. But in reality it is difficult to mobilize them. People are not coming for meetings."[43] They often cite that "people are ignorant," by which they mean that their efforts to persuade on some issues are ineffective. They also point out that once disputes take place within the local leadership, the losers would be resentful for a very long time. In addition, even if they are eager to bring development, there has been little assistance by the higher levels of the government, including the distribution of financial resources. Sometimes, even if the money is made available, this can be monopolized by a chairperson without the knowledge of other councillors. Moreover, their determination for good work is apparently hampered, at least partially, by their personal need to secure their own income and food, because lower-level councillors are not remunerated. Asked if payment would improve the situation, one councillor responded:

Yes, we will be more motivated to try to convince the people who are ignorant and those who are stubborn. We will be more willing to make more visits to these villagers. They may indeed be convinced over the importance of development works. As you know, it is

---

[40] Focus group discussion, Lumbugu, Rakai, 25 August 1999.

[41] Focus group discussion, Nama Mukono, 19 August 1999. How is democracy understood by people in Buganda? See Karlström, 1996; Ottemoeller, 1998; and Tidemand, 1994a and 1994b, pp. 123-29.

[42] Focus group discussion, Kilowooza, Mukono, 18 August 1999.

[43] Focus group discussion with councillors, Kasambya, Rakai, 12 July 2000.

also difficult to reconcile the personal needs for income and time devoted to being a councillor. Thus, if we are paid, no matter how modestly, that would be better for us.[44]

When they are asked whether they would like to be reelected as councillors in the next election, the reactions are mixed. Although it is far from conclusive, women and elderly councillors appear not to be willing to stand for reelection, while men, especially the middle aged, have more interests in seeking reelection. A study conducted in 1996 asking people at the grassroots to become LC 1 councillors found that both in Mukono and Rakai Districts more women were hesitant than were men. This may be due to the heavy burden placed on the more disadvantaged like women and the elderly (Golooba-Mutebi, 1999, Tables 8.4 and 8.5, in chapter 8). A woman councillors said, "Well, we want to let others have their chances. This is time-consuming work and it is purely voluntary. We wish to take a rest in the next term."[45]

4 Different Perceptions of Decentralization Processes

The relationship between leaders and followers at the grassroots reveals a significant gap in the expectations of what others should provide. This gap signifies that there is a lack of coherent understanding among stakeholders. Views of stakeholders on the processes of decentralization measures vary considerably on certain aspects.

The first aspect is a central-local trajectory. At the national level, political representatives may not necessarily support decentralizing endeavors, which would reduce their influence on policy making to the benefit of local political leaders. Likewise, as long as decentralizing measures do not curtail the influence of civil servants at the center on decision making, they do not oppose it. They are already at the center, and they do not have to be sent to take up local posts. On the other hand, some may lose their jobs since the central government is undergoing civil service reform which reduces the number of personnel. The administrators at the local level also have mixed views on decentralization attempts. These attempts, on the one hand, enhance their autonomy, which is liked by all. On the other hand, they may stay at their current local posts for a prolonged period and can no longer be easily transferred to central ministry posts. With limited possibilities of new appointments elsewhere, many of them feel "stuck" where they are.

The second aspect relates to political-administrative relations. While political leaders generally support decentralization, civil servants are, in fact, one of the most vocal opponents of decentralization measures. The promotion issue is one concern. But more fundamentally, the elitist administrators do not wish to be di-

---

[44] Focus group discussion with councillors, Kasambya, Rakai, 12 July 2000.

[45] Focus group discussion, Ksege, Rakai, 1 August 2000. Another reason found by Golooba-Mutebi was lack of education among rural people, especially the inability to write (1999, chapter 8).

rected by elected politicians who they think would be much less educated. This resentment was obvious particularly in the earlier stage of decentralization.[46]

Third, another complication is intra-local relations. Generally LC 5 councilors and administrators are supportive of decentralization schemes since these measures improve resource utilization. With decentralization, they can control the budgets and personnel more fully. But at the level of LC 3, leaders have mixed views: councillors are generally supportive. The technical staff/administrators are ambivalent. They are, on the one hand, supportive because their salary payments are more prompt than before. But, on the other hand, they are skeptical since district and sub-district offices are not helping them to provide necessary support to discharge their duties. Transport, for instance, is a big issue for extension staff at this LC 3 level. But one would be extremely fortunate if LC 5 offices provided some means of transport.

At LC 1 and 2 levels, most people have heard of "decentralization." However, except the leaders,[47] people at the grassroots generally do not clearly understand it. One reason is because generally at the grassroots, there have not been many visible changes in service provisions, which makes ordinary people skeptical about decentralization. Although people's understanding is improving year after year, there are still a significant proportion of the poor without an adequate understanding. A rural woman said, "We have heard of it, but do not know what it means clearly. But the LC is familiar to us."[48] This succinctly summarizes the current situation, and this appears to be quite common in a number of villages in Uganda. Even in Rakai and Mukono Districts, which are considered to be more advanced in the degree of decentralizing measures than other districts, the situation is still the same. Consequently, many people at the grassroots level do not know fully what their roles are vis-à-vis their councillors and administrators.

This inadequacy is crucial, because lack of common understanding not only prevents stakeholders from reaching consensus but also tends to create misguided blame on others. If and when the LC system does not function as anticipated, the stakeholders blame somebody else. Ordinary villagers at the grassroots would blame the councillors for their lack of leadership and dedication. They regard it as the job of the councillors to carry out development duties, and they tend to "sit back and wait" for the LCs to act (Golooba-Mutebi, 1999, chapter 5). Councillors blame the higher authorities, including the central government, for its lack of support (Golooba-Mutebi, 1999, pp. 91 and 135). These complaints are understandable, but do not necessarily focus the stakeholders' attention constructively.

---

[46] Tidemand (1994b) reports that during a meeting of the Ministry of Local Government in 1992, one civil servant argued that "now there is a heavy responsibility on the politicians. Civil servants to be transferred to the districts have (in future) to be of high quality. Therefore this should also apply to politicians. If he is a peasant, he can't be accepted by officials." This received a wide applause from his colleagues, he noted (p. 159).

[47] An LC 3 councillor said, "It is to bring power back to the people at the grassroots. People can express their views." Joggo, Mukono, 18 August 1999. This expression is re-iterated by another LC I councillor in Ndebba (21 August 1999).

[48] Focus group discussion, Mukono Town, Mukono, 19 August 1999.

5 Corruption as a Threat to Accountable Institution

One of the ultimate reasons for mutual mistrust is the widespread belief of corruption among public officials. Corruption has, unfortunately, become an inevitable reality in Uganda, especially once the state became tarnished during the long-lasting civil war, when civil servants could no longer earn living wages. The NRM is fully aware of this danger. Because the LC system is the linchpin of the NRM polity, widespread corruption would weaken the foundation of the regime.

Thus the government has been endeavoring to put an accountability system in place. Indeed, it was hoped that decentralization attempts would curb corruption. But whether this intention has been realized or not is an open question.

It may be stunning that an overwhelming majority of both the public and service providers consider that corruption is rampant in the public services. According to National Integrity Survey 1998, 70% of households thought there is a high level of corruption; 26% considered that there is some corruption; and only 4% responded there is no corruption (Flanary and Watt, 1999, p. 523).[49] The corruption is clearly related to the different degrees of satisfaction with regard to different levels of the government (Table 3.2). The higher the level of the LC, the more corrupt in attitude, and produces less satisfactory results for grassroots people.

Many people at the grassroots are disgusted with this widespread corruption,

Table 3.2 Different types of corruption in local and central government

Local government	Central government
■ **Embezzlement** ■ **Nepotism**, which results in incompetent and unqualified officials in post ■ **Location favouritism**, where funds and projects are directed to the councillor's constituent area while other less advantaged areas are neglected ■ **Lack of transparency** of District Tender Boards in awarding tenders, particularly in Moyo where market management tenders were reportedly awarded to councillors and their friends or relatives. Also in land allocation, and gazetting by local councils and the church ■ **Failure to monitor** programmes, and therefore to account for funds and activities	■ **Involvement in foreign wars** seen as directing funds away from service delivery improvements ■ **District favouritism**, particularly of South over North ■ **Failure to deal with corrupt officials** when they have been found guilty ■ **Lack of electoral transparency** particularly with regard to nepotism, false and misleading electoral promises, lack of accountability to the electorate, and lack of information after elections

Source: Uganda, MoFPED [2000g] *Uganda Participatory Poverty Assessment: Learning from the Poor*, (Kampala: MoFPED), p. 108. Reprinted with permission.

---

[49] For corruption, see CITE International, 1998; Doig, 1995; Ruzindana, 1997; Ruzindana and Gakwandi, 1998; Stapenhurst and Kpundeh, 1999; Svensson, 1999; and Tangri and Mwenda, 2001.

because they think this inhibits development at all levels. Therefore, people generally have no sympathy with those who are corrupt. They think "the poor should be rewarded and added to the rich."[50] They expressed a strong desire for accountability and transparency of public bodies in all their activities. On the other hand, what is very revealing is that numerous people at the grassroots explained that corruption is so widespread that once they are in a position in the public services they would do the same. Asked whether they would behave like a corrupt public servant, if they were in such position, a man at one village gave a frank admission:

> Yes, probably. This is a social problem. Even if one corrupt person is punished, the next person will also get corrupt. Corruption is widespread from the top to the bottom. So it is endless. Unless the top big corruption is tackled, it is not meaningful to punish the small corruption at the bottom. The government should find a solution.[51]

This corruption, however, may be misunderstood because many rural people do not clearly know the boundaries of licit and illicit demands by officials. In one meeting, this issue of corruption was raised. One attendant replied, "We believe the councillors are asking what they are not allowed to ask."[52] This statement indicates that the poor tend to think when they are asked something surprising, it must be a request for bribe. With limited information to distinguish legitimate from illegitimate claims, they tend to associate surprises with corruption.

In addition, the following question was asked in various villages. "Some may say that the councillors get more benefit from *not* resolving problems since they can keep receiving their allowance for attending more meetings. Do you believe this?" The answer to this question was unanimously "yes" in all places, which shows the magnitude of mistrust over corrupt practices. One of the essential issues is to provide accurate information to people at the grassroots level on what kind of behavior constitutes such illicit demands.

Furthermore, this issue of corruption is related to perhaps an even more controversial one of patron-client relationships. This is relevant not only in Uganda but also in Africa in general. Some argue that during economic crises this relationship becomes more prevalent (Chabal and Daloz, 1999). During the election campaigns candidates, especially those who stood for LC 5, tended to present various small gifts to voters. But people at the grassroots did not necessarily vote for those who presented gifts to them. Thus, the expectation among the grassroots people that their leaders will become their "patrons" who will extend economic benefits to the poor and the disadvantaged is not the determining factor for elections. For the relationship between LC 1 leaders and grassroots people, this kind of neo-patrimonialism tends to be irrelevant, simply because the resources allocated for the LC 1 are too small to forge such relationships. At the LC 5 level, some may wish to have such relationships as other avenues to acquire wealth are

---

[50] This proverb was mentioned during the focus group discussion, Panyangas, Tororo, 31 May 2000.

[51] Focus group discussion, Kyungu, Mukono, 26 May 2000.

[52] Focus group discussion, Osia-Magoro, Tororo, 31 May 2000.

limited, but the relationship between LC 5 leaders and grassroots people is currently too remote to form such neopatrimonial relations. Ironically, in the future, as interactions between them increase, this may become a real possibility, which would have significant implications for politics and development.

6 Lack of Sufficient Information

The perception gaps among stakeholders and the public mistrust of their leaders can be narrowed significantly by improved dissemination of accurate information. As long as significant perception gaps remain unbridged, they are unlikely to create a common ground for mutually beneficial outcomes. Sharing essential information among different stakeholders is one prerequisite for them to become more willing to participate in joint activities for the benefit of society at large.

Stakeholders at all levels desperately need more information. Even councillors themselves do not necessarily have an adequate understanding of their roles, and this is particularly true at lower levels of the LC system, although understanding improves gradually as they gain more experience. For instance, a training workshop in 1999 in Kibaale District recommended the distribution of the constitution and the Local Governments Act, 1997 to all the councillors (Kamal, 1999). This district is where capacity is relatively well developed with donor assistance. It is quite likely that in other districts and at lower levels of the LC hierarchy the situation may be more problematic.

People at the grassroots level desperately need more information. There are a number of methods by which policy messages can be sent to the public, but most of them have problems. Newspapers are expensive by the local income standard. In remote areas such as Rakai, there are very few newspaper vendors. Radio programs sometimes broadcast the announcements of council meetings, but the timing is not necessarily convenient for listeners, particularly for farmers.[53] Notices of meetings can be sent by memo from one person to another, but this does not ensure that the memo reaches the intended people or that messages are understood.

Because of these problems, people are eager to receive any explanation of the current decentralization processes and their own role in them. Interestingly enough, grassroots people generally have more exposure to national budgets than to budgets of local governments (Kintu, 2000). Once adequate information is provided, it appears that more people are willing to participate in council meetings, as well as to contribute their time and energy to group activities, which can improve their lives. But lack of information, including feedback from previous discus-

---

[53] A farmer pointed out that "Radio has some hours to inform us on council meetings, we think it is 15 minutes on Monday early morning, but normally this broadcasting time is very inconvenient for us. We are too busy to listen to the radio. But the content of the radio is also not very attractive, and it is in a sense too political" (focus group discussion, Kilowooza, Mukono, 18 August 1999).

sions, tends to foster people's suspicion that "the leaders are eating our money."[54] Many people at the grassroots level consider that the leaders are just using them for their own benefits. A rural woman said, "We are used as their ladder." Another young man even said, "We feel that we are neglected. This is a bad feeling. We even feel that we should perhaps vote for 'no-confidence' on them."[55]

Generally, the level of understanding demonstrated by people at the grassroots appears to be improving year by year, particularly in those areas where local leadership is effective. This improvement is indispensable to removing mistrust between leaders and followers. On the other hand, lack of information, mutual mistrust between leaders and people, together with the fact the agenda is mostly decided by the upper level, convince people that the authorities are hiding something. In Uganda's political culture, essential information probably still needs to be provided "from above." People are not used to raising political questions. Then, councillors themselves need to explain more fully on how the LC system is supposed to work and what kind of roles people themselves have to play.[56]

7 Summary and Conclusion

The LC system in Uganda has evolved out of the historical context of post-independence. Optimism associated with the newly born state was soon replaced by centralized and personalized rule, typical of post-independent African states. When the NRM came to power in 1986, the state institutions were virtually collapsed. Due to this institutional vacuum, a novel hierarchical system of the Resistance Council was installed after the initial experiment during the guerrilla war.

As Uganda recovered from the long civil war, legislation was undertaken to lay out the foundations of state institutions. Decentralization clearly occupies a centerpiece of the NRM's reform agenda. The renamed Local Council system is indivisible from the no-party "movement" polity. The system has changed the way in which elections are held, development plans are prepared, bureaucracy is administered, civil servants are managed, and donors provide funds.

Perceptions of decentralization measures do not conform to a uniform view, which discourages partnership formations. Each stakeholder has its own understanding, and tensions are observed along the central-local trajectories, politico-administrative relations, and among different layers of the LC hierarchy. The di

---

[54] This expression of "eating" is often used by many informants. Thus, Bayart (1993) developed "the politics of the belly" as an adequate metaphor to describe African politics.

[55] Focus group discussion, Lumbugu, Rakai, 25 August 1999.

[56] The discussions held for this study provided unique opportunities for some to receive explanations of decentralization for the first time. For example, an explanation was provided concerning taxes. This explanation, in fact, convinced some people to pay tax locally. One woman said, "In the past I was unwilling to pay my tax, because I was not clear how the money was used. Now, I am willing to pay it since I now know how it is used" (focus group discussion, Joggo, Mukono, 18 August 1999).

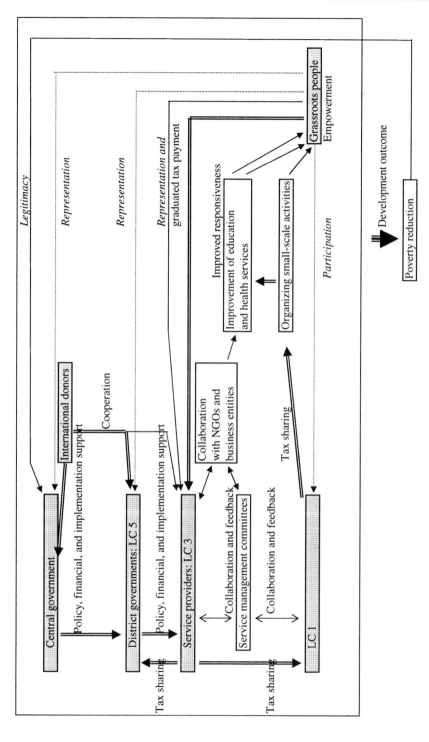

Figure 3.3 Processes of decentralization measures in Uganda

vergent views partly derive from insufficient access to information. The limited information flow also encourages corruption that is widespread and socially "accepted," albeit unwillingly.

Many of the councillors are from the middle class in rural areas. But women's advancement is significant due to affirmative action. The level of participation in LC meetings differs depending on the area as well as on the subjects, but generally it is reasonably high given the rural realities on the continent. The lower level LC has become the hub of dense personal networks of rural Uganda.

The way in which ordinary people engage public authorities has changed. Diverse actors now interact to improve their living standards, some organized as collective action in general or as partnerships in particular. A comparison of Figures 3.1 and 3.3 attests to this diversity of actors. (Figure 3.3 is a graphic presentation of "decomposed" decentralization in which complex processes of transformation are evolving.) The views emerging from both qualitative and quantitative surveys illustrate complex interactions, by which both the potential and limitations of the LC system will be assessed in the next chapter.

4 Poverty, Empowerment and the Local Council: Views from the Grassroots

The LCs are close to the people and in resolving disputes, they are the most important ones to approach. The people respect and obey them because they are the ones responsible if anything goes wrong. They are recognised by government and entrusted with the law – they are overall.

A man made a statement during
the focus group discussion, Chema, Kapchorwa District,
Uganda, MoFPED, 2000g, p. 106

This chapter presents the views of people at the grassroots about how the Local Council system should, as well as does function. In order to obtain a wide range of views, the three districts were selected for this study. These three districts represent, interestingly enough, slightly different degrees of poverty and development within Uganda. Generally Mukono, being close to Kampala, outperforms the national average, while the other two districts do not. Tororo faces more problems than Rakai. But all three districts are improving in the Human Development Index in the 1990s (UNDP, 1998). Therefore, comparisons among the three districts are useful for observing the similarities and differences of the impact of decentralization efforts (Tables 4.1 and 4.2).

Table 4.1 District human development profile

	Income index	Education index	Life expectancy index	Human Development Index
Mukono	0.285	0.62	0.4483	0.44
Tororo	0.174	0.505	0.392	0.375
Rakai	0.2231	0.548	0.4033	0.3784
National Average	0.2098	0.605	0.4323	0.4046

Sources: UNDP [1998] *Uganda Human Development Report 1998*, (Kampala, UNDP), p. 15; and UNDP [1997] *Uganda Human Development Report 1997*, (Kampala, UNDP), p. 13.

Note: Data of Mukono and Rakai are from 1996, while that for Tororo is from 1995.

Table 4.2 District human poverty profile

	Not expected to survive to age 40 (%) (1996)	Illiteracy (P2) (%) (1995)	No access to safe water (%) (1995)	No access to health services(%) (1995)	Underweight children (%) (1996)	Human Poverty Index (1996)
Mukono	33.1	38.1	86	55.7	25.9	43.8
Tororo	37.8	46.9	80.5	55.6	34.4	47.4
Rakai	36.7	35.2	94.6	60.7	25.9	46.2
National Average	36.3	38.4	51.5	51	31.8	39.3

Source: UNDP [1998] *Uganda Human Development Report 1998*, (Kampala, UNDP), p. 22.

In these districts, two types of sessions were held. The first one was focus group discussions on certain topics, which ranged from the assessment of the LC system to the poverty situation. It was assured that remarks made by rural people during the discussions would remain anonymous so that participants expressed their views freely without fear of government reprisals. The second type was a short survey questionnaire, which contained ten questions. On most occasions (but not all), informal discussions were held first, and were then followed by the survey questionnaire. It was considered that informal discussions would help respondents become familiar with the kinds of research issues, and that this procedure would be able to lead to more accurate responses to the questionnaire (An appendix is provided for further explanation of the methodology.)

Explanations of this chapter follow the structure of the questionnaire. It can be concluded that people in Uganda generally value the LC system as an essential institution, especially in rural areas. The LC 1 is a source of information as well as a mechanism to settle local disputes. They also consider that the LC system is generally, although not conclusively, supportive of their needs. 62% of respondents in the three surveyed districts answered that the LC system is responding to the needs of ordinary people, while 34% responded negatively. According to the responses, the LC can be useful in linking grassroots people with other stakeholders. As one moves up the LC hierarchy, ordinary people's access to information regarding the activities of the upper levels of local authorities is very limited. This limitation makes grassroots people less satisfied with the performances of the upper-level councils.

1 Assessment of the LC System

This section, which consists of four questions, asks respondents to evaluate the LC system. Since the LC system is a hierarchy of committees and councils operating at five levels, the questions are intended to differentiate as much as possible respondents' views according to the various levels of the LC. It may be possible that some feel content with, for instance, LC 5 but not with LC 3. The first question asks their view of the overall performance of the LC as a whole.

> 1. Are you satisfied in the way the LC system as a whole (LC 1 - 5) operates?

The responses were as follows: 32% "very satisfactory"; 46% "somewhat satisfactory"; 9% "somewhat unsatisfactory"; 10% "very unsatisfactory"; and the remaining 3% "do not know." A predominant view was that people consider the LC satisfactory but not very much so, although negative responses were definitely in the minority. This can be supported by the following remarks made by a man in Tororo:

> When we have common problems, we bring them to the LC. Issues like orphans are brought to the LC. Some selected members of the councillors try to resolve these problems. Women bring the issues of domestic violence to female councillors informally. Problems are also brought to the LC when they cannot be resolved by other associations. We bring the issues to the attention of clan and elderly people if we do not wish to make problems publicly known. Clans normally take care of issues like: organization of burial and funerals; problems with neighboring clans; arrangement of "dowries"; assistance to raise money to send some bright children to schools; ceremonies not to eat dog meat; and sexual harassment and related matters. Land disputes are brought to the LC, if the lands concerned are between neighbors. But clans would deal with them if they arise, for example, from problems of inheritance between brothers or people who share kinship relations.[1]

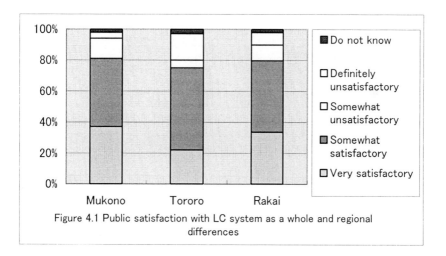

Figure 4.1 Public satisfaction with LC system as a whole and regional differences

---

[1] Focus group discussion, Panyangas, Tororo, 31 May 2000. For a conflict resolution mechanism of the LC system, see Khadiagala, 2001, and Tidemand, 1994b, particularly chapter 6, and 1995.

There were some differences concerning this pattern of response in the three different districts where responses were obtained, as illustrated by Figure 4.1. The residents in Mukono appreciated the LC system more than those in Rakai and Tororo. But it should perhaps be noted that the difference was not as great as was anticipated.

If age differences are taken into account, an interesting tendency emerges (Figure 4.2). The overall appreciation of the LC system is relatively higher in the middle-aged groups of those in their 30s and 40s, and lower among youth in their 20s as well as among the elderly in their 50s and over 60s. For the youth and the elderly, the LC system is less appealing. This is in line with the views expressed by several people at the grassroots. A frustrated and angry young man made derogatory remarks during the discussion about the government: "We have no voice in the government. Nobody listens to us."[2] A similar kind of disappointment is attested to by the elderly as well. The following remarks made by a rural man in Mukono represents their views:

> The government should look after us through the LC. If they have support from the upper authorities, the LC should help us. But often there is no such support, and the LC 1 cannot solve the problems that we face. We feel that we are marginalized and thus we are angry, and frustrated. The leaders are selfish at all levels. We are used as a ladder for them to gain their personal benefits. During the election, they came and promised many things, but they never bother to fulfill [these promises] once the election is over.[3]

The level of education is also an interesting factor helping to differentiate responses at the grassroots level, as shown by Figure 4.3. Those who have never been to school replied slightly more positively than those who have. This is in a

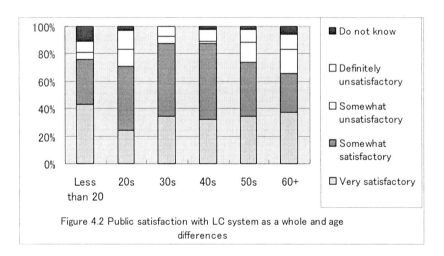

Figure 4.2 Public satisfaction with LC system as a whole and age differences

---

[2] Focus group discussion, Kidoko West, Tororo, 1 June 2000.

[3] Focus group discussion, Bontaba, Mukono, 8 June 2000.

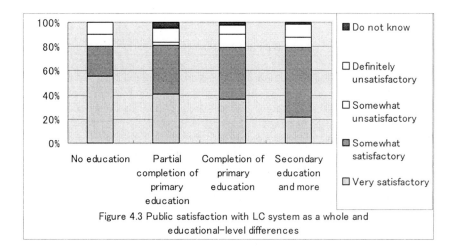

Figure 4.3 Public satisfaction with LC system as a whole and educational-level differences

sense paradoxical, but it can be interpreted that for those who are not educated at all, sources of information are very limited, and thus they do not know much about what the LC system performs. The less educated have lower expectations of the LC system. In contrast, the more educated tend to have more channels of information and have higher expectations of the LC system. They can thus be disappointed once these expectations are not met.

Then the following sub-questions were asked.

1.1. Are you satisfied in the way the LC 1 (village) operates?

The responses were: 43% "very satisfactory"; 30% "somewhat satisfactory"; 12% "somewhat unsatisfactory"; 13% "very unsatisfactory"; and the remaining 2% "do not know."

1.2. Are you satisfied in the way the LC 3 (sub-county) operates?

The responses were: 24% "very satisfactory"; 30% "somewhat satisfactory"; 20% "somewhat unsatisfactory"; 17% "very unsatisfactory"; and the remaining 9% "do not know."

1.3. Are you satisfied in the way the LC 5 (district) operates?

The responses were: 21% "very satisfactory"; 28% "somewhat satisfactory"; 15% "somewhat unsatisfactory"; 20% "very unsatisfactory"; and the remaining 16% "do not know."

These three answer patterns indicate that people at the grassroots are most familiar with the LC as a village-level forum. As their familiarity decreases, their
views become more negative. This is because one cannot provide a positive response to something he or she does not known well. (The responses to the questions can reflect both subjective and objective views on the LC performances.)
Although the interpretation of data needs to be done carefully, the overall trend is
clear. People rate the LC 1 highly, and, normally, LC 3 and LC 5 are not as highly
regarded as LC 1. A rural woman in Tororo stated, "As far as LC 1 and 2 are concerned, their mobilization is good. Through mobilization, UPE [Universal Primary Education] and water protection are improved. The clearing of roads can be
done. LC sometimes brought meals for those who did the labor work. RUWASA
[Rural Water and Sewage Authority] was working with the LC."[4]

This tendency of more satisfaction with LC 1 becomes much clearer if differences in districts are examined (see Figure 4.4). It is interesting to note that while
in Mukono and Tororo a general pattern of approval of the performance of the LC
declines as the council becomes more remote from the grassroots, in Rakai District, this pattern does not hold. In Rakai, people regard LC 5 (district) more
highly than LC 3 (sub-county). This is largely because Rakai District Council is
very appealing to ordinary people for its rehabilitating of infrastructure, including
roads and schools, with significant assistance from the Danish International

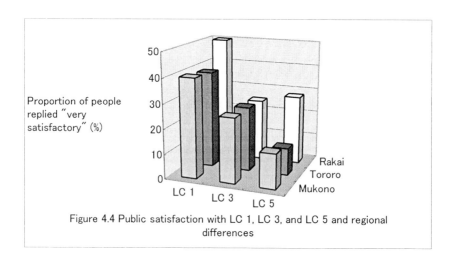

Figure 4.4 Public satisfaction with LC 1, LC 3, and LC 5 and regional
differences

---

[4] Focus group discussion, Osia-Magoro, Tororo, 31 May 2000. This tendency of lower
appreciation of higher level RCs/LCs is also reported by earlier studies. Tidemand
(1994b), for example, notes "[d]efinitely the district remains for the vast majority of villagers as a distant institution" (p. 166). See also his reference on page 103 and Table 7.2
on page 165.

Development Assistance (DANIDA).[5] A similar kind of visible improvement in ordinary people's lives has not taken place in Mukono or Tororo, and this disappointment results in less satisfaction among the people toward higher LCs.

The degree of appreciation for the LC 1 is relatively higher in Rakai than in Mukono or Tororo. On the other hand, Mukono and Tororo are basically showing similar responses from their respective residents. This is slightly contrary to what one would intuitively expect, since Mukono is very proud of itself as a very organized area. This notion is widespread even among the people outside of Mukono. But the response pattern indicates that Rakai residents demonstrate more satisfaction with LC 1 than those in Mukono and Tororo. A main reason for this difference is considered to be that the different tiers of LC system are better linked there through the assistance of DANIDA.

The different age groups show varied assessments of the different levels of the LC system. It is interesting to see, as illustrated by Figure 4.5,[6] that while the youth tend to appreciate LC 1, LC 3 and LC 5 without too much difference in de gree, the elderly appreciate mostly the LC 1 and appreciate LC 3 and LC 5 considerably less. The reasons are not very clear. It can be speculated that because the elderly have more limited mobility than younger people, they may appreciate more the LCs that are located very close. Another possible explanation may be

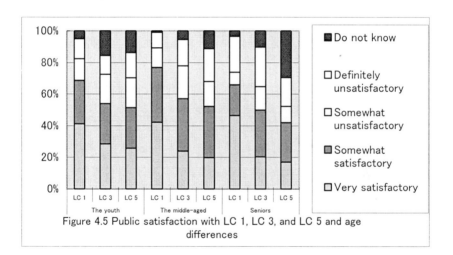

Figure 4.5 Public satisfaction with LC 1, LC 3, and LC 5 and age differences

---

[5] This was confirmed by some people in Rakai: during the focus group discussion, Nvubu, Rakai, 2 August 2000.

[6] Here instead of dividing all the respondents into numerous age brackets, the respondents were divided into three: 1) youth below 25; 2) middle age 26 to 49; and 3) and seniors above 50. The graph was based on the number of respondents who said "very much so" to respective questions.

that since the elderly have more social networks than do the youth, upper levels of local councils would not be as valuable as their own networks.

Education is again an interesting factor, which is almost parallel to the age dimension. The two graphs of the age factor (Figure 4.5) and the education factor (Figure 4.6) show some elements of similarity. Generally, the more educated one is, the less satisfaction one has with regard to the higher levels of the LC system. The proportion of respondents replying "very satisfactory" to different LC levels is reduced as they become more educated.[7] The reason for this is not so obvious. Intuitively it can be reasoned that the more educated have more exposure beyond their immediate local communities, and they would thus have more relationships and interactions with higher levels of local authorities. This process contributes to nurture higher expectations of what the LC should be all about. On the other hand, they may be more easily disappointed once their expectations are not met. The answers obtained here show their frustration. Similar reasoning may apply for the unsatisfactory responses given by the elderly.

Overall, these graphs indicate a consistent pattern of answers; in line with the recent findings of the Uganda Participatory Poverty Assessment Project (UPPAP) people appreciate the role of the grassroots LC but their satisfaction decreases with the upper levels of local authorities.

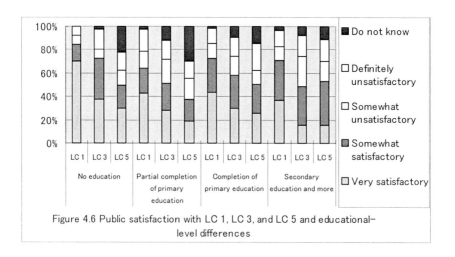

Figure 4.6 Public satisfaction with LC 1, LC 3, and LC 5 and educational-level differences

---

[7] As we look at the responses of "somewhat satisfactory," the situation is slightly modified, even though the general trend in which higher education is associated with lower satisfaction holds here. Interestingly enough, those with secondary education and more, rate LC 5 slightly more satisfactory than LC 3.

2 Participation in the LC System

Participation of various stakeholders is considered essential for successful decentralization. Therefore, the following question was asked:

2. Do you feel that participation in LC 1 meetings is useful?

The responses were: 71% "very useful"; 20% "somewhat useful"; 4% "somewhat useless"; 4% "definitely useless"; and the remaining 1% "do not know." The answers illustrate that the grassroots respondents overwhelming feel participating in LC meetings is useful. The following comments expressed by a rural man are typical of the majority feeling:

When the meetings are called, we participate. We discuss our common problems and try to resolve them. Discussing our problems is helpful, and meetings can resolve some of the issues. But some people do not participate. Apparently they are not interested in meetings. Maybe they think that the meetings are irrelevant. They may think it is a waste of their time to attend such meetings. But when they are more sensitized, they are coming to attend the meetings slowly.[8]

The responses suggest that the meetings are useful for obtaining relevant information on government policies and activities.[9] People repeatedly express appreciation of the value of explanation and guidance by LC 1 councillors concerning home hygiene matters including toilet construction and cleaning practices. This is an encouraging sign that people appreciate the value of attending meetings held at the level of LC 1. The following opinion expressed by a woman makes this point:

Security is improving. The sanitation within the house and the neighborhood is improving: toilet, kitchen, and bathroom. Road maintenance is much better. The youth are now sensitized. Mobilization for the meetings is better. Some modern farming methods are taught. People drink less alcohol now than before. Safe drinking water is more available than before.[10]

Even though the youth who do not attend the meetings regularly, they do not disagree with the value of attendance itself.[11]

On the other hand, this process is far from free of problems. The people themselves are fully aware of the problems. The following remarks by a woman is a typical response:

---

[8] Focus group discussion, Kilowooza, Mukono, 18 August 1999.

[9] Ottemoeller (1996) earlier also found that attendance is oriented more toward information gathering than participation in debates and resolution of policy matters (chapter 7).

[10] Focus group discussion, Mulanda, Tororo, 20 June 2000.

[11] This is in line with the earlier study in which indicated that people attend the LC meetings to find out what is going on in their community and what is needed to be done, especially communal work (Ottemoeller, 1996, chapter 7).

LC 1 and 2 may not know their roles precisely. It is, for them, a voluntary work. When LC 1 meetings are called, the agenda is normally fixed already. People are not given chances to propose their agenda. Often, LC 1 meetings are used for explaining government services to us, but they do not take our views back. The people at the grassroots just listen to the explanations by the government officials. We are just like that. But we generally think that it is useful to participate in meetings.[12]

Regional differences are illustrated by Figure 4.7. It is interesting to note that the residents in Tororo accord the least value to participation in the LC system than other areas. This appears to be related to the disfunctional situation of the LC system there largely caused by the debt of the district government which affects other levels of local government. The history of this district in accumulating a debt of more than one billion Shillings is complicated. But one crucial reason for this debt accumulation is that when two districts were carved out of Tororo and became independent local governments, they did not take any share of the debt. The debt remained totally on the shoulders of Tororo residents. As a result, Tororo is now asked to repay the debt with a narrower local revenue base than before. As a result, in Tororo, the debt reduces resources available for public services and for remuneration of officials, including the councillors who are not paid regularly. If service providers say, "I do not want to become an LC official again,"[13] then it is not difficult to understand that recipients are not pleased either.

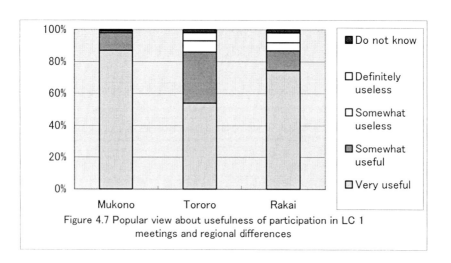

Figure 4.7 Popular view about usefulness of participation in LC 1 meetings and regional differences

---

[12] Focus group discussion, Mukono town, Mukono District, 19 August 1999.

[13] Both the LC 3 Chairperson and the Sub-county chief in Kwapa, in Tororo District, expressed this feeling (personal interview, 2 June 2000).

The age factor is again significant for differentiations, as presented in Figure 4.8.   The overall tendency is that both the youth and the elderly consider participation at LC meetings less useful than do the middle-aged groups. One reason for this dissatisfaction is that neither the youth nor the elderly are fully persuaded that the LC system addresses their needs and concerns. For the youth, they are more preoccupied with gaining cash income. Even if they think that attending meetings is useful, they put higher priority on their individual activities, especially economic ones. A young man in Rakai bluntly said, "The meetings do not produce any direct material benefits."[14] They also think that since the youth do not have much experience and cannot contribute much at meetings, they prefer to let the more experienced participants decide what is good for local communities. For the elderly, the reasons for unfavorable responses are slightly different. They have different needs than the youth. For instance, many of them are concerned with health. The LC often discusses health matters at the village level. But usually improvements in local health facilities are beyond the available means of lower level LCs, and usually nothing much can be done. An elderly man typically commented:

At our age, we do not have enough strength to cultivate our land. Thus, we do not have sufficient income. Working at our age is tough. When we were young, the tax that we paid was used for medicine, etc. Life was far better when we were young. Prices of commodities were much less in the past. But now the taxes we pay do not benefit us. Even so, we are still paying the tax at our age by squeezing our income.[15]

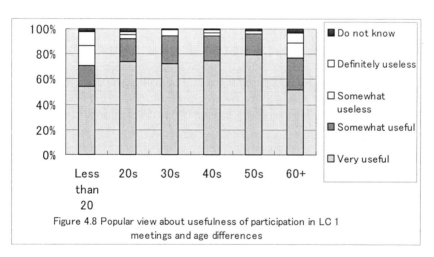

Figure 4.8 Popular view about usefulness of participation in LC 1 meetings and age differences

---

[14] Focus group discussion, Kasambya, Rakai, 12 July 2000.
[15] Focus group discussion, Bontaba, Mukono, 8 June 2000.

3 Poverty Reduction

The ultimate purpose of decentralization is to reduce the pervasive poverty in the country, which continues to be a serious problem despite impressive macro-economic growth in Uganda in recent years. The following two questions ask if people at the grassroots level see any changes in poverty both in terms of fewer material deprivations and of broader empowerment. These two questions do not ask directly if poverty has been reduced by the LC system, but are intended to give some kind of clues as to whether the LC system can contribute to poverty reduction.

3. Do you feel you are less poor in terms of material deprivation than before?

The responses were: 29% "very much so"; 39% "somewhat yes"; 13% "somewhat no"; 16% "definitely no"; and the remaining 3% "do not know." The answers present a very mixed picture. As the people at the grassroots themselves said, the poverty situation shows both positive and negative trends at the same time, and this question forces the respondents to simplify the answer. Thus, it is not surprising that the answers appear to reflect these mixed results. On the one hand, there are a number of improvements. This includes improved security and restored peace, both undoubtedly positive achievements to mitigate the poverty. A woman in Tororo reported: "We think that naked children are rare now. They wear some sort of cloth. We can also do small business."[16]

Yet on the other hand, agriculture, for example, has become more problematic than before. Soil fertility has been declining,[17] and the weather pattern is now more unpredictable. Thus, surviving on small-scale cultivation has become harder than before. Although the UPE is generally welcomed, and parents appreciate the fact that they can now send more children to school, the UPE at the same time puts more pressure on households to obtain a regular cash income to pay various fees required by schools. Thus, life is never easy, as exemplified below by comments by a rural man:

> In the past, cattle were considered to be wealth. But now there are fewer animals; especially cattle are fewer. Diseases often affect the animals. It is difficult to sell them when we need to sell. There are some training programs to treat animal diseases, and these programs are helpful, but the life is never easy. ...We used to have plenty of food in the past. All crops nowadays have problems. For instance, cassava, bananas and coffee are all affected by some kind of diseases.[18]

Another man also typically commented:

---

[16] Focus group discussion, Osere B, Tororo, 19 June 2000.

[17] Although many non-farmer Ugandans still believe that the soil in Uganda is very fertile, the farmers are fully aware of the declining soil fertility.

[18] Focus group discussion, Kibona, Rakai, 25 July 2000.

It is getting worse. Any investment does not materialize benefits. Education is not lead-
ing to a good job in the future. Education is good, but the future prospect remains bleak.
... Due to HIV/AIDS, the middle aged working force is dying. It is possible to get
HIV/AIDS regardless of education.[19]

Nonetheless, based on the responses given to this question, on the whole people
say that there are more positive than negative trends. This itself is encouraging,
although it does not mean that poverty has been eradicated completely. What is
interesting is that the perception and the realities of poverty seem to be fairly
closely linked. Responses from the questionnaire reflect perceptions, which in
turn shape realities.

The regional difference is that more people in Rakai respond positively that
they are now less poor in material terms than before compared to the other two
districts. It has to be noted that this is a relative change in poverty perception by
the people at the grassroots level, and does not reflect the absolute comparison of
poverty in the three areas. The higher level of poverty reduction perceived in Rakai seems to indicate that because the situation in Rakai was so perverse, being affected by the HIV/AIDS epidemic and other factors, relatively small changes are
now significantly felt by the local population. In Tororo, in contrast, the popular
perception perhaps confirms the general observations made by local officials that
the poverty situation is deteriorating instead of improving.[20] The poor and the
disadvantaged are becoming more isolated and vulnerable than before, and not
much empowerment in general is noticed. In short, while the relative situation in
Rakai has improved in recent years, a similar improvement is not felt by people in
the other two areas.

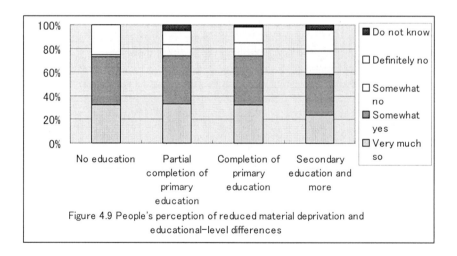

Figure 4.9 People's perception of reduced material deprivation and
educational-level differences

---

[19] Focus group discussion, Osia-Magoro, Tororo, 31 May 2000.
[20] Several officials in Tororo District Council mentioned this worsening situation during
my visits there in 2000.

Education also affects the way in which people respond to this question (Figure 4.9). Changes in the material dimension of poverty, as reflected in this question, may not be so different for those who are without schooling and those who have been to primary school. However, for those who have been to secondary school and higher, the situation is not getting much better. Like the earlier pattern of responses, the more highly educated people express less satisfaction in their answers.

4 Empowerment of the Socially Weak

Poverty is not just material deprivation. It involves such dimensions as insecurity, vulnerability and isolation. Thus, the following question was designed to reflect the views of people on this dimension of poverty. In decentralization theory, it is assumed that by bringing services closer to the people, through their active participation, especially of the poor and the disadvantaged, decentralization will enhance more democratic decision-making processes as well as empowerment.

4. Do you feel that you are more confident, more connected to the community, and have more people to help you when you need help than before?

The responses were: 46% "very much so"; 29% "somewhat yes"; 12% "somewhat no"; 11% "definitely no"; and the remaining 2% "do not know."

Interestingly, the answers given to this question do not differ tremendously from those to the previous question. The responses were mixed. The way in which this question was asked is perhaps too complicated to solicit clear answers. A common response by a woman was, "If we have some relationship with other groups, for instance, NGOs and CBOs, they are more helpful."[21] Thus, about three-quarters of the respondents positively replied that their social relations have improved. This improvement can be interpreted as a sign that decentralization enhances social networks that are empowering to the poor, as anticipated by decentralization advocates. However, there are counter-trends, as expressed by a man in one focus group discussion:

In the past, people worked together and helped each other. But now it is difficult. Extended family system for mutual help is no longer functional. When I am facing a financial problem, it is most likely that my neighbors are also having the same problem. Thus, I cannot ask help from my neighbors.[22]

This statement echoes views expressed in some other areas.[23] Thus, it may be the case that the situation may not be as promising as the graph here indicates.

---

[21] Focus group discussion, Osere B, Tororo, 19 June 2000.
[22] Focus group discussion, Kibona, Mukono, 16 July 2000.
[23] Focus group discussion, Nvuvu, Rakai, 2 August 2000

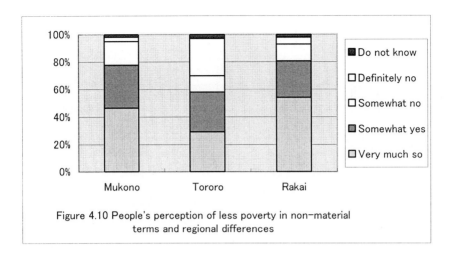

Figure 4.10 People's perception of less poverty in non-material
terms and regional differences

The regional difference becomes even more evident from the responses given to this question of the non-material dimension of poverty than to the previous question that addressed material poverty (Figure 4.10). People in Rakai express more satisfaction than those in Mukono and Tororo when evaluating their non-material poverty improvement.

The different views of different age groups are interesting to note. Persons in their 50s respond most positively to this question, while the most senior group, aged over 60, expresses the most negative views. This contrast is very revealing. This needs to be considered carefully, but maybe social networks built through experience reach their peak for people in their 50s. This interpretation largely corresponds to life expectancy in Uganda, which is now 40 years according to 1998 statistical data (UNDP, 2000c). If people grow older than 60, they start losing their friends and relatives, and social networks shrink (perhaps drastically). This results in less rosy views held by people over 60. Some senior men in Rakai mentioned the double burden that they face. While in the past children were considered as a means of social security, this is no longer the case due to changes in family structures. In addition, because this area is particularly affected by HIV/AIDS, they are often the ones to look after the family, as indicated by the following comment made by a rural woman:

Elderly are often asked to look after children/orphans who lost parents due to HIV/AIDS. Extended family system was helpful in the past, but no longer. With the increased demand for income, the elderly are financially poorer than before. Without money, people cannot help these days.[24]

---

[24] Focus group discussion, Nvubu , Rakai, 2 August 2000. For an illuminating life story of a woman who lost her children due to HIV/AIDS, see Concern Worldwide et al., 1999, pp. 38-46.

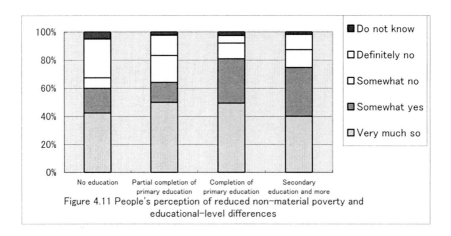

Figure 4.11 People's perception of reduced non-material poverty and educational-level differences

For reducing non-material aspects of poverty, education appears to matter significantly as suggested by Figure 4.11. Generally, the level of education is positively related to more satisfactory answers regarding the level of confidence and less isolation within local communities. The number of people who responded that their non-material poverty has been reduced "very much" combined with those who replied "somewhat reduced" increased significantly as the level of education rises. Therefore, it can be reasoned that education is crucial for mitigating non-material aspects of poverty.

5 Process of Local Consultation

In order to examine whether decentralization enhances development effectiveness or not, two aspects are considered here. The first one is a process aspect. Development becomes more effective by participation of those who have often been excluded. With their participation, decision-making processes become more inclusive and democratic, which contributes to obtaining desired results. Decentralization attempts are also considered to enrich social networks, as the LC system, being an essential institution, needs to interface with the local population on diverse matters.

| 5. Are you pleased with the process of LC consultation on local issues? |

The responses were: 41% "very pleased"; 31% "somewhat pleased"; 11% "somewhat unpleased"; 14% "definitely unpleased"; and the remaining 3% "do not know." Generally, what is clear from the responses is that the people are pleased with the process in which they are allowed to voice their concerns and issues. This feeling is especially significant for the poor and the disadvantaged.

The LC system introduced a kind of affirmative action for women, the youth and the disabled. Interestingly enough, there is no significant difference of views between men and women on this question. A woman pointed out that compared with the past system of chieftainship, "elders now involve us, and it is good that we can participate in discussions."[25]

The process of the LC system is not as appreciated by the youth as it is by the middle-aged group. This repeats the overall pattern of age and LC assessment. What is interesting is that for the elderly, the consultation process appears to be an important aspect. Their degree of appreciation is higher than that of the youth, and indeed higher than that of the middle-aged respondents.

As to the quality of consultation, it seems that the forum of LC meetings is not as interesting for grassroots participation as the ones called by NGOs. The following responses made by a women is illustrative of this view:

> Community-Based Organizations (CBOs) do sensitization and organize seminars and meetings. This enhances cooperation among members and makes members united for development. LC meetings, on the other hand, tend to explain government policies, but the meetings are not really interesting compared with those organized by CBOs. The CBO meetings are more social in a sense that members feel little constraint in participation.[26]

The statement indicates that it is desirable to improve the way in which LC meetings are organized.

6 Outcomes of Consultations

Following the previous question which focuses on the process aspect, the next one looks at outcomes. It is assumed that with decentralization measures, more pro-poor growth can be achieved, and the results will contribute to mitigate poverty. More specifically, it is believed that five major national priorities - education, health, agriculture, roads, and water/sanitation - will be better catered to under the decentralized service provisions in Uganda.

6. Are you pleased with what the LC (1-5) has done?

The responses were: 22% "very pleased"; 41% "somewhat pleased"; 16% "somewhat unpleased"; 17% "definitely unpleased"; and the remaining 4% "do not know." Like the previous question, answers given to this question indicate mixed views, but more positive than negative. A woman in Rakai noted:

> The LC can settle disputes. For example, land disputes, crop damages caused by animals, and domestic violence, etc. The LC can assist local communities in advancing

---

[25] Focus group discussion, Osere B, Tororo, 19 June 2000.
[26] Focus group discussion, Allupe, Tororo, 30 May 2000.

some ideas for development: feeder roads, schools, health units, water sources, etc.
They also communicate our views to the upper authorities. The LC is also good to ensure children going to schools. However, local councillors have time-consuming jobs.
This [work] is not paid. It is not easy to organize community works. This difficulty
partly arises from the lack of awareness of the people.[27]

What is essential here is to compare the responses given to this and the previous questions. More people appreciate the role of the LC as a forum for consultation, but less as a problem-solving institution (as seen in the previous chapter).
People generally consider it helpful to discuss common problems in communities
and to try to resolve them. On the other hand, the current LC system faces various
obstacles, and the LC system alone cannot resolve most of the problems. Many of
these issues cannot be effectively resolved at the village level, and the problems
need to be brought to upper levels of the hierarchy. In most cases, the upper authorities do not provide any meaningful explanations or remedies to lower levels.
Thus, the situation is that issues are discussed but no solution is produced. This
situation appears to explain why there is a significant difference in grassroots' appreciation of LC consultations and LCs' actual implementations after such discussions. The following expressed by a rural man illustrates this point:

> The LC system is not a bad one, but LC councillors are doing their jobs on a voluntary
> basis, and thus it is not easy to get the issues resolved. Sometimes it is a waste of time.
> Some councillors are doing their own work for their income instead of working as coun-
> cillors.[28]

It is interesting to note that this is the only question over which there is a significant difference of views between male and female respondents. Although this

Figure 4.12 Popular view of satisfaction with LC outcomes and gender
differences

---

[27] Focus group discussion, Njeru, Rakai, 1 August 2000.
[28] Focus group discussion, Nusube, Mukono, 26 August 2000.

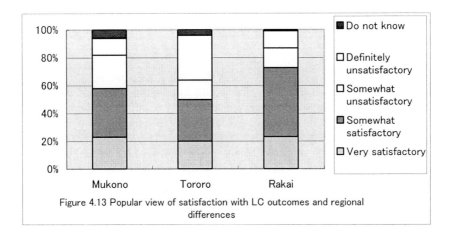

Figure 4.13 Popular view of satisfaction with LC outcomes and regional differences

may be a relatively small difference, there are more negative views among women while men tend to answer "somewhat pleased" to this question, as suggested in Figure 4.12. But at the same time, there are more women than men who replied "very pleased." Although the reasons for this difference are not fully known, it may be that women have more dissatisfaction with the LC system because it cannot resolve women's priority issues. For instance, sexual harassment and domestic violence are areas where gender bias tends to be apparent in the local power structure behind the LC system. This bias prevents full resolution of these kinds of disputes.

The regional differences of views for this question largely confirm the earlier pattern. The residents in Rakai, Mukono and Tororo express overall satisfaction with the outcomes of the LC system, as illustrated by Figure 4.13.

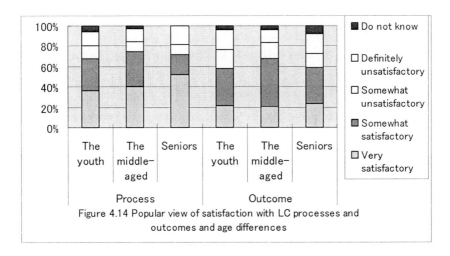

Figure 4.14 Popular view of satisfaction with LC processes and outcomes and age differences

The responses given to the previous question and this one by different age groups are interesting. Figure 4.14 compares how different age groups express their respective satisfaction with LC consultation processes and what the LC system has actually accomplished. Overall, what is clear is that all age groups express more satisfaction with the processes than with the outcomes. Relatively, both in the processes and outcomes, the middle-aged group accorded the highest degree of satisfaction followed by the seniors and the youth. The gap in satisfaction between processes and outcomes is sharpest for the elderly, moderate for the youth, and least extreme for the middle-aged people. This corresponds to a similar pattern of different levels of appreciation given to the LC system by different age groups. Again, although the reasons are not entirely clear, it can be interpreted that senior people are least satisfied with what the LC can actually accomplish to meet their specific concerns and needs, which may be different from the rest of the local population.

7 Responsiveness of the LC System

With decentralization, it is anticipated that public services will better match the concerns and needs of ordinary people. Decentralization will increase responsiveness, advocates argue. Thus, the following question was presented:

7. Do you feel that the LC system as a whole is responding to the needs of ordinary people like yourself?

The responses were: 25% "very responsive"; 37% "somewhat responsive"; 16% "somewhat unresponsive"; 18% "definitely unresponsive"; and the remaining 4% "do not know."

Since this question asks the respondents to indicate their answers taking the LC 5 through LC 1 into account, responses present a mixed picture. On the whole, it is clear that more people view the LC positively than negatively. But it is relevant to note here that the difference between positive and negative views is relatively narrow. Thus, the LC system in Uganda today is at a stage that, on the one hand, is appreciated by the people, and on the other hand, still requires significant improvements to fulfill needs and concerns of the ordinary people at the grassroots level.

The differences in responses by the three districts are in line with a similar pattern observed for earlier questions (Figure 4.15). Tororo residents considered that the LC is least responsive to their needs than the residents in the other districts.

As for the age factor, in general the middle-aged group considers the LC more responsive than do the youth and the senior age group. The youth appear to think that the LC is slightly more responsive than do the elderly, but the difference between these two groups is not significant. The views of men and women do not exhibit significant differences concerning this issue of responsiveness.

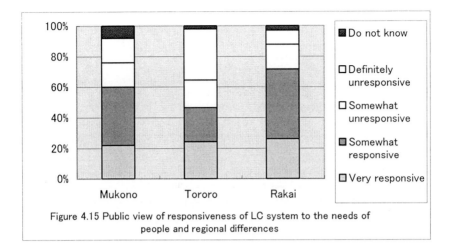

Figure 4.15 Public view of responsiveness of LC system to the needs of people and regional differences

On the other hand, the level of education is significant in varying the views of respondents as illustrated by Figure 4.16. Generally, as the level of education increases, fewer people respond with "very much so" to this question. It may be the case that the more educated people are, the higher their expectations of political and social systems; therefore, the current practices and situations may disappoint those with higher levels of education.

Responsiveness for the grassroots people depends on the character of leaders. One village in Tororo, where this researcher visited, never had a single meeting since the last election of 1997/98. This is a very exceptional case. When people in some other areas heard this, a man expressed such views as follows:

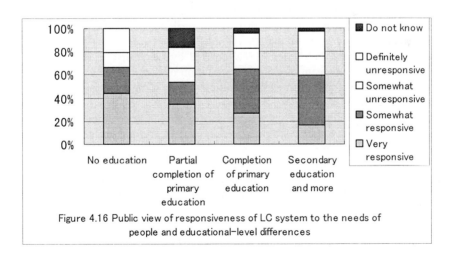

Figure 4.16 Public view of responsiveness of LC system to the needs of people and educational-level differences

Here we have good leadership, and therefore when we have problems we can always raise them and discuss among ourselves. We are sorry to hear that in some other places the situation is significantly different.[29]

8 Concluding Assessment

The views expressed by people at the grassroots hint at both positive and negative aspects of the LC system, which is intended as an interface between local authorities and the people. On the one hand, it is encouraging that people value the LC as a forum for discussion, and they also appreciate the importance of participation. LC 1 at the village level is central to people's notions and networks. This may be because it works mainly as a dispute-resolving institution in local communities. The overall assessment of the LC system is different in different districts. The resources made available for local authorities appear to affect the level of appreciation.

On the other hand, there are a number of problems, as already noted. One of the most notable is the prominent view about corruption as examined in Chapter 3. But this is a part of a wider problem. A woman expressed such views as follows:

The fee that we are asked to pay when we ask the help of the LC is too high. The LC does not deal with cases without payment. A proportion of the local tax, which should be allocated for our villages, does not reach us here. It is not used for the common people. Moreover, relief food distributed (rice, for example) is too little, and it is given unequally and unfairly. Assistance to orphans is also implemented unfairly.[30]

Undoubtedly, the LC system needs to be improved in various ways. This challenge is particularly acute when the more educated consider the LC system less satisfactory. This is a serious sign that the local governance system needs urgent attention. The challenge may mean that the LC system is becoming ineffective for the educated as a viable institution.

Some of the possible solutions are suggested by the people at the grassroots themselves. Many of them are aware that the job of the councillors is unpaid at lower levels, and the voluntary duties conflict with their personal requirements of securing food and income. They also mention that the general lack of understanding among the poor themselves makes collaboration with the councillors difficult. Remedies for these problems would be helpful for facilitating partnership formations (as will be examined in subsequent chapters in this study).

In addition, age is clearly a serious fault-line to be considered. Both the youth and the elderly have different concerns and needs than the middle-aged, and their

---

[29] Focus group discussion Kibona, Mukono, 16 July 2000. This was reported by Ottemoeller earlier. He noted that personality and style of leadership influence the way in which respondents evaluate the performance of the RC (1996, chapter 7).

[30] Focus group discussion, Mulanda, Tororo, 20 June 2000.

needs remain relatively unmet by the LC system. In fact, focus group discussions tend to reveal more negative aspects of the LC system than does the questionnaire. The remarks made about the LC system by persons attending the discussions often touch on their dissatisfaction with the LC system. The youth issue is one of the themes of the next chapter, in which the representation of the socially disadvantaged in the LC system is scrutinized.

5 The Representation of the Disadvantaged: Women, Youth and Ethnic Minorities

Generally, men do not understand women's issues. For instance, some men refuse to let their wives attend project meetings. But the understandings by men seem to have improved over the years. It is slightly better now than before. In the past, men suppressed women a lot. It is still happening, but it is less now.

A woman made a statement during
the focus group discussion Lunbugu, Rakai, 25 August 1999

There are certain social groups which are more disadvantaged and vulnerable than others. In this chapter, the examples of women, the youth, and ethnic minorities in Uganda are discussed. The first section reviews gender disparities and how women relate to the LC system. The second part analyzes the relationship between youth and the NRM. In the third section, the issue of ethnic diversity and its implications for the LC system are examined. More emphasis is placed on gender than on age and ethnicity issues, partly because the NRM places significant emphasis on the role of women, which is clearly stated in the constitution as well.[1] This research suggests that the decentralized state has a mixed impact on the formation of partnerships for respective disadvantaged groups.

There are both similarities and differences between women, the youth and ethnic groups in their relationships with the hierarchy of LC system. In addition to the structure of the LC system, both women and youth have their respective pyramidal council structures. These systems reflect NRM's desire to mobilize these social groups and promote their participation in local decision making. But given the limited alternative opportunities for both women and the youth to participate outside these council systems, they also feel constrained by the structures. While for women, even if the affirmative action scheme, under which one-third of LC members must be women, has some controversial aspects, it has promoted women's involvement in politics both nationally and locally. But as women become more active in politics, new tensions with other stakeholders are generated.

---

[1] This unequal treatment also reflects the current priorities within the academic community as well. Unfortunately, there has been little previous research on the subject of the youth in development (Uphoff et al., 1998, p. 82).

In contrast, the youth have not been mobilized in a similar way that women have been. Most of the youth engage in their individual activities for income-generation without much collaboration. They are not organized as a coherent social group in their battle for a better future. They are thus quite frustrated, and some feel that even the Universal Primary Education (UPE) is not benefiting them in obtaining better jobs. With this kind of disillusionment and apathy, they do not believe in the efficacy of the LC system. But this does not mean that they are against social mobilization itself. In some exceptional cases, the youth have been organized and started to show a willingness to collaborate with others for something mutually beneficial. The youth problem is now recognized by the NRM, and the youth may slowly follow the path of women. This path is a long and gradual process of struggle to attain political freedom, economic benefits and social justice.

But the difference between women and youth in their relationships with the LC system partly originates from the historical background against which the RC system was established. The RC system, on the one hand, was intended to be a democratic institution in which all local residents would be able to participate. On the other hand, social order and stability under the RCs was conceived according to the interests of the original leaders of the RCs who were middle-sized land-owners. While these men did not feel very threatened by women's participation in the guerrilla struggle and in the RC, it was urgent for them to control the youth who were often considered to pose threats to the acceptable social order. Consequently, while women used this opportunity within and outside of the LC system to advance their positions, the youth could not exploit it as much as women did. This original difference has influenced the way in which these socially disadvantaged groups have related to the LC system and the state.

Ethnicity is different from the gender and youth dimensions. On the one hand, ethnic differences do not cause political and social problems in normal circumstances. Usually there is no conscious engagement by different ethnic groups in the LC system as in the case of women who attempt to use the LC for their empowerment. On the other hand, ethnicity is highlighted when some issues, especially related to unequal access to public resources, surface. Then these issues are often politicized in a crude zero-sum manner, and both people at the grassroots and their elected leaders need to face ethnic issues squarely. A set of preventive measures is crucial before ethnicity becomes politicized. One of the most essential prevention measures is to ensure that the LC system gains legitimacy by including representatives of not only dominant but also marginal ethnic groups.

1 Women and the NRM

Many developing countries suffer from gender inequalities, as illustrated by the opening quotation. Uganda is no exception. According to government statistics, 55% of women are illiterate compared with 36% of men. Women contribute to more than 80% of food production. Although 97% of women have access to land, only 7% actually own land. Women-headed-households are more likely to be poor than other households (Uganda, MoGCD, 1995).[2] Recently, the HIV/AIDS epidemic has tended to reinforce gender inequality in terms of women's health as well as their socio-economic status (Obbo, 1998; and Wallman, 1996).[3]

In order to reduce such gender imbalances, the NRM government has been taking measures. The NRM created the Ministry of Women in Development in 1988. In 1993, with the passage of the National Women's Council Statute, the government established the National Association of Women's Organizations of Uganda (NAOWU), which took over what was formerly the National Council of Women created earlier by Idi Amin in 1978. The NAOWU is basically a parastatal umbrella organization for women's NGOs. This 1993 statute also established a hierarchy of Women's Councils from village to district levels, which is parallel to the LC system. This Women's Council hierarchy is overseen by the National Women's Council at the central level. The two parallel councils are linked through the secretary of women at each layer of the pyramid structures, who is a member of the LC and attends the Women Council meetings as well.

Through these structures the NRM has been promoting women's participation in decision-making processes at various levels. The new constitution expresses explicitly concern for gender equality. At the national level, and the number of women ministers has been steadily increasing since 1986. Women represent 25% of the national parliament since the 2001 election (Inter- Parliamentary Union, 2003). The proportionate representation of women in national institutions is considered to be one of the highest in Africa (Goetz, 1998, p. 253).

At the district level, all 45 chairpersons of LC 5 (governors) are men, while 40 out of 45 vice chairpersons of LC 5 are women. A recent survey on the gender ratio of district councillors reveals that on average 40% of councillors are female with the highest being 59% in Bugiri District and the lowest 28% in Masindi District (Uganda, MoFPED and UNDP, 2000b, Table A 1.2; and Uganda, MoFPED, 2001, p. 25).[4] This signifies that most of the female district councillors have secured their seats through the Local Governments Act, 1997, which requires that at least one-third of the councillors must be women.[5] The affirmative action taken by the NRM is, therefore, quite significant in boosting the representation of women.

The reasons why the NRM has been enthusiastic to support women derive from several factors. First, during the guerrilla war, women's contribution was signifi-

---

[2] Appleton (1996) calls for more careful interpretation of data rather than accepting it uncritically.

[3] For a review of the gender situation in Uganda, see Gopal and Salim, 1998; Musisi, 1995; Snyder, 2000; Tripp, 1994, 1998a, 1998b, 2000, and 2001; and World Bank 2001b.

[4] The reason why Masindi and other districts are below the legal obligation of one-third is unknown. Some female councillors may have passed away, and by-elections may have not yet been conducted to fill the vacant posts.

[5] The Electoral Commission reports that 2.6% of candidates are female among those directly elected by the constituencies. Other women candidates are elected on the affirmative action basis (Uganda, the Electoral Commission, 1999).

cant as solders, intelligence personnel, nurses and other support staff. They also provided food for the guerrillas and participated in the secret RC meetings (Tidemand, 1994b, p. 78). These efforts on the part of women helped the NRM to obtain power, and therefore the government would like to reward their contribution (Mugyenyi, 1998, p. 134).[6]

Second, the NRM itself was committed to opening up social and political space in order not to destabilize Ugandan society. A new form of women's participation in the RC system originally was in line with this rationale, and it "did not appear too threatening" to elder village leaders who on the other hand saw women's participation in council matters as quite unusual (Tidemand, 1994b, p. 79).[7]

Third, these reasons, however, do not preclude the political calculation that in order to secure electoral victory, women, constituting half of the population, are an important constituency. Thus, increasing women's representation would make an important political appeal to this crucial constituency.

The relationship between women and the NRM regime is, however, ambiguous. On the one hand, women are generally supportive of the LC system and the NRM (as seen in the previous chapter). Thanks to the less authoritative nature of this regime and to the social stability and economic recovery brought by the NRM, many associational activities of women have been made possible. With the NRM rule, various small-scale development activities at the grassroots can take place, some of which are very relevant to women's daily needs. Although this process represents a struggle between men and women over respective gender roles, women appear to have increased their autonomy in grassroots activities fairly significantly.

On the other hand, women are sometimes very critical of the NRM as long as it curtails autonomy of women and/or to reinforce gender inequalities. When women attempt to go beyond what the regime is currently prepared to accept, fierce tension is created. The creation of the parallel Women's Council can be seen as another attempt by the NRM to ensure that women's activities and grassroots movements do not go beyond the boundaries defined by the NRM.[8]

It is noteworthy that the current no-party polity in Uganda works in two contradictory ways for women to mobilize themselves. On the one hand, the restrictions placed on political parties enable women to overcome party differences and become united for common gender concerns within the polity. On the other hand, since the parties are not allowed to operate, women do not have realistic alternatives to secure electoral success. This restriction tends to reduce political influence that women otherwise may enjoy.

---

[6] According to Tamale (1999), "women's significant contribution to the five-year guerrilla struggle may have added to Museveni's realization that indeed women can perform as well, if not better, than men in traditionally 'male' jobs" (p. 19).

[7] Vincent notes that leaders' positions in a village in the late 1960s were taken by men (Vincent, 1971, p. 231).

[8] See Tripp 2000, particularly chapter 4, for tensions between women's desires for autonomy and the NRM attempts at control.

Under these circumstances, in order to attain gender equality women work both inside and outside of the LC system. Within the LCs, women councillors struggle to press their issues, although this process still faces various obstacles. Women often use the LC system wisely; women councillors within the LC system organize their activities to enlarge the autonomous space that women can enjoy. The LC system is useful to mobilize grassroots women, especially if mobilization is called for by women councillors. Outside the LC system, women also demand autonomy from the state. If the current government attempts to limit women's opportunities to participate in decision making, women undoubtedly oppose such attempts. Women sometimes seek alternative forums if they consider the LC system unsuitable for their purposes. Women defend the autonomy of small, informal and unregistered local associations in order to avoid government influence.

This kind of dual strategy has been an evolving process. Initially, women were reluctant to politicize their activities since in the past these activities were counterproductive in inviting state repression against women. But as women gain more influence in politics, and as the limitations of the NRM polity become clear for attaining gender equality, women are starting to voice their concerns more loudly and clearly. This boldness is backed up by some successful women, especially those professionals in urban areas.

1.1 Women and the LC System

There are various points through which women interface with the LC system. One of them is elections. While the method of universal adult suffrage is normal for selecting representatives, an electoral method for choosing representatives for specially designated, socially weak groups was lining behind the candidates (literally on the ground) until recently. This method was problematic. Men, intending to preserve the existing local power structure, inclined to prefer women who were linked with dominant village men, and those women who could be readily influenced by powerful men. Additionally, men often preferred to have female candidates with a pretty face! That is why the amendment to the Local Governments Act was passed by the parliament in 2001, in which women councillors would also be elected by universal adult suffrage through secret ballot.

This raises a wider problem of Ugandan political culture in which women are new players of the game. It has been pointed out that in "general, female candidates running in the 1996 parliamentary elections faced greater public ridicule than men."[9] Several women during the fieldwork for this research stated that during the election period some rumors to undermine their candidacies were spread widely.[10]

On the occasions of elections, women do not necessarily vote for women only because they are women. Women acknowledge that while they feel more comfortable with fellow women candidates, being a woman is not a determining factor

---

[9] This is commonly cited at the grassroots level. See also Tripp, 1998a, p. 88.
[10] Personal interview, Mary Mugyenyi, 2 September 1998.

in choosing suitable representatives. Other factors like personality, education, and the opinions expressed by candidates are very influential in the voting process. Capabilities and qualifications matter more than gender.

A woman chairperson at LC 3 in Mukono agreed that gender was not the sole determining factor for elections. But she explained that the gender dimension was nonetheless evident. Once she was elected, some men ridiculed her. According to her, these incidents signified that even though men have become increasingly aware of women's issues, discrimination still persists. She felt that women had advantages in raising issues of women and children in the LC system, which would often be beneficial for local communities. She maintained that it was a good opportunity for both herself and her husband to think about these issues both personally and publicly. But disadvantages included the burden placed on the family in that some of her family members would have to assist her in looking af-ter the daily family needs. She hesitantly concluded that it might be difficult for women to contest elections in the future.[11]

Dispute settlement is another area in which women and the LC system interact. In numerous villages women maintained that the LC has contributed significantly to resolving incidents of domestic violence against women. A recent statistics in-dicate that 41% of women are exposed to domestic violence in Uganda (UNDP, 1998, p. 26; and cf. Uganda, UBOS, 2001a, pp.36-38). Women need to pay a fee when they ask the LC to intervene to resolve domestic violence. This fee tends to be relatively expensive for rural women who do not have a regular cash income for their own use.[12] Although the exact degree of improvement in this issue is hard to gauge, women appear to appreciate the role of councillors, especially fe-male ones, in trying to mediate disputes over domestic violence in rural areas. It would be an exaggeration to say that the LC system would be able to resolve all disputes for women (Khadiagala, 2001). But the LCs' contribution in dispute set-tlements is no trivial matter.

1.2 Women Councillors within the LC System

The proportional representation of women in the councils has increased signifi-cantly. While in the RC system (until around 1995) only one out of nine council-lors was a woman, now about 40% of councilors are women. When the RC in-cluded at least one woman councillor, it was often reported that women's voices were not seriously heard by male colleagues who dominated local power struc-tures.[13] Now the number of women councillors has increased so that men are more exposed to women's views. If women are united within the LC system, the chances are more likely that men will no longer treat women's issues insignifi-

---

[11] Personal interview, Beatrice Yiga, Chairpeson, Kwapa Sub-county, Tororo, 18 August 1999.

[12] This is called a court fee. The amount tends to vary slightly from one area to another, but it is around 2,000 Ush (US$ 1.3). This is sometimes confused with a bribe.

[13] These accounts are numerous. See, for instance, Mulyampiti, 1994; and Tripp, 1998b.

cantly as they did in the past. Asked whether decentralization measures have done anything good for people in Uganda, one woman spoke for other women when she said: "For women, it has brought a positive change. In the past, women were rarely represented, and women were not engaged in policy making. Now women are engaged in such functions."[14] Some female councillors, particularly at the higher levels, are using the numerical improvement effectively. For instance, some female LC 5 councillors in the Mukono District Council are less hesitant to voice their gender concerns openly.[15] These open tactics sometimes invite overt and covert resistance by male counterparts. But clearly, some successful women are now more willing to take a direct approach in contrast to the low-keyed and informal method of engagement which was used in the past.

On the other hand, resistance by men for the further advancement of women is clearly persistent. There appears to be a significant perception gap between men and women in general, and male councillors and their female counterparts in particular. Some male councillors would not say it openly, but privately acknowledge that within the LC system there are already "enough" women councilors, and the LCs have to be very careful about women's issues. But female councillors contend that although men have demonstrated improved understanding of women's and children's issues compared to the past, women still wish men would become more sensitive on gender issues. The numerical increase in female representation at the LC decision-making processes does not automatically guarantee that the decisions are more gender sensitive. "A feminine presence in politics is not the same as a feminist one" (Goetz, 1998, p. 251). Translating the increased numerical representation into effective policies is challenging. Therefore, the situation of women in Uganda is at a crossroads, being influenced by a mixture of factors.

Difficulties in such a transformation are symbolized by the way in which the women councillors in the affirmative action scheme are dealt with within the LC system. Once they join the LC, there is no legal distinction between those who are elected by the constituencies and those who are sent through affirmative action. The women councillors on the affirmative action ticket, however, are often treated in reality as junior partners within the LC system. There are some exceptional cases when, for instance, women representative councillors (or youth representative councillors) join the executives of LCs, if they are considered well qualified by the chairperson, but such examples are rare. Some of those who are elected by constituencies outside of the affirmative action scheme consider that they are in a more suitable position to direct the councils. Again, this is not said openly but this kind of feeling is undeniable. This subjugation is an especially acute problem for women councillors, since most of them are elected through affirmative action. One woman councillor in Tororo stated, "It is difficult to raise issues in the council meetings. Some do not pay serious attention. We women realize that it is bet-

---

[14] Focus group discussion, Joggo, Mukono, 18 August 1999.
[15] Personal interviews, Victoria Kakoko Sebagereka, Secretary for Health, Community Services and Child Welfare, Mukono District Council, 13 August 1999; and Mary Nalugo Sekiziyuvu, Deputy Speaker, Mukono District Council, 13 August 1999.

ter to discuss the issues among women first in order to obtain more support at the official meetings."[16]

A second problem is the relations between women councillors and the Women's Councils which are parallel to the LC system. There is a specially designated secretary for women at all levels of the LC hierarchy in order to institutionalize women's representation by linking the LC and Women Council systems. Whether this functions effectively or not is a different issue. This primarily depends on the political relationship between this secretary and other councillors. Quite often, the women secretary tends to be marginalized and does not function as an effective link between women constituencies and other political leaders. Her position may become more promising if she can obtain support from other women both within and outside of the LC system. But contacts between women leaders and grassroots women are limited. As a result, linkages between the LC system and the Women's Councils remain weak.

Additional issues preventing women in the LC system from becoming fully effective include the fact that many women councillors still need more training and support. They particularly need more skill training in leadership, lobbying and budgeting. While the budgeting process is essential to secure funds to meet their gender needs, budgeting seems to be an extremely difficult subject for most of the councillors, especially female councillors. Budgeting is probably the single most important area, in which many women councillors really wish to be trained. Complaints such as the following were often heard, as typically expressed by a young man: "We receive explanations only after the office makes budgets. It is difficult to understand the language of budgeting."[17] Since budgeting is like a language, unless one is used to it, one cannot understand it. There is no particular "smartness" required to "master" it, but one needs to be reasonably "fluent" in it.

There have already been some training programs provided for councillors. For instance, the training programs provided by the Decentralization Secretariat, of course, include women councilors as a part of targeted beneficiaries. But as before, training for women needs to be adjusted to their needs and responsibilities which they bear both inside and outside the home. Women's double burden of being councillors and mothers and/or wives is really demanding, and the designing of training programs should cater to these women's burdens. One of the consequences of these difficulties is reelection. There appears to be a tendency among those who do not seek reelection of being councillors of disadvantaged backgrounds, including many women.[18]

---

[16] Personal interview, Bira Osuna, Women Councillor, Kwapa Sub-county, Tororo, 2 June 2000.

[17] Focus group discussion, Ndeeba, Mukono, 21 August 1999.

[18] See Chapter 3 of this study. For instance, focus group discussion, Ksege, Rakai, 1 August 2000.

1.3 Women outside the LC System

Since women are aware that penetrating the LC system is never easy, they also pursue gender equity outside the LC system as well. There seems to be a gradual evolution of strategies. Women at first avoided consciously making political claims in the late 1980s and early 1990s. Women generally did not seek direct confrontation with the state since it might backfire against them in reducing their autonomy. This indirect strategy was also employed partly because they feared direct engagement with the state would lead women into corruption and/or co-optation by existing power structures (Goetz, 1998, p. 256).

But some women's groups pursue different approaches today because avoiding confrontation has its own limitations. One of the critical issues is that without directly addressing power relationships between men and women in the society, some women's concerns cannot be fully realized. In fact some of these concerns are getting even more serious under the economic austerities implemented by the government with the support of international financial institutions. This situation is well captured by the following observation:

> During economic restructuring and democratization, male politicians have sought to convince women that their interests were served by the current politicians, while at the same time they deny women additional benefits. This has pushed women toward greater boldness in addressing the economic and political elements that determine and affect their status in societies that have distinct cultural traditions and historical experiences (Mikell, 1997, p. 5).

Women's groups, particularly those led by more educated and professional women leaders, are now more likely to engage the state directly to advocate women's political as well as socio-economic agendas including legal rights in access to land and protection against domestic violence. Debates over women's access to land under the Land Act, 1998, are one such example where women openly voice their views, even if the direct method often invites reactions by critics, some of whom are deeply opposed to women's advancements.

1.4 Small-scale Grassroots Activities

The way in which women engage the LC system is affected by what is happening on the ground, as varieties of small-scale development projects are now operated at the grassroots level. Quite a few of them are organized by the LC system and certainly influence women's activities significantly. Often these projects support women's practical needs: securing food, water, schools for children, and rural health clinics. As women gain more confidence in organizing their activities, they may feel less constrained to get connected with other women. Some are willing to get in touch with the elite women of the local authorities. A crucial point to note is that women are far more networked than any other category of people in Uganda, especially where government services remain haphazard. One woman in Tororo spoke for the group when she said frankly:

> We are in a poor area. We would like to meet with women in richer areas to learn from them. We would like to ask them to transfer their skills and knowledge to us, for example, modern agricultural practices. We wish to know how they become rich.[19]

Clearly, in this process of networking, women leaders and followers have a role to play for mutual empowerment, although the relationship between women leaders and grassroots women are not free from friction.[20] In this sense, small-scale development activities conducted by grassroots women are far from trivial.

The process of organizing grassroots activities also involves negotiations and accommodations between men and women over respective roles. In numerous instances, women still face objections by men. A woman typically insisted, "Husbands do not like their wives to attend and join group activities. These husbands do not know what the group is doing. They are just ignorant."[21] Another woman continues, "It is apparent that men discussed this among themselves over drinks. My husband was asked by his friends, 'How did you allow your wife to join the group?'"[22] Since these are common incidents, yet another woman commented:

> Men's understanding of women's issues is much better. But again there are some men who have not yet sensitized. ... But the challenge in the future is that decisions over allocation of household resources (including income) should be made jointly with women instead of men telling women about the results of their decisions. Although this decision making issue is better than before, we still need more men to understand this.[23]

Although these small-scale development activities entail negotiation and bargaining, they can generate encouraging outcomes for both men and women. Some *men* joined women's activities, and one such man made interesting replies:

> When I wanted to join the group, my friends laughed at me and asked me why I am following women. But now it becomes easier to work together between men and women. Just like the LC has both men and women councillors, it is no problem to have men and women in these groups.[24]

The group activities create learning opportunities for both sexes to reconsider their gender roles. The processes present valuable opportunities for mutual self-reflection on gender roles and possible mutual collaboration between men and

---

[19] Focus group discussion, Allupe, Tororo, 30 May 2000.

[20] Women do not have monolithic solidarity (Kyeyune and Goldey, 1999). Relationships between women in leadership positions, particularly at the national level, and ordinary poor women in rural areas, are ambiguous. On the one hand, the poor women would appreciate it if female leaders can help them, but often they tend to be far from grassroots women both physically and psychologically. See Goetz (2002) on this relationship.

[21] Focus group discussion, Allupe, Tororo, 30 May 2000.

[22] Focus group discussion, Mulanda, Tororo, 20 June 2000.

[23] Focus group discussion, Allupe, Tororo, 30 May 2000.

[24] Focus group discussion, Mulanda, Tororo, 20 June 2000.

women. The processes also create tension and friction, and sometimes the results are "hijacked" by some ruling men. However, although there is no guarantee that these processes end up empowering both men and women, the people who were not given this kind of social autonomy before have started to take advantage of the social space created within the NRM polity for such "win-win" results.[25] Because the LC system provides opportunities for people to reflect on gender roles, the group activities are significant to forge links inside and outside the LC system.

Women, in addition, are strategically important to create positive-sum outcomes, paradoxically because the existing socio-political structure has not been beneficial to them (Tripp, 2000). The neo-patrimonial relationship, in which material benefits are politically traded between leaders and followers, has been common in Africa, and at the same time have been creating undesirable social consequences, especially for the poor (Chabal and Daloz, 1999). Because women's groups are largely left out of this relationship, women may have the potential to break these widespread yet damaging social relationships by their demonstrated ability in networking with other disadvantaged groups who are critical of the past socio-political relationship.

2 The Youth and the LC System

Similar to sexism, ageism is another dimension of social division in Uganda. Although ageism has been a serious issue, a position for the youth remains unarticulated. Young people are in a sensitive position in various African countries including Uganda.

> It is true that in Africa today, the role of the youth has been minimized to social halls, games and at best in partisan political party youth wings. Young people must be encouraged to break out of this mould and start taking a long-term view of the society that they live in. They must start shaping the socio-political and economic landscape that they live in today and the one that they would like to live in their old age. The youth need not wait until the political tempo picks up around election time for them to get busy. Plenty of issues abound in our societies that affect the youth today and will affect them tomorrow (Kinuthia-Njenga, 1996).[26]

As this quotation explains, the youth in Uganda are treated in a contradictory fashion in the society. On the one hand, they are often told that they are the future leaders of this relatively young country. But on the other hand, the youth face

---

[25] One factor that affects the way in which grassroots activities are organized is donors' assistance. While in Rakai donors have been active in promoting gender issues, there is little comparable assistance in Tororo.

[26] This echoes Bayart (2000) in his observation that the youth are not incorporated into societies economically or institutionally despite education. Instead, they have become synonymous with the unemployed and the ones who blame foreign companies for their economic hardships (pp. 227-228).

unique difficulties in overcoming pervasive poverty in both urban and rural areas. They desperately seek cash income and work hard mainly as individuals. They recognize the merits of being organized into youth groups to do something together, but in reality they rarely carry out such joint activities (as noted in previous chapters). They are energetic, ambitious, and some are even arrogant. But they are also deeply apathetic toward any government institutions, including the LC system and Youth Council. With limited access to various kinds of information and lack of social experience, they appear to have their own logic for understanding political, social and economic events. For people who have limited exposure to different areas and localities, their mind set is fairly fixed. Thus, if a particular LC that they know is not effective, the entire LC system for them is unreliable.

As in the case of women, the youth also participated very actively in the bush war as spies and guards at roads warning the guerrillas with drums. But the youth did not participate actively in committees during the war. It appeared as if the committee functions were reserved for elders. "An unmarried youth without a home would rarely, if ever, be given leadership responsibilities" (Tidemand, 1994b, p. 112). Generally, the elders wished to control the youth who were often considered to be cruel, often misbehaving, stealing and even killing (ibid., chapter 4). "The beer-drinking youth and the girls that fail to marry are ultimately linked up with the extreme breakdown of law and order" (ibid., p. 99). Although, as with women, the position for the youth was created in the early years of the RC system, the decision to include youth in RCs, particularly in the form of the "Secretary for Youth," appeared to come from the NRM rather than from peasants at the grassroots (ibid., p. 79). The contradiction between NRM's rhetorical support for and its deep suspicion of the youth influenced the way in which representation of young people was formulated at the initial stage of the RC system.

Even though this background may still be reflected in the ambiguous relationship between the youth and the LC system today, the post-conflict years have witnessed several changes. In order to mobilize youth in the country, the NRM passed the National Youth Council Statute in 1993 (the same year the Women's Council Statute was passed).[27] The statute created yet another parallel hierarchy of five-tier councils and committees exclusively for the youth, who are defined as between 18 and 30 years old. This Youth Council is overseen by the National Youth Council at the central level. Just as in the case of women, the secretary for youth links the LC system and the Youth Council. The Youth Council is indeed a very elaborate structure. On the other hand, precisely because the society is so deliberately mobilized by the NRM, critics are adamant that these parallel state organs curtail associational autonomy. The Youth Council is severely under-funded and does not appear to provide any realistic encouragement to youth either in assisting economic activities or solidifying social bonds among the youth. It is commonly agreed that there has been little evidence that the Youth Councils have

---

[27] There have been some government attempts to provide assistance to the youth. For instance, the Youth Enterprise Scheme was a government sponsored micro-credit project for the youth to start small-scale income-generating activities. But these attempts rarely reached the targeted poor youth, and the funds were used ineffectively.

successfully engaged in economic activities that empower the youth (UNDP, 1998, p. 56).

Frustrated youth is indeed a social problem. A woman councillor in one village in Rakai stated:

> One particular difficulty of being a councillor is a youth problem. The youth here are not active. They do not produce much. Some are changing their attitude, but others are not. Although men are hard workers in this area, the youth is not. Financial scarcity is also a problem in this area.[28]

This situation is in sharp contrast to that of women. Women also face severe burdens both in productive and reproductive arenas (looking after their own economic independence as well as welfare of the next generation). But they are well organized and willing to be networked with other women. This networking has been successful in poor districts such as Tororo. The youth, on the other hand, particularly young men, do not demonstrate any capacity to organize similar social networks. Youth networks may revolve around football matches, but do not secure incomes for their families.

2.1 Frustration of Grassroots Youth

The views emerging from the grassroots youth are pretty overwhelming. Within the LC system, there are a couple of youth councillors who need to be included mandatorily in each LC: one male and one female. This arrangement is also a kind of affirmative action, and the youth councillors are supposed to represent the youth as a social group. The secretary for youth links the LC and Youth Council systems, just as in the case of women. But they are often, if not always, less influential councillors. Their ineffectiveness is acknowledged by the youth in the communities. A young man typically made the following observation:

> We know that there are youth councillors. It is useful to bring the problems to youth councillors. But they do not have power to discuss and resolve the problems that we are facing. Some youth councillors do not know what they are supposed to do. Some times, other councillors ignore youth councillors. Corruption is rampant, and the LC councillors are consuming the money for their personal use. Laymen cannot do anything about it.[29]

This disillusionment is a common reaction of youth in almost all areas covered by this study. The disillusionment certainly leads to lack of trust in the LC and the Youth Council systems. Another man commented as follows:

> We, the youth, report things to LC 1 councillors. They report and discuss things at a higher level. LC 1 discusses the issues with LC 3. They always say they do something

---

[28] Focus group discussion, Ksege, Rakai, 1 August 2000.
[29] Focus group discussion, Kiddo West, Tororo, 1 June 2000.

for us, but normally nothing happens. Some explanations may be given, but we are kept waiting and waiting for a long time and during the period nothing happens.... District has some money for the youth. But we never see any money. Chairpersons of LC 1 and 2 sometimes come and discuss the ideas with us. They promise things. But no actions are seen afterwards. Sometimes, they plan to collect some money for youth, but we never see anything. Maybe money stops at the LC 3 or 5 levels. What is missing is the feedback. If they sincerely explain the situation to us, that is better than keep making false promises.[30]

Confronted with this kind of situation, a youth councillor in Tororo confessed that when it was necessary to provide balls for the youth to organize football games, he had to buy them using his own personal money.[31] The youth councillors themselves are fully aware that the link between the Youth Council and the LC systems is very fragmented and ad hoc at best. The level of interaction appears to be far lower than in the case of women.

What is remarkable perhaps is that most of the youth do not recognize the inherent contradiction that they are fostering. They, on the one hand, complain that they need to be involved in decision-making processes, which affect their own livelihood. They also complain that they are ignored in society in general and within the LC system in particular. On the other hand, they themselves rarely attend LC meetings. In one case, in a village in Rakai, only 1 out of about 20 youth attended more than two meetings during the last year, while only 3 out of 22 attended the last meeting. When they were asked why they did not attend the LC meetings even when they knew about the meetings in advance, some youth said "we do not have much to contribute to the meetings." Some did not attend due to self-reservation, shyness, fear of the public, and other personal reasons. Even if they did not attend the meetings, they think they can still follow the issues once the meetings are over. As long as these decisions are not harmful to the youth, they tend to let others manage local matters.[32]

This kind of contradiction indicates that they are only interested in a limited number of topics, and have very narrow perspectives on social issues. They complain that the government should do something about their problems. The remarks of youth reveal that they have their own understanding of society. In a village in Tororo, an informal discussion exclusively with the youth, mainly with males, unfolded a high degree of frustration. Their brand of logic was extremely straightforward. Their reasoning involved a simple yet powerful syllogism. First, the government has lots of money, and that is well known. The money is more than enough to help the youth. Second, young people are not getting any share of this state money. Third, the money must have been used by politicians and bureaucrats. Therefore, most of the politicians are corrupt. There is no doubt about it, the youth insist.

Yet at the same time, young people think they are more capable than the current elder leaders. That is partly why they get so frustrated when they are not given

---

[30] Focus group discussion, Lumbugu, Rakai, 25 August 1999.

[31] Personal interview, Obbo Andrew, Kwapa Sub-county, Tororo, 2 June 2000.

[32] Focus group discussion, Kasambya, Rakai, 12 July 2000.

chances to harness their energy and talents. This can be taken as a sign of arrogance. A young man in Rakai said, "Some of the leaders are too old to be capable."[33] In contrast, they believe that they are more capable to mobilize the community and lead the villagers. This self-confidence may not be backed up by their active involvement in community activities, but the youth would probably believe (somewhat paradoxically) that precisely because they do not participate, they are capable.

What compounds their problems is that various organizational links that are supposedly provided by civil servants and extension workers are in reality non-existent. For instance at the district level, a department in charge of community development has an officer whose job includes assisting to empower the youth. But this department is grossly under-funded. Even if an officer is posted, s/he cannot visit the areas where the officer is supposed to be in charge. Thus, the existence of such an officer itself is hardly known to most of the grassroots youth. A group in Mukono located very close to this department office pointed out that they did not know such officer at all.[34] Perhaps the grassroots youth may be relatively familiar with agricultural extension workers. But, for instance, veterinarian staff often demand service recipients to pay the transport costs when they are called in to communities. The youth, who are without regular incomes, can hardly afford to contact this kind of government staff. If the youth can be linked with other situations even through government workers, it would likely to increase their social exposure, which may prevent them from forming their own self-fulfilling prophecies.

The chairman of the National Youth Council (the council at the national level) appears to be fully aware of this complicated situation in which the youth are immersed. He stated frankly, "It has been difficult to work with the youth." He cited four reasons. First, since youth are impatient, this leads to inconsistent demands, which in turn makes coordination difficult. Second, some youth are still suspicious that they may be used for politicians' selfish gain. Third, poverty in general forces them to think only in the short term, which makes it difficult to conduct longer-term planning to harness their energy. Fourth, the insurgencies, which are still active today in different sections of the country, employ the youth as rebels. These factors make building social bonds among the youth virtually impossible.[35]

2.2 Potential for Positive-sum Solutions?

Are there any solutions for the youth problems? One solution is to increase the amount of funds that the LC and the Youth Council systems use for youth activities. Since the lack of funds is one of the causes which in effect paralyzes the LC

---

[33] Focus group discussion, Kasambya, Rakai, 12 July 2000.

[34] Personal interview, Namawojjo Twekembe Youth Group, Mukono,19 August 1999.

[35] Personal interview, Dan Fred Kidega, Chairman, National Youth Council, Kampala, 17 August 2000.

system and keeps it from addressing any youth issues, increased funding can at least partially mitigate their severity. The LCs may, then, be better able to resolve the youth problems.

However, a more promising approach is to transform their social attitudes. Although the youth are difficult to mobilize, this does not mean that the youth do not believe in forming groups and organizing collective activities. Even though managing such a process would be more difficult for the youth than, for instance, women, some youth believe in such activities. Some are already engaged in group self-help activities, often with the assistance of NGOs. A young man expressed his hope for such group activities:

> We think it is a good idea to have joint activities, for instance, income-generating activities. But since there is no money, nothing can take place. We wish to work with somebody who can help us. The government officers come and visit. But they are not helpful to the people at the grassroots. They just pass around and never stop to see the local problems. So we just work in darkness.[36]

Among another group of youth who are organized to help other members of the village by constructing housing for primary school teachers in Mukono, a young man made the following observation:

> When we bring our problem to the LC councillors, they just say, "You should work harder." We elected our leaders, but they never returned any benefits to the grassroots.... We feel that the youth are ignored. But LC 1 does not have any money, so we cannot expect that they can solve the problem for us. So the alternative is that we mobilize ourselves and we work together. That is what we are doing.[37]

This statement is an example of those youth who are relatively self-conscious. Although other youth do not exemplify a similar attitude, the quotation suggests that it is still possible for the youth to reach this stage. A young man in Mukono said, "We think it may be a good idea to work with other youth for mutual benefits. But we simply do not know how to start such a process."[38]

Here both the government and NGOs have respective roles to play to start such a process. The problem of the youth is acknowledged by the national government, and it thus carried out a series of seminars in each district in 1999 and 2000. The seminars can be interpreted as yet another NRM attempt to co-opt young people into "pro-NRM cadres," but generally such efforts are welcomed. In some areas this seminar presented the first opportunity for the youth to meet with others in the same district. The seminar was a good learning experience for the youth. The relationship between the youth and the NRM remains ambiguous just like the one between women and the NRM. Nonetheless, if the state attempts to engage the youth, it would provide a fresh opportunity to reshape state-youth relationships. Even though the outcome is uncertain, it may be more desirable than the current

---

[36] Focus group discussion, Lumbugu, Rakai, 25 August 1999.

[37] Focus group discussion, Bontaba, Mukono, 8 June 2000.

[38] Personal interview, Namawojjo Twekembe Youth Group, Mukono, 19 August 1999.

de-facto disengagement, which has no prospect for producing mutually beneficial outcomes. If the state initiates to open state-youth channels, the youth may be able to take advantage of the social space opened up by the NRM, following the pathway of women.

3 Ethnic Diversity

Ethnicity is another source of social division, especially in Africa.[39] In Uganda, 56 groups are officially recognized as indigenous ethnic groups,[40] which are categorized into the minority "Nilotic North" and the majority "Bantu South." The Baganda (who are the people of Buganda) is the largest ethnic group, constituting almost one-fifth of the total population, followed by Banyankole (Bantu), slightly more than 10%; Bakiga (Bantu), 8.7%; Basoga (Bantu), 8.5%; Iteso (Nilotic), 6.2%; Langi (Nilotic), 6.1%; Bagisu (Bantu), less than 5%; and Acholi (Nilotic), less than 5% (Government 1991 census quoted in Tripp, 2000, p. 127). Central Sudanic peoples, who constitute less than one-tenth of the population, are also found in the north.

In Uganda, the main north-south ethnic division largely derives from the uneven development in respective areas. While in the south the favorable climate supports agriculture, in the semi-arid areas of the north the main lifestyle is pastoralism. The south benefits from accommodating the administrative center of the country. The main export cash crops are grown in the south, and this is also the area where most of the commercial activities take place, taking advantage of the relatively well-maintained infrastructure. Thus, the northerners tend to consider that their concerns are marginalized within the country. Because the Baganda is the largest ethnic group, they are the target of criticism by the northerners. The British rule (1894-1962) reinforced this tension; the colonial officers considered it useful to ally with the Baganda who had more cohesive administrative organs than other ethnic groups. This alliance, thus, alienated other ethnic groups.

The multiple ethnic society was indeed one of the causes of social instability since the independence of the country. Especially, the Baganda and their position within Uganda have been a political issue ever since independence.[41] However, in Uganda ethnicity alone does not result in conflicts (Tripp, 2000, p. 126). Usually

---

[39] Ethnicity is "a subjective perception of common origins, historical memories, ties, and aspirations; ethnic group pertains to organized activities by persons, linked by a consciousness of a special identity, who jointly seek to maximize their corporate political, economic, and social interests" (Chazan et al., 1999, p. 108). For ethnicity and conflicts, see, for instance, Bates, 1999; Ottaway, 1994 and 1999b; Rothchild, 1997; Uganda, MoFPED, 1998; and Wilmsen and McAllister, 1996.

[40] Third Schedule of the Constitution of Uganda, and also quoted in Uganda, MoFPED, 1998, Vol. 2, p. 302.

[41] The NRM government allowed the restoration of traditional kingdoms in Uganda, with the reinstallation of the Buganda kingship on 31 July 1993. See detailed discussions by Karlström, 1999a.

conflict occurs when ethnicity is combined with other factors such as access to political privileges and economic resources. Ethnicity is complicated by the fact that
it is often correlated with other social characteristics such as religion. The ethno-
religious divisions were often used by political parties in the past to justify their
claims. This is why the NRM decided to ban political parties and installed a non-
party polity of "movement." (Opponents of the NRM argue that the NRM itself is
no different from other political parties since the current political system serves its
self-interests.)

The NRM's original guerrilla war started in the western part of Uganda. With
the formation of the NRM government, a major ethnic division arose between the
westerners and the rest of Ugandans, particularly between the west and the north,
where political and economic marginalization has not been fundamentally resolved. The NRM, despite its rhetoric to resist sectarian divisions along ethnic
lines, has increasingly played the "ethnic card." Observers tend to agree that there
are an increasing number of appointments of senior government posts to a few
NRM loyalists who enjoyed special patronage with the NRM leadership (ibid., p.
58).

3.1 Ethnic Politics at Local Levels

Relations between ethnicity and the LC system are very controversial. The LC
system does not have any particular quota allocated for different ethnic groups for
balanced representation. Unlike the cases of women and the youth, there is no
parallel hierarchy of the council system for different ethnic groups. Instead, the
LC system is the only formal mechanism for representation of ethnic groups. Informally, clans and kinship associations play limited roles, but they do not have
political functions. Thus, the issue of how ethnic minorities can be represented in
the LC system is of great concern. One study concluded that the ethnic element
did not significantly come into the management of LC matters (Tukahebwa,
1997). The situation today is slightly different at different levels of the LC system.

When people at the grassroots level were asked about the issue of ethnicity,
they unanimously denied that ethnic differences influence how people form their
views.[42] Often they report that marriages of people across ethnic divisions are
quite common and that differences of ethnicity do not matter significantly. However, one needs to be careful in interpreting this assertion. In one meeting, a local
school teacher was presenting his views. It took a long time for a relatively well-
educated person to realize how the same situation could be interpreted differently
from the viewpoint of different ethnic groups.[43] What becomes evident is that
people at the grassroots have very little exposure to different lifestyles of different
ethnic groups in the country and have little understanding of, or sensitivity to, dif-

---

[42] This is a common response in villages visited by this researcher, including Kiwoomya,
Rakai, 26 August 1999.
[43] Focus group discussion, Mataba, Mukono, 21 August 1999.

ferent ethnic groups with which they form a nation-state. Therefore, ethnicity re-mains a very contentious issue even if people do not openly admit that it consti-tutes a significant social division at the grassroots.

On the occasions of elections, people appear to consider a variety of factors and ethnicity is not necessarily a determinant of their voting. Just like gender is not especially crucial for women, one does not necessarily support candidates of the same ethnic background. Nonetheless, elections raised this notion of ethnicity more acutely than before. It is often the case that the notion of whether certain candidates are "sons of the soil" comes to the minds of many.[44]

The election results of various LC 1 and 2 leaders are not very informative, since there is basically no comparable data on ethnic background.[45] There have been very few cases, if any, in which the election process has resulted in an ex-treme situation whereby ethnic minorities were eliminated from the LC system. On the contrary, some LC leaders do not necessarily come from the dominant eth-nic group in respective localities. Having political leaders from different ethnic backgrounds is quite common in various areas.

In Mukono and Rakai, where the Baganda is the dominant ethnic group, at all levels of the LC system, councillors usually come from a mixture of ethnic ori-gins, although the exact proportion differs from one area to another.[46] The mix is partly because migrations within Uganda, and to a lesser extent from neighboring Rwanda, have been fairly frequent. As a result, even in the Buganda area there are other ethnic groups and cross-ethnic marriages have been taking place.[47] Thus, at the grassroots level, apparent domination of one ethnic group over others is usu-ally absent from day-to-day management of LC matters. "Ethnicity is a mask of confrontation, and social life requires that confrontation be avoided wherever pos-sible in everyday life" (Vincent, 1971, p. 10).[48] Although this observation was made 20 years ago, the same reasoning applies today to villages. Generally, it is concluded that at least at the LC 1 level the ethnic element is not overwhelming the LC system. This situation can largely be explained by the fact that LC 1 lead-ers are middle class peasants and live together with other villagers in the same community. The degree of homogeneity between the leaders and followers is

---

[44] Personal interview, Sallie Simba Kayunga, lecturer at Makerere University, 7 August 1998.

[45] It was reported earlier that in two districts, the proportional representation of "non-sons of the soil" decreased (Kasozi, 1997, p. 62).

[46] For instance, LC 3 councillors in Nyenga, Mukono replied that their ethnic background was quite mixed (Focus group discussion 14 August 1998).

[47] Personal interviews, Shiro Kodamaya, Prof., Hitotsubashi University, Japan, June-August 2000. He was conducting a poverty study in Mpigi District during this period.

[48] Vincent (1971), based on her fieldwork in the 1960s, noted: The villagers "pride them-selves on their nontribal ethos if such considerations are forced upon them, claiming that the distinctive character of their community lies in the very fact that it is, indeed, made up of individuals from many backgrounds. They live together harmoniously and find it a better place for this very fact" (p. 110).

relatively high, and the homogeneity reduces the likelihood that ethnic differences become entangled with political and economic privileges.

The picture is slightly different at higher levels of the LC system. At the LC 3 level, the chances in which political and economic stakes are combined with ethnic divisions slightly increase compared to the LC 1 level. However, usually there are no major ethnic crises which affect the LC system. Almost the only possibility in which ethnicity hinders otherwise normal LC management is the personal relations between the LC 3 chairperson and the civil service counterpart. In sub-counties examined by this study, usually there was a cordial working relationship between political leaders and civil servants and no incidents were observed that might have derived from ethnic divisions. But there is an anxiety that if some misuses of funds are revealed, accusations may become associated with ethnic differences.

The main problem of ethnic divisions lies at the LC 5 level, where the situation is more complicated. Although ethnicity is obviously not officially proclaimed as a reason behind managing politics, its effects are certainly seen in one way or another. For instance, Table 5.1 shows the correlation between ethnicity and the number of LC 5 chairpersons. Although this table is a crude estimate since there are no "pure" districts where only one ethnic group resides, two findings become obvious from this table. First, ethnic groups are more or less proportionately represented in the 45 seats of district chairpersons. There is neither over- nor under-representation to any extreme extent. There are extremely few cases in which a chairperson is elected whose ethnic background is different from the major one in each locality. Second, the leaders of the Baganda were elected only within the Buganda area, and no Baganda chairperson is found outside the Buganda "kingdom area." This apparently confirms that the ethnic factor certainly affected the way people voted, either consciously or unconsciously.

Additionally, when the chairperson of LC 5 nominates his/her executive members for the approval of the council, the tendency is to establish some kind of balanced representation among different ethnic groups. Otherwise, if a dominant group takes all the posts, this kind of "winner-take-all" nomination is unlikely to be considered fair and legitimate by political representatives and their constituencies. Although ethnic rivalries and/or prejudices may not surface in normal circumstances, once unsatisfactory decisions are taken, ethnicity can create negative influences over day-to-day management of council affairs. One study reports that 20% of district councillors witnessed ethnic-related controversies in the management of council affairs. There have been some incidents complicated by ethnicity (Tukahebwa, 1997, p. 50). For instance, when certain key decisions, such as elections, were considered to be biased by certain ethnic connections, such decisions created fierce conflicts among different ethnic groups. These earlier findings are largely confirmed by this study.

Since the public resources to be allocated at the district level are relatively large, access to such resources provides a source of controversy. A case in point is Tororo. Ethnically, while Mukono and Rakai are primarily Baganda, Tororo is often called a "cosmos of Uganda" where varieties of ethnic groups live together.

Table 5.1 Ethnicity and posts of chairpersons in districts

Name of ethnic group	% in total population*	Anticipated number of representatives by population	Anticipated number of representatives by geographical areas	Actual number of elected representatives **
Baganda	19%	8.4	12	8
Banyankole	10%	4.6	3	5
Bakiga	9%	3.9	2	1
Basoga	9%	3.8	3	4
Iteso	6%	2.8	4	5
Langi	6%	2.7	3	2
Bagisu, Bamasaba	5%	2.1	2	1
Acholi, Labwor	5%	2.1	2	0
Lugbara, Aringa	4%	1.6	1	0
others	29%	12.9	13	19
TOTAL	100%	45	45	45

Sources; * 1991 Population Census; ** information provided by the Electoral Commission, August 1998.

This district has a large amount of debt, and this overshadows the way in which the LC 5 operates. The political stalemate between executive and non-executive members of the council in the middle of 2000 is a prime example in which the different degrees of access to resources were compounded by the multi-ethnic nature of society in this area. When some were well paid while others were not, this gap created a source of friction. The difference was then linked to complicated ethnic relations in this area. Officially, ethnic differences were not mentioned in a move for a non-confidence vote against the executive members, but were one of the background reasons.

3.2 Decentralization and Ethnic Politics

These concerns underline the fact that ethnic rivalries may come into the processes of decentralization and complicate the LC system in the future. First, some areas may become better off by managing their resources effectively, while other areas may not improve living conditions significantly. If this unequal development is linked to ethnic considerations, then this can be a dangerous background against which politicians may justify inappropriate actions. This particularly applies to the north-south tension. The sense of marginalization among the northerners within Uganda has not been fundamentally addressed by post-independence governments, including the NRM. Although this issue is very complicated, the root cause appears to be a large discrepancy in living standards between the north and the south. Therefore, this issue calls for the attention of the central government as well as the local authorities in the north. Unless coherent political and economic solutions are provided at the national level, efforts by the local governments alone will not resolve this unequal status.

The second source of concern is that the NRM continues to allow new districts to be formed (Kasozi, 1997, p. 62). One of the reasons is that this process creates more ethnic homogeneity in each district. For the NRM, the increased number of locally elected representatives who support the LC system may benefit their political agenda in the short run. But fragmenting the country into more districts can backfire in the long run, if such "purification" triggers ethnic rivalries in the country. The results of such rivalries are well known to people within and outside Uganda.

The LC system, therefore, has certainly an essential role to play in mediating ethnic relations in Uganda, since the LC at the grassroots is "a half public, half civic" forum in which all people can participate. Some point out optimistically that decentralization has enhanced social reconciliation and harmony between and within local authorities in Uganda (ibid., p. 43). This observation may be too optimistic, but this harmony is needed to prevent ethnic divisions from being intertwined with political and economic resources and privileges. As has been pointed out, "although ethnicity is by its very nature [an] oppositional construct, it need not lead to conflictual situations and perhaps does so only under certain political stimuli" (Wilmsen and McAllister, 1996, p. viii). Therefore, in order for the LC to be effective, certain measures need to be taken. Because ethnicity is primarily one form of social exclusion, devising inclusive processes for various ethnic groups in decision making is essential to prevent ethnic politics from becoming counterproductive to development. Local elections alone are not sufficient to create this desired inclusiveness. It would be more suitable to have a reasonably well-balanced (if not strict proportional) representation of different ethnic groups at different LC levels, particularly at LC 5.

In addition, the ways in which resources are allocated by the LC system need to become much more open and transparent in order to prevent suspicions and accusations from arising. More accurate information of how these funds are managed needs to be provided to the public. In the past, ethnic affiliations were often used as a channel to pass important information from one person to the other. Thus, in some cases ethnicity serves as a form of social network to harness development. But if ethnicity becomes a discriminatory factor in access to essential information, then ethnic connections become a political issue. In Africa, the magnitude of this perverse nature of ethnicity is more prevalent than in other areas (Bates, 1999). Thus, more transparent information dissemination is critical. Diversifying information access and dissemination channels other than ethnic affiliations is essential. If the rural poor can obtain alternative access to government policies and services which affect them, then the political significance of ethnicity will be reduced.

These measures are fundamental to nurture more trusting relations among different ethnic groups and reduce tensions among them. Successful prevention of minority ethnic groups from being marginalized both materially and socio-culturally would be the first step to prevent "ethnic politics," which often tends to be a crude form of zero-sum relations: some ethnic groups gain at the cost of others. In addition, grassroots movements to build networks of people across ethnic divisions would also be a promising avenue for pursuing ethnic harmony in Uganda.[49] These movements can work as information channels. Often women's groups are cross-ethnic entities and sometimes prove to be effective in forging such networks, although women's efforts alone cannot resolve the ethnic issue entirely. Once youth networking becomes effective, it may also contribute to ease ethnic tensions, but its prospect remains slim currently. Nonetheless, potential for multiple channels of information exist, which needs more attention in the future.

4 Summary and Conclusion

This chapter has highlighted the fact that there are interesting similarities and differences among women, the youth and ethnic groups in their relations with the LC system. The establishment of the LC system as an institution for inclusive decision making does not necessarily lead to equal participation of all marginalized groups in local politics. The groups discussed in this chapter have not started forming significant partnerships with different stakeholders. Even if women are well networked, there are rarely significant men-women alliances on social issues. The youth remain fragmented socially. Ethnic minorities have their internal associations such as clans, but inter-clan associations are uncommon except for socio-cultural exchanges.

The historical context in which the original RC leaders treated women and the youth differently affected the way in which these social groups engage with the LC system today. While a more accommodative stance taken by the original RC leaders has paved the way for women's increasing participation in political matters, the youth, considered to be trouble-makers by the RC leaders, evaluate the LC as useless. At the same time, these leaders were not ready for any significant redistribution of political power and economic resources to women and the youth within rural communities (Tidemand, 1994b, chapter 4).

However, at the moment, these legacies are changing, and society in Uganda is now undergoing an important transition on the issue of socially disadvantaged groups. This transition in not simple, and there are negotiations and bargaining going on between men and women, between the old and the young, between dominant and minority ethnic groups, over the allocation of authority, power and resources. In this process, some have come up with multiple strategies to engage

---

[49] Some call these "popular movements," which are essentially participatory collective actions to advance demands of the marginalized often outside of formal institutions (Brohman, 1996, p. 258). The term "popular" may be preferred since it can represent a wide range of economically disadvantaged, politically disfranchised, environmentally threatened, and culturally marginalized peoples and groups.

the LC system. A notable example is women. For young people, the LC system is highly irrelevant. They have not come up with any strategic assessment of how to deal with the LC system. Ethnicity and the LC system maintain a subtle relationship. The social space created by the LC system allows people some choices, which ironically raised ethnic consciousness. Ethnicity remains in the background in normal situations, but tends to become "explosive" when other issues ignite the situation.

But this transition process is not necessarily a zero-sum situation in which some gains are indispensable losses for others. On the contrary, this can be a mutually empowering positive-sum process with mutually beneficial outcomes, although it involves a lot of effort by various stakeholders to construct "win-win" relationships. The small-scale development activities at the grassroots present such opportunities, even if they are not free from obstacles. The experiences of three socially weak groups in this chapter emphasize that processes to achieve these results will remain gradual, and long-term perspectives are more appropriate. Long-term approaches can accommodate trial and error for people to interact with others with whom they do not share common perceptions. Men and women still have different views on respective roles. The youth have little understanding of what kind of social order is deemed desirable by elders. Different ethnic groups do not know very well how each other lives in different places. In order to improve mutual understanding, a long-term learning process is essential. In this process, the lower level LCs may be fairly useful for such learning experiences, especially if respective LCs can be networked with others in different places to exchange accounts of their varying experiences.

In order to facilitate this process, one conclusion is that possible risks associated with social divisions should not be ignored, even if the social divisions themselves are not necessarily the source of the problems. Instead, efforts are needed to face these challenges squarely. Thus, it is essential to use the LC for harnessing social harmonies. Problems become acute when they are entangled with other diverse issues, especially unequal access to state resources. Therefore, we next turn our attention to the issue of financial resources in the decentralization process in Uganda: fiscal decentralization.

6 Fiscal Decentralization: Re-centralization by Other Means?

Within a very short time, Uganda has achieved one of the most decentralised and stable systems of [sub-national governments] in the entire Sub-Saharan [African] Region. A strong political commitment towards decentralisation and the use of a consultative process among stakeholders (comprising politicians in central government and SNGs, government officials, private sector representatives, donors, non-governmental organisations and the civil society) in the design and implementation of the legal framework have facilitated these results.

Marios Obwona et al., 2000, p. 16

Finance is a major terrain in which stakeholders compete and collaborate. Fiscal decentralization affects the prospects of partnership formations among often contending stakeholders. Uganda has used a phased approach in fiscal decentralization. In FY 1993/94 a first group of 13 districts were allowed to make certain decisions on tax collection and revenue allocations. In FY 1994/95, a second group of another 13 districts followed, and then a third batch of 13 districts in FY 1995/96. During this initial phase, an experiment was made to share revenues among different levels of local governments. The earlier experiences assisted the formulation of the Constitution, 1995, that provides three forms of central government transfers to local governments. First, unconditional grants are provided for discretionary use by local authorities. Second, conditional grants are funds already earmarked for specific activities by the central government. The third form is equalization grants for districts, which cannot provide public services up to national standards. In FY 1997/98, all districts were financially decentralized in terms of recurrent expenditures. In the meantime, the Local Governments Act, 1997, clearly provided the policy framework of decentralization. Local Governments Financial and Accounting Regulations, 1998, offered detailed guidelines for managing revues and expenditures. The LC 3 (sub-county) is now in charge of local tax collection, which is shared with other levels of local government.

During this process, the expansion of local capacity was pursued. The Decentralization Secretariat, established in 1992, provided various kinds of training, including financial management for local government personnel. The Local Government Finance Commission (LGFC) was established in 1995 to advise the president on matters related to fiscal management and resource allocations between central and local governments. The LGFC contributed to the implementation of the equalization grants, which were finally put in place in FY 1999/2000.

Fiscal decentralization in Uganda evolved very quickly in a relatively short period, and the country has probably achieved the most systematic fiscal decentralization on Sub-Saharan Africa (Steffensen and Trollegaard, 2000).[1] What is noteworthy is that Uganda has a clear central government policy on decentralization and has possibly the most detailed legal and regulatory framework in the developing world. Uganda also enjoys a relatively open decision-making process to allow public participation, which has improved accountability.

Currently, approximately 20% of the total government budget is spent by local governments in Uganda (ibid., p. 239), which is very high in the African context. Local governments spend approximately 4% of GDP (based on FY 1997/98 data), which is again one of the highest among African countries. The corresponding figure for industrialized countries on average is about 11% (ibid., p. 240). These figures indicate that Uganda's fiscal decentralization has advanced significantly, as illustrated by the opening quotation of this chapter. The increased local disbursement of public funds now benefits local economies in many parts of the country, while in the past central government disbursement benefited primarily the metropolitan economy. This change of spending patterns has contributed to more equitable economic growth.

In this chapter, the evolution of fiscal decentralization is scrutinized.[2] As briefly touched on in Chapter 3, the amount of fiscal transfers from the central to local governments has increased significantly. But ironically for the local governments, more and more funds are coming in the form of conditional grants, in which a degree of discretion is denied. Although some efforts have been made to coordinate the different budgeting processes of central and local governments, the central government and donors maintain firm control over budgetary allocations, which tends to undermine the political autonomy granted by decentralization policy. At the district level, more efforts are urgently needed to improve financial management practices. The amount of inter-government transfers in Uganda is considerable, but much more needs to be done in order to use them more effectively and efficiently.

1 Central Government Transfers to Local Governments

The amount of fiscal transfers from the central to local governments clearly shows a high level of government commitment. As Table 6.1 indicates, the total

---

[1] Steffensen and Trollegaard (2000) examine fiscal decentralization for infrastructure and service provisions in Ghana, Senegal, Swaziland, Zambia, Zimbabwe, and Uganda.

[2] For a review of fiscal decentralization, see, Ahmad, 1997; Bird and Vaillancourt, 1998a; Bird and Smart, 2002; de Mello, 2000; Smoke, 2001; Steffensen and Trollegaard 2000; and Oates, 1999.

Table 6.1 Fiscal transfers to local governments (actual transfers)
(amounts in thousand shillings)

	1993/94	1994/95	1995/96	1996/97	1997/98	1998/99	1999/00
Total transfers (real price)	31,568,762	65,972,138	103,196,909	145,313,597	149,998,741	203,788,169	223,999,103
Unconditional grants as % of total transfers	25.3%	30.2%	34.8%	27.6%	26.4%	22.8%	20.1%
Conditional grants as % of total transfers	74.7%	69.8%	65.2%	72.4%	73.6%	77.2%	79.4%
Total transfer as % of GDP		1.4%	2.1%	2.9%	2.8%	3.6%	3.7%
Local government expenditures as % of GDP*	na	na	3.1%	5.3%	4.0%	na	na
Local government revenues as % of GDP*	na	na	3.2%	5.7%	4.5%	na	na
Total transfer as % of total central government recurrent budget	na	17.0%	25.0%	30.0%	30.0%	34.0%	36.0%
Total transfer as % of total central government budget	na	8.0%	12.0%	14.0%	14.0%	17.0%	16.0%
Fiscal year inflation rate**	6.5%	6.1%	7.5%	7.8%	5.8%	6.7%	6.7%

Source: * Table 4.1 of Obwona, Marios, et al. [2000] *Fiscal Decentralisation and Sub-National Government Finance in Relation to Infrastructure and Service Provision in Uganda* (Kampala: Economic Policy Research Centre, March), Annex.; ** Uganda, UBOS [1999] *The Statistical Abstract 1999*, (Entebbe: UBOS), p. 79; and all other figures are based on the Decentralization Secretariat records.
Note: 1998/99 and 1999/00 figures are based on the average of previous years.

resources transferred from the central to local governments have steadily and significantly increased. In real terms, taking inflation into account, the conditional and the unconditional grants increased 5.6-fold and 7.5-fold from FY 1993/94 to FY 1999/2000, respectively. The total transfers (in real values) increased during these seven fiscal years about seven fold. The proportionate share of inter-governmental transfers within the overall recurrent central government budget also grew steadily, and in FY 1999/00 the share was 36%. All these figures mean that a substantive amount of funds are now transferred from the central to local governments, and a significant part of the transfers is to meet recurrent costs. The resources are distributed to sub-national units of the government according to a formula; LC 5 to receive 35 % of the total inter-governmental transfers; LC 4, 3.25%; LC 3, 42.25%; LC 2, 3.25%; and LC 1, 16.25%.

While apparently impressive progress has been made in the 1990s, there are some concerns. One of the essential issues is the balance between different forms of grants. As Table 6.1 clearly indicates, the growth of conditional grants outpaced that of unconditional grants. In the earlier period of fiscal decentralization, unconditional grants represented nearly one-third of total transfers. But this relative share declined consistently, and now is only one-fifth. Eighty percent of central government grants are now conditional grants. Most of the conditions attached to these funds are really stringent, and local governments complained about them. This dominance of conditional grants can potentially undermine the rationale behind decentralization, in which more autonomy is to be granted to local authorities.

One reason for the increase in conditional grants is that many are funded by the Poverty Action Fund (PAF). The PAF was created when Uganda was entitled to benefit from the debt relief of the Highly Indebted Poor Countries (HIPC) initiative in 1998. This is ironic, because if debt relief was a donors' sign of commending Uganda, the PAF could have been designed to give discretionary funds for Uganda. The primary objective of the PAF is to reduce the pervasive poverty still remaining in Uganda in spite of the impressive macro-economic growth in the early 1990s. The PAF particularly focuses on the five priorities of education, health, water and sanitation, agriculture, and feeder roads. The PAF supports 11 forms of conditional grants. In FY 2000/01 Ush 330.3 billion (approximately US\$ 210 million) was budgeted for inter-governmental fiscal transfers from the PAF, which constitutes approximately 84% of the total transfers from the central to local governments. (The exchange rate between US\$ and Uganda Shilling was about 1 \$=1,500 Ush in the middle of 2000.)

There are other considerable challenges in Uganda's fiscal decentralization. Human resource capacity is still weak thus making it difficult to staff the local administration fully, and information technology has just been introduced to manage various aspects. Some of the many local governments may not be viable financially. In addition, perhaps the most serious challenge is to ensure that the policy of decentralization is in fact turned into improved essential services in order to meet the increasing demands of the growing population. Prospects for sustainable services, including an option for cost recovery measures by users, as well as adequate participation by the private sector, are still remote.

Furthermore, while the process of decentralizing recurrent expenditures has been more or less finalized, development expenditures have devolved only recently. One of the remaining tasks lies in the area of capital budget decentralization, which needs to be implemented with accompanying efforts to ensure accountability. Even though past efforts are commendable, much more needs to be done to enhance accountability at all levels of government, particularly because a large amount of development funds is at stake.

2 Participatory Budgeting Process

Participation in fiscal decentralization has slightly different connotations from other discussions over decentralized service provisions. Conceptually, it can be argued that with the increased participation of a wide range of stakeholders, the budgeting process and financial management can become more efficient and effective, and thereby enhance service provisions.

The experience of Uganda indicates a mixed picture on this issue. On the one hand, Uganda has succeeded in re-orientating expenditures in order to improve the living standard of the poor, especially in the priority areas as identified in the PAF. For instance, education has been receiving significant budget augmentation for the purpose of poverty alleviation. Other sectors such as agriculture and health have also been undergoing significant pro-poor re-orientation (Foster and Mijumbi, 2002, p. 10).

On the other hand, local governments' heavy dependence on the grants transferred from the central government, especially in the form of conditional grants, leaves little room for the LC system to maneuver. As a result, the national budgeting process has been largely driven by the central government with little participation of local stakeholders even after the commencement of fiscal decentralization in 1993. When participation of the officials of the LC system is limited, the poor and the disadvantaged have little, if any, opportunity for voicing their concerns in the budgeting process. Currently, local communities are empowered to the extent that they complain about abuses of funds, but are not empowered to "influence directly the public spending decisions which most affect their lives" (ibid., p. 35). This limitation seems to be a concern even within some sections of the central government (Gariyo, 2000).

2.1 Conditionality Negotiation

A recent development is, however, significant in making this process more inclusive. Some forms of the conditionality attached to the inter-government transfers are now discussed between the central and local governments. This consultation derives from the increased awareness by local governments of their rights granted in the Local Governments Act, 1997 (Article 84-3). In the past, local governments tended to accept directives by the central government. Yet the act clearly states that the local governments are entitled to voice their concerns over conditionality. For instance, PAF conditionalities for implementation in FY 2000/01 were negotiated and agreed to by the Ministry of Finance, Planning and Economic Development (MoFPED) and the Uganda Local Authorities Association (ULAA).[3] While conditionality is still rampant in other grants, this consultation is a major step forward in tipping the balance between the central and local governments. The ULAA is likely to insist on more consultations in the future, aiming for an even more equitable relationship with the central government. This

---

[3] The ULAA was established in April 1994 and its objectives are: 1) to represent and advocate the rights and interests of the local authorities; 2) to guide local governments by providing expertise on relevant matters; 3) to asses central government policies and proposals that affect local authorities; and 4) to represent Uganda in international forums on local authorities (personal interview, Raphael Magyezi, Secretary, ULAA, 30 August 1999).

engagement is, therefore, a beginning of a partnership, which should be based on equal participation of partners. The partners do not have to own equal resources, but they are indispensable to each other for common purposes. The central and sub-national units of the government both need reciprocal relations to achieve effective results.

2.2 Harmonizing Central and Local Government Budgeting

In the past, despite decentralization policy, ministries of the central government prepared their annual plans and budgets. Local authorities made their own preparation. There was no coordination between these two budget operations conducted by different units of the government. In FY 1999/00, a new mechanism, the Budget Framework Paper (BFP), was introduced. Both the central government, particularly the MoFPED, and local governments were asked to prepare their respective BFPs. The BFPs explain the policies of each unit of the government, specifying available resources and planned activities for three years. The BFP was a lengthy process involving various stakeholders, covering the period from October through May.

The BFP is a first attempt to coordinate the two different types of budgeting of the central and local governments. The way in which the BFP meeting is conducted is still heavily influenced by the MoFPED, and therefore not satisfactory for the local governments. The MoFPED still decides in a "top-down" manner the national budget ceiling for the next three years, which has to be followed by the local governments. In addition, this process is really time-consuming, and places a significant burden on the local governments whose limited human resources are already stretched thin. BFP preparation requires that departments in district offices prepare their sectoral plans in advance, but it is never easy to carry out this preparation process.

Nonetheless, the BFP is a useful tool toward establishing more equitable partnerships between the central and local governments (Lind and Cappon, 2001, p. 70). In the process, both the central and local governments respect each others' autonomy, while attempting to create synergetic effects as well. The willingness for negotiation demonstrated in this context testifies to the fact that some elements of partnership undoubtedly exist. Such a partnership is beneficial for both the central and local governments. For the central government, it enhances macro-economic stability, while for local authorities, it provides more predictable resources than before. Local governments mostly welcome the BFP initiative as a sign that the central government has become more willing to involve local governments in a crucial exercise of budgeting (ULAA, 1999). This exercise also improves the local budgeting process itself. The Chief Executive Officer (CAO) in Masindi District noted:

> In the past Local Governments did not seriously relate their budgets to resource constraints. A few technocrats often drew district budgets on their own in a non-participatory integrated manner, and as a result, Local Governments were hardly able to

contribute effectively to their mission. The introduction of Local Government Budget Framework Paper has played a pivotal role in strengthening the process of planning and budgeting by relating resources to district priorities (Wanyenze-Gimogoi, 2000, p. 2).

The BFP process is a unique initiative in African countries, and other countries are paying close attention to how Uganda refines it (Steffensen and Trollegaard, 2000).

Encouraged by the positive responses by various stakeholders, the MoFPED has shown a willingness to change the BFP process to a more mutually consultative one in the future (Uganda, MoFPED, 2000f). In order to deepen this BFP process, there are some important challenges. One such example is to harmonize the budgetary and planning cycles among different levels of the local government, particularly between districts and sub-county offices. The present BFP process involves the central government and district officials. But in order for the districts to prepare more valuable input to the process, all local governments need to engage in detailed budgetary dialogues (Wanyenze-Gimogoi, 2000). But again the dilemma is that at lower levels the capacity is much weaker than at the district level, and therefore much support for engendering capacities is urgently needed.

The BFP process poses more fundamental questions of how the rules of fiscal decentralization can and should be decided. In the future, local governments would like to be more involved in consultations with the central government in its decision-making process concerning the central government grants. They are especially keen to be informed of how the allocations of inter-governmental transfers are made, in what way the amounts are decided, and when the transfers are scheduled. The local governments wish to participate in the process to decide rules and procedures for the grants, instead of merely being passive recipients.

Although the current BFP process is a step forward, it does not fully address these concerns which have been repeatedly expressed by locally-elected representatives, technical planners, administrators, and service providers such as teachers and health managers at the grassroots level. It would be helpful for local governments if the current practices (which are in essence informal and informative) evolved into more formal and legally guaranteed ones. Additionally, any improvements in greater transparency and openness in the way in which the current BFP is carried out would be beneficial to stakeholders. Local newspapers increasingly carry articles about local government budgets, and will become more helpful by widely disseminating essential information on how important decisions over financial allocations are made.

2.3 Local Government Development Program

Another significant development in fiscal decentralization is a project, the Local Government Development Program (LGDP), under which discretionary funds are made available to local governments on a much larger scale. The LGDP is an evolution of the earlier District Development Project assisted by the United Nations Capital Development Fund (UNCDF) and implemented in five districts from

1998 to 2000. This project, with a total cost of about US$ 13 million (UNCDF et al., 1997, p. vi.), experimented in providing development funds to local authorities ranging from LC 5 to LC 1. In most villages these funds are used for procuring desks and chairs for local schools. In some areas community work was organized with these small funds. For example, in one village in Mukono, a well was constructed from a protected spring. This project was decided by an LC. Then, the local people contributed their labor, while the councillors contacted the higher administrative units for possible assistance. Fortunately, it was the time that the UNCDF assistance started in Mukono District, and the district office allocated a portion of the project funds to this small-scale initiative.[4]

The results have largely been encouraging (Uganda, MoFPED, 2001, p. 45), and the World Bank and other donors scaled up this type of assistance throughout Uganda. The LGDP commenced in 2000 and provided US$ 80.9 million over the next three years. In the peak of the second year, the LGDP financed approximately 7% of the government development budget (World Bank, 1999c, p. 4).

The LGDP's overall objective is to create more transparent and accountable management practices in both the central and local governments in order to improve essential public services. The funds have been released to local authorities, that have not yet received donor assistance including 30 districts, Kampala City (Obwona et al., 2000, p. 294) as well as 13 municipalities.[5] The recipients need to demonstrate credible development plans, because many plans are merely wish lists of activities without realistic assessment of implementation. At the same time, the project will assist those districts which have difficulty attaining such credibility in order that these districts not be penalized.

The modality of the LGDP is innovative, since donors provide financial assistance to the basket fund of the LGDP, which is in turn channeled to local governments using the normal official fiscal transfer mechanism. This way of transfer is, therefore, intended to enhance "ownership" of the government of Uganda.[6] This principle is widely welcomed by donors, but actual collaboration with the LGDP scheme varies from one donor to another. Some donors were not initially pleased to contribute to the LGDP basket fund, since they did not entirely trust the capacities of local governments to account development budget properly. They instead preferred to maintain leverage, as is often traditionally exercised by donors. As the LGDP has been implemented, the initial hesitation has been lessened, and increasing number of donors have started to channel funds through the LGDP framework. Even such donors as the Danish International Development Assistance (DANIDA), which has been a pioneer in assisting Rakai, has become willing to join the LGDP framework. LGDP has grown as the module of inter-

---

[4] Focus group discussion, Joggo, Mukono, 18 August 1999.

[5] A document of the British High Commission, Kampala, August, 2000.

[6] The term "ownership" is often used to express the notion that increasing capacities of developing countries is considered to be more effective by working through existing institutions rather than through new ones imposed by donors for project-specific purposes.

governmental fiscal transfers, whose effect is system-wide.[7] The Ministry of Local Government (MoLG) is keen to consolidate the LGDP framework even further. It was scheduled that the current project phase would end in 2003, and the formulation process had already been initiated to move to LGDP II without any gap between the then current and the next phases.[8]

3 Equity Concerns in Fiscal Decentralization

Fiscal decentralization also needs to address the issue of equity among local governments in their access to resources. For this purpose, the equalization grant plays an indispensable role. Since this grant is for relatively poorer districts which fall behind the national average in service standards, the implications for poverty reduction are also significant. The equalization grant was implemented in FY 1999/00 after a long preparation period by the LGFC (Uganda, LGFC, 1998a, 1999a, and 1999b). The amount of Ush 2 billion (about US$ 1.3 million) was released to 13 local governments, and the next year Ush 4 billion (about US$ 2.6 million) was budgeted.

The equalization grant is, in principle, a fund that local governments can use discretionarily as long as the use is in line with the national priority areas for poverty reduction: education, health, water and sanitation, agriculture, and roads. Since it is new and the amount is very limited, its impacts cannot be fully assessed. Generally, it has not substantially influenced the overall performance of public services. Its implementation is a step in the right direction, since similar grants have worked in other countries.[9] But local authorities will surely ask the central government to increase this grant in the future. Much needs to be done if the equalization grant is to become really meaningful. Unless the central government is fully committed to supporting it, the difficult issue of regional equity in Uganda will not be resolved.

---

[7] Hesitation, ironically, comes from districts which may face reduced financial support by the change of donor orientation.

[8] Similar to the LGDP, the Plan for Modernisation of Agriculture (PMA) is also a supplemental new initiative to provide discretionary funds to local governments. The PMA's goal is to transform subsistence farming into modern agriculture, in line with the globalization of markets, and to reduce poverty in rural areas. Under provisions of the PMA, there is a component to allocate non-sectoral conditional (discretionary) funds to sub-county offices (LC 3) (Uganda, MoFPED, 2000f). The implementation of the PMA started in FY 2000/01, and it is too early to gauge its impact.

[9] Crook and Manor (1998) report that Chile and West Bengal, India are performing examples (p. 302).

4 Local Government Financial Management

The capacities and practices of local authorities in financial management vary significantly. Some are more advanced than others. Quite often different management styles and reporting formats are adopted, which make comparison across local governments very difficult. But the following generalization can be made: Despite substantive progress in financial management by local authorities, the current situation is still far from ideal.[10]

On the revenue side, several issues should be pointed out. First, most local governments heavily depend on central government transfers as a source of revenue. It is estimated that 70-80% of total local government revenue comes from the central government (Table 6.2). Excluding Kampala City, which enjoys an exceptionally large resource base, local revenue constitutes less than 20% of total revenue for local governments (Uganda, MoFPED 2000f, p. 150). In addition to the small revenue base, the level of income for local governments (including central government transfers) tends to be unstable. This instability makes budgeting unpredictable.

Second, it is commonly observed that most local governments suffer from a narrow tax base, low tax rates, and inefficient tax collection. They also overestimate collectable taxes and other income. These factors lead to a shortage of funds in the implementation stage of the budgets. On average, the local governments collect less than 60% of their estimated local revenue (Obwona et al., 2000, p. 297). In FY 1997/98, among the budgets of 28 districts, only two made reasonably realistic estimates of revenue (Uganda, MoLG, 1998a and 1999). The corresponding figures in Mukono and Rakai are 60% to 75%, while Tororo had a wide fluctuation from 48% in FY 1998/99 to 157% in FY 1996/97.

Third, districts are in a relatively better position to secure funds (both central government grants and locally generated revenue) than are sub-counties and other lower levels of local governments. The revenue sharing among different levels of local authorities established by the guideline is not always adhered to, mainly due to lack of funds. Arrears in transmitting funds are quite common, although its magnitude has not been fully revealed (Obwona et al., 2000, p. 298).

Fourth, although there are significant variations in the composition of revenue sources, most districts obtain approximately 70% of their local revenue from the graduated tax. This tax is essentially a poll tax levied on all Ugandan citizens who are 18 years old and over, with a slight degree of modification depending on

---

[10] Most of the district financial offices are staffed by four or five account clerks, but do not have computers. The records are filed manually. Among the three districts analyzed by this study, only Rakai was equipped with a computer. At the LC 3 level, the capacity is extremely limited. There is usually one sub-accountant who keeps records in designated books. He (literally) possesses no more than basic calculus skills. At LC 3 level, chairpersons, the political heads, sometimes do not have basic calculus skills.

Table 6.2 Local government expenditures and revenues (real terms)[11]

(Ush Million)	1995/96	1996/97	1997/98	1998/99
Revenues				
Central Government	647,349	695,395	699,420	809,012
Local Governments	177,800	335,755	269,233	366,057
Total revenues	825,149	1,031,151	968,653	1,175,069
% Share of Local to				
Total Revenues	21.5%	32.6%	27.8%	31.2%
Total Expenditures				
Central Government	697,866	807,443	929,567	1,474,231
Local Governments	172,023	308,774	241,036	301,741
Total Expenditures	869,889	1,116,217	1,170,604	1,775,972
% Share of local to				
Total Expenditures	19.8%	27.7%	20.6%	17.0%
Capital Expenditures				
Central Government	75,073	111,444	120,219	662,176
Local Governments	31,026	17,830	38,984	18,326
% Share of Capital to				
Total Local Govt				
Expenditure	18.0%	5.8%	16.2%	6.1%
Recurrent Expenditures				
Central Government	622,793	695,999	809,348	812,054
Local Governments	140,997	290,944	202,052	283,415
% Share of Local to				
Central	22.6%	41.8%	25.0%	34.9%
% Share of Recurrent to				
Total Local Govt				
Expenditures	82.0%	94.2%	83.8%	93.9%

Sources : Obwona, Marios, et al. [2000] *Fiscal Decentralisation and Sub-National Government Finance in Relation to Infrastructure and Service Provision in Uganda* (Kampala: Economic Policy Research Centre), Annex Table 4.2.1.

the level of income and household assets.[12]

On the side of expenditures, the following issues can be highlighted. First, the share of recurrent expenditures, including wages, in total spending by local governments is quite high (Table 6.2). It is estimated that as a national average, more than 85% of funds are spent on recurrent costs, thereby leaving scant funds for de-

---

[11] Table 6.2 indicates a slightly confusing situation. It shows that total local government expenditures are *less* than their total revenues, while total government expenditures (combining both central and local authorities) are consistently *more* than their revenues. It is probable that revenues shared among different levels of local governments are miscalculated. It is suspected that this revenue is counted more than once as appropriate income by different levels of the LC system (Personal Interview, Robert Kalemba, Chief Finance Officer, Mukono District, 20 August, 2002).

[12] Exemptions apply for the sick, full-time students, people in the army or police force, and women without full-time employment (Livingstone and Charlton, 2001, p. 84).

velopment investment. Total wages constitute slightly more than half of total re-current expenditures (Obwona et al., 2000, p. 293). Most unconditional grants and nearly half of conditional grants are to pay these wages. In Tororo, Rakai and Mukono, on average about 54% of total central government transfers are for wage and allowances (respective LC records).

Second, the way in which districts allocate funds for priority program catego-ries for poverty reduction also varies from area to area, although the available data is limited. It is calculated that education, health and feeder roads are the major ar-eas for resource allocations with an approximate share of 60%, 13%, and 4%, re-spectively, in total spending of local governments in FY 1997/98. The other sec-tors which receive noticeable allocations include water and sanitation, and police and prisons (ibid., pp. 19 and 293).

Third, while the guidelines clearly state that allowances and emoluments for councillors cannot exceed 15% of the income of the previous fiscal year, some lo-cal authorities apparently go above this ceiling (Uganda, MoLG, 1998a and 1999).

Fourth, more than half of the districts do not operate balanced budgets, contrary to the requirement of the Local Governments Act, 1997.[13] The amount of deficit varies from one local authority to another, but accruing a deficit by local authori-ties appears to be not uncommon. This probably signifies the low level of aware-ness among district councillors who approve local budgets. Consequently, some local governments may not be able to maintain a "hard budget constraint" (Uganda, MoLG, 1998a and 1999).[14]

It is clear that a lot still needs to be done in the area of accounting and budget-ing, even though the level of performance in financial management at local levels has improved considerably in recent years. What is also of concern is that many local accounts have not been properly audited, primarily because of the lack of human resources by the regulatory authorities. There has been some progress in this area in the last few years, but it is still far from acceptable.

5 Data from Selected Local Governments

5.1 District and Sub-county Revenues and Expenditures

The comparison of Mukono, Tororo, and Rakai reveals some interesting find-ings illuminating the workings of fiscal decentralization. Per capita revenue and expenditure figures in the three districts differ. Mukono is considered to be a

---

[13] The analyses done by the MoLG (1998a and 1999) reveal that more than 60% of dis-tricts operate deficit budgets.

[14] One of the commonly debated issues in fiscal decentralization is "hard budget con-straints." Local governments should not expect that the central authority will bail them out in case they run up deficits.

wealthy district, where the private sector is relatively strong. An official in Tororo stated that "one tax payer in Mukono can pay what four tax payers contribute here."[15]   Based on financial and demographic information, it is estimated that one person in Mukono in fact pays Ush 2,046 which is just about three times as much local tax as a person in Tororo (Ush 672). A person in Rakai pays Ush 1,143 in taxes.   But because Rakai receives a large amount of assistance from the DANIDA, the per capita revenue of this district is 12% larger than Mukono and 26% larger than Tororo.   Per capita expenditure figures in Mukono and Tororo Districts are not much different, both being in the range of Ush 16,000 (about US$ 10).   At the district level, spending is less in Tororo than Mukono, but it is not extremely different.

The per capita figures for the different sub-county offices demonstrate that the allocation is really small at the LC 3 level.   Given that this includes administration costs and councillors' allowances, there is very little left for substantive development activities.   At the LC 3 level, the resources allocated in Tororo are much less than Mukono, although it does not appear to be any more disadvantaged than sub-counties in Rakai.

An explanation is necessary concerning the difficult situation which Tororo is facing.   This district is well known for a large amount of domestic debt.   When the current Tororo District Council took office in 1998, it inherited a debt of Ush 1.2 billion (about US$ 1 million).   The amount has been slightly reduced to approximately Ush 1.1 billion.[16]   In FY 1999/98, the district paid about Ush 217 million as a payment for debt which represented 3.1% of total expenditures.   The debt undoubtedly reduced the resources which could otherwise be used for development activities.[17]

Given the average tendency in which less than 15% of total expenditures is spent on development activities by local governments, including both district and sub-county offices, it is estimated that financial resources available per person in rural areas for developmental activities is from Ush 2,400 to 2,800 per year (US$ 1.6-1.8).[18]   A large proportion of this money is used for classroom construction in many cases.   But in reality, disbursements of the funds are often hindered by the upper levels of the LC system, particularly by districts for their administra-

---

[15] Personal interview, Anthony Jabo Okoth, Chairperson LC 3, Tororo District, 20 June 2000.

[16] Personal interview, Alianga Mattew Jassa, Chief Finance Officer, Tororo District, 9 August 2000.

[17] The history of this district accumulating more than one billion Shilling in debt is complicated.   As stated in Chapter 4, when two districts were carved out of Tororo, they did not take any share of the debt.   Consequently, Tororo must now repay the debt with a narrower local revenue base than before.   On the other hand, with the LGDP funds, the district revenue may be augmented by an additional Ush 1 billion, which is more than a 10% increase in total revenue.

[18] The estimate is largely in line with that of Livingstone and Charlton (2001). They figured that in FY 1993/94 per capital local revenue was not much more than US$ 1 (p. 85). See also Francis and James (2003, p. 331).

tion costs, and the full amount rarely reaches lower LCs for the intended local development activities. (Further discussion on education and health will be made in
subsequent chapters.)

Another rough calculation of the amount of funds which should be theoretically
made available for each village in the three districts is illuminating. Each village
is entitled to receive 16.25% of locally generated revenue.[19] In Mukono, roughly
Ush 240,000 (US$ 160) is the average amount which should be used for LC 1 ac-
tivities. The figures for Rakai and Tororo are Ush 100,000 (US$ 66) and Ush
72,000 (US$ 48) respectively. In reality, not all of these figures are made avail-
able, due to various claims made by higher-level authorities. In addition, in each
village, the councillors may not know the entitled amounts (Francis and James,
2003, pp. 331-332). Even if they do, they often use some of it for administrative
purposes including organizing meetings, visiting higher levels LC offices, and
purchasing stationary. Some village leaders who are not sincere take all the funds
for personal consumption. In other villages where leaders are relatively honest
and their financial transactions are transparent, the councillors attempt to minimize administration costs.

A very crude estimate thus may be that approximately Ush 30,000 (US$ 20) is
set aside for administrative costs. In a relatively wealthy district such as Mukono,
a village is left with US$ 140, which can be used for something meaningful. The
corresponding amount in a Rakai village is US$ 46. These amounts can be used
productively. In Mukono, several villages used this fund as "seed money" for collective improvement of the local communities. Such development can take the
form of classroom construction, road maintenance, and water source protection.
In Rakai, more villages become aware of this seed money.[20] In Tororo, the corresponding amount of US$ 28 per village may be too small to be used effectively by
one village. There, many villages do not use this seed money, which may not
reach villages at all in some cases. These rough estimates highlight the importance of using the small amount of funds meaningfully, especially in Tororo, particularly by collective action possibly coordinated at the LC 3 level (Barnes,
1999).

5.2 Historical Patterns of District Incomes and Expenditures

Financial comparisons of three districts are interesting. Real income (adjusted
for inflation) for these districts shows an overall growth trend, thanks largely to inter-governmental transfers. In all the districts, the income levels of FY 1996/97
and FY 1997/98 slowed down, partly because the FY 1996/97 lasted only for nine

---

[19] In villages, this is known as "25% allocation." 65% of total local revenue is made available for LC 3, whose 25% should be allocated to LC 1 units.

[20] A bag of cement in rural areas cost about one US dollar. Also construction of a small
room (12 x 14 feet) in rural areas, for instance, costs about Ush one million (US$ 670),
excluding the labor costs.

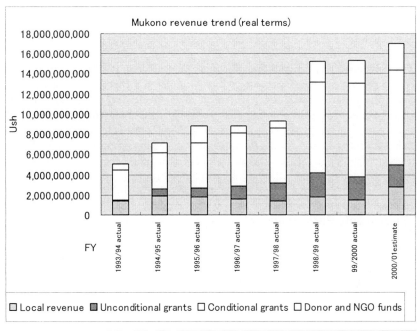

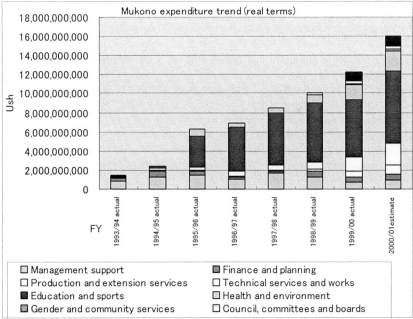

Source: Mukono District Council records.

Figure 6.1 Mukono District revenue and expenditure trends (real terms)

months in order to synchronize the fiscal years of the central and local governments. Locally generated revenues in all three districts show fluctuations over the years. As shown by Figure 6.1, Mukono is a typical example to demonstrate the increase of total revenue which is mostly funded by the central government and donors.[21]

The comparison of expenditures uncovers that allocation of funds for different activities fluctuates most in Tororo, while Mukono and Rakai show more stable patterns. In all three districts, education has been the leading recipient of district funds in recent years. Other areas, such as gender and community services, have much less allocation in the three districts. There is no significant variation of overall spending patterns among the three districts. This is not surprising, because districts depend mostly on central government transfers, a majority of which are activities pre-determined by the central government itself.

5.3 Sub-county Performances

Sub-county performance is assessed based on available information from two sub-county offices in each of the three districts. On the revenue side, the main income source is the graduated tax, just as in the case of districts. Limited information based on the sampled sub-counties reveals that it is not uncommon for these sub-counties to collect only about 40-45 % of anticipated tax revenue. The highest collection rate in this limited examination is 85% in Kawolo Sub-county in Mukono in FY 1997/98, but even there the collection rate in the next fiscal year dropped to less than 50%. In Nama Sub-county, Mukono, the collection rate fluctuated between 43% and 54%. Even if the revenue amount varies from one year to the next, the overall pattern of revenue sources remains largely the same in this sub-county.

What is noteworthy is a new development of an NGOs' direct financial assistance to the level of sub-county. An international NGO, Concern Worldwide, started assisting some sub-county offices in Rakai with a financial provision of Ush 25 million per year each.[22] The use of these funds is decided through consultation between sub-county officials and Concern representatives. Because the actual sub-county revenue in FY 1998/99 was slightly above Ush 10 million, the additional Ush 25 million was, therefore, really a big boost in the resource base.

---

[21] All three districts maintain expenditures lower than incomes. The performance of Rakai is more credible than the other districts (Uganda, MoLG, 1998a), partly because DANIDA demands more consistent accounting. In Tororo and Mukono, the expenditure side does not include transfers to lower units of local authorities. Mukono's recent budget speeches show that transfers to lower LCs are categorized as the last "buffer" to balance their budget in the case of lack of revenue. This means that in several districts, if not most, transfers to lower LC levels are not consistently recorded. As a result, total expenditures tend to be less than what they should be. These factors make it appear that most of the local authorities maintain a hard budget constraint.

[22] Personal interview, John Sserwada, Concern Worldwide Rakai Office, 5 July 2000.

On the expenditure side, because the recording format in Rakai District is different from Mukono and Tororo, comparison is difficult. But in Nama and Kawolo, both in Mukono District, spending patterns are very similar. There, general administration, employee costs, remuneration for councillors, and transfers to other local governments constitute approximately three-quarters of total spending. Only a quarter of total expenditures are left for the activities of sub-county offices. In Nama, based on the budget estimates of FY 1997/98 and 1998/99, the most significant expenditure was for feeder roads (Obwona et al., 2000, Annex, Table 4.2.3 (j)). In all sub-counties, remuneration for councillors seems to exceed the legal limit of 15%. In the two sub-counties in Rakai District, management support services account for slightly more than 60% of spending, and if all other expenses are considered, once again little money is left for local activities. When the sub-county office cannot realize anticipated revenues, public services are affected first; salaries and remuneration are relatively less affected than other categories.

6 Major Issues in Fiscal Decentralization

The Ugandan experience in fiscal decentralization is encouraging. Uganda has adopted a phased approach. Recurrent expenditures were first transferred from the central to local governments, and development expenditures have lately been transferred to sub-national governments. Critics may argue that without transferring adequate (discretionary) funds for development budgets, granting autonomy to local governments does not result in improved service provisions, which is one of the stated objectives of decentralization (Bird and Vaillancourt, 1998b). The phased approach, however, has contributed to the installation of the LC system in which local people express their views and react to government policies. Given the historical legacy and lack of experience in democratic management of public affairs in this country, the phased approach is appropriate (Smoke, 2001). Grassroots people become familiar with the way in which funds are allocated for local use. This gradual learning process is essential in creating the required local capacity to plan and manage small-scale local activities. With limited postindependence experience on the part of essential stakeholders, notably local authorities, granting significant financial autonomy from the outset may have been counterproductive.

On the other hand, the experience in Uganda so far highlights important issues. The next steps should be carefully considered, and consistent action needs to be taken at both central and local levels. First, the way in which funds are transferred from the central to local governments needs to be critically reviewed, particularly because more than half of the current grants are salaries of local personnel. The number of grants for remuneration can be reduced by consolidating numerous grants. For instance, there are at least six different grants for health services, some of which are for services and others for salaries and allowances. But since they are all administered by the Ministry of Health and its counterpart at the district level, these grants can be consolidated.

In FY 2002/03, a pilot activity is being tested in eight districts for this consolidation of grants; inter-governmental fiscal transfers are to be based on two main aggregated funds (recurrent and development transfers) instead of more than 20 different grants. It is aimed that in the future, a development transfer system would handle conditional grants, while a recurrent transfer system would deal with unconditional grants. This proposal is apparently much welcomed. But the precise way in which future transfer modalities are to be shaped is still under review.[23]

Second, the review of grants needs to be fully coordinated with another restructuring of civil service reform. Administrative restructuring needs to be coordinated between the central and local levels in order to provide an optimal mix of services. While civil service reform has been implemented mainly in the central government, similar reform is also necessary at the local level. This is a neglected area. Much effort so far has been expended to create capacities of local governments, especially at the district level. But more emphasis in the future should be placed on reallocating staff among various departments within the same levels of local governments.

So far attention has been paid mostly to workable relationships between the central government and districts. The central-local relationship itself is very crucial, but relatively more attention needs to be paid to improving the relationships between districts and sub-counties that must be in the forefront of effective and efficient public service delivery. Again, a similar improvement is critical to forge a more trusting relationship between sub-counties and grassroots people. Unless people at the grassroots level fully understand how different levels of government work, and unless they become willing to collaborate through the LC system, pumping more money into the local administrative structure will not be fully appreciated by the people. Nor will the money result in services which are more responsive to ordinary people. More information disclosures will help grassroots people understand how their respective LCs allocate financial resources and how the decisions made by LCs match grassroots preferences. Improved access to information would be useful in constructing a more accountable relationship between local leaders and the poor and the needy at the grassroots level. A recent government decision requires that the amount of central government grants for education, health, water and sanitation, and agricultural services needs to be displayed at relevant local government offices and facilities (Foster and Mijumbi, 2002, p. 6). Although this requirement does not guarantee self-explanatory information for those who have never been to school, it apparently is a step forward to change the current perception; the poor are still deeply suspicious of their leaders. In order to consolidate the accomplishments so far, some serious effort needs to be made in the following areas of concern.

---

[23] The Local Government Budget Committee and Local Government Releases and the Operations Committee will be established to oversee fiscal transfers from the central to local governments.

6.1 Fiscal Decentralization and Political Intervention

Those who oppose fiscal decentralization base their criticism on political manipulations of otherwise rational decisions. Evidence from Uganda presents a mixed picture. On the one hand, as stated by the secretary in charge of the finance and administration committee in Rakai, unless one is very bold to intervene, councillors tend to be hesitant to bring radical changes into the way in which budgeting is conducted. He said that it was only from the second year that he presented his own ideas for discussion with administrators.[24] In this example, the secretary had experience in the banking sector, and his background appears to have helped create cordial working relations with civil servants, who otherwise tend to look down on ill-educated political leaders.

On the other hand, procurement practices by districts sometimes encounter accusations of political intervention (Francis and James, 2003, p. 331). Any item or service worth more than Ush 500,000 (US$ 330) needs to be put through the tendering process, and most of the districts make annual plans for such tendering. The tendering is usually conducted regularly, and the notices are publicly advertised in national and/or local newspapers. Although the processes are largely reported to be transparent, some districts appear to be more successful than others. In some cases, political influence was noted in the decision-making process (Uganda, MoFPED, 2000m, p. 30). In Kapchorwa, the councillors reportedly formed firms in order to participate in the tendering process (Uganda, MoFPED, 2000j, p. 19). One person who served on the Local Government Tender Board in Tororo mentioned that a limited number of councillors intervened in the procurement process. He felt this was very uncomfortable and then later resigned from such service.[25] As in Tororo, if business opportunities are limited, political intervention may take place, unless preventive measures are taken.

Even if this kind of intervention is real, it can be argued that it is still preferable to decentralize procurement practices. Centrally-conducted purchases in the capital are also subject to similar political influence. Thus, it may be argued that even if there are some problems in local procurement practices, fiscal decentralization enables relatively large amount of funds to be spent in each district, which serves more equitable development than fiscal centralization in which benefits are mostly concentrated in the capital. There is a certain validity to this argument, but what is truly needed are mechanisms to ensure accountability both at central and local levels. (More discussion of this topic will be made in the last chapter.)

6.2 Tax Reform and Fiscal Decentralization

Within fiscal decentralization, granting taxing authority to local governments is a critical question. The central government of Uganda, like other African gov-

---

[24] Personal interview, Ephralim Kamugisha, Secretary for Finance, Planning and Administration, Rakai District, 7 July 2000.
[25] Personal interview, Muhamedd Hussein Shire, Tororo, 21 June 2000.

ernments, is reluctant to delegate important sources of taxes to local governments, primarily because such delegation reduces the income to the central government. It is a classic zero-sum consideration; locally collected taxes benefit localities at the expense of the central government. This issue was particularly acute in Uganda, where even on the African continent tax revenue as a share of GDP is very low.[26]

As a result, local governments generated only approximately 20% of their total revenue locally, primarily by the graduated tax. It is basically a poll tax, modified by consideration of ownership of livestock and other assets. But this tax is a typical example of a property tax which suffers from a number of problems in design as well as implementation (Smoke, 2001, p. 23). Although it is called a "graduated tax," it is very regressive in nature. Its assessment is resented by many grassroots people (Uganda, MoFPED, 2000g). It is widely perceived to be unfair because the tax is not closely related to income levels and also because administration is arbitrary and inconsistent (Livingstone and Charlton, 2001, p. 89). Because most of the LC 3 offices do not possess the capacity to assess incomes and properties in rural areas, the flat tax rate is mostly employed both by payers and collectors.[27] This tax is also very expensive to administer. Approximately 30-40% of the amount is spent on administration itself (Barnes, 1999, p. 8; and Francis and James, 2003, p. 330). The administration cost far exceeds benefits of the graduated tax.

Tax reform is a fundamental issue. In order to secure genuine autonomy, the fiscal independence of local governments from central government is ideal. Given the under-developed rural economies in Uganda, however, such complete independence would be unrealistic. The most promising alternative would be to grant local governments a new source of local taxes. One possibility is a tax on agricultural land. Because rural areas are predominantly agricultural, this kind of tax deserves serious consideration, although a land tax is not culturally familiar to the Ugandans, and land distribution is not entirely equal either. In fact, most of the LC leaders are middle-class land-owners who are anticipated to resist such a new tax. But it can be the only realistic source of new tax for local authorities. A rough estimate shows that if this tax were levied at the rate of Ush 1,200 (US$ 0.8) for those who possess more than one acre of land, this tax would generate what is currently collected by the graduated tax (Livingstone and Charlton, 2001, pp. 95-96).

Until such fundamental tax reform is carried out, local governments will have to depend on the graduated tax. What is compounding the problem is that since service provisions have not yet significantly improved, local residents are not fully convinced of the necessity to pay local taxes annually. In addition, when resources are limited, much of the taxes are used for salaries of officials, instead of

---

[26] In FY 1997/98 Uganda met only 11% of GDP from taxes, and the proportion is much lower than the 26% in Kenya, 14% in Tanzania, and 20% in Zambia (Livingstone and Charlton, 2001, p. 84).

[27] For instance, in Mbale District, 86% of payers paid Ush 5,000-6,000 (Livingstone and Charlton, 2001, p. 89).

being allocated for services. If one of the objectives of decentralization is to foster responsiveness by local governments to improve essential public services, then the incongruence of priorities between grassroots people and local leaders is a serious obstacle (Barnes, 1999).[28] The level of dissatisfaction among the poor cannot be exaggerated. As a result, locally generated revenues in the three districts of this study do not show a steady growth. In short, where the LC is ineffective, local residents do not feel the value of paying the taxes. This dissatisfaction adds more frustration to the notorious graduated tax at the grassroots level. Initiatives for collective action at the grassroots level, however, can change this situation. As reviewed in Chapter 3, some people become more willing to pay taxes, if and when they are convinced that what they pay contributes to improving their lives.[29]

6.3 Lack of Capacity without Experience?

Currently, local governments are overly dependent on the central government for resources, particularly conditional grants. One main reason is that the central government and the donors are not fully convinced that local governments are capable of managing large amounts of funds. This may be understandable given the past performance of local governments. On the other hand, unless they are given chances to manage funds, their capacity for financial management and accountability will not be improved. The experiences of Rakai and other places demonstrate that although it is not free of problems, it is essential to let local governments handle their budgets. Through this process, capacity development would take place gradually. As noted by an earlier observer, "it is only the pressure of decentralization which motivates the action necessary to improve capacity -- and motivates the existing staff and the local level to recognize their own potential and demonstrate their real abilities (Conyers, 1990, p. 30).

This issue can be especially mitigated by increasing capacities for monitoring and supervision by the central government as well as districts. The most recent development of the Monitoring and Accountability Fund by the PAF is welcomed as a step in the right direction. The MoFPED also recently introduced "results-oriented management" to the PAF. These are steps forward to improve financial efficiency. In order to obtain "the value for money," additional improvements are needed in several areas. But the relationship between different levels of the government needs to be changed from the center being the controller of local governments to a more mutual partnership. As long as this overall relationship remains unchanged, a mere increase of funds for monitoring and supervision would not be

---

[28] As seen in Chapter 3, when the question is asked, "Some may say that the councillors get more benefit from *not* resolving problems since they can keep receiving their allowance for attending more meetings. Do you believe this?" An overwhelming majority of grassroots people answered "yes."

[29] One woman expressed, as cited in Chapter 3, "In the past I was unwilling to pay my tax, because I was not clear how the money was used. Now, I am willing to pay it since I now know how it is used" (Joggo, Mukono, 18 August 1999).

likely to yield improved service provisions. As long as the upper levels of government continue to control the lower levels, decentralization measures are less likely to enhance the responsiveness of local authorities. This unchanged relationship between different levels of the government jeopardizes poverty reduction, an ultimate objective of decentralization.

In order for them to form partnerships, it is necessary for both the central and district governments to change their respective orientations. The central government and local authorities have different perspectives on inter-governmental fiscal transfers. The central government attaches high priority to macro-economic stability, and believes it is preferable if the total amount of fiscal transfers is determined annually reflecting national budget priorities. Local governments, on the other hand, consider such a method inflexible, and feel the transfers should reflect local demands (Bird and Smart, 2002).[30] One possibility is to deepen mutual consultations over the way in which inter-governmental fiscal transfers is made. The extent of local government participation should be increased, and it is important to ascertain how inter-governmental fiscal transfers will ensure that economic growth is being translated into improvement of service provisions, particularly for the poor (Obwona et al., 2000, p. 174). With increased consultation, efforts to link the transfer formula with economic performance can show promise. This collaboration is one concrete step to make growth more "broad-based" and beneficial to the poor, as current rhetoric advocates.

Another possibility to overcome this difficulty is the process of learning from the experience of decentralization. Engaging in joint activities with different levels of the government is, thus, tremendously valuable. According to the current revenue-sharing formula, a small proportion of local taxes is supposed to be allocated to the grassroots level, and this method provides a useful opportunity to engage in such joint activities. Where communities are organized for using these small funds, a sense of local accomplishment and pride is fostered. It is not always easy to organize this kind of activity and some mistakes can be made, but they generate useful lessons for both higher and lower levels of the government. What is encouraging is that as awareness among taxpayers gradually increases year by year, more communities appear to be engaging in such activities. This is a useful path by which a delicate balance can be struck between stringent financial regulations and broader socio-political objectives for autonomy to be granted by decentralization. By so doing, a current danger pointed out by some observers, in which financially desperate local governments may opt for activities which can be more readily financed by conditional grants (Obwona et al., 2000, p. 295), can be overcome.

As central and local governments experience this learning process, it is recommended that half of total local revenues should become free of conditions decided by the central government. In general, conditional grants are suitable for encouraging local governments to increase expenditures on particular activities, whereas

---

[30] Bird and Smart (2002) also suggest that one of the most adequate ways to satisfy these competing requirements is to establish a fixed proportion of all central taxes to be transferred to local governments (pp. 900-901).

unconditional grants are well-suited for supplementing deficient revenues among local authorities (Smoke, 2001, pp. 25-26). For relatively simple tasks like feeder road maintenance, conditional grants may be suitable for monitoring and accountability. Thus, conditional grants have a certain role to play even under increased local autonomy. The NRM's increasing allocation for poverty priorities is commendable (Foster and Mijumbi, 2002). On the other hand, the current predominance of conditional grants is not favorable. It is, therefore, desirable if half of the funds made available to local governments become discretionary. Discretion needs to be matched by improved accountability, and local governments are urged to provide sufficient explanations over how the financial allocations are made and how effectively and efficiently public funds are spent.

This issue of an appropriate proportion of different forms of inter-governmental fiscal transfers is related to a much wider issue of the role of development finance, which can take many different forms ranging from grants to loans to bonds. Promising avenues for local governments to secure independent sources of income include automotive taxation, sumptuary taxes, business activity taxes, and entertainment taxes (Shin and Ho, 1998, p. 109). However, often various tools for investment finance in many developing countries are provided without a coherent strategy. Therefore, designing the right mix of different transfer programs that suits Uganda's particular political, social, economic and cultural context needs to be reexamined carefully (Smoke, 2001).

6.4 Incentives for Better Performance

Discretional funds are one form of incentive to improve performances of local governments. Other adequate incentive mechanisms are needed to enhance mutual collaboration among stakeholders. This incentive issue raises an important concern of monitoring and support relationship between different levels of the government.

> The "carrot" of central financial support for local efforts must be accompanied by the "stick" of withdrawn support if performance is inadequate, which of course requires both some standard of adequacy and some way of knowing whether performance is satisfactory (Bird and Vaillancourt, 1998b, p. 14).

The data from the three districts raise some concern over this issue of incentives. If local governments overwhelmingly depend on the central government, they may become less enthusiastic to increase locally collectable revenue. The low level of local tax revenues in all three districts examined so far tends to supports this view. This situation may derive from a reasoning in which this inter-government revenue sharing encourages "free riding"; it makes good sense for local governments to let the central government to secure necessary funds. If this is the case, it may endanger macro-economic stability in the medium- to long-term.[31] In Uganda, since more donors are willing to support decentralization measures, the current situation does not as yet affect macro-economic stability. Yet, this kind of "moral hazard" on the part of local authorities may become a serious issue in the future, which cannot be overlooked.[32]

Adequate measures for introducing incentive mechanisms should be taken to prevent this problem. Some interesting local experiments have been reported in Uganda. For example, in Kabaale District, LC 2 and 3, which achieved the highest tax collection, was awarded a bull or a bicycle (Barnes, 1999, pp. 11 and 15). This example shows an innovative incentive to encourage good performance. It is, therefore, worth considering that the ULAA establish a similar kind of symbolic award to improve financial and administrative management. Another interesting incentive mechanism can be found in the District Development Project funded by UNCDF. In this case, a 20% increment in funds was made available to local authorities in the subsequent year if their performance was good, while the grants were reduced 20% if unsatisfactory. The project also adopted a matching funding mechanism for local governments, in which the increased allocation by the project would need to be matched by increased local contributions. The project motivated the local leaders to think more carefully about resource mobilization issues. Although the evidence is sporadic, this mechanism seems to contribute to a more carefully planned budgeting and execution.[33]

More measures are needed at the central level as well. In order to avert the free-riding problem, adequate "stick" mechanisms are needed. As many local governments fail to balance their budgets by overspending their resources, time is ripe to put a sanctioning mechanism in place in an overall process of performance monitoring of local financial management. It is recommended that the release of central government transfers be tied to actual performance of the grants for intended purposes instead of automatic regular releases as are common now. Of course care needs to be taken when introducing these "carrot" and "stick" measures. Particularly in the case of "sticks," the incentive mechanisms should not punish the innocent and the poor; instead, the incentives should be for officials

---

[31] De Mello (2000) argues that this so-called "common pool" problem is a serious obstacle when many governments attempt to implement policy objectives of fiscal decentralization.

[32] Very interestingly, a drama, which explained the role of the LC system to people at the grassroots, was performed in several villages in Rakai in the middle of 2000. In this drama, a corrupt LC 1 chairman mentioned that even if he embezzles tiny amounts of funds in his village, it does not matter since the central government and DANIDA will give the district a large sum of money.

[33] In this process, sub-counties competed with one another to demonstrate impressive results in order to gain more financial assistance the following year. This competition improved compliance with financial regulations (personal communication from Martin Onyach-Olaa, National Project Manager, 15 January 2001).

and administrators to fulfill their duties and requirements.[34] As demonstrated by the District Development Project, this type of incentive is crucial for improving accountability not only in narrow financial terms but also in a broader social and economic context.

This raises the wider issue of monitoring and accountability between the central and local governments. An accountable relationship should not be unilaterally determined by central governments asking local authorities to return "auditable" reports. The central government should also be scrutinized by local governments in its management of various functions: issuing appropriate guidelines of financial regulations, supporting local governments to meet increased workloads, and ensuring prompt financial transfers. On the other hand, while the central government has resources which can be used as "carrots and sticks," the local governments do not have a similar sort of leverage. Then the question arises as to how more reciprocal accountability relationships can be constructed in such resource-skewed relationships among stakeholders.

One possible method is the use of publicity campaigns. For instance, if some activities are not realized, not because of the failure of a local government but because of the failure of the central government in delaying the release of funds, that information should be made available to affected constituencies. People at the grassroots level have a stake in this process, and they should be fully informed of this kind of failure. With accurate information, if they present their views to the authorities, possibly in collaboration with other stakeholders, this may work as a leverage. This is not financial leverage, but perhaps constitutes a more "democratic" form if this is pursued in an open and transparent manner.

Another possibility for creating a more reciprocal accountability relationship is through more active associations among local authorities. In this area, the experiences of the ULAA have been encouraging. Its advocacy campaigns, especially in pointing out slowness and contradictions of policies of the central government, have been effective. More donors have, in fact, become willing to support the ULAA both technically and financially. The success of the ULAA is a prime example that increased leverage can be exercised by forming strategic alliances by the less influential even if the scope of influence by one local authority may be small. This avenue is promising for other partnerships and should be expanded in the years to come.[35]

---

[34] The hard budget constraints should normally be maintained. The debt issue of Tororo, however, merits special consideration, because the poor are the main sufferers. Although in principle a central government should not bail out local governments from debt, this case probably requires support by the central government.

[35] Bird and Smart (2002) argue that equalization grants pose a disincentive for local governments. They suggest that a way to resolve this is through a matching grant system, although they are aware that determination of the matching ratio is very difficult in practice. When local authorities increase budget allocations to priority services, this increase is matched by central government support in a form of subsidy (p. 905).

7 Summary and Conclusion

Although the Ugandan experience in fiscal decentralization deserves much credit, the remaining challenges are critical. The current form of fiscal decentralization, which depends mostly on conditional grants, appears to contribute to achieving beneficial results, which are largely in line with the nationally identified priorities. Usually budgetary allocations match the people's aspirations, but more money is spent on administration costs and salaries than on actual activities. Although the degree of participation of local authorities and grassroots people in fiscal transfers is minimum, a recent initiative of the BFP is a significant beginning for a central-local partnership.

The local population has less information on local budgets and finance than on those of the central government (Kintu, 2000). While decentralization theorists anticipate increased public scrutiny over funds, this kind of improvement is very limited. Issues are being discussed within the LC system, but the feedback mechanism is extremely weak from upper to lower levels. It has only negligibly improved accountability.

People believe that leaders are corrupt (which is often not true in reality at lower levels of LCs). Although the equalization grant is now in place, its scale is too small to make a significant impact. The equalization grant raises an equity issue in Uganda. The living conditions within Uganda vary considerably, particularly between the north and the south, but how this problem can be overcome is not addressed in the current decentralization strategy. It is also too early to see net resource increases by the private sector in response to calls made by local governments. These issues negatively influence popular perception of the LCs' responsiveness.

Nonetheless, the central government is also keen to improve the way in which it conducts budget consultation by bringing a wider range of stakeholders into a consultation process and in a more participatory way. If the consultation process can be backed by urgent support to local governments to increase their capacity to prepare for it, it would enable the central-local partnership to prosper.

This discussion brings us back to the starting point of this study. It is most critical to establish an adequate balance of services to be provided by the central and local governments in tandem. What services should really be provided by the central government directly or through local agents? What services can and should be more efficiently and effectively provided by local governments? The balance between central and local governments is less important than appropriate allocation of service provisions. Funds are a means of providing such services. Thus, we turn our attention to the essential services of education and health in the next two chapters.

7 Decentralized Primary Education: Potential of Community Contributions

UPE has brought some good changes. For instance, children who could not go to school before can now go to school. But it has also brought the deterioration of the education standard. There are too many pupils per teacher. Teachers are making many demands, which was not the case before. If parents cannot pay the cost of school items, the school sends children back home.

A woman made a statement during a focus group discussion,
Mukono, 19 August 1999

People in Uganda consider education to be critical to overcome pervasive poverty, which has persisted over generations. They cite lack of education as one of the major reasons for poverty. The poor often say that people with education have a better life. This is why communities continued to assist local schools during the period of social turmoil and the virtual collapse of public services in the 1970s and the early 1980s. The NRM has also been making education one of its priorities for development. In 1996, during the presidential election, incumbent President Yoweri Museveni promised the Universal Primary Education (UPE) as a new policy for poverty reduction. The UPE was formally launched in December 1996, and its implementation started the following year. It is essentially a subsidy to cover the cost of tuition for four children per family.[1]

This implementation took place within the overall framework of decentralized services. The reform was originally intended to improve the cost-effectiveness of public services by bringing these services closer to the people. With the Constitution of Uganda, 1995, and the Local Governments Act, 1997, significant powers and functions have devolved from the central to local governments. The Local Council system connects local authorities and grassroots people. At both district (LC 5) and sub-county (LC 3) levels, there is a committee in charge of educational matters, on which councillors sit with technical staff to discuss, plan and carry out activities.

---

[1] The amount is Ush 5,000 (about US$ 3) for each pupil from the first to third grade and Ush 8,100 (about US$ 5.4) per student from fourth to seventh grade per year (Uganda, MoES, 1998c). This standard is applied nationally.

In this manner primary and secondary education sub-sectors have been decentralized, and this Ugandan experience in decentralizing education so far highlights several important lessons. Although the central and local governments attach a high priority to both UPE and decentralization, a precise mechanism for implementing these two initiatives together remains vague. The local authorities, schools, and communities are asked to collaborate to realize primary education for all pupils. Most of the standard-setting functions for education, including qualification of teachers and curriculum development remain in the hands of the central government, especially the Ministry of Education and Sports (MoES). On the other hand, local governments (particularly districts) are now in charge of teacher management. Schools and communities are asked to collaborate in providing certain support.

The situation in Uganda presents both impressive achievements and unresolved difficulties. The UPE has contributed significantly to increasing pupil enrollment and has expanded access for education among the public, particularly for the disadvantaged. This expansion was made possible by the efforts of the LC system to solicit support for education at the grassroots level. Yet declining quality, lack of teacher motivation, poor supervision and support by the central and local governments to schools, *inter alia*, constitute major bottlenecks impending further improvement of education. The total amount of resources allocated for education increased significantly, but whether decentralized services have significantly improved the efficiency and effectiveness of resource utilization is another issue. There is an urgent need for consistent and coordinated remedial action, particularly because more children are expected to seek education from primary to secondary schools in the immediate future.

1 Background of Education Sector

Education is essential to enhance the self-esteem of people, including children. Education equips people with practical skills such as literacy, which contribute to economic growth. But the process of education itself enables people to become more aware of a wide range of social and political issues. This raised awareness can help people fulfill their potential not only in the economic sphere but also as human beings. Attending school forms an indispensable part of ordinary practices in which education is provided. Although what is taught and how it is taught affect learning, securing opportunities to attend school is much more preferable to no schooling at all. Even if education in Uganda is obviously not free from problems such as inadequate curriculum, securing opportunities for schooling is still better than no education at all. Thus, the increasing school enrollment is a step forward.

In response to the UPE initiative, the central government has allocated substantial resources for education. Education is a major sector of the national budget. It currently represents over 31% of the discretionary recurrent budget, and 27% of the entire central government budget (Uganda, MoFPED, 2000f, p. 70). As a government priority for poverty reduction, education has benefited from the Poverty Action Fund (PAF), which has been supported by debt relief granted by a series of the Highly Indebted Poor Countries (HIPC) provisions since 1998. Since FY 1997/98, over 75% of conditional grants have been directed toward the education sector (ibid., p. 149). Within the education sector, approximately 70% of the budget is allocated for primary education. Consequently, the MoES estimates that government spending increased from US$ 8 per primary school student in the 1980s to US$ 33 in FY 1997/98 (Uganda, MoES, 1999, p. 19).

With the UPE, a massive turnout of pupils made school classrooms very congested and highlighted other important issues. In response to this situation, the Education Sector Investment Plan (ESIP) was originally launched in 1997 and adopted the following year.[2] The ESIP is a sector-wide approach (SWAP), in which priorities are identified and required investment is programmed through close collaboration between the Ugandan government and donors.[3]

One essential factor of the ESIP is proper division of functions and responsibilities among key stakeholders including the MoES. Roles of MoES under the decentralized structure are:

a) to develop, approve and adjust education policy through wide stakeholder discussion;
b) to ensure that policy decisions are communicated to all stakeholders;
c) to monitor the effectiveness of the education system and to ensure the best value for money; and
d) to support the decentralized levels in all aspects of education management and monitoring including general and specific capacity building activity.

The central government is, thus, still responsible for developing curriculum nationally and for setting the required standards for teachers and school buildings. The rationale behind this is to ensure that students in different places can have equal access to comparable levels of education.

The major roles of district governments, particularly respective offices of the District Education Officer (DEO), include the following broad categories:

a) education planning and management;
b) teacher management; and

---

[2] Its five major components are: a) increasing access to, and quality of, primary education (US$ 466 million); b) expanding opportunities for secondary education ($ 100 million); c) expansion of technical and vocational education and training ($ 67 million); d) support to reform higher education ($ 66 million); and e) strengthening institutional capacity in planning and management of education ($ 11 million) (Uganda, MoES, 1998a).

[3] The SWAP has four features: 1) individual projects are planned within agreed sector priorities; 2) the government prepares a medium-term financial framework; 3) the adoption of a management structure for common implementation arrangements; and 4) institutional development and capacity building (Teskey and Hooper, 1999, p. 3). For a review of SWAP, see Brown et al., 2001; Foster 2000; and World Bank 2001a.

c) installation and operation of the Education Management Information System (EMIS) (Uganda, MoES, 2000d, pp. 2-3).

The goals for decentralizing education include efficiency and effectiveness of education services, particularly primary education. The DEOs have generally welcomed their redefined role, partly because decentralization provides more predictable resources with which to manage educational issues, and also because the decentralized framework encourages more active interaction among local stakeholders including local people.[4] With this interactive process, it is expected that accountability at various levels of authority will be improved. The goal of decentralized education, at least at this moment, does not include allowing each DEO to modify nationally determined curriculum or to select languages used in teaching classes, although some schools may have already become flexible on these issues.

Based on this new division of labor between the central and local governments, the MoES has been restructured, and this process is still continuing. An idea to establish a network of officers at the MoES headquarters to cater to the needs of local governments is under review. This is called a "decentralization desk." Compared with other ministries, responses of the MoES toward service decentralization were very slow. One senior official at the ministry explained that in the educational sector, schools were already given a relatively high degree of autonomy, and it was considered that the education sector was already "decentralized."[5] In the meantime, other ministries, notably the Ministry of Health (MoH), went ahead to streamline their functions and structures in line with decentralization policy. The reorganization in other ministries left the MoES relatively behind, but the MoES is now attempting to catch up with them through this decentralization desk initiative.

2 Major Achievements

2.1 Successful Collaborative Pattern

Motivated by a zealous dedication to education on the part of the people of Uganda, stakeholder participation in education improvement has been reasonably impressive. The central government formulated its policies relatively clearly and fulfilled its commitment by providing significant funds. This government action was welcomed by the population in general who appreciate the value of education.

---

[4] Personal interviews, Yona Doya, DEO, Tororo, 29 May 2000; James Ssemugabi, DEO, Rakai, 26 July 2000, and S.D. Otto-Akwee, Educational Officer, Mukono, 22 May 2000. But the extent of decentralization from DEOs down to lower levels of the hierarchy is less than in the case of the health sector.

[5] Personal interview, Joseph Eilor, Principal Education Planner, MoES, 14 August 2000.

The local authorities, especially the offices of DEO, carried out local planning for facilities and manpower. The LC system functioned as a liaison between local authorities and grassroots people, and thereby improving school facilities. The relationship between educational officers and political leaders (councillors) initially was not so cordial. But as they worked together, they nurtured mutual understanding, and both sides now claim, in general, that the working relationship is not a major problem.[6] The councillors particularly play an essential role in mobilizing the support of grassroots people in this process.[7] For the councillors, classroom construction is politically ideal, because it takes a relatively short time for visible results to be realized, and because such activities match peoples' aspirations.

At the grassroots level, individual schools are now managed by School Management Committees (SMCs), each consisting of nine members. The SMCs are in charge of routine tasks in managing schools. Although it is not clearly defined legally, the common understanding is that the SMCs are supposed to collaborate both with the Parent Teachers Associations (PTAs) and with the LC system. The decisions made by the SMCs are reported to ordinary people either through PTA networks or gatherings of their respective LCs, particularly LC 1 (village level), depending on the issues.[8] If collaboration of people is needed in such activities as constructing additional classrooms, then the respective LCs ask the local population to contribute their time and energy to such activities. Although information dissemination is not always optimal, the LC system appears to be functional in eliciting some forms of participation by ordinary people, particularly where leadership is effective. The councillors' efforts are appreciated by school teachers.[9]

Such collaboration has worked reasonably well in Uganda, although there have been problems for stakeholders in discharging some of their duties and obligations. The LC system raises various issues at local meetings. Among them, education tends to attract relatively high attendance by people in the three districts studied. The fact that the poor themselves collaborate in the mobilization undertaken by the LCs attests to the fact that they are at least partially willing to support initiatives for improving primary education. The case of education is reasonably straightforward for the poor who understand the value of such initiatives. Given the past community involvement in sustaining local schools even during the hardship period, their involvement is reasonably high. Thus, collaboration in improving their local schools has been successful. The collaborative partnership between service providers and recipients is a prime example of transaction costs being lowered. As a result, many classrooms are built by utilizing limited resources efficiently.

Some may argue that labor contributions by the grassroots people, mobilized by political leaders, are not considered as a proper form of participation. Rather, this

---

[6] For instance, personal interview, Edward Festo Kaweesi. Chairman LC 3, Nama, Mukono, 13 June 2000.

[7] Personal interview, Sam Frederick Bemba, Councillor LC 5, Mukono, 13 August 1999.

[8] Group interviews, SMC members of Katale-Busawulla Primary School, Wakiso District, 20 August, 2002; SMC members of Kyoga Primary School, Mukono, 23 August 2002.

[9] For instance, interview at Najjembe Primary School, 11 August 1999.

form of "participation" is in fact a manipulation. Although this argument has a certain validity in developing countries, the grassroots collaboration in rural Uganda is different. There, collaboration is not forced by political leaders. The population in general is keen on education, and their labor contributions often reflect their willingness. In fact, in some areas, communities build small-scale schools and ask the government to assist in managing them.[10] At the grassroots level, both the people and their leaders are satisfied once they accomplish their goals of building classrooms because their children can now be educated.[11] The process itself gives self-confidence, especially to the poor. As long as the autonomy of ordinary people is respected, this case constitutes a form of partnership.

There is another argument which asserts that the same collaboration could have been possible even without the LC system. Many primary schools were established by churches and religious bodies in Uganda.[12] They have undoubtedly played a very influential role in managing schools. They might have been able to mobilize the same people for similar activities as the LC system has done. Although it is difficult to conclude firmly, these funding bodies also tend to contribute to sectarian divisions in Uganda (Golooba-Mutebi, 1999). In places such as Tororo, schools were established by Protestant and Catholic missions, respectively, which tended to separate communities along denominational lines. The collaboration is different in the case of the LC system, because it is through this system that all people can participate in decision making either directly or indirectly through their elected representatives. Thus, the LC appears to be successful in mobilizing people without significantly dividing Ugandan society.

2.2 Increase of Enrollment and School Facilities

The UPE has markedly increased the number of pupils enrolled. Net primary enrollment increased from 53% in 1990 to 94% in 1998, according to one set of statistics (McGee, 2000c, p. 91). The gross enrollment ratio grew from a low of 67% in 1992 to a high of 124% in 1997, as shown in Table 7.1.[13] The reason why this is more than 100% is that some dropouts returned to school to repeat some classes. These figures undoubtedly demonstrate that the UPE assists children of poor families who could not otherwise attend or complete primary schools as compared to the non-poor who have done so to a greater proportion in the past

---

[10] NGOs were supportive of local communities as well. For instance, in Rakai, World Vision constructed about 300 classrooms (interview at the Rakai office, 7 July 2000).

[11] The sense of accomplishment was common. For instance interview, Nakamute Primary School, Mukono, 08 June 2000.

[12] For a good overview of the role of churches in Uganda, see Gifford, 1998, chapter 4.

[13] In Rakai District, it is reported that the number of pupils increased from 69,000 in 1996 to 142,298 in 2000 (personal interview, James Ssemugabi, District Education Officer, Rakai, 26 July 2000). In Mukono, enrollment has risen from 158,583 in 1996 to 293,716 in 1998 (personal communication, Ikuko Suzuki, researcher at the University of Sussex, 9 September 2001).

Table 7.1 Gross enrollment ratio (GER)

	Enrollment P.1 to P.7			Population aged 6-12 years			GER(%)		
	Male	Female	Total	Male	Female	Total	Male	Female	Total
1990	1,263,585	998,005	2,201,590	1,660,901	1,558,000	3,324,994	77	61	69
1991	1,303,306	1,236,243	2,539,549	1,670,905	1,666,201	3,337,106	78	74	76
1992	1,203,670	1,160,408	2,364,078	1,719,528	1,783,993	3,503,521	70	64	67
1993	1,492,630	1,182,335	2,674,965	1,741,794	1,807,093	3,548,887	85	65	75
1994	1,407,797	1,190,895	2,598,692	1,763,787	1,829,911	3,593,698	79	65	72
1995	1,587,216	1,325,257	2,912,473	1,790,502	1,859,115	3,649,617	86	72	72
1996	1,647,742	1,420,883	3,068,625	1,996,182	1,988,785	3,984,967	86	74	80
1997	2,855,093	2,315,813	5,170,886	2,077,312	2,069,513	4,146,825	137	112	124
1998	2,868,564	2,595,289	5,591,000	2,159,144	2,149,100	4,308,244	129	114	122

Source: Uganda, MoES records.

(Foster and Mijumbi, 2002, p. 16). The return effect is particularly strong for girls. This enlarged access to education among the poor has an important effect in addressing the equity issue in society. Thanks to the UPE and donor support, Rakai, a relatively disadvantaged area, in recent years has recorded the fourth highest completion rate of primary education in the country.[14]

Generally, the UPE is highly appreciated by people at the grassroots level. People fully acknowledge that it has reduced the financial burdens of schooling. There has been a particular impact on disadvantaged children, especially girls, orphans and the disabled (Uganda, MoFPED, 2000g). As one woman stated, "It [the UPE] is good because children get educated up to the primary level. For a widow, government support for children is really appreciated."[15] The UPE has, therefore, contributed to the empowerment of the disadvantaged, as seen in Chapter 4.

This rapid increase in enrollment was facilitated by the decentralized schoolroom construction activities. This achievement resulted from the successful collaboration of various stakeholders at various levels. The MoES adopted a new School Facilities Grant (SFG). The tenders were given by local governments to local contractors. A number of local governments also made supplementary contributions by allocating locally generated revenue for classroom construction. At the sites of construction activities, community involvement was generally high. Although there were some problems associated with this process, this collaboration pattern facilitated the rapid construction of numerous classrooms.

As a result, many communities now have primary schools within reasonable proximity. It was often stated by grassroots people that in the past children had to walk for long distances to school, but now that is no longer the case.[16] The na-

---

[14] Personal interview, James Ssemugabi, District Education Officer, Rakai, 23 August 1999.

[15] Focus group discussion, a woman in Osia-Magoro, Tororo, 31 May 2000.

[16] Focus group discussion, Kibona, Rakai, 25 July 2000.

tional average of distance to schools is approximately 1.5 km in rural areas and less than 1 km in urban areas (Uganda, UBOS, 2001b, p. 17).

3 Urgent Issues in Primary Education

3.1 Ill-defined Roles of Stakeholders

Although the stakeholders' collaboration has produced impressive results, the processes need to be consolidated if decentralized education intends to be effective and efficient in a sustainable way. The current division of labor between the MoES and the DEOs is relatively well understood. But relations among sub-county offices, LC 1 (village) councils, schools, SMCs, PTAs, and people themselves are not clearly defined. For ordinary residents, SMCs are distant organizations. People obtain information related to school financial management, for instance, from PTA meetings, other parents, and teachers, in this order, and few, if any, mention SMC members (Uganda, UBOS, 2002, p. 105). Members of the SMCs and local residents do not necessarily share a common understanding of what their roles are, although the situation appears to be improving year after year.[17] The PTAs are indispensable in operating schools, but the SMCs are now in charge of overall school management. PTAs may not be pleased with their loss of influence vis-à-vis the SMCs. It is, therefore, crucial for each stakeholder not only to understand their role but also to discharge respective responsibilities in order for education to mitigate poverty.

This situation is aggravated by a serious lack of capacity at local levels. For example, many SMC members are not skilled enough to fulfill their official duties. Quite a few of them are not capable of basic accounting. As a result, many chairpersons of the SMCs often tend to give approval to head teachers without much knowledge about issues. The SMCs consequently cannot verify whether financial transactions made by schools are appropriate. In other cases, conflicts between SMC chairpersons and head teachers delay actions required for securing accountability (Uganda, MoES, 2000e). What makes the matter more troublesome is that in rural areas, the likelihood that the same people hold more than one leadership positions is quite high. In this situation, diversion of public funds for private use cannot fully be prevented. The situation, consequently, does not encourage transparency of management practices.[18]

---

[17] Group interviews, SMC members of Katale-Busawulla Primary School, Wakiso District, 20 August, 2002; SMC members of Kyoga Primary School, Mukono, 23 August 2002.

[18] Suzuki (2002) reports that following the direction of the MoES in 2000, DOEs started to advise schools not to nominate councillors as SMC members (p. 256). Whether this recent development has been implemented in rural villages remains to be seen.

In addition, the SMCs are in charge of the management of local schools, and the decisions made by the SMCs are supposed to be reported back to local communities through the LC 1. But the feedback does not happen so often. The formal coordination between the LC system and the SMCs on agenda setting and information dissemination to the public is also limited, although informally some councillors are also members of SMCs.

Another complication faced by the LC system is the erosion of community cohesiveness. As discussed briefly in Chapter 1, community is a social manifestation of small-scale personal interactions usually organized for effective collective action. In Uganda, parents can choose to which schools they wish to send their children. With the deterioration of educational quality due largely to the increased enrollment, wealthier parents, particularly in urban locations, tend to send their children outside of their villages.[19] It costs considerably more for this education,[20] but the educational standard of (urban) private schools is higher than the government ones. The administrative boundary of the LC and the area where parents send children to schools, thus, do not necessarily coincide. Even if parents live in the same neighborhood, their notions of "community" are different (Suzuki, 2000). Although, generally speaking, local people appreciate schools as an essential common concern, the situation where neighbors send their children to different schools may undermine the social bonds under which local villagers attempt to resolve their common concerns such as education. Financially, wealthier families may feel less enthusiastic in supporting nearby schools if their children are not enrolled in them. But they are the ones who have more resourecs to make contributions than the poor.[21] This situation may suggest that community development remains an empty slogan. Because cohesion is a sense of common identity and interests which unites people for collective action, eroding community cohesion is a serious issue. If this tendency deepens, the LC system may not become very effective in improving such essential services as local education. This ineffectiveness may undermine public confidence in government schools.

---

[19] An effect of the "exodus" from public to private schools is the reduced enrollment at public schools in urban areas of Mukono. Particularly, the number of pupils enrolled in grades one and two have decreased fairly significantly between 1998 and 2000 (personal communication, Ikuko Suzuki, researcher at the University of Sussex, 11 September 2001).

[20] A recent survey reveals that private education can cost about five times as much as public education (Uganda, UBOS, 2002, p. 69).

[21] The role of the local elite in effective local management is a delicate one. On the one hand, they can provide resources, knowledge, and personal networks. On the other hand, they can dominate decision-making processes at the cost of the disadvantaged. Reinikka and Svensson (2001) argue that the wealthier the parents, the more likely local schools receive the full amount of grants.

3.2 Equitable Access to Education

Although UPE has massively increased enrollment, there are still those who cannot attend primary schools. It will probably require special assistance in addition to the UPE policy, if equitable access to education by all children is to be ensured. A recent survey points out that about one-third of six to nine years old boys and girls have never been to school despite the UPE (Uganda, UBOS, 2001a, p. 14). There seems to be several reasons for this. First of all, some parents still do not fully appreciate the importance of education, and this results in their children not being sent to school. In order to cope with this problem in various areas local councillors are attempting to convince the parents of the importance of education.[22] But when parents themselves did not receive education, persuasion by councillors tends to be unsuccessful.[23]

Second, the economic burden is still high for the very poor despite UPE subsidies.[24] Ironically, in order to cope with the massive increase in pupils at schools, parents are often asked to pay various fees. This increased payment request surprised parents in the initial years of UPE implementation, since UPE was described originally as "free education" fully supported by the government. In fact, various fees are asked at schools in addition to the costs of uniforms, stationary and scholastic materials.[25] The variety of fees include developing school facilities, pupils' lunch, teachers' welfare, building churches in the cases of schools originally built by Christian missionaries, extra lessons, and contributions (for instance, of water, fuel, and labor). Among these, what is officially accepted is a lunch fee. But due to poor supervision by the MoES and DEO, schools collect diverse fees. One recent study estimates that even after the UPE, parents contribution to school matters ranged from Ush 3,000 to 5,000 per pupil per term (about US\$ 2 to 3.3) (Suzuki, 2002, p. 250).

It is reported that in some cases up to 20% of household income is spent on education including the payment of all kinds of fees.[26] For those very poor families, particularly for female-headed households, widows and orphans, these additional cash requirements are grievous, and thus many children cannot remain in school.[27] A parent expressed the typical opinion that "teachers are paid a salary, why pay more. UPE came to relieve us of such extra payments!" (Uganda, MoF-

---

[22] For instance, this is confirmed by the focus group discussion in Osia-Magoro, Tororo, 31 May 2000.

[23] Focus group discussion in Rakai, 25 August 2000. Interview, Kidoko Primary School, Tororo, 1 June 2000.

[24] In 2001, discussions were held by the MoES to make the standardized UPE allocation more flexible to meet the needs of pupils with disabilities, pupils in remote and/or small schools (personal communication, Ikuko Suzuki, 15 September 2001).

[25] It costs about Ush 4,000 – 6,000 for uniforms, Ush 100–350 for books, and Ush 100 for a pencil.

[26] For instance, focus group discussion Osia-Magoro, Tororo, 31 May 2000.

[27] Thus, grassroots people wish to be empowered so that they can fulfil required financial obligations (focus group discussion, Kibona, Rakai, 25 July 2000).

PED, 2000g, p. 77). This kind of harsh reaction applies to the eastern and northern parts of the country more acutely. Public expenditure per pupil in Tororo and Rakai is about half of that in Mukono (Uganda, MoES, 2000g). A villager typically commented on this situation as follows:

> Fees asked by the school cannot always be paid by all parents. In cases of non-payment, the pupils are sent back to the house. Parents are asked to pay the cost of salary of teachers who have not been paid by the government, the cost of meals, the church fee, and examination fee. We are aware that the government should not ask the parents to pay the examination fee. But we have no choice. If we do not pay, kids are sent back to the house. Maybe the money goes to the pocket of the headmaster. He is eating our money. Therefore we directly pay to the teacher who teaches our respective children.[28]

The third reason for poor school attendance is the poor status of child nutrition. Many children do not have adequate school lunches and do not stay at schools. The MoES admits that "up to 80% of primary school children do not benefit from a mid-day meal. A major weakness is the absence of a policy on the issue of child nutrition and school feeding. There are no budgets allocated to this, and it clearly affects the achievement of improved quality" (Uganda, MoES, 2000b, pp. 15-16).[29] The nutritional status of pupils is different for boys and girls. A recent study conducted in eastern and northern Uganda reveals that the proportion of malnourishment among dropouts is considerably higher among girls than boys (Tumushabe et al., 2000, p. 76).

The fourth issue concerns gender disparity. Thanks to UPE, more girls are now attending classes than before. Female enrollment increased from 39% in 1970 to 47% in 1999, according to MoES figures (Uganda, MoES, 1999, p. 11). Yet, a gender gap clearly remains (Uganda, UBOS, 2001a). Especially for poor families, completion of school by girls still remains a more formidable challenge than for boys. More girls tend to drop out than boys (McGee, 2000c). A recent study confirms that while approximately one-third of male pupils drop out between the first and the third grades, the comparable figure for female pupils is one-half (Tumushabe et al., 2000, p. xix). The statistics also reaffirm that girls find it more difficult to complete primary education, especially at the higher-grade levels.[30]

Gender discrimination is a national tendency, but regional disparity is also significant. The enrollment gap by gender in northern and eastern Uganda, for instance, in Tororo, where economic conditions are harsh, is more acute than in Mukono and Rakai (Uganda, MoES, 2000g). In addition, in Tororo female pupils in grades six and seven drop out more than males, while this tendency is not noticeable in Mukono and Rakai (ibid.). For female students, pregnancy, marriage and family responsibilities are important reasons for dropping out, while male dropouts tend to lose interest in learning (ibid.). The situation needs to be under-

---

[28] Focus group discussion, Bontaba, Mukono, 8 June 2000.

[29] Quite a few schools send children back to their homes for lunch, because schools cannot organize lunch services (interview at Ssese Primary School, Mukono, 14 August 1998).

[30] A possible reason may be that fathers still tend to be the final decision makers on school matters rather than on other matters (Uganda, UBOS, 2002, p. 51).

stood accurately, and more concerted efforts should be made to rectify gender disparities. Sporadic efforts made by local councillors at the grassroots can yield ad hoc results at best and would not represent a sustainable solution. A new National Strategy and Plan of Action for Girl's Education, adopted in 2000, is, therefore, a welcomed step.

3.3 Quality of Education

People at the grassroots level are aware that a variety of factors contributed to the deterioration of educational quality, even if they are generally thankful to the UPE.[31] The participatory exercise conducted in one locality analyzed the problem (participants discussed issues related to education and drew a picture analyzing the causality between different points). Its result unfolds that although poor school quality itself is not a major cause of school absence (Uganda, UBOS, 2002, p. 57), quality improvement at primary schools is much desired (Uganda, MoFPED, 2000g, p. 73).

The first issue is teachers. The increase of pupils has outpaced the increase of newly recruited teachers, even though efforts have been made for additional recruitment. The pupil: teacher ratio set by the MoES at the inception of the UPE was 110:1 for the first three grades (P1 - P3) and 55:1 for grades four through seven (P4 - P7). These ratios were then revised to 80:1 for P1 through P3 while the ratio of 55:1 remains unchanged for P4 - P7. But in reality this can be 100:1 and even 200:1. The situation in Tororo is slightly worse than in Mukono and Rakai (Uganda, MoES, 2000g). Furthermore, in order to cope with the increase in pupils, many of new teachers who were hastily recruited in 1997 and 1998 were not adequately qualified. In 1998, only 45% of teachers were certified to teach (Uganda, MoES, 2000a, p. 2). Currently, with donor support, a project is implemented to improve qualifications of teachers.

A second problem in the quality of education is that school materials and facilities are far from sufficient. The supply of textbooks almost tripled between 1995 and 1999 (Uganda, MoES, 2000f, p. 10). But, the pupil: book ratio is still targeted to reach around 6:1 (Uganda, MoFPED, 1999b, p. 141). Textbooks in Rakai are more available due to donor assistance than in Mukono and Tororo (Uganda, MoES, 2000g). In addition, schools frequently cannot meet the minimum required sanitation standards. Quite a few classes are held literally "under trees." It is estimated that 60 - 70% of pupils attend classes in incomplete or temporary structures (Obwona et al., 2000, p. 304). Unfortunately, this situation will continue despite increased funding by the government and donors. It was estimated that in FY 2002/03 nearly 45% of classes would still lack classrooms (Uganda, MoFPED, 2000f, p. 73; and Uganda, MoES, 2000f, p. 6).

As a result, crowded classrooms with inadequate furniture and a poor state of scholastic materials do not encourage effective learning. As the number of children enrolled at primary schools has increased, more children have actually

---

[31] Focus group discussion, Mukono town, Mukono, 19 August 1999.

dropped out since 1997 than before, especially in the lower grades.[32] A recent comparison of 1996 and 1999 showed that the proportion of successful pupils in some subjects fell significantly (Foster and Mijumbi, 2002, p. 17; and Uganda, MoFPED, 2001, p. 125).[33] As a result, the MoES is now concerned that UPE is not leading to an overall improvement of scholastic achievement.

Some efforts have been made to cope with the increased demand. In many areas, the LC often discusses this issue of the deteriorating quality of education. But given the limitation of additional support by the government, the councillors often explore possibilities of attracting donors, particularly international NGOs. Their efforts, however, face difficulties. Information related to which NGOs are active in supporting local schools is not easily available. This inadequate access to information is an acute problem particularly in rural areas far from Kampala. Fortunate villages, whose councillors may have some knowledge about NGOs and/or connections with them, may succeed in obtaining collaboration with the NGOs.[34]

3.4 Lack of Transparency and Inappropriate Financial Accounting

A study to trace government grants indicates that at various levels there are serious problems of accountability of public funds. A significant portion of the grants are retained by the DEO offices in order to meet their own expenses (Ablo and Reinikka, 1999, p. 14). At schools, record keeping is grossly inadequate. Most head teachers do not have sufficient skills in basic accounting. They do not return the monthly expenditure reports to DEOs, which is a requirement for accountability. The monthly enrollment figures are mostly not sent to DEOs, who then have to rely on old figures to estimate the grants. Procurement practices are subject to over-pricing and the purchase of sub-standard goods (Uganda, MoES, 2000e). SMCs are apparently not functioning efficiently to safeguard the effective utilization of funds.

This poor situation has alarmed the MoES, which has issued a guideline for the use of UPE funds.[35] With this clarification, accusations of embezzlement and misuse of UPE funds by head teachers have considerably decreased. One recent review points out that the situation in 2000 significantly improved compared to previous years (Foster and Mijumbi, 2002, p. 17).

Although the MoES guideline is a major step forward to improve the transparency of fund management, there are still remaining problems. First, understanding

---

[32] The main reason is the educational costs (Uganda, UBOS, 2002).

[33] Appleton (1999) suggests that one reason for deterioration of educational quality is that with the UPE more pupils come from less favorable backgrounds (pp. 20-21).

[34] In addition, the issue of quality of education applies to the post-primary level as well, since it is anticipated that more students will attend secondary schools in the immediate future.

[35] According to the guideline, the use of the conditional UPE grant is to be as follows: 50% for instructional and teaching materials; 35% for co-curricula activities; 15% for school management (including utilities and maintenance); and 5% for administrative costs.

of the UPE guideline is not necessarily high at local levels. Some DEO offices appear not to understand fully the rationale for formulating work plans for UPE grants and SFG. Second, the UPE guidelines are considered to be too rigid by many head teachers, and, thus, they do not consistently follow the guidelines.

But inadequate accountability of funds cannot be explained only by the lack of capacity at the local government level. District officials complain that the central government does not explain fully how financial allocation was made. Many head teachers do not know the criteria used for calculating the grants and rarely receive notices of the funds being received at the districts. This undermines school planning and effective utilization of the funds. For instance, the MoES did not explain why the 9th UPE conditional grant scheduled to be transferred in FY 1999/00 was not in fact released to the districts (Uganda, MoES, 2000e). There is clearly a need for mutual consultation among the MoES, DEO, and head teachers.

3.5 Incentive Mechanisms of Rewards and Sanctions

Grassroots people tend to be sympathetic to teachers who face increased workloads due to UPE. The lack of teacher motivation is apparently felt by local communities. Some examples of low teacher morale include repeated absenteeism, lateness, and other inadequate behavior in the classrooms. Some teachers even drink alcohol on duty or fall asleep, although these are rare examples. Still, some are not enthusiastic in teaching regular courses but diligently prepare supplementary sessions, for which they charge additional fees. These malpractices are caused by the general factor that teachers themselves are poor. Children sometimes say, "Teachers do not teach since they are hungry too" (Uganda, MoFPED, 2000g, p. 74). It is clear that lack of teacher motivation is a serious concern since an inadequate ability of teachers is generally associated with a high repetition rate of pupils (McGee, 2000c, p. 101).

A fundamental problem is the issue of incentives, which has not been addressed by decentralized education services. Organizational restructuring has to go hand in hand with improving the overall framework of incentives for personnel in order to have a broad and sustainable impact. Unless teachers believe in their job, individual abilities are not translated into organizational improvement (Teskey and Hooper, 1999, p. 8). Pay needs to be adequate and prompt.[36] Good performance should be rewarded, while poor ones sanctioned. It is critical to pay more attention to how teachers can be motivated for better performance and what particular criteria and methods should, and can, be used for such performance assessment. As the following statement by the MoES illustrates, most teachers do not appreciate the supervision by head teachers:

---

[36] Teskey and Hooper (1999) further point out that a main incentive mechanism within the ESIP is per diems and travel allowances. While it is desirable for Kampala-based staff to contact local governments and schools, this is pervasive because civil servants can double their income by being absent from their desks for three days (p. 11).

What gripes me about this so-called supervision is that the head teacher only comes into my classroom once a year for an hour. It is a scary, unpleasant experience. I wouldn't mind if I was being supervised by someone who has been a success in the classroom; but it is usually someone who was a poor teacher who has been pushed into an administrative position; and to top it off, that person usually has had no training whatsoever in how to supervise (Uganda, MoES, TDMP Draft, undated, p. 16).

Because many teachers dislike this kind of supervision, most, if not all, schools abandon such supervision entirely. As a result, interaction between teachers and head teachers is at a minimum. But, as the quotation illustrates, teachers are not against supervision itself. Instead, they do not favor the way in which it is carried out currently. Participatory action research conducted in three rural primary schools in 1998 found that in one school where the concerns of teachers were taken into account by informal mutual learning, improvements in teaching methods were realized (Uganda, MoES, 1999). If supervision responds to teacher concerns and aspirations, teachers would welcome such supervision. Unfortunately, the present supervision, however, does not foster effective career development of teachers.

Compounding the problem is the fact that opportunities for promotion at primary schools are limited. A limited number of teachers can be promoted to become either head teachers or deputy head teachers. Thus, there is in reality virtually no opportunity for teachers to develop their careers beyond ordinary classroom teachers. This limited possibility of promotion discourages teachers to attend seminars and training workshops and make extra efforts to apply what they learn through these training opportunities.[37]

The most fundamental problem is that the current system does not encourage good teachers and punish bad ones. Again it is admitted by the MoES, "it is observed that although recognition is a strong and effective incentive, in the current system, good/exceptional performers hardly get recognized. On the contrary, it is the most vigilant and in some cases *non-performers* that catch the eyes of decision-makers" (emphasis in original, Uganda, MoES, TDMP Draft, undated, p. 21). The provisions for sanctioning non-performers are clearly provided within the regulatory framework, but they are rarely exercised. There appear to be a number of reasons for this, but fundamentally there is no guarantee that sanctioning non-performers will result in replacement by better teachers.

In order to mitigate this situation, the financial incentive is perhaps most effective. The central government has increased teacher salaries in recent years. The level of salaries was more than tripled between 1991 and 1995. Decentralization measures have also speeded up the release of salary payment to teachers.[38] These

---

[37] Another discouraging factor for teachers is a big wage gap between them and head teachers, even if their duties are not tremendously different. For instance, at grade three schools, teachers earn about Ush 83,000 (US$ 55) per month while a head teacher can earn about Ush 213,000 (US$ 142) (Uganda, MoES, TDMP Draft, undated, p. 20; and Uganda, MoES, 2000b, p. 51).

[38] One interesting development is that Rakai District has been piloting the decentralized payroll and has tremendously reduced the bureaucratic time and procedure required to

developments are really welcomed by teachers.[39] However, even the increased salary could not keep pace with the rising costs of living. The salary increase started at a very low level, and as of 1995 it did not reach the "living wage" (Ablo and Reinikka, 1999, p. 17). It is anticipated that teacher wages continue to grow from Ush 100 billion (US$ 70 million) in FY 1998/99 to Ush 175 billion (US$ 115 million) in FY 2002/03 (Uganda, MoFPED, 2000f, p. 72). In FY 2001/02 a new allowance for hardship areas was budgeted. These schemes will certainly mean a net increase in total funds for teacher salaries, but will be shared by an increased number of teachers. The increased total for teacher pay, therefore, will not resolve the remuneration issue entirely.

Given the financial constraints of both the central and local governments, a massive increase in the teachers' pay scale is not realistic.[40] Other possible incentive schemes include housing and transport allowances, provision of other fringe benefits, additional teaching guides and textbooks, and opportunities for long- and short-term training (including study tours). Accommodation particularly appears to be effective incentive in remote rural areas. It is a welcome sign that 15% of the School Facility Grant (SFG) can be used for construction of teachers' houses from FY 2001/02.[41] Exchanges and secondment of teachers between different schools is also a possibility which deserves investigation (secondment refers to the release of teachers from regularly assigned positions for temporary duties with other organizations).

In order to respond to the need for incentives and improved accountability, the central government introduced new School Performance Awards in the 2000 school year at the sub-county level. Although details of these new awards are not known, "attention will be paid to accounting and record keeping, promotion of girl's education, and promotion of education for special needs children" (Uganda, MoFPED, 2000f, p. 75). These awards are obviously a desirable step forward, and their effects should be evaluated carefully.

3.6 Financial Trends

There are three issues related to financial considerations. First, the financial allocation by districts to their education sector is a priority, which is clearly attested to by the expenditure pattern of the three districts. In all three districts analyzed by this study, educational expenditures (in nominal terms) increased from FY

---

process local payment. This pioneering experience appears to be very encouraging and may be adopted on a nation-wide level later on.

[39] Interviews at Ssese Primary School, Mukono, 14 August 1998 and Kidoko Primary School, Tororo, 1 June 2000.

[40] Parents in the past supplemented teacher salaries. In the early 1990s, approximately 30% of their salaries came from parent contributions (Ablo and Reinikka, 1999, p. 16). However, due to competing requests for community contributions, recently it is becoming more difficult for parents to keep providing the salary "top ups" for teachers.

[41] Personal interview, Joseph Eilor, Principal Education Planner, MoES, 31 July 2002.

1993/94 to FY 2000/01, although the level of increase is varied from one district to another. Real growth, adjusting for inflation, shows a consistent increase. The only exception is FY 1999/00 in Mukono. The share of education of total district expenditure reveals interesting differences in the various districts (Figure 7.1). In Mukono, it rose from a very low level of approximately 5% in FY 1993/94 and FY 1994/95 to a peak of 66% in FY 1996/97, and then declined to the 50% range in subsequent years. In Tororo, it increased from 4% in FY 1995/96 to nearly 70% in FY 1999/00. In Rakai, it started from a comparatively high level of 43% in FY 1994/95 and increased slightly until FY 1998/99 and remained around that proportion from FY 1999/00 to FY 2000/01. The differences in the three districts appear to indicate that although education is heavily funded by central government transfers, some local resources are also utilized for education.[42] One possible reason why the Rakai figures vary from the other two districts is due to assistance by the Danish International Development Assistance (DANIDA) which placed some emphasis on rehabilitating educational facilities. A decline in the percentage of educational expenditure around 1996 may be related to the financial limits that local authorities faced in generating local revenues for discretionary activities. In any case, education is very different from, for instance, the health sector, which showed a clear decline in its financial allocation by all three districts (which will be analyzed in the next chapter).

A second financial issue is the relation between decentralized services and equity. Critics often argue that decentralized services widen the gap in services between rich and poor areas. A comparison of expenditures on education in the three districts does not support this criticism. The allocation pattern for the education sector is fairly stabilized as seen in Figure 7.1. Although total spending by each district was led by Mukono, followed by Tororo, and then Rakai, the per capita expenses in FY 1999/00 were are approximately Ush 5,500 (US$ 3.6) in Mukono, Ush 8,500 (US$ 5.6) in Tororo, and Ush 6,700 (US$ 4.5) in Rakai.[43] The wealthiest district, Mukono, did not rank first. The primary reason why Tororo ranked first is the grants allocated by the central government. This rough estimate suggests that as long as the central government grants provides the resources needed by the local governments, the equity concern between the rich and poor areas does not constitute a major problem.

Third, although the bulk of funds for education are provided by the central government, the majority of the funds are in the form of conditional grants, which must be used for purposes earmarked by the MoES. Teacher salaries and classroom construction are both funded by conditional grants. Unconditional grants are mostly used for salaries of local personnel working at district offices. In Mukono District, for instance, in FY 2000/01 an estimated 68% of education expenses were for wages and 32% was for non-wage items (Mukono District Council, Uganda,

---

[42] The locally generated resources are used for purchasing bricks and iron sheets (interview, Ssese Primary School, Mukono, 14 August 1998).

[43] Since the data on the total pupils who should be enrolled at schools are not available, the comparison was made on a per capita basis. In addition, since education is very "labor intensive," these per capita figures include wages.

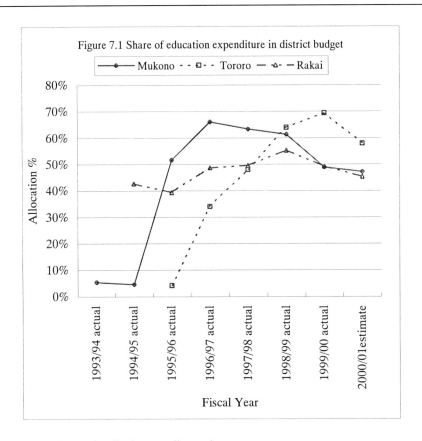

Figure 7.1 Share of education expenditure in district budget

Source: Respective district council records.

2000b).[44] Local governments are not left with significant discretionary funds which can be used for education.

This conditionality is partly created by donors, since they are the major resource providers. The donors are aware that districts and schools often complain that the UPE guideline is too rigid. Donors, nonetheless, appear to generally support the principle that the UPE funds should be released as conditional grants given the weakness in accountability for the funds, although they do not necessarily agree entirely with the details of the conditions. The MoES appears to agree with donors in its overall assessment, that at least at this moment the capacity of the DEOs and schools cannot be fully trusted:

> In view of the independent reports of misappropriation, mismanagement, [and] diversion of funds disbursed by the center to the districts, the center should maintain a system of

---

[44] At the time of this writing, only estimated figures available in contrast to the actual ones.

conditional grants with clear guidelines on the utilisation of such funds, as well as sanctions on the defaulting districts, schools and individual officers (Uganda, MoES, 2000b, p. 49).

4 Major Challenges in Decentralized Primary Education

4.1 How does Decentralization Fit with the Education Sector Investment Plan and UPE?

The current education sector displays a mixed situation: there have been some achievements but other remaining issues need urgent attention. At this juncture, more strategic thinking is much needed to clarify overall policy. In order to secure the achievements made so far, a more coherent strategic vision is need to allocate what functions (enrollment choice by students, teacher qualifications, academic freedom, curriculum and instruction, assessment of learning, facilities, and funding) can best be performed by what levels (MoES, districts, sub-county, schools, and communities). The UPE policy was initially launched by the president as an election promise and was essentially a political initiative. On the one hand, this initiative can give essential political support needed to implement such a demanding policy of decentralizing education services. On the other hand, the policy has to be supported by administrators, teachers, and the people in general. Therefore, a wide range of consultation with different stakeholders is desirable to sustain educational reform. The consultation process inevitably raises a very delicate question of national cohesion and equity, on the one hand, and local diversity and flexibility, on the other. It would be desirable if all essential stakeholders could discuss these issues and come to a shared vision. This consensus may be more effective if it is written in a formal document, which could serve not only as a standard for judgment, should there be any disputes, but also as a source of information for stakeholders. This consensus has to be disseminated widely among stakeholders, particularly at local levels.

Policies of the central government should match the aspirations and concerns of the local governments, schools and people as much as possible. The local stakeholders' understanding of policies and procedures is, however, far behind those at the central level. Local voices are not fully heard at the central level. As a result, the MoES may have its own agenda, although it means well. For example, the MoES is sometimes criticized for organizing "too many uncoordinated workshops for the district officials" (Uganda, MoES, 2000b, p. 50). Unless local voices are reflected, the people do not feel much relevance to government activities. The perceived irrelevance does not encourage people to be more involved in efforts to sustain educational facilities and results.

Even the often-praised ESIP is not well understood locally. While the MoES sees it as an overall policy framework, some local government leaders treat this as just another (big) project. The ESIP is seen as a national initiative led by the central government. The fundamental problem is that there has not been sufficient consultation carried out with local stakeholders on the ESIP in its approach and local implications. As a consequence, the precise roles of local governments, schools, parents, and communities are not well defined, let alone fulfilled.

Basically, both decentralization and ESIP are generally welcomed. But these two policies are not without contradictions. As in other sectors, the idea of the sector-wide approach (SWAP) is largely welcomed both by the central government and donors. The SWAP has enhanced coordination between the central government and donors as well as among various donors themselves.[45] But it may contradict the spirit of decentralizing service provisions. The SWAP can lead to a situation where major policies and financial allocations are decided by the center with little consultation with local stakeholders. This means that local governments, schools, and parents serve as implementers of centrally decided activities. This kind of treatment can frustrate local political leaders, planners, and service providers.

Therefore, the MoES needs to clarify its strategy on how to implement the ESIP with decentralizing services. The MoES has lately proposed a study to enhance capacity in districts, and Ush 50 million was budgeted out of the PAF in FY 2001/02.[46] These are good signs. But the MoES must present a much clearer vision of the core functions of the MoES, and the essential responsibilities of districts as well as schools. Otherwise, at local levels, the ESIP will continue to be just another donor project.

Strategic thinking is also needed to determine a suitable public-private mix in education services in Uganda. At the moment there are no government grants to assist private schools. As the MoES is aware, "Many private schools and colleges have been left to struggle on their own without assistance from the government" (Uganda, MoES, 2000b, p. 51). Thus, it may worth assisting private schools in order to seek more collaboration between public and private institutions. This is a delicate issue, and care should be taken. An appropriate public-private mix should be sought, taking into account equity in access to education, quality of education, cost-effectiveness of expanding service coverage, capacity building for managing service delivery, and increasing incentives for service providers.

Another important issue, which has not fully thought out, is equity. With decentralized services, wealthier areas can devote more resources to develop education while poorer areas cannot. This is not a crucial issue now but may become so in the years to come. In fact, this anxiety is shared by various stakeholders, including many people at the grassroots level. Yet the MoES does not include equity as an explicit goal of decentralizing education services, even though UPE and the slogan "Education for All" imply equitable access to education for every pupil. This issue poses a serious challenge for Uganda, especially because the northern area faces more profound difficulties than the southern part of the country. Even if there are special educational projects implemented in the north, it is far from

---

[45] In fact, Uganda's ESIP is cited as an impressive example in the review of SWAP practices (Brown et al., 2001; and Kuteesa, 1999).

[46] Personal interview, Joseph Eilor, Principal Education Planner, MoES, 31 July 2002.

certain whether the issue of equity in different localities can be solved by individual projects. It would be preferable if the equity issue were clearly presented within the overall policy framework itself, and action then taken subsequently. Unfortunately, the current policy remains silent on this issue.[47]

4.2 More Community Involvement

In Uganda, education is much valued and considered a priority for poverty reduction. It is well known that schools were maintained thanks largely to the significant contributions of PTAs even during the 1970s and the 1980s when Uganda suffered from serious social turmoil (Passi, 1995). This community involvement has contributed to a relatively transparent institutional environment in which public services are provided. This transparency is notable compared with health care services (Ablo and Reinikka, 1999; and Okuonzi and Birungi, 2000).

Unfortunately, when UPE was announced, ordinary people thought that the government would now provide free education and people would have no (financial) role to play. This interpretation was very unfortunate, and discouraged people from being continuously involved in educational issues. Nonetheless, where communities have remained involved, or became re-involved, the likelihood of ensuring transparency and accountability is higher than in those without any community participation. Where community participation is relatively high, decentralization is often appreciated.[48] Community involvement is also needed to make School Management Committees (SMCs) a success. The current form of SMC under the overall framework of the LC system is still new, and the roles and responsibilities of the committees are not fully understood by the committee members or by communities. Given the history of community involvement, there is a good chance that the SMCs can be useful.

On the other hand, in order to improve education even further in the future, there are some obstacles which need to be overcome. One is the tension arising from increased community involvement in planning and implementation of activities. Decentralizing education so far has focused more on improvement of school facilities, especially construction of classrooms. Once this kind of local need is met, it is likely that with decentralizing service provisions local people may demand more flexibility in the educational system and more discretion to modify curriculum and possibly even to select the language of instruction. At the moment, this kind of modification is not allowed by the MoES or DEO. But communities may demand more autonomy, beyond which point the central government and regulatory authorities are ready to accept. Then stakeholders involved in de-

---

[47] In some relatively rich areas, a modest amount of locally generated revenues are used for education unlike in poor areas. Additionally, in the more affluent areas, the private sector has started to construct some schools. The private investments take place in urban areas and places along the main road networks. The poor regions do not benefit from local contributions or private investment.

[48] Interview, Kidono Primary School, Tororo, 1 June 2000.

centralized educational services will face a difficulty in balancing national standards and local autonomy.

Another critical problem may be the potential breakdown of communities themselves. As decentralization and privatization of the economy provide more freedom for people, parents, especially the wealthy ones near urban centers, will not necessarily send their children to nearby local schools which the LC system wishes to improve and maintain. While in the health sector, some people who used to seek services at private facilities are now coming to public health facilities, in the education sector, the trend appears to be the reverse. In order to prevent further degradation of education quality in public schools, optimal public-private collaboration merits more serious consideration. Furthermore, as social openness may damage the cohesiveness of local communities, what kinds of remedies are possible? What implications does this lost cohesion have for such important services as education? What role would each stakeholder play in resolving these issues? The MoES, among other stakeholders, does not appear to be ready to face these tough questions, which may surface in the not very distant future. This is why in the future, much clearer vision and rules will be necessary, articulating what kind of autonomy is given to what level of institution, as well as how the integrity of the educational system is to be maintained and enforced.

4.3 Enhancing Incentives for Teachers

One critical area that urgently needs action is incentives for teachers. Since there are limited means to resolve this issue, closer cooperation among schools, communities and the private sector may present a possibility. Community participation may play a role in improving teacher incentives. One good incentive for teachers is a housing provision. In various areas, often with NGO assistance, community members build teacher accommodations.[49] Given the constraints on available incentive options, this seems to be one promising approach.

If community members recognize the value of education and are willing to devote their time and effort, it is likely that they would also be interested in teacher performance. Then good performers would more likely be recognized socially in the community. Therefore, a recent decision by the MoES requiring that from FY 2001/2002 districts earmark up to 15% of the School Facilities Grant (SFG) for teachers accommodation (Uganda, MoES, 2000f, p. 6) is a step forward, and may present a good opportunity for mutual collaboration among DEOs, schools, NGOs, and local people. Such a collaborative approach is indeed more necessary in difficult areas in the eastern and northern parts of the country than in the central areas.

In addition, effective training for teachers can serve as a good incentive. Head teachers require various kinds of administrative and supervisory skills. Classroom

---

[49] For instance, in Mukono, the Food for the Hungry International (FHI) have been organizing such assistance through community participation (interview, Miyuki Numata, Director, FHI, 8 June 2000).

teachers need more innovative and effective teaching methods and practices. Here, again, collaboration between the government, particularly DEOs, and NGOs are crucial. It is reported that ACTIONAID provided in-service training for under-qualified primary school teachers in Mubende District through distance education. This assistance was evaluated favorably by the MoES and planned to be expanded to the northern region in Uganda (Gaynor, 1998, pp. 23-24). This project appears to be a pioneering effort in how NGOs can play a role in providing much-needed in-service training suited to locally specific conditions. Another example of innovative NGO assistance is the operation of the Concern Worldwide, which started to provide discretionary funds to selected sub-counties in Rakai. Their use will be determined by consultation between the councillors and the representatives of the NGO. Although in the next few years the fund will likely be spent on improvement of physical infrastructure, this resource may be used for training activities once infrastructure needs are met.

Collaboration with private service providers can be used as an incentive as well. Some community schools have been taken over by the government. Yet this seems to be the only collaboration between public and non-public sectors at the primary education level. Enhanced collaboration between the government and private service providers should be encouraged. Currently the offices of DEO in each district are unable to establish effective collaborations between public and private schools. This is largely because their capacity is stretched thin. If DEOs are unable to provide adequate support to public schools, they cannot start establishing relations with private schools. It would be valuable if the DEOs can establish a regular forum for both public and private schools in which relevant issues of in-service training as well as supervision and support by head teachers to other teaching staff are discussed. The opportunities to exchange practical experiences may be useful to improve teaching practices.

This forum would also be useful for arranging exchange programs between different schools, which might contribute to enhanced incentives as well. For a group of students from one school to visit other schools would be an interesting learning experience, not only for students but also for teachers. This kind of exchange can be a relatively inexpensive incentive for teachers. Such school visits can be arranged in collaboration with the Uganda Local Authorities Association (ULAA), even though the ULAA has not been significantly involved in sector-specific exchange programs. Through the process of exchanging practical experiences, secondment of teachers to different schools may become a useful practice.[50]

These incentive schemes should be combined in order to implement accountability in which "carrots" and "sticks" are applied consistently. Rewards may include a wider variety of programs: in-service training, special study leave, hard-

---

[50] Secondment of government-recruited teachers to private schools was practiced from around 1996 to 1999, but then stopped. A main reason for the suspension was that the "brain drain" of teachers from pubic to private schools due to wage differences. Faced with this problem, MoES was unsure on how to establish meaningful collaboration with private schools. Although this danger is still relevant today, it is worthwhile reconsidering this option strategically.

ship allowances, housing subsidies, better promotional prospects, and improved facilities at schools. But unless rewards are granted to those who provide better teaching, they would not function as incentives. Thus, sanctions for non-performers should be implemented simultaneously.[51] For this to take place, certain types of enforcement based on clear standards are necessary. Supervision would be more relevant and effective if it is performed not in a formal and bureaucratic way but in informal appraisal processes through, for instance, peer evaluation, self-evaluation, group reviews of performances, and regular informal discussions with supervisors (Gaynor, 1998, p. 30).

4.4 Information and Monitoring

Close collaboration among various stakeholders can be possible only when more essential information is widely shared among them (Reinikka and Svensson, 2001).[52] Not only the various levels of government, but communities, NGOs, and the private sector should be involved in this information sharing. Lack of effective communication among stakeholders tends to invite mutual suspicion and lack of cooperation.

The need for information sharing points to a broader issue of educational information management and stakeholder roles in it. The government is aware of the problem and is making some efforts in this direction. The MoES is now installing a new Education Management Information System (EMIS). Although the EMIS itself is welcomed, a more fundamental solution should be found by looking at communication requirements more broadly rather than just trying to find a narrow technical solution by the EMIS. What would be a more systematic (rather than ad hoc) consultation mechanism for essential stakeholders to be involved both at the central and local levels? How does information assist various stakeholders to fulfill their roles and responsibilities? What role can be played by the people at the grassroots level on this issue?

Information requirements are clearly related to the issues of monitoring, support, and supervision. With decentralized service provisions, one nationally determined standard for monitoring and evaluation may not be suitable. As an increasing number of schools and communities demand more flexibility and freedom in teaching, the issue of flexibility in pedagogical standard-setting will perhaps become a critical issue. On the other hand, there is a definite necessity to ensure that flexibility will not be abused. If incompetent administrators and teachers can achieve positive evaluation results by corruption, the system of monitoring and evaluation itself is in danger. Thus, there is a delicate balance between

---

[51] Even though underpaid teachers are understandably not very motivated, prolonged absence of teachers from classrooms without acceptable reasons, for instance, cannot be tolerated (Gaynor, 1998, p. 17).

[52] Reinikka and Svennson (2001) note that often quantitative information is helpful to improve results because officials cannot dismiss comparable data as unimportant anecdotal evidence (p. 2).

accuracy and flexibility in performance assessment (Florestal and Cooper, 1997, p. 25).

The current state of poor accountability at schools is at least partly attributed to poor supervision and support, particularly by DEOs. Therefore, monitoring capacities need to be engendered at various levels of the government. Cost-effectiveness needs to be kept in mind since, at least from the perspective of school teachers, the current accountability process is very expensive (Uganda, MoES, 2000e). This perception is based on reality in a situation where an increased workload due to decentralized education services is not awarded by corresponding allowances and/or recognition of teaching service. It would be useful to engage in consultative dialogues among the MoES, DEOs, and head teachers on defining appropriate cost-effective approaches to provide sufficient accountability without overwhelmingly increasing the burdens of teachers.

The central government has started to allocate funds for districts to improve monitoring of decentralized services. Using PAF funds, a new conditional grant of District Monitoring and Accountability Grant was allocated in FY 2000/01 for the use of districts. The amount was estimated to be Ush 0.8 billion (about US$ 533, 000) in the first year and thereafter Ush 2 billion (US$ 1.3 million) per year (Uganda, MoFPED, 2000f, p. 75). A separate fund will also be made available out of PAF for ministries, the Auditor General and the Inspector General of Government (ibid., pp. 152-153). This budgetary provision is welcomed.

But funds do not automatically guarantee that the required skills of DEOs, head teachers, and SMC members will be improved. The funds should not be used to deliver a "top-down" judgment to accuse those who fail to meet standards. Instead, they should be spent to support essential stakeholders who desperately need more capacity building. Such support needs to be provided in a more transparent way with much more information shared among stakeholders. Otherwise, providing top-down supervision does not lead to more effective institution development which can respond to the aspirations of people in local communities.

The people are the ultimate evaluators of policy outcomes in democratic societies. Even though democracy in Uganda is far from mature, the role of the people in monitoring and supervision needs to be defined. The LC system is a mechanism to link people with various levels of the government. But for the LC system to be effective, more coherent provisions need to be implemented both at the central and local levels simultaneously, and more information should be shared and generated by people themselves. As reported in the experience of Brazil, when the public acts as an outside monitor, decentralization measures have a greater chance of success (Tendler, 1997, p. 140). Thus, using the LC system for building an effective public monitoring mechanism is at least one promising approach to enhance monitoring capacities with the involvement of grassroots people.

5 Conclusion

Education is now becoming a victim of its own successful UPE. Because the government has been keen on decentralized educational services, there have been various developments gradually evolving throughout this process. On the one hand, UPE has enabled poor families to send their children to school, which otherwise would not be possible. Communities are willing to support education, including classroom construction. The large number of primary school classrooms built by community support is surely a commendable achievement that is appreciated by diverse stakeholders. In this process, costs are shared by service providers and recipients, who started to form a kind of partnership to reduce total expenses. Both the processes and outputs contribute to empowerment of local communities. Thus, the MoES recently reaffirmed that decentralized and community-based school construction activities will continue (Uganda, MoES, 2000f, p. 4). With the current efforts to recruit required personnel for teaching and administration, the public sector will be more likely to respond to the increasing demands in the near future. The private sector has also started building private community schools.

On the other hand, there are critical issues in the area of education, which need to be urgently resolved. Appreciation of decentralized education varies according to stakeholders. The LC system, particularly LC 1, often discusses educational issues, but locally available means are limited, and solutions tend to be provided from the central government. The nationally determined standards do not leave much local autonomy, which is not satisfactory for local political leaders. School facilities are standardized, and the curriculum is nationally decided. Thus, tailor-made local solutions are not provided. With deteriorated education conditions, rich families send their children to schools outside of villages. Communities are also losing cohesiveness, ironically, because of UPE. The issue of incentives for teachers remains largely ignored. As a result, it appears that responsiveness, one of the main objectives of decentralization, has improved only slightly.

But since sporadic progress is being made in various areas, if more strategic thinking can guide these elements of progress more coherently, the decentralization experiment in primary education can be successful. Decentralized education services call for a delicate balance of different aspects to be cohesive. Experience in Uganda suggests that although decentralizing such an essential public service as education is far from free of obstacles, it does present the potential for improving public services and poverty reduction. The situation of education can be better understood if the experience of the health sector is considered as a contrasting example, which is the topic of the next chapter.

8 Decentralization and Health Services: Challenge for Public Confidence[1]

Our government dispensary does not have most of the popularly needed drugs. But they still charge us the consultation fee of Shs 500. Thus, most of the people prefer to go to private clinics, although their charges are more expensive. Even if people go to the government medical unit, they often go to other clinics to get drugs.

A woman made a statement during a focus group discussion,
Mukono, 19 August 1999

Just like education, health is also important for mitigating poverty in Uganda. Health can be broadly defined as a state of physical, mental and social well-being and not merely the absence of disease. The poor certainly acknowledge that poor health is one of the major causes and consequences of poverty. Thus, maintaining good health is one of the essential conditions for people to use their abilities fully.

Yet there are important differences between the education and health sectors. Health services were in the past provided by the public sector, but were abandoned during the civil strife in the 1970s and 1980s. In response, people largely turned to individual and family-level coping measures. As a result, Uganda's recent health indicators are not impressive even compared with those of other African countries. In spite of the measures to improve health services taken by the NRM in collaboration with donors, establishing affordable health care for all Ugandans in the near future is a difficult task.

Decentralizing health services is one essential measure to reverse this undesirable situation. Similar to education, health service decentralization was originally intended to improve the cost-effectiveness of public services by bringing them closer to the people. Significant powers and functions have been devolved from the central to local governments. With the LC system, both district (LC 5) and sub-county (LC 3) offices have respective committees in charge of health matters. The elected councillors meet with technical staff to discuss, plan, and carry out activities. The local civil servants must answer to the councillors, who in turn are held accountable by their constituencies.

---

[1] A preliminary version of this chapter appeared in *Uganda Health Bulletin*, Vol. 7, No. 1, 2001.

The Ministry of Health (MoH) launched in 1998 an innovative policy of Health Sub-District (HSD), in which both curative as well as preventive health services are provided in an integrated manner from the nearest service delivery points to the population. The HSD is a decentralized service delivery strategy and forms one of the essential pillars of recent National Health Policy (Uganda, MoH, 1999) and the Health Sector Strategic Plan (HSSP) (Uganda, MoH, 2000). Just like education, the new National Health Policy adopts a sector-wide approach (SWAP), which is largely welcomed by the donors. Following the example of educational SWAP, regular review mechanisms have recently been put in place in such forms as Joint Review Missions, Health Policy Advisory Committee, and Health Development Partners Forum (Uganda, MoH, 2001).

Nonetheless, the current state of decentralized health services demonstrates impressive achievements as well as remaining challenges. On the positive side, the restructuring of the MoH has helped to create a more conducive institution for supporting the local authorities in health services. Interactions between the LC system and local populations have resulted in noticeable improvements of home hygiene and sanitation, as noted in Chapter 4. With increasing interaction between the service providers and recipients, people have started to appreciate gradually the value of health services, as an increasing number of people seek treatment at public clinics, although the magnitude of increase varies from one area to another.

In addition, the health service has been improving its responsiveness to the needs of local people. The increased responsiveness basically derives from collaboration between the providers, while in the case of education it mainly comes from the collaboration of grassroots recipients. In this process, the LC system has not yet worked as effectively as in the case of education. Because there is widespread public mistrust of health workers at rural clinics, people at the grassroots are not so willing to collaborate. Instead, meaningful collaboration has started to develop among public and private service providers. This kind of public-private partnership is more effective in the case of health than in education. In short, education is a "demand-driven" example of successful utilization of the LC system while health is "supply driven."

On the other hand, the remaining challenges for better health services are daunting. First, service providers in rural clinics face severe disincentives for better performance. The accumulated salary arrears are substantial. The payments do not provide an adequate living wage. This underpayment induces illicit activities (i.e. requests for bribes and illegal sales of public medicines for private benefit), which are certainly perceived negatively by service recipients. As a result, rural people are not persuaded by the LC attempts to mobilized local communities for the purpose of improving health services, although such improvement is desirable if accomplished. This public mistrust in health services calls for more fundamental reform, some of which needs to be taken at the national level. The central government is urged to take necessary measures to improve incentives for service providers who would become more motivated to provide improved services. It is, thus, argued that the likelihood of decentralized health services bearing effective results increases if reform measures are pursued both at the national and local levels simultaneously as well as coherently. Other recommended measures include improved funding arrangements, wider information availability, and participation of the people in monitoring policy results.

1 Background of Health Sector

Maintaining good health is a prerequisite for overcoming poverty. It is indispensable not only for earning income but also for maintaining self-confidence. Thus, preventive as well as curative aspects of health care are closely related to the general welfare of the poor in developing countries. In the developing world, non-medical elements such as nutrition, safe drinking water, family planning, and the general level of education strongly affects the health status of people. In Uganda, community-based preventive activities are often advocated by the government, but rural people have not fully understood the notion of preventive services. Since preventive and curative services started to be provided recently in an integrated way, people's access to health facilities has increased. Even though the quality and quantity of health services are far from ideal, the prospect for improved accessibility is welcomed by the people in rural areas.

In Uganda, access to health facilities has certainly been limited. Only approximately 49% of the population live within five kilometers of health facilities (Uganda, MoH, 1999, p. 3). The government and private sectors - mission facilities, non-governmental organizations (NGOs), traditional healers and practitioners - provide health services roughly equally.[2] The government is strong in immunization, modern delivery, and reproductive health care including HIV/AIDS, while private providers account for the majority of curative care (Hutchinson, 1999, p. 17). But approximately half of Ugandans do not seek medical treatment when they fall sick (de Torrenté and Mwesigye, 1999, p. 25). It is estimated that the poor spend from one-quarter to one-half of what non-poor spend on health care (Hutchinson, 1999, p. 20). The deteriorated health service is a result of long lasting civil strife and the virtual collapse of public services. Unlike the case of education, community involvement to support health services in the difficult period was very limited, if at all.

Health service decentralization is a strategy taken by the NRM to reverse this situation (Okuonzi and Lubanga, 1997). Since the first 13 districts were decentralized in 1993, the MoH has been involved in the process. Thus, the MoH states that "decentralization has been warmly embraced and has contributed to improvements in service delivery through increased community participation and better supervision" (Uganda, MoH, 2000, p. 13). This statement symbolizes the view of service providers in the decentralizing process. They are pleased with decentralization, which has brought more effective control over limited resources.

---

[2] Similar to other African countries, there are three categories of private service providers: private non-profit; private for profit; and traditional medical practicners.

In order to put service decentralization fully in practice, the MoH carried out an organizational restructuring. The newly redefined roles for the MoH vis-à-vis districts include the following:

a) policy formulation, setting standards, and quality assurance;
b) resource mobilization;
c) capacity development and technical support;
d) provision of nationally coordinated services, e.g. epidemic control;
e) co-ordination of health research; and
f) monitoring and evaluation of the overall sector performance.

The MoH now considers that this reorganization enhances its responsiveness to local governments.

In contrast, the responsibilities of the district governments, especially the offices of District Director of Health Services (DDHS), include:

a) implementation of National Health Policy;
b) planning and management of district health services;
c) provision of disease prevention, health promotion, curative, and rehabilitative services, with the emphasis on the Minimum Health Care Package, and other national priorities;
d) control of other communicable diseases of public health important to districts;
e) vector control;
f) health education;
g) ensuring provision of safe water and environmental sanitation; and
h) health data collection, management, interpretation, dissemination, and utilization (Uganda, MoH, 1999, p. 16).

The districts are now "responsible for implementation of a package of health services to the population of Uganda under an autonomous decentralized system" (Uganda, MoH, 2001, p. 10). The offices of DDHS generally welcome the decentralization policy as it improves the planning and management of limited resources for running health facilities. They also appreciate that interactions with service recipients are now better facilitated in collaboration with the LC system and other stakeholders like mission hospitals and NGO health facilities.[3]

At the local level, an institutional pillar for health service delivery in this decentralized policy context is the Health Sub-District (HSD), first proposed in 1998. Each county (LC 4, equivalent to MP constituency) is supposed to have a hospital or an upgraded health center from where both curative and preventive health services are provided for a population of approximately 100,000 in collaboration with lower-level health facilities. The HSD is a relatively well-equipped

---

3 Personal interview, Ellys Tumushabe, DDHS, Mukono, 25 May 2000; Walimbwa, Acting DDHS, Tororo, 29 May 2000; and Robert Mayanja, Deputy DDHS, Rakai, 6 July 2000.

facility to promote decentralization of health services even further.[4] The MoH until recently controlled the curative services of district hospitals directly under its supervision, while preventive services devolved to the DDHS. Now the MoH has put the district hospitals also under the supervision of the DDHS, and hospitals are in turn to supervise and support the lower level medical units.

This HSD policy is significant in at least three aspects. First, the integration of curative and preventive services, including primary health care (PHC), is sought at the level of actual local service delivery. Second, with the HSD, some functions and responsibilities are transferred away from the DDHS to lower levels where hospitals are actually located. Third, the HSD can be publicly or privately managed. While in the past the public medical units and private clinics were operated more or less as parallel systems, this new policy attempts to enhance collaboration of public and private medical service providers (Uganda, MoH, 1998).

Following the earlier experiences of decentralizing health services, and also reflecting the desire on the part of the central government for more consistent collaboration with donors, the MoH has recently updated its health policy. In 1998, the Minimum Health Care Package was proposed. In 2000, the National Health Policy as well as the Health Sector Strategic Plan (HSSP) were adopted. Like the example of education, this series of initiatives is a sector-wide approach, in which a medium-term framework is negotiated with donors, and the normal government institutions are used for donor-funded projects instead of creating separate management for each project. Donors generally welcome this evolution of policy planning, because this process has contributed to a much more articulated strategic vision and has produced a more reliable estimate of financial resources necessary to provide essential health services for Ugandans. Unlike the education sector, the HSSP is new, and its annual review mechanism for monitoring progress has been put in place only recently.

2 Limited Local Participation in Health

The collaborative pattern among stakeholders in health services is not as evident as in the example of education. Similar to the case of education, the LC system interfaces with the local population in the health sector. This interaction has improved the sanitation and hygiene standards of homes in many rural areas in Uganda, as discussed in Chapter 4. Immunization campaigns work well in collaboration with the LC system, which mobilizes mothers and children for vaccinations. In the case of Polio, the area which achieves the highest immunization rate during each campaign period receives much publicity in the news media, and the councillors are eager to call for local collaboration for such achievements.

On the other hand, community involvement in health matters has been limited in the past. The services used to be provided freely in the past, when such services were available in the 1960s. This past experience still creates a nostalgic feeling

---

[4] It should have an operating theater, admission ward and minimum of 30 beds.

among the people, especially among the elderly.[5] There has, thus, been little pre-vious experience among grassroots people to be involved in supporting rural health units. Health does not attract much attention by local residents in LC meet-ings. Consequently, even if the LC system calls for some forms of collaboration with the local people in supporting health facilities, some people consider that such work should be done by the councillors themselves. As a result, the level of community participation in health is more limited than in education, where local people usually show a high degree of collaboration with the LC system (as seen in the previous chapter).

The absence of adequate collaboration is also seen in the way hospitals and health units are managed by the Health Unit Management Committees (HUMCs). Similar to the School Management Committees in the case of education, the HUMCs are organized for routine management of health facilities.[6] The HUMCs typically consist of nine members and collaborate with the LC system. LC 3 members in charge of health matters are consulted by HUMCs. The discussion re-sults of the HUMCs are supposed to be communicated to the local population through the LC 1 meetings. But in reality, most of the grassroots do not clearly understand the roles and functions of the HUMCs. Often the poor at the grass-roots do not even know of the existence of the HUMCs. The link between HUMCs and ordinary people is weak as in the case of education. But the problem is much more acute in health. This weakness partly results from the somewhat more technical nature of discussions in health matters than in education. For ex-ample, asked why health workers enjoyed the liberty to open and close the health unit when and as they pleased, a member of the HUMC responded in 1996:

> Those people are so difficult. We can't control them. Whenever we try to reprimand them they threaten to leave, saying they are educated and can find work elsewhere. Now we simply keep quiet and let them do as they please. Many of us on the committee are uneducated; how can we question those who are? (An interview, quoted in Golooba-Mutebi, 1999, chapter 6).

In addition, many of the necessary improvements, for instance, the more effi-cient procurement of medicine, are not attainable by local communities. Thus, there is a tendency for not reporting these issues to community members. This se-crecy in fact works negatively; the precious medicines are often consumed by

---

[5] Focus group discussion, Mukono town, Mukono, 19 August 1999.

[6] In Mukono District, the role of the HUMCs are defined as follows: 1) to undertake needs assessment of the HUMC and to prepare operational plans for improvement of efficiency of services and maintenance of the facility; 2) to mobilize additional resources for the HUMC; 3) to ensure efficient utilization and management of resources in each HUMC; 4) to promote good public relations between health workers and communities and to re-solve possible conflicts; 5) to improve the welfare of health staff; 6) to develop collective supervisory and advisory roles in the HUMC; 7) to fix the charges for various services provided by private service providers, where they exist; 8) to monitor and evaluate per-formance of the HUMC continuously; and 9) to report regularly about the activities of the HUMC to the relevant authorities (Golooba-Mutebi, 1999, chapter 6).

committee members and their relatives.[7] Therefore, the way in which the HUMCs work at the moment does not ensure the accountability of funds allocated for the use of respective health facilities.

3 Achievements in Health Services

Nonetheless, limited improvements in health services have been realized. Generally, managers of district hospitals are pleased with the HSD initiative since it has improved planning and management of health facilities. Since decentralized services make the hospitals more clearly responsible for these functions, procurement of drugs and allocation of personnel can now be initiated locally. Even if the available funds are limited, districts manage the local initiatives. These improvements enhance responsiveness to local constituencies.[8] For example, hospitals now have a department of community health.[9] The hospitals transferred their staff from curative responsibilities to this new department to provide PHC activities. The most common activities organized by this department include educational activities for the purpose of disease prevention at the hospitals, nutrition improvement, prevention of sexually transmitted diseases (STDs) including HIV/AIDS, mother and child health, immunization, and school visits for improvement of school and home hygiene. School health is gradually receiving more attention than in the past (Uganda, MoH, 2001, p. 40). Thus, the integration of curative and preventive health services has started and is generally welcomed by people, although it is too soon to evaluate the outcomes.

Second, this kind of reorganization on the part of public hospitals facilitates public-private collaboration. Some initial forms of government-private service partnerships have appeared. Missionary hospitals and NGOs are invited to the process of annual budgeting of districts. The degree of involvement of private service providers varies from one area to another, but clearly districts and offices of the DDHS are now more willing to share information with mission hospitals and NGOs and to plan budgets by taking into account the activities of the private service providers in respective jurisdictions. NGOs appreciate this kind of col-

---

[7] This special treatment may affect perceptions of the HUMC members on local health issues. On the one hand, most villagers believe that since the HUMC members and the councillors live in the same area and use the same facility, the HUMC members are fully aware of the poor quality and misconduct of health workers. On the other hand, if the committee members and relatives are treated more favorably than in the case of others, such special treatment reduces their exposure to the unpleasant experiences that ordinary people endure (Golooba-Mutebi, 1999, chapter 6).

[8] For instance, interview at Kalisizo Hospital, Rakai, 10 July 2000.

[9] Confirmed by interviews with Joachim Zziwa, MD, Medical Superintendent, Kawolo Hospital, 15 August 2000; with Sarah Kasewa, MD, Medical Superintendent, Rakai Hospital, 7 July 2000; and Obonyo John Hyachinth, MD, Medical Superintendent, Tororo Hospital, 21 June 2000.

laboration,[10] which is now being further "decentralized" from district to sub-county level. In Rakai, some sub-counties started to do this kind of budgeting together with NGOs operating in their areas. This is a welcomed development since neither partner loses institutional autonomy. On the contrary, participating agencies appreciate the comparative advantages, which form the basis of discussions and negotiations.

Cooperation is also taking place in the area of service delivery as well. In Tororo and Rakai, government and missionary hospitals collaborate in referring patients to more suitable hospitals depending on their needs.[11] In outreach programs, staff members of missionary hospitals join government teams. In Mukono and Rakai, international NGOs (for instance World Vision) built rural health facilities, where the MoH subsequently sent medical personnel. In Tororo, some NGOs (such as Plan International) provided medicines to public health facilities. In Rakai, NGOs trained traditional birth attendants and referred their patients to government hospitals for prenatal care.[12] This kind of collaboration is also a benefit of partnership, since the end results are more than the sum of the parts. Even if the degree is limited, there has been a start in creating synergy between public and private service providers, which is beneficial for the recipients of services.

As a result, more people are now aware of what of kinds of services are available at public hospitals. Comparing data in 1992 and 1999 reveals improvement in maintenance of clinics, closer local health facilities, and slightly improved availability of medicine, bandages, needles, and vaccines. This improvement has resulted in a slight increase in the utilization of public health facilities (Foster and Mijumbi, 2002, p. 19). Data at Kawolo Hospital in Mukono (Table 8.1) and the records of Rakai District attest to the fact that public utilization of hospital ser-

Table 8.1 Public utilization at Kawolo Hospital, Mukono

	total patients	out-patients	deliveries	operations	immunization	family planning	user fees collected (million Ush)	antenatal care
1997	4,846	27,141	1,596	450	1,334	10,057	16	3,125
1998	4,924	30,787	1,318	382	2,276	42,731	22	3,196
1999	6,639	30,047	1,888	466	3,043	9,598	32	3,943

Source: Mukono District Council records.

---

[10] Personal interviews with Harriet Wanyoto Mabonga, The AIDS Support Organization (TASO) Center Manager in Tororo, 29 May 2000; and with Deograttias S. Kituusibwa, Program Manager, Rakai AIDS Information Network (RAIN), 28 August 1998.

[11] Personal interview, James Eyul, MD, St. Anthony's Hospital, Tororo, 23 June 2000.

[12] Personal interview, Sarah Kasewa, MD, Medical Superintendent, Rakai Hospital, 7 July 2000.

vices is increasing steadily. The increased utilization appears to indicate that information on health facilities has become more widely available among rural people, and, moreover, it is a sign that people have started to show a greater appreciation of health services. In Rakai, some have changed where they seek their treatment. Instead of visiting private clinics, some now go to government facilities.[13] This shift is no trivial improvement. This increasing attendance at public health facilities contributes modestly to the empowerment of the poor who were often reluctant to seek such treatment in the past, although available data is sporadic.

Furthermore, collaboration between health workers and local communities has been enhanced through various activities including those of outreach. Often these activities are organized through the LC system. Although this is a controversial point and no definite conclusion can be made, it is safe to state that there has been some progress. A senior nurse at Tororo Hospital remarked, "We are now more familiar with people in the local community. Patients are no longer treated as strangers as they used to be."[14] These activities have contributed to nurturing more trustworthy social relationships between service providers and recipients, who otherwise may face serious mutual mistrusts. Such relationships create mutually satisfactory solutions for both health workers and the poor. Through this kind of relationships among stakeholders, and through learning processes in partnerships, public facilities are gaining what they cannot acquire alone: public confidence. This significant improvement in customer relations could not have been attained if multiple types of stakeholders did not start to interact frequently due to decentralized service provisions.

4 Unresolved Problems in Health Services

4.1 Dissatisfaction with Services

Even though these improvements are significant, the remaining challenges are daunting. First of all, people are not pleased with the quality of services that they are asked to pay for at rural health facilities, as seen in Chapter 4.[15] Dissatisfaction with health service quality is a fundamental problem. The most commonly expressed complaint is the unavailability of drugs. Although decentralized services have enabled locally suitable purchases of medicines, the amount available in rural clinics is far below demand. At government hospitals, until recently pa-

---

[13] Personal interview, Robert Mayanja, Deputy DDHS, Rakai District, 6 July 2000.

[14] Personal interview, Ruth Oloko, Senior Nurse, Tororo Hospital, 21 June 2000.

[15] People's dissatisfaction was often revealed during interviews for this study.

tients were first requested to pay for registration.[16] They were asked to wait for a certain period for treatment. Then they were told that necessary medications were not available and advised to get them elsewhere. The private clinics, which tend to charge higher fees, have more drugs than government facilities. At these private facilities, patients pay at the end of treatment.

People also express dissatisfaction with the attitudes that health workers often demonstrate in clinical facilities. They are arrogant and unfriendly to patients. Often they are accused of showing a "don't care" attitude.

> A man came with a very deep wound on his head arising from a fight the previous night in a bar. He could hardly stand for a few minutes due to the terrible pain. The nurse who came to attend to him asked him to walk back to the shops and buy a razor blade, then shave off the hair where the wound was. When he finished this then he could come back for treatment (Uganda, MoFPED, 2000g, quoted in Uganda, MoFPED, 1999b, p. 126).

This notion that the workers at government health facilities are inhuman is a significant obstacle for improving the relationship between service providers and recipients.

One reason behind this inadequate treatment is that many rural health facilities are not sufficiently staffed either in terms of quantity or quality. Since the start of decentralized health service, the MoH admits that only about 65% of the posts are filled (Uganda, MoH, 2001, p. 75).[17] In addition, many of which are filled are in fact by non-qualified nursing assistants or nursing aids (Okello et al., 1998, p. 16). It is estimated that only approximately 34% of the positions are filled by qualified personnel (Uganda, MoH, 2000, p. 19). Additionally, many such personnel are not well motivated. While decentralization has contributed to a more prompt release of their salary,[18] it has also virtually eliminated reassignment possibilities including Kampala. It is also estimated that the average salary arrears of health staff is two and a half years (Hutchinson et al., 1999, p. 120)! The housing situation is not encouraging either. Unlike the case of teachers, few medical personnel are helped by communities with accommodation.[19] Rural facilities are hardly equipped with transportation for outreach activities. Equipment tends to be in short supply to maintain proper storage of medicines. Water sources are often located inconveniently in villages. Although these issues are often reported from lower level facilities to DDHS offices and to the MoH, remedial action rarely takes place, and staff at rural facilities are frustrated with decentralized measures. It is, thus, no wonder that they are not dedicated to their work as good work remains unrewarded. Therefore, it can be concluded that decentralization has largely ignored the issue of inadequate incentives, which are crucial to efficient

---

[16] Although the exact fee differed from one area to another, usually the consultation fee for new patients was Ush 1,000 (US$ 0.67).

[17] There may be two reasons. One is that vacant stations are unpopular. Second, there is a shortage of qualified staff (Uganda, MoH, 2001, p. 75).

[18] Interview at Najjembe District Health Unit, 11 August 1999.

[19] For instance, interview at Kwapa Health Unit, Tororo, 2 June 2000.

use of resources and improved services at health clinics. "In essence, decentralization runs the risk of recreating an inefficient centralized system within each district" (ibid., p. 75).

4.2 Corruption by Health Service Providers

People are disgusted with health facilities, simply because they think health workers are corrupt (Cockcroft, 1996).[20] When they seek treatment at public facilities, it often tends to be uncomfortable. They often report that when they seek treatment, they are asked: "Do you have a brother?"[21] If they indeed have a brother (bribe), they can be treated; otherwise, no treatment. Therefore, health clinics are notorious for corruption. The people's level of disgust is quite high.

What fueled their anger was the user charges, which were normally used in various health facilities till lately. People considered it as a double payment; they were asked to pay direct service charges on top of indirect taxation (Lucas and Nuwagaba, 1999, p. 18). The user charge was often considered to be in a gray area between licit and illicit payment requests (ibid., p. 14). The heart of the problem was that the user charges at government rural health facilities were to supplement the underpaid government health workers, while the similar charges at private clinics are used to maintain an adequate drug supply (Okello et al., 1998). It is also well known that health workers divert drugs supplied by the government to supplement their income. One estimate is that the rate of drug "leakage" is from 40 to 94% with a median of 78% (Hutchinson et al., 1999, p. 117).

Grassroots people sometimes tend to show sympathy for the workers at the health facilities, who they know are ill-paid. Ordinary people are, nonetheless, adamant about the attitude of the health workers. This is because they are on the government payroll and supposed to receive a cash income, while the poor at the grassroots do not have cash income regularly. The fact that user charges did not lead to service improvements but instead went into the pockets of corrupt medical personnel did not please the poor at all. Thus, the abolishment of the user fee in 2001 was a step forward, but its effect on popular perception still remains to be seen.

The present situation contains many institutionalized malpractices at all levels of health services. Both supervisors and supervisees at the local levels are tremendously underpaid and not motivated to adhere to the established regulatory standards. When performance is unrelated to payment, the regulations are empty slogans. In order to reverse the present situation, efforts are particularly needed at the national level. Unless the wage bill itself is augmented significantly, the morale of health service staff will remain low. Sporadic reward and sanction mechanisms are ineffective, unless the fundamental cause is rectified by the central gov-

---

[20] This is also raised, for example, in a focus group discussion, Katana, Rakai, 2 August 2000.

[21] This is a common expression which was often reported during my field research. Lucas and Nuwagaba also confirm this expression (1999, p. 16).

ernment. Moreover, it would be desirable if the release of central government grants becomes tied carefully to actual performance of health services, although this tying should not punish the service recipients who already have lost their trust in public health facilities.[22]

4.3 Individual Responses and Lack of Community Activities

The ineffective regulatory mechanisms are compounded by the people's notion of health issues. Most people think that health care is a personal or family problem rather than a community issue. When people are in need of caring others, they often attempt to cope with family members and rarely try to seek assistance from outside their family, even when such assistance is available (Lucas and Nuwagaba, 1999). Community responsibilities are considered to be limited to helping patients to be transported to nearby health facilities and also to help organize funerals (ibid., pp. 16-17). People in the same community are clearly reluctant to offer financial assistance for the needy on the occasions of illness, since such lending is unlikely to be repaid.

This notion may make community efforts for health improvement difficult. If any assistance is given to create a community fund to help the sick, it may not succeed. On the other hand, this does not necessarily mean that people do not pay attention to health issues. Grassroots people desire accessible health facilities in their vicinity. They also wish that sufficient drugs would be provided in the health facilities and that trained health staff treat patients more sympathetically (Uganda, MoFPED, 2000g, pp. 69-70).

This discrepancy between the importance placed on health care and the notion that it is a family matter derives from the lack of community involvement in supporting health care facilities. This lack of experience prevents ordinary people from understanding fully that some kind of community support and management can be feasible and that outcomes of such initiatives are mutually empowering for both health service providers and recipients. The LC system has a crucial role to play in bridging this important gap. When the LC system is assisted by donors and NGOs, people together with the councillors often express their willingness to engage in such attempts to improve accessibility to affordable rural health services. One sub-county in Rakai District, where financial assistance is provided by an international NGO (Concern Worldwide), now plans to build such a clinic at a

---

[22] The MoH reports that performance-based release of the PHC grants (which were introduced in FY 1997/98) is currently under discussion. First, the MoH and offices of DDHS have agreed broadly on various performance indicators which may become required for releasing funds in the future. Second, at the national level, the MoH and the MoFPED have agreed on three indicators (immunization rate, OPD attendance, and percentage of supervised deliveries) not as conditions to the release of funds but as annual targets to be achieved (personal communication, Sam Okuonzi, Coordinator, District Health Services Project, MoH, 12 September 2001).

new location. But, typically, the LC structure also faces formidable challenges to fulfill this role, including financial constraints.

As a result, interaction between councillors and grassroots poor on health matters is much less significant than in the case of education. What appears to be symbolic is that the poor sometimes attempt to elect intentionally those who are not necessarily well-qualified as leaders. It was pointed out in several places that when the poor who cannot afford to build toilets in their homes do not wish to be pushed for home hygiene improvement, they vote for those who also do not have toilets in their homes. If the ones without toilets are elected, they are least likely to bring the toilet issue up in LC discussions. Thus, the poor do not have to face embarrassment during public discussions.[23]

4.4 Inadequate Financial Resources

The financial resources allocated for health under the decentralized services present a paradox. When it was anticipated that the local needs were going to be well matched by action by local governments, it was also considered that the local governments would increase financial allocation for such important areas of the health sector. However, the way in which the LC system operated did not conform to this expectation. In fact, financial allocation by district authorities covering recurrent health costs has actually *declined* both in absolute and relative terms after the decentralization policy was put in place. This reduction particularly applies to PHC.

It is widely known that politicians prefer short-term results. Thus, they tend to be reluctant to support preventive health care activities such as PHC, which take a long time for their impact to become measurable. Their decision for cutting preventive health costs may be understandable when curative services are also suffering from a severe shortage of funds. But the overall reduction of health expenditures signifies that the health sector is not a priority area for local governments.

This unexpected reduction made the MoH very uneasy. In response to this worrisome situation, the MoH started to provide a conditional grant for PHC since the FY 1997/98. This grant is calculated by three criteria: 1) district population; 2) infant mortality rate; and 3) district area/size. The grants are released quarterly from the central to district governments. The MoH reviews whether district reports satisfactorily meet accountability and other criteria.[24]

Figure 8.1 clearly demonstrates both the decline and the revival of the financial allocations of the three districts, although it does not disaggregate expenditure

---

23 For instance, personal interview with Robert Sasemberya, Medican Assistant, Najjembe Sub-county, Mukono District Health Unit, 11 August 1999.

24 The criteria cover both managerial and technical aspects (personal communication, Sam Okuonzi, Coordinator, District Health Services Project, MoH, 10 September 2001).

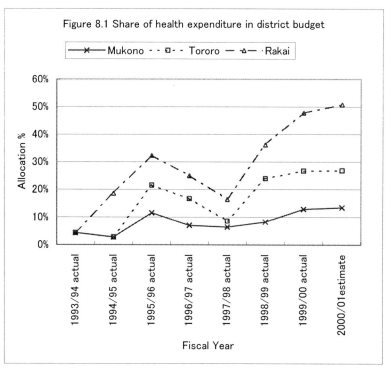

Figure 8.1 Share of health expenditure in district budget

Source: Respective district council records.

patterns between curative and preventive care.[25] The PHC grant was a very strong message to local authorities on the importance of health. After the installation of this grant, the local governments reversed the tendency of reducing financial allocation and supplemented it with locally generated revenue. Without the new grant, commitment to health could not have been revived as readily as it has been.[26]

In addition, if the rationale behind decentralizing health services was to create a "tailor made solution" to meet the different needs of different areas, then it may be anticipated that financial allocations for services may vary from one area to another. However, as Figure 8.1 demonstrates, the three districts do not indicate any significant differences in the overall pattern of resource allocation for health. Although the magnitude of financial allocation varies from one district to another,

---

[25] The expenditure for health is based on the actual expenditures of respective directorates in charge of health.

[26] The HSD policy commenced in 1998 also affected the way in which funds are spent. Since the HSD brought district hospitals under the control of DDHS, local government expenditures from FY 1998/99 started to reflect the expenses of district hospitals as well.

the overall trend is very similar, which is contrary to the original logic of decentralization. Rakai District shows a relatively larger amount of allocation for health than the other two districts. A main reason may be that HIV/AIDS is more serious in Rakai and still more prevalent than in the other areas (Uganda and UNICEF, 1999, p. 6), which attracts more assistance from donors.[27]

The fact that the overall trend among the three districts is similar is not surprising given that approximately 80% of the local government budget comes from the central government, of which nearly 80% are conditional grants. Financial allocation is heavily influenced by the priorities of the central government and donors. There are several donor-funded vertical programs that are implemented nationwide. Within the health sector alone, conditional grants finance about 45% of the total sector budget (Obwona et al., 2000, p.169). As a result, local governments are left with a very small amount of discretionary financial resources.

Ironically perhaps, this small allocation in the three districts does not indicate that a widening gap in health services between wealthier and poorer areas is a major concern among the three districts. Since this equity issue is one of the essential points raised by critics of decentralizing services (Green, 1999, p. 220), the following estimate is presented. Per capita health expenditures in FY 1999/00 in each district is calculated based on the records of the respective district governments: it is approximately Ush 1,400 (US$ .93) in Mukono, Ush 1,700 (US$ 1.13) in Tororo, and Ush 2,900 (US$ 1.93) in Rakai. Roughly, the non-wage expenditures in each district is about Ush 1,000 (US$ .70) in Mukono, Ush 1,300 (US$ .86) in Tororo, and Ush 2,200 (US$ 1.50) in Rakai. The reason why Rakai ranks first is due to donor assistance to combat the HIV/AIDS epidemic in this district. The difference between wealthy Mukono and poor Tororo is fairly small, and it may be surprising that Tororo spends slightly more on a per capita basis than Mukono.[28] Thus, as in the case of education, the equity concern is not substantiated, at least at the moment, as long as the central government and donors continue to provide necessary funds to local governments. But the situation needs to be revisited, particularly because the expenditure pattern for the health sector has not yet been fully stabilized, and because other developments related to the implementation of the new National Health Policy may affect the situation in the future.

4.5 Different Health Visions of the Central and Local Governments

The financial issue poses much broader issues. First of all, it is clear that the MoH and local authorities have different visions and priorities concerning health

---

[27] One such example is the European Community-funded Rural Health Programme (Kisubi and Mugaju, 1999).

[28] On the other hand, the debt incurred by Tororo District significantly affects the health services in the District, including local procurement of medicines (interview, Tororo Hospital, 21 June 2000).

issues.[29] Differences may also derive from political considerations of local leaders and technical viewpoints held by civil servants. While the former need short-term results for political appeal for constituencies, the latter emphasizes longer-term sustainable solutions for health. What is urgently needed are thorough discussions between national and local leaders including both political as well as administrative cadres over a wide range of health issues. They need to voice their concerns and seek consensus as much as possible for coherent planning of health policies and strategies. Although decentralization receives attention within the MoH, when it devised a national policy and strategy, the involvement of local stakeholders was negligible (Brown et al., 2001, p. 38). Therefore, it is no surprise that the MoH and local authorities have different views at balancing, for instance, curative and preventive care. As long as there are significant differences in priorities among different stakeholders, decentralized health provisions may not result in coherent policy outcomes.

In addition, local councillors may not have an adequate understanding of PHC. The MoH itself acknowledges that PHC is difficult to be understood locally since the concept originated from donors. Therefore, more dialogue is recommended between DDHS offices and councillors. It would be helpful if the technical staff of DDHS collaborates more with the councillors to forge a reasonable complementarity between curative and preventive health care. Even if they have differences of opinion, the divergence of views should not preclude more dialogue and consultation. As in the case of the national vaccination campaigns, if significant achievements in preventive care can be publicly recognized, that would enhance the collaboration by councillors. Thus, it would be possible to have a mutually agreeable balance between preventive and curative care among stakeholders.

5 Examination of Essential Issues

The impact of decentralization on the health sector presents a mixed picture. While some progress has been made, the remaining issues represent considerable challenges. It is, therefore, crucial to consolidate the progress made so far and tackle the remaining challenges. It is essential that various actions be coordinated and implemented coherently.

5.1 Seeking Optimal Public-Private Collaboration in Health Services

First, the government and people of Uganda have to agree generally on what kind of priority they would like to put on to health care reform. Particularly, the balance between curative and preventive care needs to be agreed on broadly, be-

---

[29] The experience of health decentralization in Papua New Guinea from the late 1970s to the early 1990s also showed tensions between the central and local governments (Kolehmainen-Aiken, 1992).

cause the view of the MoH does not necessarily mesh with that of various local authorities. Currently the MoH places more emphasis on PHC than districts. Thus, it is clearly necessary for the leadership of the MoH to initiate consultative processes to establish an agreeable consensus on health reform. Once such a consensus is reached, it would be possible to achieve credible results. The earlier experience of Uganda in combating the HIV/AIDS epidemic demonstrates that once the national consensus is supported by political commitment, impressive results can be achieved.[30] It is equally essential that the consensus be translated into organizational structures and policy instruments. The reform efforts at the central and local levels also need to be mutually consistent.

At the center, the MoH especially needs a carefully thought out strategy. Although a recently released Health Sector Strategic Plan (HSSP) indicates a broad approach, the HSSP needs to be reviewed critically. A number of factors need to be addressed in this thorough review. One of the most fundamental questions is what would be the essential areas in which the government should continue to provide services in a situation where much of the satisfactory curative services can be provided more cost-effectively by the private (often for profit) sector. It is estimated that the cost of public services is about one-and-a-half to two-times that of private ones (Hutchinson et al., 1999, p. 117). Even with the current HSSP, available government and donor resources are not expected to be more than $ 6.5 per person, which is obviously insufficient to fulfill health policy (Foster and Mijumbi, 2002, p. 18). In addition, as noted earlier, people seeking health services are less satisfied by public facilities than private ones. Then what should be the role of public health facilities in Uganda?

This situation probably justifies a critical re-examination of specific modalities in enhancing a public-private mix in health services. This examination can establish the appropriate ratio of public to private health facilities. In the long run, more private providers may be needed, since they are much more cost effective. If one of the goals of decentralization is more efficient and effective utilization of resources, the option of privatizing curative health services should be carefully considered. Privatization means more involvement of missionary, NGO, and traditional medical facilities, which are valued by the people.

Even though privatized services may be more appropriate in the long-term, some transitional measures are necessary. Several options are viable for the transition period. Currently, the government can send personnel to mission hospitals on a secondment basis. Secondment should be further encouraged, because it can function as an incentive to public health workers. Many of them at the moment feel that they are "stuck" in remote rural facilities without many opportunities for career development. Unlike the education sector, "brain drain" from public to private entities in the health sector does not happen very frequently. Exposure to more efficiently managed private facilities is also a learning experience for them. Given the financial constraints of the government, relatively inexpensive incentive measures such as secondment should be fully explored.

---

[30] Close examination of Uganda's successful attempts to combat HIV/AIDS is beyond the scope of this study. See Okware et al., 2001; Parkhurst, 2002; and Reid, 1995.

As an additional measure for a more effective public-private mix, adequate consideration needs to be given to the allocation of equipment or funds to health facilities operated by private entities. This kind of support is a de facto government subsidy to private providers. Although few countries explicitly provide this kind of subsidy, it is worth considering this option for enhancing partnerships between public and private service providers to improve the cost-performance of the health sector in general. Even if NGOs per se are not necessarily any more efficient and/or effective than the government in providing services,[31] contracting out some services may merit serious consideration. A small amount of conditional grant is already given to mission hospitals, and probably more of such allocation should be made in the future. The central government decided that in FY 2000/01 the government budget support to NGO hospitals (mainly mission hospitals) was to be almost doubled from the previous level (Uganda, MoFPED, 2000f, p. 85). This decision was welcomed as a move in the right direction.[32]

5.2 Coherent Policy Coordination at the National Level

Once the role of public health provision is clarified, it needs to be orchestrated in a manner consistent with other important reforms. Other initiatives which are important for coordination include inter-governmental fiscal transfers in health care, the issue of user charges, the SWAP, and the urgent need for improving the capacity of the MoH to support local health providers who face increasing demands.

First, the issue of financial resources for health care has to be scrutinized. The MoH must identify the required resources in order to implement the new National Health Policy. It is also necessary for the MoH to establish an appropriate balance between conditional and unconditional grants in health activities to achieve the goals of the policy. For local governments, more discretionary funds are preferable. But given the past decline of financial resources allocated to health by local governments, the MoH is reluctant to reduce significantly conditional grants. Because the local resource base is too small to generate substantial funds for essential activities, securing financial resources is primarily the responsibility of the central government and donors. The MoH, thus, should increase the total resources available for local authorities. The new policy framework helps the MoH engage with donors to enlarge donor assistance to the health sector. It is encour-

---

[31] De Torrenté and Mwesigye argue that missionary hospitals are operated more or less permanently and are more suitable for sustainable services in the long run. But international and national NGOs often operate with very short-term goals largely influenced by their availability of funds, and are not suitable for substituting for government in such essential services as health (de Torrenté and Mwesigye, 1999).

[32] Reflecting these considerations, the MoH established an office to coordinate activities with the private sector. A working group was appointed to develop policy on public-private partnership. This activity is assisted by the Italian government (Uganda, MoH, 2001, p. 72).

aging that donors generally support the new policy. Once the overall resources channeled to the health sector are increased, it is recommended that about half of the transfers be in the form of conditional grants and the remaining half in discretionary funds. This recommendation satisfies both the central government that requires more total resources and the local governments which are currently frustrated with the very small amount of discretionary funds left in their hands.

Second, the MoH must look into the impact of the abolishment of user charges in 2001. The charges were often interpreted as a source of corruption by the public, and could not realistically be considered as a tool for resource mobilization. The level of rural poverty would not allow user charges as a means for financial sustainability to run health facilities. Thus, the MoH policy of abolishment is probably in the right direction. On the other hand, with the abolishment, the number of people seeking treatment at public clinics has increased dramatically, and some facilities cannot effectively cope with the upsurge. This situation is analogous to the deteriorating quality of educational services due to the UPE. This increase undoubtedly has made health staff much busier. Many, especially middle- to low-level staff, are demoralized since salaries did not increase significantly.[33] Even if the abolishment is considered appropriate, further consideration is, thus, needed for creating appropriate incentives for more effective health facilities. As in private facilities, fees collected at government health units can be used for improving the quality of care. If patients can see tangible improvements, they would be willing to pay for them, which benefits health workers as well. Whether the abolishment will prove to be as a positive incentive remains to be seen.

A third area for the MoH to coordinate institutional reform relates to contradictions between decentralization and the new sector-wide approach (SWAP) in health services. The SWAP is generally welcomed both by the central government and donors as a way for better coordination of different activities funded by numerous donors. Although the donors' receptive attitude is considered to be a merit, the way in which the SWAP is organized is in fact contrary to the notion of granting more decision-making authority to local governments. If the SWAP is fully implemented, a situation is envisaged in which local governments carry out centrally-decided health activities. This situation would frustrate local governments, notably local political leaders who find it difficult to establish a politically accountable relationship between themselves and local constituencies.[34]

Fourth, for the sake of coherent reform, the MoH has an important responsibility to support, monitor, and supervise both public and private local service providers. One of the reasons why decentralized health services now generate mixed results is weak supervision and support from the center. As already pointed out as a

---

[33] Personal interview, Sam Okuonzi, Coordinator, District Health Services Project, MoH, 5 August 2002.

[34] The contradiction between the two apparently needs much more attention. Brown et al. (2001) evaluate the education sector in Uganda more favorably than the health sector, and briefly touch on the contradiction without much examination. Foster and Mijumbi (2002) and World Bank (2000b) also provide little analysis. This issue, furthermore, points to a related issue of who "owns" health policies (Okuonzi and Macrae, 1995).

"paradox of decentralization," for service decentralization to be effective, a strong central government is needed (Tendler, 1997). Capacity building at the local levels is necessary, but this does not mean that institutional building should be concentrated only at the local level. In fact, the central government also faces a new challenge in discharging different responsibilities. This necessary central-level improvement does not happen automatically, and much more training is needed to enhance the capacity of the central government, especially the MoH in a new decentralized structure.[35]

All of these reform efforts would need coordination, since these issues are interdependent. Unless the central government and donors can increase the total resources needed for health, any immediate shift from conditional to unconditional grants in inter-governmental resource transfers is unrealistic. Both the MoH and donors have to be convinced that local governments can handle financial resources adequately, before such augmentation of resources can be dispensed. This ability in turn depends on how much support the MoH can provide to local governments.

The MoH's support is most needed in the northern part of Uganda. Central government support is much needed to provide a comparable quality of health services in different localities. In the three districts examined by this study, the magnitude of inequity is not a major concern. This does not, however, mean that decentralized services can be successful in all places in Uganda. Ecological systems in the north and the south are fairly different, and people are engaged in different life styles and must deal with different diseases. Thus, to ensure equal access to health care is a tremendous task considering the north-south gaps. Unfortunately, the current national policy has no deliberate approach to this equity problem. This concern is similar in the case of education. But the health sector in Uganda is far behind that of neighboring countries, therefore, the current situation needs to be reversed as soon as possible.[36]

5.3 Action Needed at Local Levels

At the local level, remedial action is crucial to overcome the current situation. First, as in the case of education, there is an urgent need for clarifying the role of respective stakeholders, especially at the local level. Even if the demarcation of responsibilities is now articulated between the MoH and the offices of DDHS, a similar division of responsibilities and tasks between the lower LCs, service delivery points, Health Unit Management Committees (HUMCs) and people at the grassroots is not precisely defined. This lack of precision in the health sector is more acute than in the case of education. The HUMCs do not function adequately, and often some of its members are not trained sufficiently to discharge

---

[35] It is welcomed that the MoH recently started to disseminate National Supervision Guidelines (Uganda, MoH, 2001). But it remains to be seen whether this dissemination has actually improved relations between service providers at various levels.

[36] The current government policy on poverty, PEAP, refers to the equalization grant in one paragraph only in its main volume of 200 pages (Uganda, MoFPED, 2000e).

their duties. The reporting of information from the HUMCs to grassroots people through the LC system is limited. This insufficient flow of information is one of the reasons for HUMC dysfunction (Hutchinson et al., 1999). In addition, the abolishment of user charges, ironically, has undermined HUMCs. Political leaders who previously enjoyed benefits (inappropriately) from the pooled resources of the user fees cannot receive similar benefits any longer. Thus, some, if not many, are now reluctant to facilitate the committee.[37] Thus, as the MoH recently acknowledged, "Public and stakeholder awareness on the Health Policy and HSSP is low and requires publicity in order to enlist the full public and stakeholder support" (Uganda, MoH, 2001, p. 38).

Second, this issue of the HUMCs highlights the fact that much more information needs to be provided concerning the health policy and services. Ordinary people do not know, for instance, the hierarchy of the health system, in which certain drugs are only available at a particular type of health unit. If people are well informed about what kind of services are available at what levels, mistrust toward health workers will be lessened. This is no trivial matter, since perceptions are crucial in forging confidence about public services by grassroots people. The following concerning the flow of information has been reported:

> Empowering people to stand up and demand their rights and quality services is obviously a key way to prepare them to take up their new responsibilities. However, local people are at a critical crossroads. Their voice is still too weak to influence the behaviour of the officer and to determine the direction of their decisions. The fact that their source of information is usually from government representatives and more often than not such information is to serve the interests of government is disempowering (Kasumba, 2000, p. 137).

As this quotation shows, management of information dissemination is not as easy as it may appear. But several options are worth examining. Local councillors need more training and awareness in order to disseminate essential information. Moreover, locally suitable communication tools can be devised, for example, drama performances. In fact, some NGOs are using dramas very effectively as an influential method of raising awareness of the rights and obligations of rural people in terms of decentralized service provisions. As was often observed by this researcher in visiting rural villages, once people are informed about their rights, duties, and obligations, some become more vocal in expressing their views and demands, especially toward the lower level LCs. This process steadily improves financial accountability. Increased awareness and improved information availability create the potential to overcome hindrances to empowerment.

The issue of information relates to the more fundamental problem of the role of ordinary people in monitoring essential public policies such as health care. The MoH is currently planning to improve the Health Management Information System (HMIS). The HMIS is often used solemnly by the technical staff. People are

---

[37] Personal interview, Sam Okuonzi, Coordinator, District Health Services Project, MoH, 5 August 2002.

treated as a source of information. But what would be an optimal relationship between the HMIS and grassroots people? Do people have any role to play instead of being treated passively as a source of health information? If their role is more than just as an information provider, then how can people's participation lead to more effective use and application of the HMIS? Ideally, collectors of information should also be among the users of the information. In reality, information is often collected by people but monopolized by officials. Feedback mechanisms are thus necessary in order to motivate collectors to maintain the accuracy of the data (Green, 1999, p. 132).

This role of people is related to an even broader issue of participatory poverty assessment (PPA). Although it is often more difficult to orchestrate popular participation in the development process than any rhetoric suggests, it would be critical to put the PPA into practice if decentralized service delivery is to be successful. As in the case of education, health issues need to be coordinated with other on-going initiatives including PPA (McGee 2000a and 2000b). With increased emphasis on the participation of people not only in project management but also in policy monitoring, what would be a more inclusive and participatory monitoring mechanism for health care improvement? On this important question, Uganda has been unique in conducting the elaborated Uganda Participatory Poverty Assessment Project (UPPAP) in recent years (Uganda, MoFPED, 2000g).[38] Building on the experiences gained through the UPPAP process as well as the LC system being in place, one realistic approach would be to link the LC system with the UPPAP process in order to create functional communication by which people can be more involved in evaluating essential government policies, including health and education.

What needs to be emphasized is that people in Uganda have already gained some experience, which can serve as the foundation to create such a public monitoring mechanism. Although remaining institutional obstacles for the LC system are obvious, the LC system has the potential to be a communication channel between people and the various levels of authority. If more efforts are made by various stakeholders in the next few years, the LC system can become a conduit for the voices of the ordinary people to reach decision makers of the central as well as local governments. This kind of hope in Uganda is very different from other countries where participatory monitoring and poverty evaluation remain mere rhetoric. When people can become a part of monitoring mechanisms of policy outcomes, they pay more attention to such results. People can also feel an "ownership" of the process of monitoring. Ultimately, people as citizens evaluate whether any policy is successful or not. This evaluation enhances their prospects for collaborating with service providers in order to attain mutually satisfactory outcomes and can also contribute to more accountability and transparency in public services.

Third, the increasing interaction and collaboration between district health management teams and private service providers should be encouraged. This is a trial

---

[38] The UPPAP attracts attention widely. See Brock and McGee, 2002; and Narayan and Patel et al., 2000.

and error process, that will encounter fresh problems. But through these experiences, some successful cases can be established as learning models. Rakai's experiences demonstrate that this process has "ups and downs" (Kasumba, 1998 and 2000). Although the process is still fragile, the partnership between the government and private (often for profit) service providers is possible and is one avenue worth exploring. If "best practices" can be recognized, they can serve as motivation for health workers who are often seeking more professional satisfaction even if they are not well paid. In fact, a recent increase of the utilization of services at government hospitals has made medical staff busier than before, but many of them also acknowledge that the situation is encouraging and more satisfactory than before.

6 Summary of the Health Sector

In Uganda, health is considered essential for overcoming pervasive poverty. But treating and caring for the sick is considered to be a family issue, and devising community-wide solutions is difficult even if many people share similar difficulties in health care. This lack of past experience contributes to a low degree of public participation in the consultation process of health services often called for by LC leaders. The level of services at delivery points is too basic to allow regional flexibility, and the standards are centrally set by the MoH.

Decentralized health services are hampered by unfavorable conditions in making much needed improvements. It was assumed that the LC system would function as a liaison between local authorities and the population. The autonomy given to the LC system was expected to lead to more flexible and tailor-made solutions for location specific health agenda. But in reality, health care under the LC system is far from effective for facilitating partnerships between service providers and recipients. Rather, progress in decentralized health care was largely initiated by the collaboration between public and private service providers. For them, decentralized health care services are recognized as noticeable progress, although the degree of appreciation is higher among district officials than the medical staff of rural clinics.

But there is an indication that more people have recently started to appreciate the services. The new initiative of Health Sub-District has significantly increased the responsiveness of health services. The integration of curative and preventive services and the public-private collaboration in service provision have initiated an appreciable impact. The increased interaction between service providers and community members, especially in outreach activities, has started to disseminate useful information to local communities. The regular interaction between service providers and recipients help to build social bonds between these stakeholders. Many people at the grassroots level frequently state that their home hygiene has improved significantly thanks to frequent discussions held at the LC meetings. With the increased number of people seeking care, more effective management of human and material resources is critical to sustaining the new trend of improvements.

The fundamental challenge lies in the area of rewards to, and sanctions of, health personnel. The basic salary and remuneration structure is far too low to attract qualified people at rural facilities. Support and supervision of service providers are weak at all levels, and need immediate action to make decentralized services meaningful. Some communities have mobilized their resources to create additional incentives for health care, but the magnitude is much less than in the case of education. In contrast to education, there are few attempts by communities to provide accommodation for health unit staff, because 1) there has been limited experience of this in the past; 2) public mistrust of health staff prevents such community actions from being organized; and 3) the linkage between leaders and villagers is not well established on health matters.

Health services in Uganda are now at a critical juncture. Although Uganda has already started to make a few significant steps, the remaining challenges are critical. The road to this goal is by no means smooth, nor short, but Uganda appears to be heading in the right direction. A more precise demarcation of roles and responsibilities between the central and local governments combined with an articulated policy and strategy for the more effective utilization of both public and private resources has just begun. The actions by central and local service providers need to be coordinated by increased funding and more readily available information. If these measures improve incentives for service providers, "consumer satisfaction" with health services is likely to improve. Then accountability of public services is likely to become more impressive than at present.

7 Conclusion of Service Provisions

It is undoubtedly a long-term process to enhance the problem-solving capacity of societies. Decentralization measures are not more intrinsically conducive to creating such capacities than centralized ones. The critics of decentralization argue that local power elites manipulate decentralized service provisions to benefit themselves at the cost of the poor. The experiences of Ugandan service decentralization in health and education present different circumstances in which local politics have intervened into service provisions. In the education sector, community involvement in school management has prevented the often-proclaimed danger of elite domination. In the case of health care, the situation is more ambiguous. Decentralization services have certainly benefited officials and their relatives who have obtained more favorable treatment than others. Although local-level political manipulation is certainly a problem, its magnitude is far less than the regular malpractices performed by service providers themselves.

As Uganda's experiences show, lack of incentives for service providers and for people at the grassroots level are closely linked. Initially, before the decentralization process, incentives were missing both for service providers and recipients. When providers are not motivated enough to improve the quality of services, recipients are rarely encouraged to improve them either. Taxpayers at the grassroots level would like to see improvements in their lives in return for the sacrifice they make in paying taxes. If they cannot see such improvements, they will not cooperate with other stakeholders. Their patience in waiting for improved public services may be running out, particularly where local leadership is ineffective.

Although this is a vicious circle, it can be broken as some examples have shown. People clearly acknowledge the centrality of the LC system in their livelihood, and are certainly aware that its effectiveness is desirable for overcoming poverty. Some communities have been successful in managing small-scale development activities using the LC system. Health workers and teachers can be more motivated to provide better services if communities acknowledge the importance of health and education. The examples of some communities in trying to provide housing for teachers are encouraging in this direction. People at the grassroots level can also be more encouraged to participate in community development activities as long as competent leadership can demonstrate the positive consequences of meaningful participation. People can realize the many opportunities participation brings to their lives, and service providers can also feel pleased to be recognized socially, if not financially. This is a "virtuous cycle" creating mutually beneficial results. The LC system in Uganda can become an effective interface between different stakeholders. Through these processes, mutually reinforcing incentives can be found. Accordingly, partnerships can be formed for mutually beneficial outcomes.

If such a cycle can be created, service provision at local levels may provide for for more "value for funds." This improvement at the grassroots level in turn would satisfy the central government because the goal of service decentralization would be achieved. The raised confidence by the center in local governments may lead to more autonomy being granted to local authorities. Therefore, the remaining issue is less concerned with the structure of the LC as such, but more with how to use created opportunities by the LC system for mutually beneficial outcomes. To turn a vicious cycle to the virtuous one is far from easy, but it is still possible with efforts by essential stakeholders.

9 Conclusions: The Way Forward

[A] powerful case for decentralization can be mounted. Physical and social conditions in Africa favour it as a pragmatic response to the problems of government. The inability of the central government to reach its citizens effectively suggests that something else is necessary. The continuing strength of the democratic norm in the city and countryside demonstrates the persistent desire of people to participate in the management of their own affairs.

Nelson Kasfir, 1993, p. 25

Decentralization measures are multi-dimensional processes of transformation, in which various stakeholders engage in the allocations of different kinds of influence and resources. In developing countries decentralization measures have been attempted in several forms to achieve numerous goals ranging from democratization to economic growth. In the African context, decentralization has been considered crucial to seek a closer fit between the state and society so that more legitimate relations can be constructed between the leaders (who have tended to personalize power and wealth) and the majority of populations (who have not significantly benefited from the modernization processes in the post-independence era).

Uganda's decentralization attempt is one of the most advanced on the continent, and the examination of its decentralization reform efforts in previous chapters have presented an overview of its achievements and challenges. When the NRM took power in Uganda in 1986, the state was virtually void of any state institutions due to the long-lasting civil war. The NRM then installed the Resistance Council (RC), a five-tier hierarchy of councils and committees from village to district levels, which was renamed the Local Council (LC) in 1995. Since the late 1980s, the RC/LC system has been functioning as a forum where local authorities interface with ordinary people at various administrative levels. As a result, this LC system is distinguished in post-independent Africa as an institution which emphasizes popular participation and democratization (Karlström, 1999b, p. 112). Uganda today probably has the most elaborate legal framework for decentralizing measures in Africa and is firmly committed to decentralization. The amount of financial resources transferred to local governments is one of the largest in Africa. Decentralization measures have contributed to empowering marginalized Ugandans to some extent. Elections also have contributed to the political empowerment of the grassroots poor. Primary education has been extended to poor children. In addition, some daily necessities are now provided through collective action, some of which is organized by the LC system. Even with underdeveloped capacities and the limited resources of local governments, effective leadership in some places has succeeded in mobilizing certain resources and skills for achieving mutually beneficial outcomes. These improvements imply that the hypothesized framework presented in Chapter 1 has proven to be useful in examining the complex processes of decentralization.

On the other hand, the decentralization processes in Uganda are double-edged. The experiences in Uganda present a mixture of significant improvements as well as remaining challenges. When several improvements were made, they in turn created new challenges. Decentralization measures have both stabilized and destabilized relations among stakeholders. This mixture is an acute reality in implementing such a complex policy in a poor country on the African continent. Therefore, Uganda is at a critical crossroads, in which either positive or negative forces can dominate in the future. Decentralization attempts are far from a panacea, which is not to mean that the old centralization can provide better results. Clearly, Uganda has already crossed the point from which they cannot return to the old days of centralization as described in the opening quotation of this chapter. The success of decentralization efforts depends on whether institutional reform can enrich social networks for the purpose of resolving common concerns, as well as on whether strategic partnerships can be formed out of the dense network of changing stakeholder relations. This formation must be facilitated by incentive mechanisms, widely available information on key facts and resources, and availability of affordable conflict-resolution mechanisms.[1]

---

[1] These three elements indeed explain the different performances in Mukono, Tororo, and Rakai. Clearly, the well-performing districts of Mukono and Rakai are well motivated, while the non-performer lacks such motivation. In Mukono, both leaders and followers pride themselves that Mukono is "the best district" in Uganda. In Rakai, a slightly different pride based on Rakai being "the pioneering district" in the decentralization schemes in Uganda is shared by almost all local stakeholders (focus group discussion, Nvuvu, Rakai, 2 August 2000). On the other hand, in Tororo, leaders suffer from a sense of victimization and grassroots people are dissatisfied with public services. The bad reputation does not attract donors. The media also treat Tororo unfavorably. Similarly, Mukono and Rakai are reasonably good in accessing and sharing information, while Tororo is again unimpressive. Mukono benefits from its proximity to Kampala in accessing information. In Rakai, the presence of the donor, Danish International Development Assistance (DANIDA), itself serves as a source of information. In contrast, Tororo is far from Kampala, and the multiplicity of languages spoken tends to complicate communication. In addition, although structurally the three districts do not demonstrate much difference in conflict resolution, pride in Mukono and Rakai plays indeed a big role to prevent conflicts from escalating. When economic opportunities are limited, as in Tororo, harsh competition tends to invite neo-patrimonial actions by leaders, which invites more conflict than consensus. Economic opportunities in Mukono ard Rakai are more promising than in Tororo.

In this concluding chapter, the lessons which bear important policy implications well beyond Uganda are discussed in order to suggest ways to improve policy design and implementation of this widespread institutional reform agenda in many parts of the world.

1 Strategic Partnership Formations

As examined in Chapter 2, post-independent African states demonstrated severe drawbacks, including an incongruence between territorial boundaries and politico-economic communities at the national level. This disharmony may have been lessened at local levels where interactions by stakeholders become more frequent and the territorial boundaries may pose less problems than at the national level. If democracy deepens through decentralized structures, this progress will be much welcomed, particularly in Africa. African states have been suffering from the monopolization of coercive forces and the personalized, yet unarticulated, exercise of power, and democratic practices at local levels present promising potential for reversing these trends. Improved service provisions that contribute to reducing poverty will also be welcomed and this would enhance the legitimacy of the state. As a consequence, decentralization measures offer certain possibilities to rectify fundamental problems associated with African states.

However, whether this hope can be realized largely depends on how decentralization measures are implemented, as the anti-decentralists have been arguing (as reviewed in Chapter 2). If decentralization endeavors are poorly planned, they may become under the control of the local elite, which would further exacerbate undemocratic problems. Likewise, service provisions may not be improved for the majority of the poor, and legitimacy is eroded even further. The various successful and unimpressive signs of the transformative processes of decentralization suggest that one critical factor to determine success or failure is whether participating stakeholders can form strategic partnerships in achieving mutually beneficial outcomes. Partnerships are reciprocal relations among diverse actors to attain common goals. Partnerships are based on the equal participation of autonomous organizations, and also produce synergy which could not be possible if organizations act independently. When such partnerships are formed, they often lead to improved efficiency and effectiveness in utilizing various resources. The collaboration of stakeholders enhances learning opportunities for effective outcomes. Outcomes of partnership endeavors are more than the sum of individual participant activity. As seen in Chapter 6, locally available resources are still limited, but this scarcity can be overcome partly by collaborated efforts. Improved management in turn improves outcomes, which are often in the form of essential services provided to the poor and the needy. Improved output contributes to poverty reduction in both material and non-material terms. More responsive service provisions undoubtedly enhance the well-being of the poor in meeting their practical needs. The process of collaboration and engagement in attaining such outcomes also reduces the feelings of isolation and vulnerability of the poor. It is no trivial achievement to empower the socially disadvantaged, as examined in Chapters 4 and 5. The pro-poor outcomes are "win-win" solutions in which improved effectiveness enhances the legitimacy and mutually accountable relations between the rulers and the ruled.

In Uganda, four types of strategic partnerships are emerging. The first is the changing *relationship between the central and local governments*. While the central government controlled local authorities in the past, it is now emerging as a still hesitant yet significant partner for local governments. The harmonization of budgeting between the central and local governments, through the Budget Framework Paper (BFP) process (as seen in Chapter 6), as well as the reorganization of some service delivery ministries in Kampala to enhance responsiveness by the central government to local authorities (Chapters 7 and 8) are examples of this central-local partnership.

The second significant strategic partnership is found in the *relationship between the government and the private/NGO sector*, particularly at local levels. Representatives of the business community, various associations and NGOs now interact with local governments to pursue mutually beneficial results. A limited number of districts established local NGO forums, which provide opportunities to exchange information between districts and NGOs (Uganda, MoFPED, 2000j, p. 19; and Uganda, MoFPED, 2000i, p. 25). When these forums convene, activity plans and budgetary information are shared. Generally, the collaboration between district authorities and development NGOs is welcomed by both sides. Each part plays its role in exercising respective comparative advantages.[2] This process is particularly noteworthy in health (Chapter 8), which certainly enhances the responsiveness of service provisions and also improves both the processes and outcomes of development effectiveness.

The third partnership is found in the collaboration *between service providers and recipients*, as examined in the case of primary education (Chapter 7). The degree of collaboration by grassroots people is high when they are convinced that such collaboration will yield common benefits. Education is a typical example. Similar collaboration is also found in other types of small-scale development activities organized at the grassroots level. Effective leadership of LC 1 can yield, for instance, the protection of water sources and rehabilitation of rural feeder roads. What is noteworthy is that the LC system, especially at the grassroots level, is an indispensable social network for most Ugandans, as discussed in Chapters 3 and 4.

The fourth type of strategic partnership is the formation of *associations of local authorities*. The Uganda Local Authorities Association (ULAA) has been particularly effective in its advocacy role and has presented their demands to the central government. The ULAA demands have influenced the ways in which important decisions are made by the central government on the allocation of resources.

Nonetheless, partnerships are apparently not free from drawbacks. The degree of participation of stakeholders even in partnerships is far from ideal. For in-

---

[2] Kisoro District reported that "when partners and partnership arrangements are healthy, it helps to bridge the gaps in the delivery of services" (Uganda, MoFPED, 2000k, p. 23).

stance, participation by local governments in the BFP process still remains at a minimum. Intentions behind restructuring the ministries have not been translated into the effective support much needed by local authorities. In addition, while new partnerships can create appreciated collaboration, they can also become a new source of complication. In cetain cases it may make some stakeholders more vulnerable to others. The partners may attempt to exploit new opportunities for their own benefit at the cost of the local population. The collaboration between districts and NGOs is still based on personal affiliations rather than institutionalized ones (Uganda, MoFPED, 2000i, p. 25).

2 Factors for Successful Partnerships

Decentralization measures provide opportunities in which interactions among individuals and organizations multiply. Through these multiple networks, partnerships emerge, even if this process is not automatic. In fact, this process of partnership formation at local levels is double-edged (Brinkerhoff, 2002, p. 41). On the one hand, local partnerships can be more easily facilitated since the results of partner collaboration can be immediately known to constituencies. On the other hand, local partnerships may be entangled with long-lasting patronage networks which may be intensely nurtured by face-to-face contacts. Political interferences may skew partnerships.

This paradox runs parallel with the one of participation. For popular participation to be realized, local government structures need to create certain social spaces in which local people feel less constrained in attending meetings and organizing activities for improving their livelihood. Participation can harness people's energy for local collective activities. On the other hand, this process may be used by some stakeholders to increase their benefits without necessarily contributing to collective gains. Decentralization measures may also weaken the social bonds of local communities. Opening up social space paradoxically both encourages and discourages collective action, as demonstrated by the primary education experience in Uganda.

Furthermore, another dilemma is the inverse relation between the level of education and the degree of satisfaction expressed over the LC system, as shown in Chapter 4. The more educated one is, the higher the expectation one has of local government reform. Thus, more highly educated people tend to get easily disappointed when such high expectations are not met. This is a serious dilemma because the more educated citizens are the likely leaders of the reformed local institutions. If they become too cynical about their performances, it is unlikely that the reforms would yield satisfactory results for the society at large.

In analyzing the diverse dilemmas of partnership formation, the field investigation suggests three elements are indispensable for creating and sustaining effective partnerships: 1) incentives; 2) information; and 3) conflict-resolution mechanisms. These are mutually related. Incentives spur stakeholders to forge partnerships, and usually to share relevant information for collaboration. The sharing of information is also a key to prevent conflicts among the stakeholders. When these three elements are present, it is more likely that strategic partnerships will be durable and produce results in a sustained manner. On the contrary, if all or even one of these factors are missing, it would become very difficult for partners to collaborate productively. These considerations have important policy implications that can be applicable to other countries as well, some of which are pursuing similar structural reforms.

These three factors also are important to link the different views held by what is called neo-liberalists and neo-populists (Chapter 2). Even if these elements alone do not resolve complicated relations between economic development and democracy, they certainly are crucial to ease the tension of different principles of economic efficiency and political justice. Information facilitates economic transactions. When information is widely shared, it fosters a common sense of identity, which forms the basis of a politico-cultural community. Conflict resolution is essential for securing property and enforcing contracts essential for economic activities. But these factors are also crucial to clarify the rules on which political actions are based. Improvements in information and conflict-management in turn influence the way in which "selfish" individuals make rational choices. Very few would like to be openly recognized as selfish, thus information availability induces incentives for fair economic activity. Political transactions are also influenced by transparency both in terms of information accessibility and impersonalized governance. These factors, therefore, are critical to resolve social dilemmas in which individual gains are not necessarily socially optimum outcomes.

2.1 Mutually Reinforcing Motivation

Creating opportunities for stakeholder participation in local affairs is necessary but not sufficient for successful decentralization. Enhanced grassroots involvement in local decision-making processes can both facilitate as well as complicate collective action. The "double-edged" nature of decentralization measures highlights the importance of incentives behind participation. The real challenge is, then, how participation can be structured to reflect the competing interests of heterogeneous stakeholders.[3]

Motivations behind decentralizing measures may be different for different stakeholders even when they form strategic partnerships. First, while the central government is still reluctant to lose its influence over local governments, the latter are keen to exercise their new autonomy. This continued desire on the part of the central government to retain its control is called the "hidden agenda of decentralization" (Regan, 1995). Whereas the contents of policy packages are more centrally determined, their implementation mechanism tends to be entrusted to local

---

[3] The paradox that decentralization measures can both solidify and fragment different types of social bonds parallels a myth concerning communities; what is often considered as a homogeneous community is often filled with inherent tensions (Cleaver, 1999; Craig and Mayo, 1995; Francis, 2000; and Guijt and Shah, 1996).

administration, as is well illustrated by Uganda's education example.[4] Likewise, the central government in Kampala often uses conditional grants predominantly for inter-government fiscal transfers. This kind of grant does not readily allow participation of local stakeholders in the decision-making process of policy content. This situation is, in fact shared by various other developing countries. As a consequence, several decentralization attempts have become de facto re-centralization, which is obviously a clear contradiction against the rationale of decentralization. Thus, skeptics have already argued:

> Decentralization in fact usually has been intended as a technique (or means) of achieving *central government programs* of economic and social development, especially in the

Table 9.1 Re-centralization vs. decentralization: its accountability implications

	De facto re-centralization	More decentralization with local autonomy
Poverty outcome	It may lead to less material poverty by carrying out poverty focused activities.	It may lead to less material poverty and possibly less non-material deprivation by carrying out poverty-focused activities.
The role of local government system	The local governments become less significant as an implementer of centrally decided activities.	The local governments become more significant as development institutions.
Political representatives	The local representatives are frustrated and may try to infiltrate into the center-local relationship.	The local representatives play a more significant role in local decision-making process.
Civil servants	The administrators become mere agents of line ministries of the central government.	The administrators become more involved in serving the local political leadership.
People at the grassroots	Ambiguous: they may appreciate the outcome, but not appreciate the process.	Positive: they may appreciate both the process and the outcome.
Accountability	Civil servants more accountable to central line ministries administratively; political accountability deteriorates between the local representatives and constituencies.	Political accountability improves between the local representatives and constituencies; this in turn may improve the link between center and the local governments.
Corruption in local governments	It may lead to less corruption if central governments improve supervision functions.	It may lead to less corruption if the constituencies become more involved in monitoring local activities.
Responsiveness of the local government system	Unlikely to be enhanced.	Likely to be enhanced.

---

[4] This tendency in which curriculum and standards for qualifying personnel are decided centrally and local governments are asked to administer these standards applies not only to Uganda but to other countries as well. See a five-booklet series of World Bank publications on *Decentralization of Education* (for example, Fiske, 1996).

countryside. As a result, it is viewed as a technical rather than political issue, and as a question of ensuring *better* control by the central rather than opening the door for true local initiative (Olowu, 1990, p. 87, emphasis in original).

This contradiction undermines the motivations of stakeholders in the processes of decentralization. The simultaneous centralization of policy packages and the decentralized delivery modality has a much wider implication for accountability, as illustrated by Table 9.1. The process in which local governments become implementers of centrally determined policy packages frustrates *political* accountability between local political leaders and their constituencies. This process, on the other hand, may be suitable to ensure *administrative* accountability between the central and local governments. While the decentralized process with increased autonomy can improve political accountability between people at the grassroots level and local leaders, administrative accountability between the central and local governments may not be as easily secured as in the centralized case. Table 9.1 indicates that accountability revolves around a very complex web of stakeholder relationships in determining who is accountable to whom (central government, local authorities, technocrats, and people at the grassroots) on what grounds (political and administrative/financial).

Although some development outcomes may be attained, different processes have much more complicated implications for accountability. In order to improve accountability, the process to produce outputs is at least as significant as the outputs themselves. Even though the central government may consider it suitable to centralize policy contents in the short-term, its long-term consequences may damage central-local relationships both politically and administratively.

Second, the often-praised partnerships between districts and NGOs are not free from problems, either. Obstacles for closer cooperation exist on both sides. NGOs consider local governments to still be very bureaucratic in processing relevant matters. Local administrators in rural Africa often demand allowances in order to cooperate with NGOs (Uganda, MoFPED, 2000k, p. 23). Political influences are sometimes exercised in the process of choosing beneficiaries (Uganda, MoFPED, 2000m, p. 28).[5] On the other hand, local governments consider many NGOs to be under-funded and unsuitable for long-term activities. The officials point out that many do not possess necessary transportation for grassroots activities. Although lack of vehicles may be a small example, it is symbolic enough to highlight the importance of sharing common motivation for sustaining partnerships. Accordingly, in various localities, NGO forums were formed for coordination but remain inactive primarily due to mutual suspicion.

This importance of motivation equally applies to the third type of partnership between service providers and recipients. Providers require adequate incentives for improving services needed by recipients, while recipients also need to be mo-

---

[5] In an extreme example, in Kotido District in Uganda, a charge of Ush 50,000 (US$ 30) for participating NGOs was levied, and the entities which could not afford the payment stayed away from meetings (Uganda, MoFPED, 2000l, p. 32).

tivated to collaborate with local service providers.[6] The more recipients and providers are linked by shared goals, the more likely they will have trusting relationships in which mutually beneficial outcomes become more likely (Golooba-Mutebi, 1999, chapter 9). Where leadership is effective and transparent, such encouraging changes, no matter how sporadic, have started to emerge.

A consistent framework of rewards and sanctions also helps to construct more satisfactory accountability relations between leaders and followers.   If accountability is a tool for ensuring more efficient and effective public services, both rewards and sanctions should be used consistently in order to establish adequate standards of performances and to improve motivation of relevant stakeholders.   If accountability has financial and political aspects, rewards and sanctions can be both monetary as well as non-monetary.   Salaries and social pressures, for example, can work as incentive mechanisms.   Thus, as already pointed out by rural development analysts, mixing different kinds of incentives is critical.   Complementing material with moral incentives is essential to ensure that development processes are cost-effective as well as performance-effective (Uphoff et al., 1998, p. 105).

Therefore, it is be essential to create this kind of complementary incentive structure.   Without such complementarities, there would be little reason for organizing public-private partnerships for mutually beneficial outcomes (Evans, 1996, p. 1123).   Creating such complementarities is possible even though it is by no means easy.   Limited government budgets render financial incentives alone ineffective.   Increased autonomy and discretion can be more promising as a useful non-monetary incentive, in which options for mutually beneficial outcomes are explored (Tendler, 1997, pp. 4-5).[7] Newly created autonomy presents a possible basis on which partnerships can be established through a coherent set of material and non-material incentives.

The complimentary incentive mechanisms are, then, necessary to foster a new culture of accountability in many developing countries.   In many parts of the developing world, accountability is a new concept; the poor have not been accustomed to raising questions over public affairs.   If such behavior had been attempted in the 1970s in Uganda, for instance, people could have easily been killed by the authorities.   Accountability being enhanced as a core value of liberal democracy as it has been in the West is far from automatic (Przeworski et al., 1999). It is a gradual process in which socio-political stability and the new social spaces opened by decentralization measures have enabled ordinary people to discuss political issues without many constraints in a number of developing countries.

---

[6] Evans (1996) highlights the fact that "public sectors typically rely on incentive systems that send very weak signals about performance to staff.... [M]any public bureaucracies give public sector workers little reason to pay attention to the people they are serving" (p. 1126). See also Carley and Christie (2000) for a similar description (p. 151).

[7] Tendler argues that in Brazil's case, the government service providers showed a high degree of dedication to their jobs primarily because their dedication was rewarded. The higher levels of the government also supported their dedication through repeated pubic campaigns (Tendler, 1997, p. 136).

Effective accountability is in essence reciprocal. It would work both upwards and downwards between those who govern and the governed. Both leaders and followers need to be held accountable for respective duties and responsibilities. In reality, however, the accountability relationship is often unequal. This inequality is at the heart of the accountability issue. Lower levels of sub-national governments and ordinary grassroots people in developing countries do not have many tools to reward or sanction political and administrative leadership. Accountability can more likely be ensured when both those who account and those who are accounted for can be in more reciprocal relationships.[8] Such prospects may increase, if both sides can have fewer discrepancies in their access to incentive mechanisms. Ordinary citizens, including the poor, are the ultimate evaluators of development policies in any democratic system. The degree of state responsiveness is one important indicator of democracy (Dahl, 1971), but the followers obviously have much less access to incentive mechanisms than their leaders. Elections are essential but not sufficient to establish a fair and reciprocal accountability for those in power. Although decentralization attempts are believed to be more conducive to forge such reciprocity, much more efforts are needed.[9]

Here, associations of local authorities and social movements can play crucial roles to offset such imbalances in their access to accountability tools. It is encouraging that, as shown in Uganda, some associations of local authorities are making effective demands on respective central governments to create such reciprocal and more accountable relationships. Women's organizations are one of the most effective social movements to voice their concerns in order to influence national policies in many parts of the world (Chapter 5). Although these examples are not free of problems, they provide some opportunities to induce accountable relations among stakeholders.[10]

In order to sustain this kind of effective change, it is essential to identify who is a good performer and who is a non-performer. It is also crucial to examine on what basis any performance can be judged. Accurate information, supported by freedom of speech and the press, is therefore much needed to make informed judgments.

---

[8] A distinction between 'answerability' and 'enforcement' in analyzing accountability may be useful. The former comes into play as "being accountable means having the obligation to answer questions regarding decisions and/or actions" (Ribot, 2001, pp. 30-31), while enforcement is the ability to apply sanctions if answers are not deemed satisfactory. See Ribot (2001) on his review of accountability issues (pp. 30-34).

[9] Ribot (2001) thus argues that the power disparity between the powerful and marginalized groups skews accountability toward more privileged groups. He therefore argues for the need of multiple mechanisms for the disadvantaged to be included in the political process (p. 33).

[10] Although decentralization attempts may tend to spread corruption, they also have some potential to contain it. A recent study (CITE International, 1998) reports that decentralization measures present a potential for more transparency by increased disclosures of illicit activities and misconduct by local officials.

2.2 Information for Partnership Formations

Information plays an essential role to foster partnerships. Stakeholders involved in rural development need to pay much more attention to information dissemination as an indispensable component supplementing technical support and organization reforms.[11] More accurate information should be provided to all stakeholders about their new roles as well as their rights and responsibilities in a newly-established decentralized context. Such information, especially related to local policies and budgets, should also be provided more thoroughly in order to enhance transparency.[12] In order for the rural poor to understand essential information, successful communication needs to be "easy to grasp – simple, succinct, attractive, self-evidently legitimate, and enhancing self-esteem" (Uphoff et al., 1998, pp. 148-49). With decentralization attempts, it is critical to devise innovative information dissemination strategies. The strategies need to overcome the difficulties encountered during decentralization processes in which bargaining and struggles take place over new patterns of power distribution and resource allocation. While in the past people in developing countries paid more attention to policies and programs carried out by their central governments, they have also started to show interest in local government activities lately. As they gradually come to understand that local governments also affect their everyday lives, ensuring fair access to essential information of both central and local governments becomes crucial for sustaining effective decentralization endeavors.

But information does not flow automatically. The current insufficient disclosure of information in various decentralization schemes in developing countries, including lack of feedback on previous meetings, contributes to a widespread notion that "our leaders are eating our money." There is significant mutual discontent between local leaders and people at the grassroots, and the people are particularly resentful because the leaders benefit from decentralization policies at the cost of the majority of populations. This kind of mutual distrust is further complicated by relationships involving male leaders and grassroots women. This mistrust is undoubtedly harmful for constructing mutually empowering results. In contrast, consensus can facilitate the process of mutual collaboration for positive-sum outcomes in which nobody loses at the cost of others.

A crucial dilemma of information dissemination is that it is still disseminated from the top to a large extent, particularly at local levels. Top-down dissemination can create opportunities for those in power to manipulate and sometimes to monopolize essential information. Such a situation is harmful to the poor who

---

[11] Long (2001) emphasizes that knowledge is embedded in social contexts. Therefore unless due attention is paid to how information is shared, disseminated, monopolized, and applied in the context of specific development activities, the simplistic notion of merely "supplying" knowledge to others is meaningless (p. 19).

[12] It is revealing to note what Rosenau (1995) stated: "It might even be said that governance in an ever more complex and interdependent world depends less on the issuance of authoritative directives and more on the release of reliable information and the legitimacy inherent in its detail" (p. 63).

tend to have many fewer sources of information than the rich and the powerful. Indeed information needs to be disseminated and shared in a particular political, economic, and social context.[13] New information strategies under decentralization attempts should be targeted to different audiences than in the days of centralized administration. This issue is not only technical but also political. Negotiations among stakeholders, including the powerful and the powerless, for attaining a mutually beneficial common vision can facilitate information disclosure. As demonstrated elsewhere, an effective information campaign can be a powerful tool in creating a new constituency who would back up desirable reforms and in attempting to overcome political opposition (Tendler, 1997, p. 137).

Information dissemination can be promoted by several channels. The first possibility rests with the central government (Mackintosh and Roy, 1999, p. 19), even if this may sound paradoxical. Because local government officials may be entangled in personal networks of local patronage, information may not be readily disseminated from local leaders to the grassroots poor. This situation can be offset by intervention from the center. The central government is more distant from local personal networks, and this remoteness presents an advantage in information dissemination. The central government is responsible for devising appropriate national policy on media. There is a common pattern in many developing countries; women are less exposed to mass media than men and the exposure also declines slowly with age. It is also clear that urban residents have more access to media than their rural counterparts.[14] To ameliorate these gaps in information access is often beyond the capacity of individual local governments, and thus should be the responsibility of the central government.[15]

The second possibility is associations of local authorities like the ULAA in Uganda.[16] This kind of association is very useful for information sharing and dissemination. If the occasional gatherings of the associations can be used for sharing innovative experiences of different places, that itself would be one effective mechanism of information dissemination. This is especially noteworthy since in some countries various levels of local governments are about to form their respective associations, and these multiple layers of associations would present promis-

---

[13] Effective communication needs to be context specific. According to White (1999), communication as an integrated component of sustainable development has to be participatory and is a "two-way, dynamic interaction, which through dialogue transforms 'grass-roots' people and enables them to become fully engaged in the process of development and become self-reliant" (p. 36). See also Agunga, 1997; Melkote and Steeves, 2001; and Moemeka, 2000.

[14] Uganda clearly fits into this characterization (Uganda, UBOS, 2001a, pp. 23-25).

[15] In Uganda, the proposed Communications Strategic Plan is a step in the right direction (Uganda, MoFPED, 2001, p. 41).

[16] It is interesting that the ULAA is planned to establish, with Kenayan and Tanzanian counterparts, the East African Local Authorities Association (Bakunzi, 2001a). In addition, in some areas, professional associations seem to be emerging. In Rakai, medical doctors started to form an association to discuss common problems (interview, Kalisizo Hospital, Rakai, 10 July 2000).

ing opportunities for attempting to overcome, if not totally eliminate, the difficulties of information dissemination from above.

Widely available information not only helps each stakeholder understand respective roles and responsibilities but also helps construct a consensus over how to turn new opportunities of local autonomy into more specific improvements in their livelihoods. Even though the poor do not necessarily share identical concerns, prospects to overcome social divisions (including gender, religion, and ethnicity) may increase if improved disclosure of public policies can accommodate competing needs of various stakeholders.

Among the social divisions, ethnicity becomes acutely political once critical information is monopolized and shared only among an individual ethnic group. This monopoly aggravates social divisions, and "the information divide" has serious implications for collaborative action. It can, however, be overcome by diversifying information channels. If there are informal interactions between local leaders and traditional authorities of various ethnic groups, such interactions may present one improved channel of information flow. Often these interactions widen social networks, and information is passed in multiple ways. If this kind of multiplication continues, establishing harmony among different ethnic groups may become a reality in the future. [17]

Women's networking is a second good example of overcoming social divisions, as witnessed in the Ugandan experience. Women are often good networkers, but have less inclination to monopolize information. Women often share information with men, because sharing benefits all family members. Information sharing plays an indispensable role in reducing gender gaps in this process. Young people are, in contrast, far behind women in networking, because most are oriented toward individual activities. Their access to information is severely limited, which discourages collective action. In order for decentralization attempts to deliver intended policy objectives, it is crucial for divergent stakeholders to build a consensus over goals. For that purpose, effective communication strategies are indispensable. This importance is highlighted even more by the erosion of social cohesiveness noticed in some villages which may be the result of decentralization processes. Social movements exemplified by women – the movements aiming to achieve broader results beneficial to more than those narrowly defined social groups – certainly have a crucial role to play in overcoming this erosion. Because community is a functional notion (as discussed in Chapter 1), improved information dissemination may present new opportunities for unconventional communities to emerge if access to information sharing fosters a common identity.

---

[17] Long (2001), however, notes a paradox. Effective dissemination of information largely depends upon "weak ties" that bridge divergent networks. Such weak ties are particularly important for obtaining access to diverse fields of information. However, accessing information normally requires that individuals secure some support from others who may share some consensus and may enforce compliance from members. The arrangement assumes the pre-existence of a relatively dense social network, that can at the same time, paradoxically, prevent new information from being shared as well as from being adapted to new circumstances (p. 181).

2.3 Conflict-resolution Mechanisms

It is often argued that local democracy can serve to balance the competing interests of different people more effectively than at the national level. Decentralized provisions are said to be more suitable to accommodate pluralism, often considered as a core value of democracy. But critics argue that pluralism in developing countries is often associated with sectarian tendencies and civil strife. Uganda is certainly no exception in post-independence Africa. The challenge is, then, instead of letting pluralism slide into mutually harmful negative-sum interactions among different stakeholders, where everybody is worse off than before, for pluralism to be more positively harnessed for mutually satisfactory and empowering outcomes in low-income countries.

One essential solution appears to lie in ascertaining how participation can overcome various conflicts at different levels. If development is a process of social change, it inevitably invites tensions and conflicts. Then, it is essential to ensure first that such conflicts do not threaten the foundation of the state, and also that conflicts can be more creatively used in sharing power and resources among diverse actors (Carley and Christie, 2000, p. 137). This issue of turning conflicts into creativity is of serious importance since decentralization processes are associated with complex interactions of heterogeneous participants. Conflicts can take various forms: debate, contest, dispute, disagreement, turmoil, and a state of unrest (Warner, 2001). They can be violent sometimes. Some conflicts are clearly based on a given political system, while others are contained by repression (Evans, 1996, p.1127). Harnessing conflicts positively requires that management capacity cope with pressures put on individuals and organizations deriving from social transformation. These capacities should be able to settle social disputes, reduce economic grievances and lessen political hostilities (Warner, 2001, p. v).[18]

Experiences in Uganda provide useful lessons here as well. First of all, effective conflict management apparatus is very context specific and usually encompasses both formal and informal procedures. As seen in the example of Tororo District in Uganda, urgent attention is needed to craft formal procedures within the legal framework in order to enhance the efficiency and effectiveness of the local government system, since many of these systems in Africa and elsewhere do not

---

[18] It should be emphasized that development processes and conflicts are two sides of the same coin (Carley and Christie, 2000; and Warner, 2001). On the one hand, general economic improvements may reduce conflicts. Where opportunities for earning income are severely limited, people who seek political offices would in fact stand for the sake of economic gains rather than for political considerations. Then harmful neo-patrimonialism tends to prevail. Stimulating the local economy can work as an indirect but effective deterrent in a low-income country like Uganda. On the other hand, development also induces conflicts over resource allocations and creates new types of contentions and disagreements.

provide any clear procedures for resolving political stalemates in local governments.[19]

But formal procedures often prove insufficient, particularly in Africa. Often disputes could have been resolved by traditional authorities such as chiefs, even though this method is also filled with numerous controversies and animosities. Legitimate conflict resolution tends to rely on what people are historically accustomed to. It is therefore essential to supplement formality with informality. In order to enhance the legitimacy of local governments, devising a coherent framework in which formal as well as informal procedures complement each other is essential, because the poor have significant reservations about the way local authorities presently function in Uganda (Khadiagala, 2001)[20] and in other places. The complement of an informal resolution mechanism is appreciated, particularly because social cohesiveness at local levels appears to be eroding due to decentralization measures.

Here the issue of incentives is relevant again. If people are motivated for mutual collaboration by any valid reason, that would act as a deterrent to creating serious disputes. As long as collaboration is valued, selfish behavior is discouraged. As long as small-scale activities at the grassroots level are organized for mutual benefit, they present the potential to turn a vicious cycle of mistrust into a virtuous sequence of enhancing trust (Carley and Christie, 2000, p. 185). In addition, external donors (including NGOs) play an important role in facilitating such collaborative processes (Charlick, 2001; and Nielsen, 2001).[21]

3 Policy Lessons

As this study has demonstrated, the examination of strategic partnership formations supported by incentive mechanisms, information sharing and conflict-resolution provisions are important in themselves. Moreover, these factors relates to much wider issues relevant for successful institutional reforms in developing countries at a difficult time partly influenced by globalization, financial scarcity for most of the states, and limited democratization as seen in Chapter 2.

---

[19] While a formal judicial system may not close the door on such resolutions, its efficacy may be questioned in numerous developing countries. Certainly the poor are often unable to afford such formal procedures.

[20] While traditional leadership often provides alternative conflict-resolution mechanisms in other places in Africa, in Uganda this is not the case. Although the chiefs and clans still operate on a very limited number of issues in Uganda, the unitary polity of Uganda, of which the LC system forms a central pillar, has deprived traditional authorities of political functions.

[21] Warner (2001) argues that consensus building leads to "win-win" solutions and provides effective guidelines for its attainment. See also Carley and Christie, 2000, chapter 9.

3.1 Cohesive Efforts at National and Local Levels

Decentralization is a complex process of social transformation. While one set of issues is resolved, another set is created. As illustrated by the examples of education and health in Uganda, decentralized services have attained some progress in efficiency and effectiveness. However, these results face another serious set of challenges for sustainability. Many complications cannot easily be resolved by individual local governments alone. The problems need to be tackled in tandem by the national and local governments.

Sustainable institutional reform efforts at the central and local levels need to be coordinated, and the reforms need to be implemented within a clearly defined and coherent framework (Harbeson, 2001; and Mamdani, 1996). This coherence is especially important, since efforts to improve incentive mechanisms, information dissemination, and conflict resolution at local levels face certain limitations unless similar endeavors are made at the national level. Therefore, concerted efforts are indispensable for facilitating strategic partnership formations.

The first issue is related to civil service reforms. For material incentives to be improved, central governments in developing countries have to reform their civil service system and improve remuneration of public service personnel. The civil service reforms in developing countries have predominantly focused on how to make a small and efficient public sector at the national level. But little attention has been paid to implement them in a way consistent with decentralized provisions. Because it is normally the responsibility of the central government to establish the pay scale, central governments are urged to determine a pay level that can provide a decent standard of living for civil servants. Unless this pay scale is established nationally, sporadic local efforts in applying non-material incentives alone cannot resolve the incentive issue fully, which is crucial for strategic partnership formation.

The second critical area which needs coordinated reform at the national level is the contradiction between the sector-wide approach (SWAP) and decentralized service provisions. Both are often supported by the central government as well as donors. As in Uganda, although there has been some effort to consolidate numerous inter-governmental fiscal transfers (Chapter 6), such efforts need to address the wider issue of maintaining positive incentives for autonomous local governments to determine locally specific activities without jeopardizing certain public services which are provided nationally. Discretional funds contribute to enhancing incentives for improved service provisions. But so far both central governments in developing countries and donors fear losing control over local governments. This contradiction is a serious concern, particularly in developing countries, which heavily depend on donor financing for essential public services. However, little research has been done and further investigation is urgently needed.[22]

---

[22] Even the recent reviews of the SWAP make little reference to this contradiction. See Brown et al., 2001; Foster, 2000; Lister and Nyamugasira, 2003, p. 103; and World Bank, 2001a.

Third, the central government policies on information dissemination and conflict-resolution mechanisms significantly affect whether local partnerships can be formed. Unless there is national-level support to enhance the transparency and accountability of the state, local efforts alone will not be able to provide all the key information to be disseminated. The most acute example is probably the issue of conflict resolution. If facilitation and mediation attempts to resolve local disputes are unsuccessful, ultimately this has to be handled at the national level. Nation-wide judicial and police reforms need to be clearly linked with other initiatives to provide "popular justice" at the grassroots level (Tidemand, 1995).

The fourth arena in which central-local harmonization is needed concerns regulations on NGO activities and policies on private sector development. If there is no genuine support by the national government for NGO activities, collaboration between local governments and NGOs will only yield limited results. Likewise, unless there is a national commitment to secure the free and fair movement of people, goods and money, liberalization attempts to assist market-oriented development at local levels will not effect a durable solution. This emphasis on simultaneous reform at the national and local levels does not mean that these efforts have to be pursued in a top-down fashion as they were in the past. A top-down mode of operations and reforming rules of relations among stakeholders are not identical.

Fifth, equity concerns need much more attention by central-local collaboration. Regional disparities may widen due to decentralization measures, and this serious concern is shared by many stakeholders including grassroots people. As in the case of Uganda, equalization grants are one step forward but their implementation is usually troublesome (Bird and Smart, 2002). Therefore, this issue cannot be left to local governments alone and needs to be addressed at the central level. This equity concern is also related to balancing national standards in service provisions and flexible local adaptations in implementation. In other words, the equity issue is also a coordination question of which levels of the government should be allowed to make what kinds of policies. Thus, central and local governments have their respective essential roles to play.

The necessity of concerted efforts by both central and local governments means that, contrary to often-held views, decentralization attempts may not reduce the size of the state. One of the assumptions of decentralization is that it makes the state smaller. This idea of small government has almost become an imperative since the 1980s when the state was considered as a key obstacle to development, particularly in Africa. But this assumption is clearly unrealistic. While local governments are more suitably positioned to identify the needs of the population, other functions (including coordination, support, supervision, and monitoring) increase along with the increased autonomy granted to local authorities. In a decentralized structure, the center needs to improve its capacity not to provide hierarchical control but to provide technical support to sub-national units of the government (Uphoff, 1986, p. 225). As a result, contrary to the notion of a minimalist state, decentralizing services would almost assuredly engender bigger governments (Mackintosh and Roy, 1999, p. 19).

3.2 Political System at the National Level

The ultimate consistency needed in orchestrating reforms at national and local levels is polity itself. The political context in which these reforms are pursued has proven to be a decisive element, as seen in the experiences of Uganda. Unless political leadership, both at the central and local levels, consider decentralization measures to serve their interests, political leadership will not commit to such reforms, and initiatives cannot be "owned" by a developing country. This consideration reinforces the notion that decentralization is normally influenced by political factors. Decentralizing service provisions cannot be neutral institutional reforms which derived from a technical blueprint used elsewhere; nor can they be easily replicated by other countries. This does not mean, however, that other countries cannot learn from the experiences of Uganda.

If decentralization attempts are intended to achieve both democracy and development, political commitment by central governments in developing countries constitutes both advantages and disadvantages. While the central governments are committed politically to decentralizing measures, social autonomy granted to local governments can indeed be limited by political ideas and objectives of those in power at the national level. This contradiction often remains unnoticed by policy makers in developing countries and donors alike. The literature on decentralization emphasizes the political commitment necessary to render decentralization attempts successful. But little attention has been paid to the inherent paradox of simultaneous political support and political interference.

Thus, in order for any decentralization measures to be successful, more attention needs to be paid to balancing national and local politics. It is contradictory to pursue an inclusive and participatory political system at local levels without concomitant democratization at the national level. A genuinely democratic decision-making process is established only if political opponents of the regime can participate in polity (Dahl, 1971). The states in developing countries face an inherent dilemma, particularly because many decentralization measures are implemented with restrictions on democratization in place (Olowu, 2001). As in Uganda, if accountability between local leaders and constituencies is hampered by local governments becoming mere administrating agents of centrally-determined activities, this political decay would pose a significant threat to political systems. In this situation, what is at stake is the legitimacy of the polity systems.[23] This danger can be avoided if more political and administrative autonomy can be granted to local governments with enhanced support, supervision, and coordination by respective central governments in disseminating appropriate information, creating mutually reinforcing incentives, and facilitating conflict mediations. This approach is consistent with the original purpose of the decentralization attempts. In order for local governments to become "democratic organs of the people," they

---

[23] Legitimacy is also multiple in a situation whereby diverse actors attempt to resolve issues collectively (Goss, 2001, p. 23).

need to harness the energies of the people more democratically and developmentally.[24]

3.3 Mutually Empowering Possibilities for the State and Civil Society

The polity issue has a wider implication for state-society relations. It is often assumed that decentralization contributes to nurturing civil society. Associational activities and movements, in reality, flourish at the level where the state is also active (cf Brinkerhoff, 2002, p. 30). Decentralizing attempts do not automatically foster autonomous associational activities at local levels, unless the local-level state is also active and it becomes worthwhile for civil society to be engaged (Tendler, 1997, p. 148). If local governments are weak, local associations will not be strong. This does not mean that all associational activities are shaped solemnly by the state, but the state does have a profound influence on how civil society is shaped. It is crucial in developing countries that local governments be in the process of building their capacities to plan and implement various activities. In this process, various associations, including NGOs, are also presently responding to these emerging local governments by enhancing their own capacities as well (Clayton, 1998). It can be anticipated that through these processes of capacity building on the part of both governments and voluntary associations at local levels, mutually empowering outcomes can be achieved (Higgott et al, 2000; and Migdal et al., 1994). This may be an ultimate positive-sum situation whereby all gain from the transformation. Small-scale service provisions are promising arenas around which this kind of mutually satisfactory solution can be achieved, although it does not mean that this process is free of problems.

This new kind of local development has the potential to transform neo-patrimonial relationships, which are so deeply rooted in Africa (Chabal and Daloz, 1999). The fundamental issue is that neo-patrimonial rule is essentially a zero-sum approach to politics, in which some gains are loses for others. This approach leaves no scope for mutual compromise, and is not only very crude politics but also harmful to consultative policy reform efforts (Hyden, 2000, p. 23). As long as neo-patrimonialism persists in Africa, this kind of zero-sum transactions will continue (Ake, 1996). Therefore, politics in Africa becomes "politics of survival" (Bratton and van de Walle, 1997). It would be naïve for one to anticipate that it will disappear shortly, but there are at least some possibilities to turn this zero-sum relationship to a positive-sum one in which mutually beneficial outcomes can be reached. Thus, although decentralization implementation needs to be improved, one can still be hopeful that decentralizing measures can provide an impetus for this deadlocked zero-sum cruelty to be reversed to more socially acceptable positive-sum consequences.

Furthermore, even if decentralization measures are not a panacea, they provide some opportunities for more congruence between structures (institutions) and

---

[24] On the implication of this polity issue for the LC system in Uganda, see, for instance, Hyden, 1998b; and Tegulle, 2001.

norms, values, and attitudes (cognitive assets) of populations. Decentralization measures provide new opportunities whereby a multiple web of interactions among diverse individuals and organizations can take place. The enriched networks of interactions themselves create a new socio-economic dynamism. In addition, if decentralization attempts are viewed as a mutual institution building process for both the state and civil society, both the state and autonomous associations have more chances to learn from each other, and foster common values. This process, in turn, can create acceptable procedures, which can guide the behavior of stakeholders for mutually useful purposes. Organizing such local learning is less problematic than at the central level. Through this learning process, integration between institutions and cognitive values can be improved. This integration is needed to rectify the imbalances between current states and societies in Africa. More balanced relations between states and societies can produce considerable economic as well as socially harmonious outcomes.[25] Put differently, the subjective arena of motivations and norms for collaboration and the objective domain of organizational setups are interdependent. Values and norms can compensate for the lack of material resources, a common situation in rural subsistence economies in developing countries. Again decentralization measures per se do not automatically produce appropriate institutional mechanisms for balanced state-society relations, but this option can still be more suitable than the old centralization. This lesson is especially crucial since even in materially "poor" areas of developing countries, such cognitive forms (norms and values) can be nurtured which compensate for material deprivation. Decentralization endeavors can, thus, be successful even on the continent of Africa.

3.4 Donor Facilitation and Coordination

Given the fact that, particularly in Africa, the majority of development funds are provided by external donors, including multilateral organizations, bilateral agencies, and NGOs, the role of these donors needs to be reexamined in the context of decentralization attempts (Charlick, 2001; and Nielsen, 2001).[26] First, decentralizing services change the method of donor coordination dramatically. In the past, donors were almost exclusively working with various ministries and agencies of central governments in low-income countries. Thus, coordination was conducted at the central level. Now, with decentralization measures, donors provide assistance not only to respective central governments, but also to sub-national units of the government. As a result, few, if any, local authorities are fully aware

---

[25] Decentralization measures are, therefore, considered to provide some hope for creating appropriate local institutions on which "social capital" can be adequately expressed and to produce streams of benefits to stakeholders (Uphoff and Wijayaratna, 2000). See also Evans (1996).

[26] Aid dependency complicates accountability. "States are not likely to be accountable to a population from whom they do not earn their income through taxation" (Ribot, 2001, p. 33).

of all donor/NGO assistance provided to lower levels of the government under them. Therefore, coordination is needed both for "horizontal" as well as "vertical" lines of functions and authorities of the decentralized administrative structure. The familiar form of coordination, which has traditionally been taking place, is a "horizontal" one, in which donor-assisted activities do not duplicate other activities at similar levels of the administrative structure. "Vertical" coordination, in which efforts can be concerted among different levels of the government, is new and has increasingly become necessary. This type of coordination may become much more demanding than horizontal coordination at the central level. This makes coordination a very complicated yet indispensable task. Some of the donors are apparently uneasy over such coordination since it deprives them of some of the leverage that they seek to maintain vis-à-vis recipient governments. This contradiction between a willingness for donor coordination in rhetoric and a real motivation for maintaining influence and control may become more apparent in the conducting of the new type of vertical coordination. Donor coordination will become a more acute process of negotiations and bargaining between various donors and government units.

Second, the donors themselves support both the sector-wide approach (SWAP) and decentralization, which are contradictory as we have already seen. This concomitant support for contradicting principles takes place in numerous developing countries. Since this contradiction originates at least partly from the donors, efforts should be made first among the donors themselves to find possible resolutions. Although the recipient governments are willing to pursue institutional reforms, their efforts alone will not be effective, unless similar attempts are made by the donors for more consistent collaboration in development.

These are extremely relevant concerns, because the sustained efforts for much deeper democratization and effective economic reforms cannot be realized without continued donor support in the developing world, particularly in Africa. The donors' role in capacity building both at the central and local levels is crucial, but may turn out to be harmful unless urgent care is taken in consistent planning and coordinated implementation of donor funded projects and activities.

4 Concluding Remarks

This study has identified puzzling aspects of decentralization, which has been a common reform agenda in many parts of the world. One possibility to resolve tensions between those who emphasize economic efficiency and others who advocate political empowerment lies in collective action. One particular form of collective action is partnership. Thus, this study has focused on examining conditions under which partnerships can be facilitated by decentralizing the states in developing countries, especially in Africa, which themselves have been suffering from mismatches with their societies.

If decentralization attempts are to make significant contributions to improving fundamental political, economic, and social conditions in developing countries, this process of transformation needs to be supported by strategic partnerships among stakeholders. Such partnerships are more readily formed if incentive structures are coherent, essential information is disclosed widely, and affordable conflict-resolution mechanisms are in place – factors to which research so far has not paid sufficient attention. With these three elements accompanying decentralization measures, partnerships can be formed, which present the possibility to ease economic and political tensions lurking behind this policy agenda, even if the easing process needs to be further investigated in the future.

With decentralization measures, negotiations and accommodations of different interests and views will continue in a different way from those of centralized provisions. But if these struggles are more transparent and conducted openly in the public realm, the chances are greater for mutual collaboration. In the past, the struggles for accessing resources were largely conducted behind the official scenes, even though these hidden struggles were extremely widespread. As long as neo-patrimonialism in Africa operates without much transparency, it will not lead to democracy or advancement in developing countries.

Decentralization measures are far from a panacea to rectify imbalances between states and societies in Africa. But they offer various new opportunities for actors to diversify their interactions with others, through which some strategic partnerships can emerge. Some forms of partnerships produce mutually beneficial outcomes, a type of collective action much needed for overcoming poverty in developing countries. Thus, decentralization policies, when managed appropriately, present some hope to overcome the pessimism often associated with the African continent.

Appendix: Methodological Notes

In order to sketch out the broad tendencies of how the LC system is viewed by people at the grassroots level, two types of survey were conducted in 1999 and 2000 in three districts of Mukono, Rakai, and Tororo. The first method to seek grassroots people's view is commonly called a focus group discussion. The second one is the quantitative survey. The following Table A.1 shows the sampling information for the quantitative survey.

The first method of the focus group discussions took place in an informal and relaxed setting without interference by authorities and outsiders. It is considered that participants generally expressed their views without feeling being constrained.

The quantitative survey was to get obtain a basic indications of how people evaluate performances of the LC system and decentralization measures in a comparable way in different places. The survey enables us to assess performances of the LC with more insights since quantitative and qualitative methods are complementary with each other.

In contacting local communities, collaboration with different individuals and NGOs were sought. Since the questions were concerned with performances of the Local Council, it was deemed more suitable to collaborate with NGOs rather than the Councillors themselves who may inhibit local people to express critical views of the LC system. NGOs were considered to be more "neutral" in introducing the researcher to local communities. In Mukono, Food for the Hungry International and an individual who had extensive connection with women and youth groups were helpful in introducing me to the communities. In Rakai various different NGOs offered me an assistance: Rakai AIDS Information Network, Concern Worldwide, Integrated Rural Development Initiatives, and Irish Foundation for Coo-operative Development Ltd. In Tororo, since NGO activities were not so widespread as in other two areas, Development Office of the Bukedi Diocese of Church of Uganda was immensely helpful. Consultation was held, prior to the surveys, with the representatives of these organizations on methodologies and the practical applications in selected areas, and potential dangers in the survey if any. Given the practical constraints of limited time and logistics, selections of communities to be visited were made carefully. Since the purpose was to investigate how rural people at the grassroots would view the process of decentralization, diverse rural communities were visited during the fieldwork.

However, some notes on caution are in order. The answers for the questionnaire were obtained from those who were willing to attend meetings called by the collaborators of the research who were well known among the villagers in the survey areas. This means that those who were not willing to come were not reached,

Table A.1 Sampling data

Total		Mukono number 100	%	number 149	%	Rakai number 179	%	Total number 428	%
Sex	Men	36	36%	51	34%	93	52%	180	42%
	Women	57	57%	87	58%	73	41%	217	51%
	Unknown	7	7%	11	7%	13	7%	31	7%
Age	The youth (less than 25)	20	20%	33	22%	49	27%	102	57%
	The middle aged (26 - 49)	58	58%	77	52%	88	49%	223	52%
	The elderly (more than 50)	22	22%	36	24%	30	17%	88	21%
	Unknown	0	0%	3	2%	12	7%	15	4%
Councillor	Councillors themselves	9	9%	11	7%	41	23%	61	14%
	Not Councillors	46	46%	35	23%	116	65%	197	46%
	Unknown	45	45%	103	69%	22	12%	170	40%
Education	No education	10	10%	22	15%	8	4%	40	9%
	Primary schooling	54	54%	58	39%	86	48%	198	46%
	Primary up to 4th grade	10	10%	17	11%	16	9%	43	10%
	Secondary schooling and more	35	35%	61	41%	71	40%	167	39%
	Unknown	1	1%	8	5%	14	8%	23	5%
Occupation	Farmer	77	77%	93	62%	110	61%	280	65%
	Others	19	19%	51	34%	45	25%	115	27%
	Unknown	4	4%	5	3%	24	13%	33	8%
Ethnicity	Muganda	16	16%			120	67%	136	32%
	Others	2	2%			7	4%	9	2%
	Unknown	82	82%	149	100%	52	29%	283	66%
Religion	Catholic	9	9%			94	53%	103	24%
	Protestant	7	7%			25	14%	32	7%
	Muslim	2	2%			13	7%	15	4%
	Traditional African	0	0%			1	1%	1	0%
	Others	0	0%			0	0%	0	0%

and this puts a certain bias in the survey. The bias might be significant, if those respondents participated in training and seminars for various activities and these experiences may have hanged the way they perceive the local situations. In short, the responses given to the questionnaire may describe more elaborated views than "average" reactions. It is plausible that these views are also more appreciative of the LC system than the negative ones which may have been held by non-attendants.

On the other hand, the degree of this kind of bias does not appear significant. Some efforts were made to cross check the relevance of the information, and the series of double-check exercises confirm that the findings were not influenced too much by the selection biases. The two sets of data gathered by the quantitative and qualitative surveys were cross checked with each other.

It was also very useful to discuss the findings of the surveys with the collaborators of the research and sometimes with the grassroots people themselves who earlier participated in the survey. The informants themselves participated in further discussing the survey findings, and this experience was very helpful. The findings were also checked with the earlier works in similar research projects. Additionally, the collaborators informed me how non-participants would possibly react to some of the essential questions.

In order to ensure fair comparability of three districts, the number of respondents are standardized based on the minimum response in Mukono District: 100.

In the case of Tororo, the samples from Mulanda are decided to be excluded because there a significant number of responded answered "very much so" to all the questions. When the questionnaire were distributed in Mulanda, the gathering was too large, and it appears that participants could not fully understand the purpose of the exercise. The responses of Mulanda are very different from other answers from the same district. Table A.1 excludes Mulanda samples. Then randomly 100 responses are picked up. In Tororo it appears that opinions vary relatively significantly depending on areas within the same district. Thus, the inclusion of Tororo is useful for comparative examinations with the two other districts.

In contrast, in Rakai, the simple tabulation and the tabulation based on the random sampling indicate basically an identical pattern of answers. In Rakai, thus, 100 samples are randomly chosen.

The suggested questions for the informal discussions and the quantitative survey questions are attached in the following. As noted in the opening sections of the discussion topics for the focus group consultations, these topics are suggested guidelines only. When participants would like to refer to other matters, it was encouraged to allow such free talks.

The Suggested Questions for informal discussions with people at the grassroots level, 1999

Please note that this is an indicative guideline only. When participants would like to talk what they wish to reveal, a sufficient care should be taken not to prevent them from doing so.

- introduce the moderator and the translator
- explain the purpose of the meeting
- ask the participants to introduce themselves: sex, age, level of education, their job/work

The topics for discussions included as follows:
1. Relationship with local political leaders
2. Decentralization
3. Service Delivery
4. Development and Democracy
5. Gender and Ethnicity

The Suggested Questions for informal discussions with people at the grassroots level, 2000

Please note that this is an indicative guideline only. When participants would like to talk what they wish to reveal, a sufficient care should be taken not to prevent them from doing so.

- introduce the moderator and the translator
- explain the purpose of the meeting
- ask the participants to introduce themselves: sex, age, level of education, their job/work

1. Diversity of social networks and the LC system
   - In your view, what are the qualities or characteristics of a good leader?
   - Comparing the LC with other social networks and organizations, how would you evaluate its performance? What are the useful things it does? What are the things not so useful?
   - When was the most recent meeting that you attended? Can you tell us the date and the month of the last meeting?

2. Service Delivery including UPE
   - When you choose your leader, do you vote for someone with good education or do you vote for someone just like yourself? What other criteria do you use for voting?
   - When you vote for an educated person, do you think s/he can represent you?
   - Do you think, for instance, views of farmers can only be represented by farmers?

3. Corruption
   - Do you think that corruption is getting worse than before? Any example?
   - What kind of corruption do you think ARE is happening in your area?
   - Are you concerned some of these examples? Why? Why not?

4. Social divisions
   - In your area, what are the examples of social divisions, which prevent people in the community/local area from getting together? Religion, ethnicity, gender, age, and disability etc?
   - What do you think of these divisions? Is it good to have them?
   - Do you think efforts should be made to overcome these divisions?

5. Information Needs
   - What sort of information you wish to receive? Central government budget; central government activities; local government budget; local government activities, donors assistance; agricultural market produce; management of local school and health clinic, etc
   - Do you wish to know how and why some officials are appointed?

Questions sheets

Date: Place:

Sex: male or female
Occupation: farmer, business, teacher, office worker; unemployed; other (   )
Are you a Councillor? Yes, No: If yes at LC (   )
Years of schooling: (   ) years
Age: (   ) years old
Religion: Catholic, Protestant, Islam, Traditional African religion, Other (   )
Ethnic group/Tribe: Muganda, and Other (   )

1. Are you satisfied in the way the LC system as a whole (LC I-V) operates?
       5 (   ) very much so;
       4 (   ) somewhat yes;
       3 (   ) somewhat no;
       2 (   ) definitely no;
       1 (   ) do not know.

1.1. Are you satisfied in the way the LC I (village) operates?
       5 (   ) very much so;
       4 (   ) somewhat yes;
       3 (   ) somewhat no;
       2 (   ) definitely no;
       1 (   ) do not know.

1.2. Are you satisfied in the way the LC III (sub-county) operates?
       5 (   ) very much so;
       4 (   ) somewhat yes;
       3 (   ) somewhat no;
       2 (   ) definitely no;
       1 (   ) do not know.

1.3. Are you satisfied in the way the LC V (district) operates?
       5 (   ) very much so;
       4 (   ) somewhat yes;
       3 (   ) somewhat no;
       2 (   ) definitely no;
       1 (   ) do not know.

2. Do you feel participation in LC I meetings useful?

        5 ( ) very much so;
        4 ( ) somewhat yes;
        3 ( ) somewhat no;
        2 ( ) definitely no;
        1 ( ) do not know.

3.Do you feel you are less poor in terms of material deprivation than before?

        5 ( ) very much so;
        4 ( ) somewhat yes;
        3 ( ) somewhat no;
        2 ( ) definitely no;
        1 ( ) do not know.

4.Do you feel you are more confident, more connected to the community, and have more people to help you when you need help than before?

        5 ( ) very much so;
        4 ( ) somewhat yes;
        3 ( ) somewhat no;
        2 ( ) definitely no;
        1 ( ) do not know.

5.Are you pleased with the process of LC consultation on local issues?

        5 ( ) very much so;
        4 ( ) somewhat yes;
        3 ( ) somewhat no;
        2 ( ) definitely no;
        1 ( ) do not know.

6.Are you pleased with what the LC (I-V) has done?

        5 ( ) very much so;
        4 ( ) somewhat yes;
        3 ( ) somewhat no;
        2 ( ) definitely no;
        1 ( ) do not know.

7. Do you feel that the LC system as a whole is responding to the needs of the ordinary people like yourself?

        5 ( ) very much so;
        4 ( ) somewhat yes;
        3 ( ) somewhat no;
        2 ( ) definitely no;
        1 ( ) do not know.

References

Ablo, Emmanuel and Ritva Reinikka [1999] "Do Budget Really Matter?: Evidence from Public Spending on Education and Health in Uganda," Assessing Outcomes for a Comprehensive Development Framework, Kampala, Uganda (Kampala, October 26-28).

Abram, Simone and Jacqueline Waldren (eds) [1998] Anthropological Perspectives on Local Development (London: Routledge).

Adamolekun, Lapido (ed) [1999] Public Administration in Africa: Main Issues and Selected Country Studies (Boulder, CO.: Westview Press).

Agrawal, Arun and Jesse Ribot [1999] "Accountability in Decentralization: A Framework with South Asian and West African Cases," The Journal of Developing Areas Vol. 33, pp. 473-502.

Agunga, Robert A. [1997] Developing the Third World: A Communication Approach (Commack, NY.: Nova Science Publishers).

Ahmad, Ehtisham (ed) [1997] Financing Decentralized Expenditures: An International Comparison of Grants (Cheltenham: Edward Elgar).

Ake, Claude [1996] Democracy and Development in Africa (Washington, D.C.: Brookings Institution).

Alfonso, Haroldo Dilla [1997] "Political Decentralization and Popular Alternatives: A View from the South," In: Michael Kaufman and Haroldo Dilla Alfonso (eds) Community Power and Grassroots Democracy (London: Zed Books).

Appleton, Simon [1999] "Education in Uganda: What to Expect from Universal Primary Education (UPE)?," Assessing Outcomes for a Comprehensive Development Framework, Kampala, Uganda (Kampala, October 26-28).

Appleton, Simon [1998] "Changes in Poverty in Uganda, 1992-1996," http://www.worldbank.org/research/sapri/uganda/appleton.pdf [accessed 6 May 2001].

Appleton, Simon [1996] "Women-Headed Households and Household Welfare: An Empirical Deconstruction for Uganda," World Development Vol. 24, No. 12, pp. 1811-1827.

Apter, David E. [1997] The Political Kingdom in Uganda: A Study in Bureaucratic Nationalism, third edition (London: Frank Cass).

Association for the Development of Education in Africa (ADEA) [1999] Prospective, Stocktaking Review of Education in Africa: Draft Synthesis Document for the 1999 Biennial Meeting, http://www.adeanet.org/biennial99/Synthesis-5%20eng.pdf [accessed 22 October 2000].

Aziz, Abdul and David D. Arnold (eds) [1996] Decentralised Governance in Asian Countries (London: Sage Publication).

Bakunzi, James [2001a] "East Africa Plans Local Government Association," New Vision 9 August.

Bakunzi, James [2001b] "KCC Joins Local Council Association," New Vision 19 July.

Barnes, Nicole C. [1999] "How Local Can Government Go? Lessons from Fiscal Decentralization in Uganda," masters thesis submitted to the Massachusetts Institute of Technology.

Barrow, Edmund and Marshall Murphree [2001] "Community Conservation: From Concept to Practice," In: David Hulme and Marshall Murphree (eds) African Wildlife and Livelihoods: the Promise and Performance of Community Conservation (Oxford: James Currey).

Bates, Robert H. [2001] Prosperity and Violence: The Political Economy of Development (New York, NY.: W.W. Norton & Company).

Bates, Robert [1999] "Ethnicity, Capital Formation, and Conflict Social Capital Initiative," Working Paper No. 12 (Washington, D.C.: World Bank).

Bates, Robert [1981] Markets and States in Tropical Africa: the Political Basis of Agricultural Policies (Berkeley, CA.: University of California Press).

Bayart, Jean-Francois [2000] "Africa in the World: A History of Extraversion," African Affairs Vol. 99, pp. 217-267.

Bayart, Jean-Francois [1993] The State in Africa: the Politics of the Belly (London: Longman).

Bigsten, Arne and Steve Kayizzi-Mugerwa [2001] "Is Uganda an Emerging Economy?," A Report for the OECD Project "Emerging Africa" Research Report No. 118 (Uppsala: Nordiska Afrikainstitutet).

Bigsten, Arne and Steve Kayizzi-Mugerwa [1999] Crisis, Adjustment and Growth in Uganda: A Study of Adaptation in an African Economy (London: Macmillan).

Bigsten, Arne and Steve Kayizzi-Mugerwa [1995] "Rural Sector Responses to Economic Crisis in Uganda," Journal of International Development Vol. 7, No. 2, pp. 181-209.

Bird, Richard and Michael Smart [2002] "Intergovernmental Fiscal Transfers: International Lessons for Developing Countries," World Development Vol. 30, No.6, pp. 899-912.

Bird, Richard and Francois Vaillancourt (eds) [1998a] Fiscal Decentralization in Developing Countries (Cambridge: Cambridge University Press).

Bird, Richard and Francois Vaillancourt [1998b] "Fiscal Decentralization in Developing Countries: an Overview," In: Richard Bird and Francois Vaillancourt (eds) Fiscal Decentralization in Developing Countries (Cambridge: Cambridge University Press).

Blair, Harry [2000] "Participation and Accountability at the Periphery: Democratic Local Governance in Six Countries," World Development Vol. 28, No. 1, pp. 21-39.

Bratton, Michael and Gina Lambright [2001] "Uganda's Referendum 2000: the Silent Boycott," African Affairs Vol. 100, pp. 429-452.

Bratton, Michael and Nicolas van de Walle [1997] Democratic Experiments in Africa: Regime Transitions in Comparative Perspective (Cambridge: Cambridge University Press).

Bray, Mark [1996] Decentralization of Education: Community Financing (Washington, D.C.: World Bank).

Brett, E. A. [1996] "Structural Adjustment, Efficiency and Equity in Uganda," In: Poul Engberg-Pedersen, Peter Gibon, Phil Raikes, and Lars Udsholt (eds) Limits of Adjustment in Africa: the Effects of Economic Liberalization, 1986-94 Center for Development Research Copenhagen (Oxford: James Curry).

Brett, E. A. [1995] "Neutralizing the Use of Force in Uganda: the Role of the Military in Politics," Journal of Modern African Studies Vol. 33, No. 1, pp. 129-152.

Brett, E. A. [1994] "Rebuilding Organisation Capacity in Uganda Under the National Resistance Movement," Journal of Modern African Studies Vol. 32, No. 1, pp. 53-80.

Brett, E. A. [1992] "Providing for the Rural Poor: Institutional Decay and Transformation in Uganda," IDS Research Reports 23 (Brighton: Institute of Development Studies).

Brinkerhoff, Jennifer M [2002] Partnership for International Development: Rhetoric or Results (Boulder, CO.: Lynne Reinner Publishers).

Brock, Karen and Rosemary McGee [2002] Knowing Poverty: Critical Reflections on Participatory Research and Policy (London: Earthscan).

Brohman, John [1996] Popular Development: Rethinking the Theory and Practice of Development (Oxford: Blackwell).

Brown, Adrienne, Mick Foster, Andy Norton, and Felix Naschold [2001] "The Status of Sector Wide Approaches," ODI Working Paper No. 142 (London: Overseas Development Institute).

Brown, Douglas and Marchelle V. Brown (eds) [1996] Looking Back at the Uganda Protectorate: Recollections of District Officers (Western Australia: Douglas Brown).

Brown, Michael and JoEllen McGann (eds) [1996] A Guide to Strengthening Non-Governmental Organization Effectiveness in Natural Resource Management (PVO-NGO/ NRMS Project).

Bunker, Stephen G. [1987] Peasants Against the State: The Politics of Market Control in Bugisu, Uganda, 1900-1983 (Chicago, IL.: University of Chicago Press) with a new afterword in 1991.

Burki, Shahid Javed, Guillermo Perry, and William Dillinger [1999] Beyond the Center: Decentralizing the State (Washington, D.C.: World Bank).

Carley, Michael and Ian Christie [2000] Managing Sustainable Development, second edition (London: Earthscan).

Cassen, Robert [1999] "Governance and Democracy in Asia," a paper presented at EIAS Workshop in Brussels, November.

Chabal, Patrick and Jean-Pasal Daloz [1999] Africa Works: Disorder as Political Instrument (Oxford: James Currey).

Charlick, Robert B. [2001] "Popular Participation and Local Government Reform," Public Administration and Development Vol. 21, No. 2, pp. 149-157.

Chazan, Naomi, Peter Lewis, Robert Mortimer, Donald Rothchild, and Stephen John Stedman [1999] Politics and Society in Contemporary Africa, third edition (Boulder, CO.: Lynne Rienner).

Cheater, Angela (ed) [1999] The Anthropology of Power: Empowerment and Disempowerment in Changing Structures (London: Routledge).

CITE International [1998] Uganda National Integrity Survey 1998 Final Report (Kampala: CITE International).

Clayton, Andrew [1998] NGOs and Decentralised Government in Africa (Oxford: INTRAC).

Cleaver, Frances [1999] "Paradoxes of Participation: Questioning Participatory Approaches to Development," Journal of International Development Vol. 11, No. 4, pp. 597-612.

Cockcroft, Anne [1996] Performance and Perceptions of Health and Agricultural Services in Uganda: A Report Based on the Findings of the Baseline Service Delivery Survey, December 1995 (Washington, D.C.: World Bank).

Cohen, John M. and Stephen B. Peterson [1999] Administrative Decentralization: Strategies for Developing Countries (West Hartford, CT.: Kumarian Press).

Comaroff, John L. and Jean Comaroff (eds) [1999] Civil Society and the Political Imagination in Africa: Critical Perspective (Chicago, IL.: the University of Chicago Press).

Commission on Global Governance [1995] Our Global Neighbourhood: the Report of the Commission on Global Governance (Oxford: Oxford University Press).

Community Development Resource Network (CDRN) [1996] A Study of Poverty in Selected Districts of Uganda (Kampala: CDRN).

Concern Worldwide with Lutheran World Federation and Irish Foundation for Co-operative Development Ltd. [1999] Insights on Poverty: Livelihood Strategies of Community Members in Rakai District, Uganda (Kampala: Concern Worldwide).

Conyers, Diana [1990] "Decentralization and Development Planning: A Comparative Perspective," In: P. de Valk and K. H. Wekwete (eds) Decentralizing for Participatory Planning: Comparing the Experiences of Zimbabwe and Other Anglophone Countries in Eastern and Southern Africa. (Aldershot: Avebury Press).

Cooke, Bill and Uma Kothari [2001] Participation: the New Tyranny? (London: Zed Books).

Craig, Gary and Marjorie Mayo (eds) [1995] Community Empowerment: A Reader in Participation and Development (London: Zed Books).

Crook, Richard and James Manor [1998] Democracy and Decentralisation in South Asia and West Africa: Participation, Accountability and Performance (Cambridge: Cambridge University Press).

Crook, Richard C. and Alan Sturtla Sverrisson [1999] "To what extent can decentralised forms of government enhance the development of pro-poor policies and improve poverty-alleviation outcomes?," mimeo.

Dahl, Robert A. [1971] Polyarchy: Participation and Opposition (New Haven, CT.: Yale University Press).

Dauda, Carol L. [1999] "Meeting the Requirements of a New Localism: Local Government in Sub-Saharan Africa, The Case of Uganda and Zimbabwe," dissertation submitted to the University of Toronto.

Davis, Daniel, David Hulme and Philip Woodhouse [1994] "Decentralization by Default: Local Governance and the View from the Village in The Gambia," Public Administration and Development Vol. 14, pp. 253-269.

Dawa, Dawin [2001] "Zambians Hail Decentralisation," New Vision 23 July.

Ddungu, Expedit [1998] "Decentralization in Uganda: Processes Prospects, and Constraints," Occasional Paper 47 (Iowa, IA.: University of Iowa).

Ddungu, Expedit [1994] "Popular Form and Question of Democracy: The Case of Resistance Councils in Uganda," In: Mahmood Mamdani and Joe Oloka-Onyango (eds) Uganda: Studies in Living Conditions, Popular Movements and Constitutionalism (Vienna: JEP Book).

Dicklitch, Susan [1998] The Elusive Promise of NGOs in Africa: Lessons from Uganda (London: Macmillan).

Doig, Alan [1995] "Good Government and Sustainable Anti-Corruption Strategies: A Role for Independent Anti-Corruption Agencies?," Public Administration and Development Vol. 15, No. 2, pp. 151-165.

Engberg-Pedersen, Poul, Peter Gibon, Phil Raikes, and Lars Udsholt (eds) [1996] Limits of Adjustment in Africa: the Effects of Economic Liberalization, 1986-94 Center for Development Research, Copenhagen (Oxford: James Curry).

Englebert, Pierre [2002] "Born-again Buganda or the Limits of Traditional Resurgence in Africa," Journal of Modern African Studies Vol. 40, No. 3, pp. 345-368.

Estrella, Marisol et al. (eds) [2000] Learning from Change: Issues and Experiences in Participatory Monitoring and Evaluation (London: Intermediate Technology Publications).

Evans, Alison [1994] "Growth and Poverty Reduction in Uganda," CDR working paper (Copenhagen: Center for Development Research).

Evans, Peter [1996]"Government Action, Social Capital and Development: Reviewing the Evidence on Synergy," World Development Vol. 24, No. 6, pp. 1119-1132.

Evans, Peter [1995] Embedded Autonomy: States and Industrial Transformation (Princeton, NJ.: Princeton University Press).

Fatton Jr., Robert [1995] "African in the Age of Democratization: The Civic Limitations of Civil Society," African Studies Review Vol. 38, No. 2, pp. 67-99.

Fine, Ben [2001] Social Capital versus Social Theory: Political Economy and Social Sciences at the Turn of the Millennium (London: Routledge).

Fiske, Edward [1996] Decentralization of Education: Politics and Consensus (Washington, D.C.: World Bank).

Flanary, Rachel and David Watt [1999] "The State of Corruption: A Case Study of Uganda," Third World Quarterly Vol. 20, No. 3, pp. 515-536.

Florestal, Ketleen and Robb Cooper [1997] Decentralization of Education: Legal Issues (Washington, D.C.: World Bank).

Foster, Mick [2000] "New Approaches to Development Co-operation: What can we learn from experience with implementing Sector Wide Approaches?," ODI Working Paper 140 (London: Overseas Development Institute).

Foster, Mick and Peter Mijumbi [2002] "How, When and Why does Poverty get Budget Priority: Poverty Reduction Strategy and Public Expenditure in Uganda," ODI Working Paper 163 (London: Overseas Development Institute).

Fowler, Alan [2000] Partnerships: Negotiating Relationships – A Resource for Non-Governmental Development Organisations (Oxford: INTRAC).

Fowler, Alan [1997] Striking a Balance: A Guide to Enhancing the Effectiveness of Non-Governmental Organizations in International Development (London: Earthscan).

Fox, Jonathan and L. David Brown (eds) [1998] The Struggle for Accountability: World Bank, NGOs, and Grassroots Movements (Cambridge, MA.: the MIT Press).

Francis, Elizabeth [2000] Making a Living: Changing Livelihoods in Rural Africa (London: Routledge).

Francis, Paul and Robert James [2003] "Balancing Rural Poverty Reduction and Citizen Participation: The Contradictions of Uganda's Decentralization Program," World Development Vol. 31, No. 2, pp. 325-337.

Friedmann, John [1992] Empowerment: the Politics of Alternative Development (Cambridge, MA.: Blackwell Publishers).

Fukuyama, Francis [2001] "Social Capital, Civil Society and Development," Third World Quarterly Vol. 22, No. 1, pp. 7-20.

Fukuyama, Francis [1995] Trust: the Social Virtues and the Creation of Prosperity (New York, NY.: Free Press).

Gariyo, Zie [2000] "Citizen Involvement in the Budgetary Process in Uganda," a paper presented at Civil Society, Donor Policy Synergy and Coordination Workshop, Glasgow Scotland, May, http://www.worldbank.org/participation/ugandabudget.htm [accessed 3 May 2001].

Gauthier, Bernard and Ritva Reinikka [2001] "Shifting Tax Burdens through Exemptions and Evasion: An Empirical Investigation of Uganda," World Bank Governance Working Paper No. 2735 (Washington, D.C.: World Bank).

Gaynor, Cathy [1998] Decentralization of Education: Teacher Management (Washington, D.C.: World Bank).

van der Geest, Willem and Rolph van der Hoeven (eds) [1999] Adjustment, Employment and Missing Institutions in Africa: Experience in Eastern and Southern Africa (Oxford: James Currey).

Gershberg, Alec Ian [1998] "Decentralisation, Recentralisation and Performance Accountability: Building an Operationally Useful Framework for Analysis," Development Policy Review Vol. 16, pp. 405-431.

Gifford, Paul [1998] African Christianity: It's Public Role (London: Hurst).

Goetz, Anne Marie [2002] "No Shortcuts to Power: Constraints on Women's Political Effectiveness in Uganda," Journal of Modern African Studies Vol. 40, No. 4, pp. 549-575.

Goetz, Anne Marie [1998] "'Fiddling with Democracy': Translating Women's Participation in Politics in Uganda and South Africa into Gender Equity in Development Practice," In: Mark Robinson and Gordon White (eds) The Democratic Developmental State: Politics and Institutional Design (Oxford: Oxford University Press).

Goldman, Abe and Kathleen Heldenbrand [1999] "Gender and Soil Fertility Management in Mbale District, Southeast Uganda: Draft Summary Report," May, http://www.fred.ifas.ufl.edu/CRSP/Abe.html [accessed 4 May 2001].

Golooba-Mutebi, Frederick [1999] "Decentralisation, Democracy and Development Administration in Uganda, 1986-1996," doctoral dissertation submitted to the London School of Economics and Political Science.

Gopal, Gita and Maryam Salim [1998] Gender and Law: Eastern Africa Speaks: Conference Organized by the World Bank and the Economic Commission for Africa (Washington, D.C.: World Bank).

Goss, Sue [2001] Making Local Governance Work: Networks, Relations and the Management of Change (London: Palgrave).

Granovetter, M. [1973] "The Strength of Weak Ties," American Journal of Sociology Vol. 78, pp. 1360-80.

Green, Andrew [1999] An Introduction to Health Planning in Developing Countries, second edition (Oxford: Oxford University Press).

Grootaert, Christian and Thierry van Bastelaer [2002] The Role of Social Capital in Development: An Empirical Assessment (Cambridge: Cambridge University Press).

Guijt, Irene and Meera Kaul Shah (eds) [1996] The Myth of Community: Gender Issues in Participatory Development (London: Intermediate Technology Publications).

Hansen, Holger Bernet and Michael Twaddle (eds) [1998] Developing Uganda (Oxford: James Currey).

Hansen, Holger Bernet and Michael Twaddle [1995] "Uganda: the Advent of No-Party Democracy," In: John A. Wiseman (ed) Democracy and Political Change in Sub-Saharan Africa (London: Routledge).

Hansen, Holger Bernet and Michael Twaddle (eds) [1994] From Chaos to Order: The Politics of Constitution-Making in Uganda (Kampala: Fountain Publishers).

Hansen, Holger Bernet and Michael Twaddle [1991] Changing Uganda (Oxford: James Currey).

Harbeson, John W. [2001] "Local Government, Democratization and State Reconstruction in Africa: Toward Integration of Lessons from Contrasting Eras," Public Administration and Development Vol. 21, No. 2, pp. 89-99.

Harbeson, John W., Donald Rothchild, and Naomi Chazan (eds) [1994] Civil society and the State in Africa (Boulder, CO.: Lynne Rienner Publishers).

Harris, Olivia (ed) [1996] Inside and Outside of the Law: Anthropological Studies of Authority and Ambiguity (London: Routledge).

Harrison, Graham [2001] "Post-conditionality Politics and Administrative Reform: Reflections on the Cases of Uganda and Tanzania," Development and Change Vol. 32, pp. 657-679.

Healey, John and Mark Robinson [1994] Democracy, Governance and Economic Policy: Sub-Saharan Africa in Comparative Perspective (London: Overseas Development Institute).

Healey, P. [1987] "The Future of Local Planning and Development Control," Planning Outlook Vol. 30, pp. 30-40.

Hearn, Julie [1999] "Foreign Aid, Democratisation and Civil Society in Africa: A Study of South Africa, Ghana, and Uganda," Discussion Paper No. 368 (Brighton: Institute of Development Studies), http://www.ids.ac.uk/ids/publicat/dp/dp368.pdf [accessed 6 May 2001].

Held, David [1995] Democracy and the Global Order (Cambridge: Polity Press).

Held, David, Anthony McGrew, David Goldblatt, and Jonathan Perraton [1999] Global Transformations: Politics, Economics and Culture (Cambridge: Polity Press).

Hemmati, Minu [2002] Multi-Stakeholder Processes for Governance and Sustainability (London: Earthscan).

Higgott, Richard A., Geoffrey R. D. Underhill and Andreas Bieler (eds) [2000] Non-State Actors and Authority in the Global System (London: Routledge).

van der Hoeven, Rolph and Fred van der Kraaij (eds) [1994] Structural Adjustment and Beyond in Sub-Saharan Africa (Oxford: James Currey).

Hollingsworth, J. Roger and Robert Boyer (eds) [1997] Contemporary Capitalism: the Embeddedness of Institutions (Cambridge: Cambridge University Press).

Holmgren, Torgny et al. [1999] "Aid and Reform in Uganda: Country Case Study," mimeo, October.

Howes, Mick [1997] "NGOs and the Development of Local Institutions: a Ugandan Case-Study," Journal of Modern African Studies Vol. 35, No. 1, pp. 17-35.

Human Rights Watch [1999] Hostile to Democracy: the Movement System and Political Repression in Uganda (New York, NY.: Human Rights Watch).

Hutchinson, Paul [1999] "Household Demand for Health Service in Uganda," Assessing Outcomes for a Comprehensive Development Framework, Kampala, Uganda (Kampala: October 26-28).

Hutchinson, Paul in collaboration with Demissie Habte and Mary Mulusa [1999] "Decentralization of Health Service in Uganda: Moving towards Improved Delivery of Services," In: Paul Hutchinson in collaboration with Demissie Habte and Mary Mulusa Health Care in Uganda: Selected Issues (Washington, D.C.: World Bank).

Hyden, Goran [2000] "The Governance Challenge in Africa," In: Goran Hyden, Dele Olowu, and Hastings W.O. Okoth Ogendo (eds) African Perspectives on Governance (Trenton, NJ.: Africa World Press).

Hyden, Goran [1998a] "Governance and Sustainable Livelihoods," a paper presented at the Workshop on Sustainable Livelihoods and Sustainable Development, jointly organized by the United Nations Development Programme and the Center for African Studies, University of Florida, in Gainesville in October.

Hyden, Goran [1998b] "The Challenges of Constitutionalizing Politics in Uganda," In: Holger Bernet Hansen and Michael Twaddle (eds) Developing Uganda (Oxford: James Currey).

Hyden, Goran and Michael Bratton (eds) [1992] Governance and Politics in Africa (Boulder, CO.: Lynne Rienner Publishers).

Hyden, Goran and Julius Court [2001] "Governance and Development: Trying to Sort out the Basics," United Nations University (UNU) World Governance Assessment Working Paper 1. (Tokyo: UNU).

Hyden, Goran, Dele Olowu, and Hastings W.O. Okoth Ogendo (eds) [2000] African Perspectives on Governance (Trenton, NJ.: Africa World Press).

Infield, Mark and William M. Adams [1999] "Institutional Sustainability and Community Conservation: A Case Study from Uganda," Journal of International Development Vol. 11, No. 2, pp. 305-315.

Inter-Parliamentary Union [2003] Information on national parliaments, http://www.ipu.org/wmn-e/classif.htm [accessed 1 April 2003].

Iversen, Dorte Salskov, Hans Krause Hansen, and Sven Bislev [2000] "Governmentality, Globalisation, and Local Practice: Transformations of a Hegemonic Discourse," Alternatives Vol. 25, No. 2, pp. 183-222.

Jabweli, Okello [2001] "Sh 30b For Local Government," New Vision 5 May.

Jackson, Edward T. and Yusuf Kassam [1998] Knowledge Shared: Participatory Evaluation in Development Cooperation (West Hartford, CT.: Kumarian Press).

Jamal, Vali [1998] "Changes in Poverty Patterns in Uganda," In: Holger Bernet Hansen and Michael Twaddle (eds) Developing Uganda (Oxford: James Currey).

Jamal, Vali [1991] "Inequalities and Adjustment in Uganda," Development and Change Vol. 22, pp. 321-337.

Johnson, Craig [2001] "Local Democracy, Democratic Decentralisation and Rural Development: Theories, Challenges and Option for Policy," Development Policy Review Vol. 19, No. 4, pp. 521-532.

Johnson, Hazel and Gordon Wilson [2000] "Biting the Bullet: Civil Society, Social Learning, and the Transformation of Local Governance," World Development Vol. 28, No. 11, pp. 1891-1906.

Joseph, Richard (ed) [1999] State, Conflict, and Democracy in Africa (Boulder, CO.: Lynne Rienner Publishers).

Kamal, Kar [1999] Report of the Second Consultancy Visit related to Institutionalisation of Participatory Approaches in Kibaale District Local Government.

Kanyinga, Karuti, Andrew S. Z. Kiondo, and Per Tidemand [1994] The New Local Level Politics in East Africa: Studies on Uganda, Tanzania and Kenya, Edited and Introduced by Peter Gibbon (Uppsala: Nordiska Afrikainstitutet).

Karlström, Mikael [1999a] "The Cultural Kingdom in Uganda: Popular Royalism and the Restoration of the Buganda Kingship," doctoral dissertation submitted to the University of Chicago, June.

Karlström, Mikael [1999b] "Civil Society and Its Presuppositions: Lessons from Uganda," In: John L. and Jean Comaroff (eds) Civil Society and the Political Imagination in Africa: Critical Perspective (Chicago, IL.: the University of Chicago Press).

Karlström, Mikael [1996] "Imagining Democracy: Political Culture and Democratisation in Buganda," Africa Vol. 66, No. 4, pp. 485-505.

Kasfir, Nelson [2000] "'Movement' Democracy, Legitimacy, and Power in Uganda," In: Justus Mugaju and J. Oloka-Onyango (eds) No-Party Democracy in Uganda: Myth and Realities (Kampala: Fountain Publishers).

Kasfir, Nelson [1999] "No-party Democracy in Uganda," In: Larry Diamond and Mark F. Plattner (eds) Democratization in Africa (Baltimore, MD.: the Johns Hopkins University Press).

Kasfir, Nelson (ed) [1998] Civil Society and Democracy in Africa: Critical Perspective (London: Frank Cass).

Kasfir, Nelson [1993] "Designs and dilemmas of African decentralization," In: Philip Mawhood (ed) Local Governments in the Third World: Experiences of Decentralization in Tropical Africa (Africa Institute of South Africa).

Kasozi, A.B.K. [1997] "Decentralization and Social Reconciliation in Uganda since 1986: A Study of Four Districts," a draft report prepared for the United Nations Department for Development Support and Management Services, August.

Kasumba, George [2000] "Rakai Case Study," In: Jossy Materu, Tony Land, Volker Hauk, and Jane Knight Decentralised Cooperation and Joint Action: Building Partnership between Local Government and Civil Society in Africa (Maastricht: European Centre for Development Policy Management).

Kasumba, George [1998] "Enhancing the Decentralisation Process in Uganda: the Role of NGOs," DENIVA News January-March.

Kasumba, George [1997] "Decentralising Aid and its Management in Uganda: Lessons for Capacity-building at the Local Level," ECDPM Working Paper No. 20, April, http://www.oneworld.org/ecdpm/pubs/wp20_gb.htm [accessed 3 May 2001].

Kaufman, Michael [1997] "Differential Participation: Men, Women and Popular Power," In: Michael Kaufman and Haroldo Dilla Alfonso (eds) Community Power and Grassroots Democracy (London: Zed Books).

Kaufman, Michael and Haroldo Dilla Alfonso (eds) [1997] Community Power and Grassroots Democracy (London: Zed Books).

Kaul, Inge, Isabelle Grunberg and Marc Stern [1999] Global Public Goods: International Cooperation in the 21st Century (New York, NY.: Oxford University Press).

Kayizzi-Mugerwa, Steve [1993] "Urban Bustle/Rural Slumber: Dilemmas of Uneven Economic Recovery in Uganda," In: Magnus Blomstrom and Mats Lundahl (eds) Economic Crisis in Africa: Perspectives on Policy Responses (London: Routledge).

Kayunga, Sallie Simba [2000] "The Federo (Federalism) Debate in Uganda," Working Paper No. 62 (Kampala: Centre for Basic Research).

Khadiagala, Lynn S. [2001] "The Failure of Popular Justice in Uganda Local Councils and Women's Property Rights," Development and Change Vol. 32, No. 1, pp. 55-76.

Kintu, Francis [2000] Report of Focus Group Research on Budget Transparency Issues under subcontract to Susan Hills, MoFPED, EFMPII, Budget Transparency Consultancy (Kampala: MoFPED).

Kinuthia-Njenga, Cecilia [1996] "Civil Society: new roles for African traditions, NGOs, women and youth in Africa," Development Journal Vol. 3, http://www.waw.be/sid/dev1996/kinuthia.html [accessed 28 February 2001].

Kisubi, Mohammad [1999] "Uganda," In: Ladipo Adamolekun (ed) Public Administration in Africa: Main Issues and Selected Country Studies (Boulder, CO.: Westview Press).

Kisubi, Mohammad and Justus Mugaju (eds) [1999] Rural Health Providers in South-West Uganda (Kampala: Fountain Publishers).

Klugman, Jeni [1994] "Decentralization: A Survey of Literature from a Human Development Perspective," (UNDP), http://hdr.undp.org/docs/publications/ocational_papers/oc13.htm [accessed 15 February 2003].

Kohli, Atul and Vivienne Shue [1994] "State Power and Social Forces: On Political Contention and Accommodation in the Third World," In: Joel S. Migdal, Atul Kohli, and Vivienne Shue (eds) State Power and Social Forces: Domination and Transformation in the Third World (Cambridge: Cambridge University Press).

Kolehmainen-Aiken, Riitta-Lissa [1992] "The Impact of Decentralization on Health Workforce Development in Papua New Guinea," Public Administration and Development Vol. 12, pp. 175-191.

Kothari, Rajni [1996] "Issues in Decentralised Governance," In: Abdul Aziz and David D. Arnold (eds) Decentralised Governance in Asian Countries (London: Sage Publication).

Kuteesa, Florence [1999] "Involving Local Government in Sector-wide Programmes," http://www.capacity.org/3/editorial2.html [accessed 25 October 2000].

Kyeyune, Grace and Patricia Goldey [1999] "Towards Effective Poverty Reduction: A Study of Heterogeneous Groups of Poor Women in Uganda," Journal of International Development Vol. 11, No. 4, pp. 565-580.

Langseth, Peter [1995] "Civil Service Reform in Uganda: Lessons Learned," Public Administration and Development Vol. 15, No. 4, pp. 365-390.

Larmour, P. and R. Qalo [1985] Decentralization in the South Pacific: Local, Provincial and State Government in Twenty Century (Suva: University of South Pacific).

Leftwich, Adrian (ed) [1996] Democracy and Development: Theory and Practice (Cambridge, MA.: Polity Press).

Leonard, David K. [1987] "Political Realities of African Management," World Development Vol. 15, No. 7, pp. 899-910.

Lewis, W. Arthur [1965] Politics in West Africa (London: George Allen & Unwin).

Lind, Jeremy and Jan Cappon [2001] Realities or Rhetoric?: Revisiting the Decentralization of Natural Resource Management in Uganda and Zambia (Nairobi: African Centre for Technology Studies).

Lister, Sarah [2000] "Power in Partnership?: An Analysis of an NGO's Relationship with Its Partners," Journal of International Development Vol. 12, No. 2, pp. 227-239.

Lister, Sarah and Warren Nyamugasira [2003] "Design Contradictions in the 'New Architecture of Aid'?: Reflections from Uganda on the Roles of Civil Society Organizations," Development Policy Review Vol. 21, No. 1, pp. 93-106.

Litvack, Jennie, Junaid Ahmad, and Richard Bird [1998] Rethinking Decentralization in Developing Countries (Washington, D.C.: World Bank).

Livingstone, Ian and Roger Charlton [2001] "Financing Decentralized Development in a Low-Income Country: Raising Revenue for Local Government in Uganda," Development and Change Vol. 32, No. 1, pp. 77-100.

Livingstone, Ian and Roger Charlton [1998] "Raising Local Authority District Revenues Through Direct Taxation in a Low-Income Developing Country: Evaluating Uganda's GPT," Public Administration and Development Vol. 18, pp. 499-517.

Long, Norman [2001] Development Sociology: Actor Perspectives (London: Routledge).

Lovell, Nadia (ed) [1998] Locality and Belonging (London: Routledge).

Lucas, Henry and Augustus Nuwagaba [1999] "Household Coping Strategies in Response to the Introduction of User Charges for Social Service: A Case Study on Health in Uganda," IDS Working Paper No. 86 (Brighton: Institute of Development Studies).

Lyon, Fergus [2000] "Trust, Networks and Norms: the Creation of Social Capital in Agricultural Economies in Ghana," World Development Vol. 28, No. 4, pp. 663-681.

Mackintosh, Maureen and Rathin Roy (eds) [1999] Economic Decentralization and Public Management Reform (Cheltenham: Edward Elgar).

Magyezi, Raphael Tibaingana [1998] "Regional Report on Decentralization: The Case of Uganda," August, http://www.mdpesa.co.za/pubs/decent4.html [accessed 9 October 2000].

Makerere Institute for Social Research (MISR) [2000] Human Resource Demand Assessment from the Perspective of the District (Kampala: MISR).

Makerere Institute for Social Research (MISR) [1997] The Quest for Good Governance: Decentralisation and Civil Society in Uganda (Kampala: MISR).

Mamdani, Mahmood [1996] Citizen and Subject: Contemporary Africa and the Legacy of Late Colonialism (Princeton, NJ.: Princeton University Press).

Mamdani, Mahmood [1992] "Class Formation and Rural Livelihoods: A Ugandan Case Study," In: Henry Bernstein et al. (eds) Rural Livelihoods: Crises and Responses (Oxford: Oxford University Press).

Mamdani, Mahmood [1991] "Uganda: Contradictions in the IMF Programme and Perspective," In: Dharam Ghai (ed) The IMF and the South: the Social Impact of Crisis and Adjustment (London: Zed Books).

Mamdani, Mahmood and Joe Oloka-Onyango (eds) [1994] Uganda: Studies in Living Conditions, Popular Movements and Constitutionalism (Vienna: JEP Book).

Manor, James [1999] The Political Economy of Democratic Decentralization (Washington, D.C.: World Bank).

Mawhood, Philip (ed) [1993] Local Governments in the Third World: Experiences of Decentralization in Tropical Africa (Africa Institute of South Africa).

Mayoux, Linda [1999] "Questioning Virtuous Spirals: Micro-Finance and Women's Empowerment in Africa," Journal of International Development Vol. 11, pp. 957-984.

McGee, Rosemary [2000a] "Analysis of Participatory Poverty Assessment (PPA) and household survey findings on poverty trends in Uganda," Mission Report, February, http://www.uppap.or.ug/pdf/Poverty-Trends.PDF [accessed 14 September 2000].

McGee, Rosemary [2000b] "Participation in Poverty Reduction Strategies: A Synthesis of Experience with Participatory Approaches to Policy Design, Implementation and Monitoring," IDS Working Paper 109 (Brighton: Institute of Development Studies).

McGee, Rosemary [2000c] "Meeting the International Poverty Targets in Uganda: Halving Poverty and Achieving Universal Primary Education," Development Policy Review Vol. 18, No.1, pp. 85-106.

Melkote, Srinivas R. and H. Leslie Steeves [2001] Communication for Development in the Third World: Theory and Practice for Empowerment (London: Sage Publications).

de Mello Jr., Luiz [2000] "Fiscal Decentralization and Intergovernmental Fiscal Relations: A Cross-Country Analysis," World Development Vol. 28, No. 2, pp. 365-380.

Migdal, Joel S. [1988] Strong Societies and Weak States: State-Society Relations and State Capabilities in the Third World (Princeton, NJ.: Princeton University Press).

Migdal, Joel S., Atul Kohli and Vivienne Shue (eds) [1994] State Power and Social Forces: Domination and Transformation in the Third World (Cambridge: Cambridge University Press).

Mikell, Gwendolyn (ed) [1997] African Feminism: the Politics of Survival in Sub-Saharan Africa (Pennsylvania, PA.: University of Pennsylvania Press).

Moemeka, Andrew A. [2000] Development Communication in Action: Building Understanding and Creating Participation (New York, NY.: University Press of America, Inc.).

Moore, Mick and James Putzel [1999] "Thinking Strategically About Politics and Poverty," IDS Working Paper No. 101 (Brighton: Institute of Development Studies).

Moser, Caroline O. N. [1993] Gender Planning and Development: Theory, Practice and Training (London: Routledge).

Mugyenyi, Mary R. [1998] "Towards the Empowerment of Women: a Critique of NRM Policies and Programmes," In: Holger Bernet Hansen and Michael Twaddle (eds) Developing Uganda (Oxford: James Currey).

Mukono District Council, Uganda [2000a] Budget Conference Held on 23. 3. 2000 in Mukono Community Centre (Mukono: Mukono District Council).

Mukono District Council, Uganda [2000b] Budget Speech 2000/2001: Recurrent and Development Budget Estimates (Mukono: Mukono District Council, 8 June).

Mukono District Council, Uganda [2000c] Budget Framework Paper 2000/2001-2002/2003 Vol. I (Mukono: Mukono District Council, 24 March).

Mukono District Council, Uganda [1998] Budget Speech 1998/99: Recurrent and Development Budget Estimates (Mukono: Mukono District Council, 29 June).

Mulyampiti, Tabitha [1994] "Political Empowerment of Women in Uganda: Impact of Resistance Councils and Committees," MA Thesis for the Department of Women Studies, Faculty of Social Sciences, Makerere University.

Museveni, Yoweri [1993] "Address on the launching of the Local Government Decentralization Programme on 2nd October 1992 at the Uganda International Conference Centre," In: Decentralization in Uganda: the Policy and its Philosophy (Kampala: Decentralization Secretariat, May).

Musisi, Kiwanuka C.G. [1998] "Central Government Transfers and Budget Process: Local Government Perspective," a paper presented at the Budget Framework Consultative Meeting, 10 November.

Musisi, Nakanyike B. [1995] "Baganda Women's Night Market Activities," In: Bessie House-Midamba and Felix K. Ekechi (eds) African Market Women and Economic Power: the Role of Women in African Economic Development (Westport, CN.: Greenwood Press).

Narayan, Deepa [1995] "Designing Community-Based Development," Paper No. 7, Environmental Department (Washington, D.C.: World Bank).

Narayan, Deepa, Robert Chambers, Meera K. Shah, and Patti Petesch [2000] Voices of the Poor: Crying out for Change (Oxford: Oxford University Press for the World Bank).

Narayan, Deepa with Raj Patel, Kai Schafft, Anne Rademacher, and Sarah Koch-Schulte [2000] Voices of the Poor: Can Anyone Hear Us? (London: Oxford University Press for the World Bank).

Ndegwa, Stephan N. [1996] The Two Faces of Civil Society: NGOs and Politics in Africa (West Hartford, CN.: Kumarian).

Nielsen, Henrik A. [2001] "The Role of Donors: How to Combine Sector Programme Support with Devolution? A Comment from a Practitioner to James Wunsch: Decentralization, Local Governance and Recentralization in Africa," Public Administration and Development Vol. 21, pp. 415-418.

Nielsen, Henrik A. [1996a] "Decentralisation Experience: From Noakhali to Rakai," In: Soren Villadsen and Francis Lubanga (eds) Democratic Decentralisation in Uganda: A New Approach to Local Governance (Kampala: Fountain Publishers).

Nielsen, Henrik A. [1996b] "Donor Support to Decentralisation in Uganda: Experiences from Rakai District 1990-95," ECDPM Working Paper Number 9, June, http://www.oneworld.org/ecdpm/pubs/wp9_gb.htm [accessed 10 December 2000].

Oates, Wallace E. [1999] "An Essay on Fiscal Federalism," Journal of Economic Literature Vol. XXXVII, pp. 1120-1149.

Obbo, Christine [1998] "Who Care for Carers?: AIDS and women in Uganda," In: Holger Bernet Hansen and Michael Twaddle (eds) Developing Uganda (Oxford: James Currey).

Obwona, Marios et al. [2000] Fiscal Decentralisation and Sub-National Government Finance in Relation to Infrastructure and Service Provision in Uganda Main Report and Annexes Draft Final Report (Kampala: Economic Policy Research Centre, March), http://www.mdpesa.co.zw/pubs/mdpcd%20files/Uganda%20Report.pdf [accessed 10 April 2001].

Okello, D. O., R. Lubanga, D. Guwatudde, and A. Sebina-Zziwa [1998] "The Challenge to Restoring Basic Health Care in Uganda," Social Science and Medicine Vol. 46, No. 1, pp. 13-21.

Okuonzi, Sam Agatre and Harriet Birungi [2000] "Are Lessons from the Education Sector Applicable to Health Care Reforms?: The Case of Uganda," International Journal of Health Planning and Management Vol. 15, No. 3, pp. 201-219.

Okuonzi, Sam Agatre and Francis X. K. Lubanga [1997] "Decentralization and Health Systems Change in Uganda: A Report on the Study to Establish Links between Decentralization and Changes in Health System," mimeo (November 1995, edited February 1997).

Okuonzi, Sam Agatre and Joana Macrae [1995] "Whose Policy Is It Anyway?: International and National Influence on Health Policy Development in Uganda," Health Policy and Planning Vol. 10, No. 2, pp. 122-132.

Okware, Sam, Alex Opio, Joshua Musinguzi, and Paul Waibale [2001] "Fighting HIV/AIDS: Is Success Possible?," Bulletin of the World Health Organization Vol. 79, No. 12, pp. 1113-1120.

Olowu, Dele [2001] Decentralization Policies and Practices under Structural Adjustment and Democratization in Africa (Geneva: United Nations Research Institute for Social Development).

Olowu, Dele [1999a] "Accountability and Transparency," In: Lapido Adamolekun (ed) Public Administration in Africa: Main Issues and Selected Country Studies (Boulder, CO.: Westview Press).

Olowu, Dele [1999b] "Local Governance, Democracy, and Development," In: Richard Joseph (ed) State, Conflict, and Democracy in Africa (Boulder, CO.: Lynne Rienner Publishers).

Olowu, Dele [1990] "The Failure of Current Decentralization Programs in Africa," In: James S. Wunsch and Dele Olowu (eds) The Failure of Decentralized State: Institutions and Self-Governance in Africa (San Francisco, CA.: ICS Press).

Olowu, Dele and Paul Smoke [1992] "Determinants of Success in African Local Governments: An Overview," Public Administration and Development Vol. 12, No. 1, pp. 1-17.

Olson, Mancur [1965] The Logic of Collective Action: Public Goods and the Theory of Groups (Cambridge, MA.: Harvard University Press).

Ostrom, Elinor [1998] "A Behavioral Approach to the Rational Choice Theory of Collective Action," American Political Science Review Vol. 92, No. 1, pp. 1-22.

Ostrom, Elinor [1990] Governing the Commons: The Evolution of Institutions for Collective Action (Cambridge: Cambridge University Press).

Ostrom, Elinor, Larry Schroeder, and Susan Wynne [1993] Institutional Incentives and Sustainable Development: Infrastructure Policies in Perspective (Boulder, CO.: Westview Press).

Ottaway, Marina [1999a] Africa's New Leaders: Democracy or State Reconstruction (Washington, D.C.: Carnegie Endowment for International Peace).

Ottaway, Marina [1999b] "Ethnic Politics in Africa: Change and Continuity," In: Richard Joseph (ed) State, Conflict, and Democracy in Africa (Boulder, CO.: Lynne Rienner Publishers).

Ottaway, Marina [1994] Democratization and Ethnic Nationalism: African and Eastern European Experiences (Washington, D.C.: Overseas Development Council).

Ottemoeller, Dan [1998] "Popular Perceptions of Democracy: Elections and Attitudes in Uganda," Comparative Political Studies Vol. 31, No. 1, pp. 98-124.

Ottemoeller, Dan [1996] "Institutionalization and Democratization: the Case of the Ugandan Resistance Council," doctoral dissertation presented to the University of Florida.

Padmanabhan, C.B. [1999] "Educational Planning for National Development: Some Reflections on the Ugandan Experience," Africa Quarterly Vol. 39, No. 1, pp. 69-79.

Parkhurst, Justin O. [2002] "A Unique Policy: The Evolution of HIV/AIDS Prevention under the National Resistance Movement," In: Nakanyike B. Musisi and Cole P. Dodge (eds) Transformation in Uganda (Kampala: Makerere Institute of Social Research).

Passi, Fabius O. [1995] "The Rise of People's Organizations in Primary Education in Uganda," In: Joseph Semboja and Ole Therkildsen (eds) Service Provision under Stress in East Africa: the State, NGOs and People's Organizations in Kenya, Tanzania and Uganda (London: James Currey).

Patrinos, Harry Anthony, and David Lakshmanan Ariasingam [1997] Decentralization of Education: Demand-side Financing (Washington, D.C.: World Bank).

Picciotto, Robert and Eduardo Wiesner (eds) [1998] Evaluation and Development: the Institutional Design (New Brunswick, NJ.: Transaction Publishers).

Pierre, John (ed) [2000] Debating Governance: Authority, Steering, and Democracy (Oxford: Oxford University Press).

Plummer, Janelle [2002] Focusing Partnerships: A Sourcebook for Municipal Capacity Building in Public-Private Partnerships (London: Earthscan).

Porter, Doug and Martin Onyach-Olaa [1999] "Inclusive Planning and Allocation for Rural Services," Development in Practice Vol. 9, No. 1, pp. 1-12.

Portes, Alejandro [1998] "Social Capital: Its Origins and Applications in Modern Sociology," Annual Review of Sociology Vol. 24, pp. 1-24.

Przeworski, Adam, Susan C. Stokes, and Bernard Manin (eds) [1999] Democracy, Accountability, and Representation (Cambridge: Cambridge University Press).

Rasheed, Sadig and Dele Olowu (eds) [1993] Ethics and Accountability in African Public Services (African Association for Public Administration and Management).

Reason, Peter and Hilary Bradbury (eds) [2001] Handbook of Action Research: Participative Inquiry and Practice (London: Sage Publications).

Regan, Anthony [1998] "Decentralisation Policy: Reshaping State and Society," In: Holger Bernt Hansen and Michael Twaddle (eds) Developing Uganda (Oxford: James Currey).

Regan, Anthony [1995] "A Comparative Framework for Analysing Uganda's Decentralisation Policy," In: P. Langseth, J. Katorobo, E. Brett, and J. Munene (eds) Uganda: Landmarks in Rebuilding a Nation (Kampala: Fountain Publishers).

Reid, Elizabeth (ed) [1995] HIV & AIDS: the Global Interconnection (West Hartford, CT.: Kumarian Press).

Reinikka, Ritva and Paul Collier (eds) [2001] Uganda's Recovery: The Role of Farms, Firms, and Government (Washington, D.C.: World Bank).

Reinikka, Ritva and Jackob Svensson [2001] "Explaining Leakage of Public Funds," World Bank Governance Working Paper No. 2709 (Washington, D.C.: World Bank).

Ribot, Jesse C. [2001] "Local Actors, Powers and Accountability in African Decentralizations: A Review of Issues," a paper prepared for International Development Research Centre of Canada, October.

Riddel, Roger, Zie Gariyo, and Hope Mwesigye [1998] "Review of National Policy on Non-Governmental Organisations for Uganda," a consultancy report for the United Nations Development Programme, Kampala, Uganda (Kampala, August).

Robinson, Mark and Gordon White (eds) [1998] The Democratic Developmental State: Politics and Institutional Design (Oxford: Oxford University Press).

Rondinelli, Dennis [2002] "Public-Private Partnerships," In: Colin Kirpatrick, Ron Clark, and Charles Polidano (eds) Handbook on Development Policy and Management (Cheltenham: Edward Elgar).

Rosenau, James N. [1995] "Governance in the Twenty-first Century," Global Governance Vol. 1, No. 1, pp. 13-43.

Rosenbaum, Allan and Maria Victoria Rojas [1997] "Decentralization, Local Governance and Centre-Periphery Conflict in Sierra Leone," Public Administration and Development Vol. 17, pp. 529-540.

Rothchild, Donald [1997] Managing Ethnic Conflict in Africa: Pressures and Incentives for Cooperation (Washington, D.C.: Brooking Institution Press).

Rowland, Allison M. [2001] "Population as a Determinant of Local Outcomes under Decentralization: Illustrations from Small Municipalities in Bolivia and Mexico," World Development Vol. 29, No. 8, pp. 1373-1389.

Rudebeck, Lars, Olle Tornquist, and Virgilio Rojas (eds) [1998] Democratization in the Third World: Concrete Cases in Comparative and Theoretical Perspective (London: Macmillan).

Ruzindana, A. [1997] "The Part Played by Structural Reforms of the State in Fighting Corruption: The Case in Uganda," a paper presented at the 8th International Anti-Corruption Conference (IACC) 1997, http://www.transparency.de/iacc/8th_iacc/papers/ruzindana.html [accessed 1 May 2001].

Ruzindana, A., P. Langseth, and A. Gakwandi (eds) [1998] Fighting Corruption in Uganda: The Process of Building a National Integrity System (Kampala: Fountain Publishers).

Sahn, David and Alexander Sarris [1994] "The Evolution of States, Markets, and Civil Institutions in Rural Africa," Journal of Modern African Studies Vol. 32, No. 2, pp. 279-303.

Samii, Ramina, Luk N. van Wassenhove, and Shantanu Bhattacharya [2002] "An Innovative Public-Private Partnership: New Approach to Development," World Development Vol. 30, No. 6, pp. 991-1008.

Sandbrook, Richard [1996] "Democratization and the Implementation of Economic Reform in Africa," Journal of International Development Vol. 8, No. 1, pp. 1-20.

Sandler, Todd [1992] Collective Action: Theory and Applications (Ann Arbor, MI.: the University of Michigan Press).

Schacter, Mark [2000] "Sub-Saharan Africa: Lessons from Experience in Supporting Sound Governance," Evaluation Capacity Development Working Paper Number 7 (Washington, D.C.: World Bank).

Schneider, Hartmut [1999a] "Participatory Governance: the Missing Link for Poverty Reduction," OECD Development Centre Policy Brief 17 (Paris: Organisation for Economic Co-operation and Development).

Schneider, Hartmut [1999b] "Participatory Governance for Poverty Reduction," Journal of International Development Vol. 11, No. 4, pp. 521-534.

Semboja, Joseph and Ole Therkildsen (eds) [1995] Service Provision under Stress in East Africa: the State, NGOs and People's Organizations in Kenya, Tanzania and Uganda (London: James Currey).

Sen, Amartya [1999] Development as Freedom (New York, NY.: Anchor Books).

Shah, Anwar [1998] "Balance, Accountability, and Responsiveness: Lessons about Decentralizaiton," Policy Research Working Paper 2021 (Washington, D.C.: World Bank).

Shepherd, Andrew [2000] "Evaluation of Rakai District Development Programme Report No. 1 Synthesis," draft report submitted for Danish International Development Assistance (Kampala: DANIDA, July 2000).

Shin, Roy W. and Alfred Tat-Kei Ho [1998] "Strategies for Economic Development under Decentralization: A Transition of the Political Economy," In: Kuotsai Tom Liou (ed) Handbook of Economic Development (New York, NY.: Marcel Dekker).

Sklar, Richard L. [1999] "African Polities: The Next Generation," In: Joseph, Richard (ed) State, Conflict, and Democracy in Africa (Boulder, CO.: Lynne Rienner Publishers).

Smith, Brian [2002] "Decentralization," In: Colin Kirpatrick, Ron Clark, and Charles Polidano (eds) Handbook on Development Policy and Management (Cheltenham: Edward Elgar).

Smith, B.C. [1998] "Local Government and the Transition to Democracy: A Review Article," Public Administration and Development Vol. 18, pp. 85-92.

Smith, B.C. [1997] "The Decentralization of Health Care in Developing Countries: Organizational Options," Public Administration and Development Vol. 17, pp. 399-421.

Smith, B.C. [1996] "Sustainable Local Democracy," Public Administration and Development Vol. 16, pp. 163-178.

Smoke, Paul [2001] Fiscal Decentralization in Developing Countries: A Review of Current Concepts and Practice (Geneva: United Nations Research Institute for Social Development).

Smoke, Paul and Dele Olowu [1993] "Successful Local Government: Methodological and Conceptual Issues Reconsidered," Public Administration and Development Vol. 13, pp. 507-514.

Snyder, Margaret [2000] Women in African Economies: from Burning Sun to Boardroom (Kampala: Fountain Publishers).

Sserwaniko, Frank [2001] "Government to bolster PAP fund," New Vision 15 May.

Stapenhurst, Rick and Sahr J. Kpundeh (eds) [1999] Curbing Corruption: Toward a Model for Building National Integrity (Washington, D.C.: World Bank).

Steffensen, Jesper and Svend Trollegaard [2000] Fiscal Decentralisation and Sub-National Government Finance in Relation to Infrastructure and Service Provision: Synthesis Report on 6 Sub-Saharan African Country Studies May, http://www.mdpesa.co.zw/ pubs/mdpcd%20files/Synthesis%20Report.pdf [accessed 10 April 2001].

Sunder, Nandini [2001] "Is Devolution Democratization?," World Development Vol. 29, No. 12, pp. 2007-2023.

Suzuki, Ikuko [2002] "Parental Participation and Accountability in Primary Schools in Uganda," Compare Vol. 32, No. 2, pp. 243-259.

Suzuki, Ikuko [2000] "The Notion of Participation in Primary Education in Uganda: Democracy in School Governance?," a paper originally presented at BAICE conference on 9 September.

Sverrisson, Alan Sturtla [2000] "The Politics of Poverty Alleviation under Structural Adjustment," draft PhD. dissertation, Glasgow Caledonian University, the UK.

Svensson, Jakob [1999] "The Cost of Doing Business: Experience of Ugandan Firms on Corruption," Assessing Outcomes for a Comprehensive Development Framework, October 26-28 (Kampala: World Bank).

Tamale, Sylvia [1999] When Hens Begin to Crow: Gender and Parliamentary Politics in Uganda (Kampala: Fountain Publishers).

Tangri, Roger and Andrew Mwenda [2001] "Corruption and Cronyism in Uganda's Privatization in the 1990s," African Affairs Vol. 100, pp. 117-133.

Tegulle, Gawaya [2001] "Movement Acting like a Party," New Vision 4 July.

Tegulle, Gawaya [2000] "The People are happy with new districts: An interview with Jaberi Bidandi Ssali, Minister for Local Government," New Vision 20 December.

Tendler, Judith [1997] Good Government in the Tropics (Baltimore, MD.: the Johns Hopkins University Press).

Teskey, Graham and Richard Hooper [1999] "Uganda Education Strategic Investment Programme: Case Study," prepared for the joint DAC Informal Network / ACBF Workshop on Institutional and Capacity Development, http://www.capacity.org/pubs/dfid/dac_case_dfid_uga.htm [accessed 15 June 2000].

Therkildsen, Ole [1993] "'Successful African Local Government': Some Methodological and Conceptual Issues," Public Administration and Development Vol. 13, pp. 501-505.

Thomas, Caroline [2000] Global Governance, Development and Human Security: The Challenge of Poverty and Inequality (London: Pluto Press).

Thomas, Vinod et al. [2000] The Quality of Growth (Oxford: Oxford University Press for the World Bank).

Thomas-Slayter, Barbara [1994] "Structural Change, Power Politics, and Community Organizations in Africa: Challenging the Patterns, Puzzles and Paradoxes," World Development, Vol. 22, No. 10, pp. 1479-1490.

Tidemand, Per [1995] "Popular versus State Provision of Local Justice," In: Joseph Semboja and Ole Therkildsen (eds) Service Provision under Stress in East Africa: the State, NGOs and People's Organizations in Kenya, Tanzania and Uganda (London: James Currey).

Tidemand, Per [1994a] "New Local State Forms and 'Popular Participation' in Buganda, Uganda," In: Kanyinga et al. The New Local Level Politics in East Africa (Uppsala: Nordiska Afrikainstitutet).

Tidemand, Per [1994b] "The Resistance Council in Uganda: A Study of Rural Politics and Popular Democracy in Afrika," doctoral dissertation presented for Roskilde University.

Tordoff, William [1994] "Decentralisation: Comparative Experiences in Commonwealth Africa," The Journal of Modern African Studies Vol. 32, No. 4, pp. 555-580.

Tororo District Local Government, Uganda [1999] Budget Framework Paper 1999/2000 (Tororo: Tororo District Local Government).

de Torrenté, Nicholas and Frederick Mwesigye [1999] "The Evolving Role of the State, Donors and NGOs Providing Health Services in a Liberal Environment: Some Insights from Uganda," Centre for Basic Research Occasional Paper No. 2 (Kampala, CBR Publications).

Transparency International [2000], http://www.transparency.de/ [accessed 10 December 2000].

Tripp, Aili Mari [2001] "Women's Movements and Challenge to Neopatrimonial Rule: Preliminary Observations," Development and Change Vol. 32, No. 1, pp. 33-54.

Tripp, Aili Mari [2000] Women & Politics in Uganda (Oxford: James Currey).

Tripp, Aili Mari [1998a] "Expanding 'Civil Society': Women and Political Space in Contemporary Uganda," In: Nelson Kasfir (ed) Civil Society and Democracy in Africa: Critical Perspectives (Oxford: James Currey).

Tripp, Aili Mari [1998b] "Local Women's Associations and Politics in Contemporary Uganda," In: Holger Bernet Hansen and Michael Twaddle (eds) Developing Uganda (Oxford: James Currey).

Tripp, Aili Mari [1994] "Gender, Political Participation and the Transformation of Associational Life in Uganda and Tanzania," African Studies Review Vol. 37, No. 1, pp. 107-131.

Tukahebwa, Geoffrey B. [1997] "The Role of District Councils in the Decentralisation Programme in Uganda," In: Makerere Institute of Social Research (MISR) The Quest for Good Governance: Decentralisation and Civil Society in Uganda (Kampala: MISR).

Tumushabe, Joseph, Catherine A. Barasa, Florence K. Muhanguzi, and Joyce F. Otim-Nape [2000] "Gender and Primary Schooling in Uganda," IDS Research Report 42 (Brighton: Institute of Development Studies).

Turner, Mark and David Hulme [1997] Governance, Administration and Development: Making the State Work (London: Macmillan).

Uganda, the Republic of [1999] Human Resources Management Manual for Local Governments in Uganda (Kampala: the Republic of Uganda, March).

Uganda, the Republic of [1998] The Local Governments Financial and Accounting Regulations, 1998 (Kampala: the Republic of Uganda, March).

Uganda, the Republic of [1987] Commission of the Inquiry into the Local Government System (Kampala: the Republic of Uganda).

Uganda, the Republic of, Uganda Bureau of Statistics (UBOS) [2002] Uganda DHS EdData Survey 2001: Education Data for Decision-making (Entebbe: UBOS).

Uganda, the Republic of, Uganda Bureau of Statistics (UBOS) [2001a] Uganda Demographic and Health Survey 2000-2001 (Entebbe: UBOS).

Uganda, the Republic of, Uganda Bureau of Statistics (UBOS) [2001b] Uganda National Household Survey 1999/2000: Report on the Community Survey (Entebbe: UBOS).

Uganda, the Republic of, Uganda Bureau of Statistics (UBOS) [1999] The Statistical Abstract 1999 (Entebbe: UBOS, June).

Uganda, the Government of, and UNICEF [1999] Country Programme Progress Report (Kampala: UNICEF).

Uganda Local Authorities Association [1999] "Position Paper of the Uganda Local Authorities Association (ULAA) on the National Budget," (Kampala: ULAA, September).

Uganda Local Authorities Association [1998] "Position Paper of the Uganda Local Authorities Association (ULAA) on the National Budget 1998/99," (Draft) (Kampala: ULAA, October).

Uganda Local Authorities Association [1996] "Position Paper of Uganda Local Governments on the National Budget 1996/97," (Kampala: ULAA, September).

Uganda Participatory Development Network (UPDN) [2000] Decentralization: What Opportunities for Participation? (Kampala: UPDN).

Uganda, the Republic of, the Electoral Commission [1999] The 1997/1998 Local Governments Councils' Election Report (Kampala: the Electoral Commission, February).

Uganda, the Republic of, Local Government Finance Commission (LGFC) [1999a] Introduction of Equalization Grant: Analysis and Recommendations (Kampala: LGFC, March).

Uganda, the Republic of, Local Government Finance Commission (LGFC) [1999b] International Experience in Local Government Budget and Grants Management System: Experiences from Denmark, Latvia, Lithuania and Malaysia Compared with Ugandan Practice (Kampala: LGFC, February).

Uganda, the Republic of, Local Government Finance Commission (LGFC) [1998a] Quick Reference Financial Data for Districts Based on FY1996/97 Actual Local Revenues FY1998/99 Budgeted Government Grants (Kampala: LGFC).

Uganda, the Republic of, Local Government Finance Commission (LGFC) [1998b] Allocation of Conditional Grants in the Five Priority Programme Areas: Equalization Grant Study Part I (Kampala: LGFC, December).

Uganda, the Republic of, Ministry of Education and Sports (MoES) [2000a] Education for All: The Year 2000 Assessment Report of Uganda, http://www2.unesco.org/wef/countryreports/uganda/rapport%5F1.html [accessed 10 December 2000].

Uganda, the Republic of, Ministry of Education and Sports (MoES) [2000b] Education Strategic Investment Plan Joint Review 3rd April to 14th April 2000 Final Aide Memoir (Kampala: MoES, April).

Uganda, the Republic of, Ministry of Education and Sports (MoES) [2000c] Proposed Plan for Decentralised Level Capacity Building (Kampala: MoES, 31 March).

Uganda, the Republic of, Ministry of Education and Sports (MoES), Education Planning Department [2000d] "Terms of Reference for A Consultancy to Support 15 Districts in the Preparation of District Level Capacity Building Programmes," prepared on behalf of the decentralisation sub-committee (Kampala: MoES, 31 March).

Uganda, the Republic of, Ministry of Education and Sports (MoES) [2000e] Report on Tracking the Flow of and Accountability for UPE Funds By International Development Consultants Ltd. (Kampala: MoES, February).

Uganda, the Republic of, Ministry of Education and Sports (MoES) [2000f] Policy Statement 2000/2001 (Kampala: MoES).

Uganda, the Republic of, Ministry of Education and Sports (MoES) [2000g] Education Statistical Abstract 2000 (Kampala: MoES).

Uganda, the Republic of, Ministry of Education and Sports (MoES) [1999] The Ugandan Experience of Universal Primary Education, July, http://www.adeanet.org/pstr99/pstr99_uganda.pdf [accessed 22 October 2000].

Uganda, the Republic of, Ministry of Education and Sports (MoES) [1998a] Education Strategic Investment Plan 1998-2003 (Kampala: MoES, November).

Uganda, the Republic of, Ministry of Education and Sports (MoES) [1998b] Education Strategic Investment Plan (ESIP) (1998-2003): Work Plan (Kampala: MoES, November).

Uganda, the Republic of, Ministry of Education and Sports (MoES) [1998c] Guidelines on Policy, Roles and Responsibilities of Stakeholders in the Implementation of Universal Primary Education (Kampala: MoES).

Uganda, the Republic of, Ministry of Education and Sports (MoES) [undated] Education Statistical Abstract, http://www.educationsectoruganda.com/ [accessed 22 October 2000].

Uganda, the Republic of, Ministry of Education and Sports (MoES) [undated] Systems Review and Audit of Expenditure for the Year Ended 30 June 1998 (Kampala: MoES).

Uganda, the Republic of, Ministry of Education and Sports (MoES), Department of Teacher Education [undated] Teacher Development and Management Plan (TDMP) (Primary Education) Formal Draft (Kampala: MoES).

Uganda, the Republic of, Ministry of Finance, Planning and Economic Development (MoFPED) [2001] Uganda Poverty Status Report, 2001: Milestones in the Quest for Poverty Eradication (Kampala: MoFPED).

Uganda, the Republic of, Ministry of Finance, Planning and Economic Development (MoFPED) [2000a] Poverty Action Fund 2000-2001, General Guidelines for the Planning and Operation of Conditional Grants: Providing Resources to Local Governments to Implement the Poverty Eradication Action Plan (Kampala: MoFPED, April).

Uganda, the Republic of, Ministry of Finance, Planning and Economic Development (MoFPED) [2000b] Background to the Budget 2000/01 (Increasing Efficiency in Reduction Service Delivery Through Output Oriented Budgeting) (Kampala: MoFPED, June).

Uganda, the Republic of, Ministry of Finance, Planning and Economic Development (MoFPED) [2000c] Guideline for the Planning and Operation of the Poverty Action Fund Monitoring and Accountability Grant 2000-2001: Maximising the Effectiveness of Local Government PAF Programmes (Kampala: MoFPED, April).

Uganda, the Republic of, Ministry of Finance, Planning and Economic Development (MoFPED) [2000d] National Programme for Good Governance in the Context of the Poverty Eradication Action Plan (PEAP) (Kampala: MoFPED, May).

Uganda, the Republic of, Ministry of Finance, Planning and Economic Development (MoFPED) [2000e] Revised Volume I of the Poverty Eradication Action Plan (PEAP) Draft 2 (Kampala: MoFPED, May).

Uganda, the Republic of, Ministry of Finance, Planning and Economic Development (MoFPED) [2000f] Public Expenditure Review Meeting: Budget Framework Paper 2000/01 to 2002/03.

Uganda, the Republic of, Ministry of Finance, Planning and Economic Development (MoFPED) [2000g] Uganda Participatory Poverty Assessment: Learning from the Poor (Kampala: MoFPED, June), http://www.uppap.or.ug/pdf/UPPAP-National-Report.pdf [accessed 2 October 2000].

Uganda, the Republic of, Ministry of Finance, Planning and Economic Development (MoFPED) [2000h] Uganda Participatory Poverty Assessment Process, Participatory Planning for Poverty Reduction: Capacity Needs Assessment Report, Bushenyi District (Kampala: MoFPED, March).

Uganda, the Republic of, Ministry of Finance, Planning and Economic Development (MoFPED) [2000i] Uganda Participatory Poverty Assessment Process, Participatory Planning for Poverty Reduction: Capacity Needs Assessment Report, Kabarole District (Kampala: MoFPED, March).

Uganda, the Republic of, Ministry of Finance, Planning and Economic Development (MoFPED) [2000j] Uganda Participatory Poverty Assessment Process, Participatory Planning for Poverty Reduction: Capacity Needs Assessment Report, Kapchorwa District (Kampala: MoFPED, March).

Uganda, the Republic of, Ministry of Finance, Planning and Economic Development (MoFPED) [2000k] Uganda Participatory Poverty Assessment Process, Participatory Planning for Poverty Reduction: Capacity Needs Assessment Report, Kisoro District (Kampala: MoFPED, March).

Uganda, the Republic of, Ministry of Finance, Planning and Economic Development (MoFPED) [2000l] Uganda Participatory Poverty Assessment Process, Participatory Planning for Poverty Reduction: Capacity Needs Assessment Report, Kotido District (Kampala: MoFPED, March).

Uganda, the Republic of, Ministry of Finance, Planning and Economic Development (MoFPED) [2000m] Uganda Participatory Poverty Assessment Process, Participatory Planning for Poverty Reduction: Capacity Needs Assessment Report, Kumi District (Kampala: MoFPED, March).

Uganda, the Republic of, Ministry of Finance, Planning and Economic Development (MoFPED) [2000n] Uganda Participatory Poverty Assessment Process, Participatory Planning for Poverty Reduction: Capacity Needs Assessment Report, Moyo District (Kampala: MoFPED, March).

Uganda, the Republic of, Ministry of Finance, Planning and Economic Development (MoFPED) [2000o] Draft Estimates of Revenue and Expenditure (Recurrent and Development) 2000/01 (Kampala: MoFPED).

Uganda, the Republic of, Ministry of Finance, Planning and Economic Development (MoFPED) [1999a] Public Expenditure Review Meetings with Donors on the Medium Term Budget Framework 1999/00-2001/02 – Decentralisation: Resource Transfers and Capacity Building (Kampala: MoFPED, May).

Uganda, the Republic of, Ministry of Finance, Planning and Economic Development (MoFPED) [1999b] Uganda Poverty Status Report, 1999 (Kampala: MoFPED).

Uganda, the Republic of, Ministry of Finance, Planning and Economic Development, (MoFPED), Uganda Participatory Poverty Assessment Project [1999c] Perspectives of Communities on Education: a Briefing Paper (Kampala: MoFPED, April).

Uganda, the Republic of, Ministry of Finance, Planning and Economic Development, (MoFPED) [1998] "Managing Ethnic Diversity in Uganda," In: Uganda Vision 2025 Volume Two: Background Papers (Kampala: MoFPED, December).

Uganda, the Republic of, Ministry of Finance, Planning and Economic Development (MoFPED) and the UNDP [2000a] Draft Final Report on the District Resource Endowment Profile Survey (DREPS) Volume I: Household Micro – Finance Survey (Main Report) (Kampala: MoFPED, April).

Uganda, the Republic of, Ministry of Finance, Planning and Economic Development (MoFPED) and the UNDP [2000b] Draft Final Report on the District Resource Endowment Profile Survey (DREPS) Volume III: Institutional Data Report (Kampala: MoFPED, April).

Uganda, the Republic of, Ministry of Gender and Community Development (MoGCD) [1995] Country Report in Preparation for the Fourth World Conference on Women 1995 (Kampala: MoGCD).

Uganda, the Republic of, Ministry of Health (MoH) [2001] Annual Health Sector Performance Report Financial Year 2000/2001 (Kampala: MoH, September).

Uganda, the Republic of, Ministry of Health (MoH) [2000] Health Sector Strategic Plan Draft (Kampala: MoH, July).

Uganda, the Republic of, Ministry of Health (MoH) [1999] National Health Policy Draft (Kampala: MoH, September).

Uganda, the Republic of, Ministry of Health (MoH) [1998] Health Sub-district in Uganda: Concept paper (Entebbe: MoH).

Uganda, the Republic of, Ministry of Local Government (MoLG) [1999] Analysis of District and Urban Councils Budget for 1998/99 Financial Year (Kampala: MoLG, March).

Uganda, the Republic of, Ministry of Local Government (MoLG) [1998a] Analysis of District and Urban Councils Budget for 1997/98 Financial Year (Kampala: MoLG, May).

Uganda, the Republic of, Ministry of Local Government (MoLG) in collaboration with Ministry of Justice and Constitutional Affairs [1998b] Legislation Manual for Local Councillors in Uganda (Kampala: MoLG, May).

Uganda, the Republic of, Ministry of Local Government (MoLG) [1997] Analysis of 1996/97 Budgets for Districts on Block Grant System (Kampala: MoLG, April).

Uganda, the Republic of, Ministry of Local Government (MoLG) [1996] Budget Implementation under the Block Grant System in FY 1994/95: Experience of the First Thirteen Decentralized Districts (Kampala: MoLG, February).

Uganda National Association of Community and Occupational Health (UNACOH) [1999] People's Participation in Health: Proceedings of the 8th UNACOH Annual Scientific Conference (Kampala: UNACOH, September).

United Nations Capital Development Fund (UNCDF), United Nations Development Programme, and Ministry of Local Government, the Government of Uganda [1997] District Development Project – Pilot Project Document (Kampala: UNCDF, June).

United Nations Development Programme (UNDP) [2002] Human Development Report 2002 (Oxford: Oxford University Press).

United Nations Development Programme (UNDP) [2000a] Overcoming Human Poverty (New York, NY.: UNDP).

United Nations Development Programme (UNDP) [2000b] Decentralised Governance: A Synthesis of Nine Case Studies (New York, NY.: UNDP).

United Nations Development Programme (UNDP) [2000c] Human Development Report 2000 (Oxford: Oxford University Press).

United Nations Development Programme (UNDP) [1998] Uganda Human Development Report 1998 (Kampala: UNDP).

United Nations Development Programme (UNDP) [1997] Uganda Human Development Report 1997 (Kampala: UNDP).

United Nations Development Programme (UNDP) and German Federal Ministry for Economic Cooperation and Development (BMZ) [2000] The UNDP Role in Decentralization and Local Governance (New York, NY.: UNDP).

Uphoff, Norman [1992] Learning from Gal Oya: Possibilities for Participatory Development and Post-Newtonian Social Sciences (Ithaca, NY.: Cornell University Press).

Uphoff, Norman [1986] Local Institutional Development: An Analytical Sourcebook with Cases (West Hartford, CO.: Kumarian Press).

Uphoff, Norman, Milton J. Esman, and Anirudh Krishna [1998] Reasons for Success: Learning from Instructive Experiences in Rural Development (West Hartford, CO.: Kumarian Press).

Uphoff, Norman and Anirudh Krishna [1999] "Operationalizing Social Capital: Explanation and Measurement of Mutually Beneficial Collective Action in Rajasthan, India," mimeo.

Uphoff, Norman and C.M. Wijayaratna [2000] "Demonstrated Benefits of Social Capital: the Productivity of Farmer Organizations in Gal Oya, Sri Lanka," World Development Vol. 28, No. 11, pp.1875-2000.

Valderrama, Camilo and Kate Hamilton [1999] "Strengthening Participation in Local Governance: Report of the Workshop 21-24 June 1999," (Brighton: Institute of Development Studies).

de Valk, P. [1990] "State, decentralization and participation," In: P. de Valk and K. H. Wekwete (eds) Decentralizing for Participatory Planning? Comparing the experiences of Zimbabwe and other African countries in eastern and southern Africa (Aldershot: Avebury).

de Valk, P. and K. H. Wekwete (eds) [1990] Decentralizing for Participatory Planning? Comparing the experiences of Zimbabwe and other African countries in eastern and southern Africa (Aldershot: Avebury).

Van de Walle, Nicolas [2001] African Economies and the Politics of Permanent Crisis, 1979-1999 (Cambridge: Cambridge University Press).

Van Rooy, Alison [1998] Civil Society and the Aid Industry: the Politics and Promise (London: Earthscan).

Villadsen, Soren [1996] "Decentralization of Governance," In: Soren Villadsen and Francis Lubanga (eds) Democratic Decentralisation in Uganda: A New Approach to Local Governance (Kampala: Fountain Publishers).

Villadsen, Soren and Francis Lubanga (eds) [1996] Democratic Decentralisation in Uganda: A New Approach to Local Governance (Kampala: Fountain Publishers).

Vincent, Joan [1971] African Elite: the Big Men of a Small Town (New York and London: Columbia University Press).

Wallman, Sandra [1996] Kampala Women Getting By: Wellbeing in the time of AIDS (Oxford: James Currey).

Walsh, A.H. [1969] "The Urban Challenge to Government: National Comparison of Thirteen Cities," International Urban Studies Project (New York, NY.: Institute of Public Administration, University of New York).

Wanyenze-Gimogoi, Margeret [2000] "Experience of Local Governments in Operationalisation of the Local Government Budget Framework Paper," a paper presented at the Poverty Eradication Action Plan Revision and Public Expenditure Review/ Donor Consultative Workshop in May 2000.

Warburton, Diane (ed) [1998] Community and Sustainable Development: Participation in the Future (London: Earthscan).

Warner, Michael [2001] Complex Problems, Negotiated Solutions: Tools to Reduce Conflict in Community Development (London: ITDG Publishing).

Werlin, Herbert [1992] "Linking Decentralization and Centralization: A Critique of the New Development Administration," Public Administration and Development Vol. 12, pp. 223-235.

White, Shirley A. (ed) [1999] The Art of Facilitating Participation: Releasing the Power of Grassroots Communication (London: Sage Publications).

Widner, Jennifer and Alexander Mundt [1998] "Researching Social Capital in Africa," Africa Vol. 68, No. 1, pp. 1-24.

Wilmsen, Edwin N. and Patrick McAllister (eds) [1996] The Politics of Difference: Ethnic Premises in a World of Power (Chicago, IL.: the University of Chicago Press).

Woods, Dwayne [1992] "Civil Society in Europe and Africa: Limiting State Power through a Public Sphere," African Studies Review Vol. 35, No. 2, pp. 77-100.

World Bank [2003] World Development Report 2003 (Oxford: Oxford University Press for the World Bank).

World Bank [2001a] Education and Health in Sub-Saharan Africa: A Review of Sector-Wide Approaches (Washington, D.C.: World Bank).

World Bank [2001b] A Database of Gender Statistics, http://genderstats.worldbank.org/ [accessed 17 July 2001].

World Bank [2000a] World Development Report 2000/2001 (Oxford: Oxford University Press for the World Bank).

World Bank [2000b] "Sector-Wide Approaches for Education and Health in Sub-Saharan Africa," mimeo (Washington, D.C.: World Bank, March).

World Bank [1999a] World Development Report 1999/2000 (Oxford: Oxford University Press for the World Bank).

World Bank [1999b] Second Economic and Financial Management Project: Project Appraisal Document (Washington, D.C.: World Bank).

World Bank [1999c] Project Appraisal Document on a Proposed Credit in the Amount of SDR 58.7 Million (US$ 80.9 Million Equivalent) to the Republic of Uganda for the Local Government Development Program (Washington, D.C.: World Bank, October 28).

World Bank [1993] Uganda: Social Sectors (Washington, D.C.: World Bank).

World Bank [undated] Local Government Development Program, http://www.worldbank.org/pics/pid/ug2992.txt [accessed 21 March 2000].

Wunsch, James S. [2001] "Decentralization, Local Governance and 'Recentralization' in Africa," Public Administration and Development Vol. 21, pp. 277-288.

Wunsch, James S. [2000] "Refounding the African State and Local Self-Governance: the Neglected Foundation," Journal of Modern African Studies Vol. 38, No. 3, pp. 487-509.

Wunsch, James S. and Dele Olowu (eds) [1990] The Failure of the Centralized State: Institutions and Self-Governance in Africa (San Francisco, CA.: ICS Press).

Young, Oran R. [1994] International Governance: Protecting the Environment in a Stateless Society (Ithaca, NY.: Cornell University Press).

Index